PREHISTORIC ANCIENT AND HINDU INDIA

A STUDENT'S HISTORY OF INDIA

PREHISTORIC ANCIENT AND HINDU INDIA

R. D. BANERJI, M.A.

GYAN

Published by

Gyan Publishing House
5, Ansari Road
Daryaganj, New Delhi-110002
Phone: 011-47034999, 9811692060
E-mail: books@gyanbooks.com

Distribution Network
gyanbooks.com
India, USA, Canada, UK, Australia, France

ISBN : 978-81-212-6545-4 (HB)
First Published, 1934

2nd Impression 2022

Printed at: Gyan Press, Delhi.

PREHISTORIC ANCIENT AND HINDU INDIA
Author: R. D. BANERJI

A STUDENT'S HISTORY OF INDIA

PREHISTORIC ANCIENT AND HINDU INDIA

R. D. BANERJI, M.A.
Late Manindra Chandra Nundy Professor of Ancient Indian History and Culture, Benares Hindu University; Sometime Lecturer Post-Graduate Department, Calcutta University; formerly Fellow of the Bombay University, &c. &c.

PREFACE

This book was written and revised by my father, but unfortunately he did not live to see it published. The duty of, in some measure, still further revising it, and of seeing it through the Press, has therefore fallen upon myself.

The work is primarily meant for students, and if it can help to create in the heart of the rising generation a just pride in their national heritage, the deceased scholar's labours will be amply rewarded.

Opinions will almost inevitably differ as to the value of sources relied upon, and the soundness of conclusions reached, by the Author. To generous critics who would have me correct some slip or make good some omission I shall feel grateful.

My grateful thanks are due to Prof. S. Bhattacharji, M.A., of the Sanskrit College, Calcutta, and to Messrs. P. Gupta, M.A., and A. Raychaudhuri, M.A., for help received during the revision of the work.

I have to acknowledge a debt of gratitude to Mr. Donald A. Mackenzie, who has so kindly contributed a Foreword to the book. Mr. Mackenzie has expressed himself as being "particularly struck by observing how far advanced the deceased author was in his perception of the trend of anthropological discovery in India".

Lastly, my thanks are due to members of the staff of our publishers, Messrs. Blackie & Son (India), Ltd., without whose interest and willing co-operation the book would never have seen the light of day.

A. C. BANERJI.

CALCUTTA,
23rd May, 1934.

FOREWORD

By DONALD A. MACKENZIE

Modern research has greatly extended our knowledge of early India. As the " miracle of Greece " no longer obtains in consequence of the revelations of the archæologists in Crete and elsewhere in the Near East, so there is in India no longer an " Aryan miracle ".

It has been established that a wonderful pre-Aryan civilization existed in the Indus valley many centuries before the period of the Aryan intrusions, and that it was of higher and more complex character than can be gathered from the patriotic writers who celebrated the achievements of the famous Vedic Age. The discovery at Harappa on the Ravi in the Montgomery district of the Panjab of " seals " lettered in a strange script, which had been unearthed from time to time, presented to modern scholars a problem that aroused speculations on the one hand and scepticism regarding these on the other, but ultimately led to the thrusting open of the door to forgotten wonders of antiquity.

In 1921 the author of this volume was engaged in laying bare Buddhist remains at Mohenjo-Daro on the Indus, in the Larkana district of Sindh, when, as Sir John Marshall has recorded,[1] he " came by chance on several ' seals ' which he recognized as belonging to the same class as the remarkable ' seals ' with legends in an undecipherable script, long known, from the ruins of Harappa, in the Panjab ". He " was quick to appreciate

[1] *Mohenjo-Daro and the Indus Civilization.* Probsthain, 1932, 3 vols.

the value of his discovery", and he at once deepened his digging on the east side of a Buddhist monastery. Here, Mr. Banerji was a pioneer, and his work resulted in the discovery of remarkable remains that antedate the Buddhist structures by two or by three thousand years. "This was no small achievement", says Sir John Marshall, and he goes on to remind us that Mr. Banerji's conclusions upon it have been remarkably borne out by subsequent research. Larger operations have since been carried out, but they do not lessen the credit due to Mr. Banerji or diminish the importance of his discoveries.

Mohenjo-Daro lies about four hundred miles distant from Harappa, and, after the discoveries made there by Mr. Banerji in 1921–22, the larger operations that were conducted fully established the existence of the pre-Aryan city of Mohenjo-Daro and that of Harappa, the eloquent relics of a homogeneous pre-Aryan civilization which, in the light of comparative evidence, has been carried back to the fourth millennium B.C.

Seals similar to those discovered in the Indus valley have been found at various sites in Elam and Sumeria (Lower Mesopotamia), and there are other indications that cultural and trading connexions existed between north-western India and the ancient civilization of the Tigro-Euphrates valley. The Aryans did not enter India till the second millennium B.C., and their culture had no connexion with that of the much earlier settlers, who were apparently the Dravidians or proto-Dravidians, later represented by various communities in southern India, speaking dialects of the Dravidian language.

The early Indus valley settlers were agriculturists and traders and their high social organization is reflected by their well-planned and well-built cities. Mohenjo-Daro was laid out with thoroughfares that, like the great pyramids of Egypt, were oriented as nearly as possible to the cardinal points, and the buildings were constructed of kiln-baked bricks. Houses had doors and windows, paved floors and drains like those in Mesopotamia and Crete, and there were bathrooms and other conveniences. A great variety of vessels were manufactured. Copper, tin and lead had come into use and ornaments were made of gold, silver, ivory, bone, imported lapis-lazuli and of faience. Yet stone was still so freely used that the archæologists regard the early Indus settlers as a people of the Chalcolithic Age—the transitional stage between the ages of stone and metal. Artifacts (articles made by man) of chert were still being manufactured for occupational purposes. Domesticated animals included the elephant and camel, as well as the pig, shorthorn and humped cattle, the buffalo, sheep and the dog. Barley, wheat and the cotton plant were cultivated, and spinning and weaving had reached an advanced stage. Clay figures and images and phallic bætylic stones suggest that Durga and Śiva worship was of a very much greater antiquity in India than has hitherto been supposed.

It was formerly customary to explain, by wrongly adopting the theory of biological evolution, the gradual development of Vedic religion into the Brahmanical complex, with Brahma, Śiva and Vishnu eclipsing Indra, Agni, Varuna and Mithra, and with the goddesses rising into prominence. The modern view, confirmed by the striking Indian discoveries, is that the process was rather one of " culture mixing ", and that the religious changes were due mainly to the fusion of Aryans and Dravidians and their distinctive cultures, the ancient Dravidians having been a refined and highly civilized people. As is shown in the chapters that follow, the Dravidians had a currency while yet the Aryans practised a system of barter, and were sea-traders before the introduction of a Sanskrit equivalent for the word " sea ".

Research in Indian pre-history and history has been further promoted by the aid of numismatology (science of coins in relation to history), by philology and by the study of art and inscriptions and a great abundance of literature in various languages. Some dynasties have been restored almost by numismatic data alone, and much light has been thrown upon the origin and development of styles in sculpture and architecture by the accumulation and critical investigation of comparative evidence. In this volume a wonderfully full and consecutive narrative is provided from early times to the period of the Musalman conquest. Many blanks have been filled in, and for each period there are useful bibliographies which will serve as guides to those who desire to specialize in particular fields of research. The various kingdoms of the north and south are given special treatment, as are also the various intrusions of alien peoples who have contributed to the ethnical complex of the great sub-continent of India. Of very special interest is the restoration of the Dravidians to their proper place in history as influential shapers of Indian civilization. Pro-Aryan writers of the past have inclined in no small measure to share the political prejudices of the ancient Vedic authors, who referred to the Dravidians as fierce, hostile and semi-savage peoples. Fusions of Aryan and Dravidian cultures and peoples came in time. In this volume it is shown that before the period of the Musalman intrusions there were prosperous, progressive and enterprising Aryo-Dravidian communities in southern India, who not only extended their sway towards the north, but to farther India, the Dutch East Indies and Malaya. Greeks, Romans and Arabs had long traded with and influenced Dravidian seaport communities, and Aryo-Dravidian seafarers and colonizers carried from time to time the elements of a complex Indian civilization with Western features to distant places, including Cambodia, whence, it would appear, there emerged at intervals fresh carriers of some of the elements of the specialized and locally developed Aryo-Dravidian colonial culture to even more distant areas.

CONTENTS

Book I—Prehistoric India

Book II—Ancient India

CHAPTER VII

CHAPTER VIII

CHAPTER IX

Book III—History of Mediæval India

CHAPTER I

CHAPTER II

CHAPTER III

CHAPTER IV

CHAPTER V

CHAPTER XI

CHAPTER XII

BOOK I

Prehistoric India

CHAPTER I

PHYSICAL FEATURES OF INDIA

India is the central peninsula of the three which lie in the south of Asia. On account of its extent, diversity of climate, **Extent.** differences in physical features, and the variety of races that inhabit the country, it can very well be called a continent. The northern part very often resembles a tract in the frigid zone, though situated in the temperate area, and the extreme south resembles, to some extent, the central part of Africa on account of its very great heat. The name India was originally applied to the country on both banks of the River Indus by the Greeks who served under the Hakhamanishiya or Achæmenid emperors of ancient Persia, or those who came with Alexander the Great. The Sanskrit name for the River Indus, *Sindhu*, became *Hindu*, *Hidu* in the ancient dialects of Iran (Avestan and Old Persian), which the Greeks turned into *Indos*, and this Indos is the source of *Indus*, *India*.

The extent of the country has varied at different times. At present many scholars think that Afghanistan did not form **Afghanistan.** a part of India at any time. But the explorations of Stein in Central Asia and of the French School of Archæology in Afghanistan prove that that tract at one time formed an integral part of India. Afghanistan may be roughly divided into three parts: Kabul and Herat in the north, and Kandahar

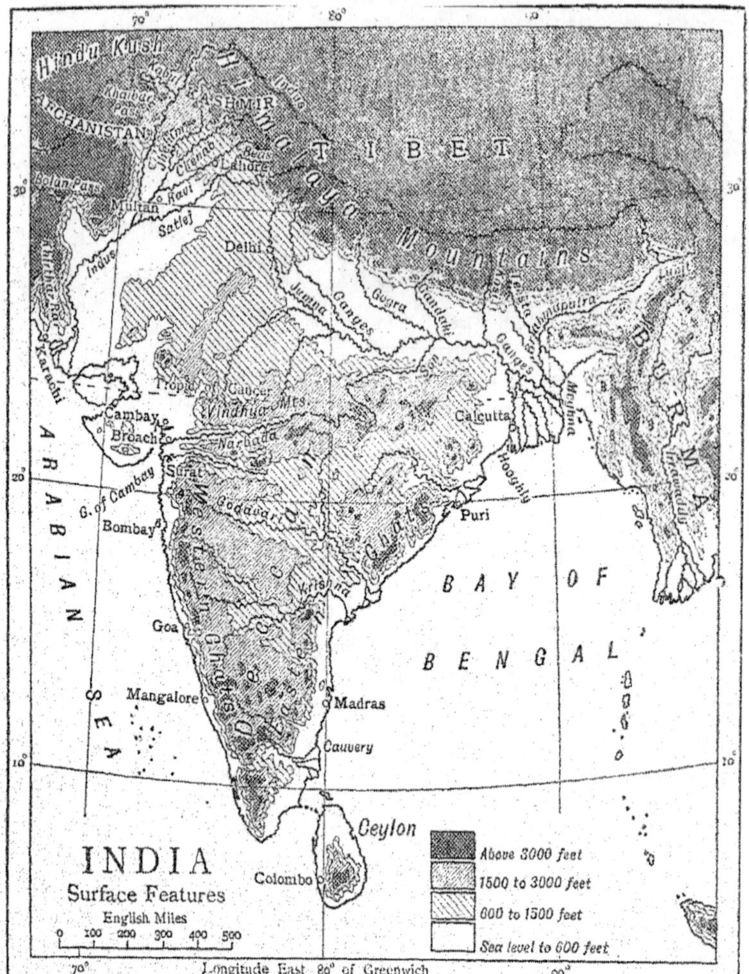

in the south. Of these three, the Kabul district is the most fertile, Kandahar stands next, and Herat last both in point of fertility and population. Kabul and Kandahar were Indian in population, language, and faith till the beginning of the sixteenth century.

Afghanistan consisted of the provinces of Aria, Arachosia, Gedrosia, Paropanisadai, and part of Drangiana. These provinces are now represented by the *Vilayats* of Herat, Balkh,

Kabul, Ghazna or Ghazni and Kandahar. They formed a province of the first and northernmost region of India.

Baluchistan has always been a different country and forms a part of the Iranian desert, though it lies so very close to the Indian provinces of Afghanistan and Sindh. This country was the borderland between India and Persia, and the northern part of it, now called Kalat, was called Draṅgāni in Sanskrit and Zranka in Old Persian, both of which terms mean "The Frontier". When the Greeks came they transliterated this term into Drangiane or Drangiana.

Baluchistan.

Geographically India is divided into four parts. The first consists of the mountainous country extending from the borders of Persia in the west to those of the province of Yun-nan in the south of China. Most of the provinces in this region are enclosed within a very long and wide mountain system called the Himalayas and the Hindu-Kush. The Himalayas form a barrier between the high tableland of Tibet and the low plains of the basins of the Ganges and the Indus river systems. Towards the north-west this mountain chain encloses the fertile valley of Kashmir, which was the bed of a lake in prehistoric times, and the small groups of valleys of the modern districts of Balkh, Kabul and Kandahar in Afghanistan. The western part of this mountain system has acquired different names; such as the Karakorum, the Hindu-Kush, the Sulaiman, and the Khirthar; but in reality they are parts of one range. The western side of these mountains is entirely different from the eastern; the latter is covered with dense vegetation, while the former is almost bare. But these western ranges contain the fertile valleys of Kabul and Kandahar. The eastern part contains the less productive and smaller valleys of Kumaun, Garhwal, and Nepal. In the north-eastern corner, these valleys, though more frequent and fertile, are not productive, on account of the dense jungle, which has not been removed since the formation of this tract.

The Four Regions.

The First Region.

The Mountain Region.

The second part, or region, consists of the basins of the seven rivers of the Panjab and the flat plains through which the Ganges and the Brahmaputra flow. In recent geological ages, this tract, with the exception of the hills in the Jhelum district of the Panjab, formed with Rajputana a sea-bed.

The Second Region. The ancient sea has gradually dried up and the basins of the great rivers have been filled with alluvium brought down during thousands of years. Rajputana has remained barren and arid, as no freshwater stream flows through it to make its soil fertile and productive. The bed of the ancient sea was uncovered, and the vast sandy plain, which once formed the ocean bed, now constitutes the great Indian Desert lying between the provinces of Malwa and the Panjab. A remnant of the ancient sea now forms the salt lake of Sambhar near Ajmer and the great salt marsh, called the Rann of Cutch (Sanskrit *Iriṇa*), between the mouths of the Indus and the peninsula of Kathiawad. The second region is bounded on the north by the jungles at the foot of the Himalayas, on the east by the mountain ranges which separate Bengal from Burma, on the west by the mountains of Afghanistan and Baluchistan, and on the south by the jungles on the northern slope of the Vindhya ranges.

The third region consists of the great plateau in the centre of the Indian Peninsula. The plateau rises abruptly at the end of the vast plain through which the Ganges, the Brahmaputra, and the Indus flow. The country between the basins of these rivers and the slope of the tableland is full of dense jungle and low hills. The Vindhya Mountains run through the centre of this belt of hills and forests. They consist of two or more parallel ranges of hills, running from Rajmahal at the western extremity of Bengal to the Gulf of Cambay. The plateau itself is a triangle, smaller than the peninsula, two sides of which are almost parallel to the eastern and western coasts of India. This plateau is much less fertile than the second **The Third Region: the Deccan Plateau.** region and consists of a vast undulating plain intersected by smaller plateaux, which very often rise in two or three tiers. The western edge of this plateau is higher than the eastern, and these two edges are bounded by mountain chains called the Eastern and the Western Ghats. The plateau slopes from west to east, and the apex of the triangle is formed by a high projection which runs due south from the Nilgiris and divides Travancore from the British province of Madras. This projection is called the Anaimalai Hills. The soil of the plateau varies in different regions. The western part is formed of lava and its soil is almost black. As one approaches the eastern edge of the plateau, he sees the change in the soil, and near the Eastern Ghats it is reddish, as is that at the end of the plateau to the south of the rivers Krishna and Tungabhadra. The plateau culminates in the Hindu state of Mysore, which is higher at the southern end than most of the plateau itself.

The fourth part or region of India consists of a broad belt of fertile land which runs along the sides of the peninsula. It is bounded on one side by the sea and on the other side by the Eastern or the Western Ghats. The western part of this belt is called the Konkan, from Sanskrit *Kaṅkaṇa*, a bracelet. The northern part, lying between the Gulfs of Cambay and Trombay, is very fertile and formed the richest portion of the Mughal Subah of Gujarat. Near Bombay the hills approach the Arabian Sea, and the tract between Bombay and Goa is not so fertile as Gujarat. But the coast land produces salt and provides for a large number of fishermen, while the valleys produce abundant crops of rice on account of the heavy rainfall during the south-western monsoon. South of Goa, the land is as fertile as Bengal and supports a very dense population. The country consists of a flat alluvial plain stretching from the Western Ghats or the Anaimalai Hills to the salt creeks near the sea coast. The eastern belt of coastland, from Ramnad near Ramesvaram to Tanjore, is also very rich and fertile and supports the densest population in Southern India. To the north of Tanjore the belt contracts, and above Madras the nature of the soil changes. The population is also less dense. The northern part of the eastern belt is much less fertile than the southern part, and the inhabitants are less enterprising than the people of the western coast. The people of Malabar are born sailors, and their sea-going craft are much more seaworthy than the cruder boats of the eastern coast. Therefore, while the natives of Konkan and the Malabar coast are bold sailors and trade with the Gulf of Persia and the Red Sea, the more primitive craft of the eastern coast are hardly fit for the open sea. The difference between the types of the sea-going craft of the eastern and western coasts of India reflects to some extent the important characteristics of the inhabitants of those parts.

The Coast land: the Fourth Region.

From a historical viewpoint the four regions differ greatly. Since early times the sea coast has been the abode of enterprising foreigners, who have crossed over from other lands. The rich fertile coast land has seen the rise of many different civilizations. The Deccan plateau and the three mountain systems which gird it have afforded a safe refuge to conquered races from time immemorial, and its barren and unproductive soil has repelled invaders, while the broad fertile plain of the basins of the Indus, Ganges, and Brahmaputra has attracted hungry nomads from outside India from the very dawn of the history of mankind. Like the third region, the secluded valleys of the mountain-girt Himalayan region have sheltered the remnants of conquered races of different historic periods. The languages, manners, and customs of the different inhabitants of these alpine valleys of India afford very great help in the reconstruction of the history of her prehistoric past.

BIBLIOGRAPHY

Cambridge History of India, Vol. I, chap. i.

CHAPTER II

THE RACES OF INDIA AND THEIR LANGUAGES

Being really a continent, India is inhabited by peoples of different races, who speak many different languages. The oldest of these peoples are the inhabitants of the Andaman Islands, who belong to the Negrito branch of the Negro race. Their language does not show any affinity to any other language of the world. The Negritoes are to be found on the sea coast of Makran, between India and Persia, in the Malay Peninsula, and in the Philippines. Formerly they lived along the entire sea coast from Arabia to China, but now they have been either driven inland or have been exterminated or enslaved and absorbed by people of many other races. The Negritoes lived entirely by fishing and hunting, and the ancient Greek writers called them *Ichthyophagoi* or fish-eaters. They pos-

The Negritoes.

sessed very rude weapons made of stone and bones of animals. Their weapons of stone are so rude and primitive that scholars call them weapons of the Old Stone Age or *Palæoliths*. They had no idea of building houses or huts, and lived in caves or in mere thatched shelters. They had no idea of throwing missiles, and we do not know as yet whether they had advanced sufficiently to make earthenware pots. Agriculture was not known among them, and they clothed themselves with skins or grass mats. The Andaman Islanders do not know how to produce corn even now, and live entirely by hunting and fishing, and on wild roots and berries. They fashion weapons from old nails or pieces of glass and shoot fish with arrows.[1]

The Palæolithic Period.

The Negritoes were followed by another race, who came from the south-eastern regions of Asia and at one time covered the entire archipelago, from the Easter Islands in the Pacific to Madagascar on the coast of Africa. In the north, the languages spoken by them are still to be found in Yasin to the north of Kashmir and in the small valleys of Nepal. Scholars call these people the *Austric*, or Southern race. This word has nothing to do with Australia. No connexion has as yet been established between the primitive inhabitants of Australia and the Austric people of Southern Asia and the islands. Some scholars think that these Austric people possessed an advanced civilization at one time. There are huge statues and pyramid-shaped altars in many of the islands of the Pacific, but these are certainly not the handiwork of the modern inhabitants. Traces of irrigation works and stone masonry are to be found in some of the islands whose present-day inhabitants do not know anything about masonry.[2]

The Austric Race.

The Austric languages fall into two broad groups, which are called the Austronesian and the Austro-Asiatic. The Austronesian or "Southern Island" languages are distributed over a very wide area and include almost all the languages spoken in the islands of the Pacific and the Indian Oceans, with the exception of those spoken on the continent of Australia. The Austro-Asiatic languages, on the other hand, are confined to

The Austro-Asiatic Group of Languages.

[1] Keane, *Man, Past and Present*, pp. 145–59.
[2] Perry, *Children of the Sun*.

a smaller area. This group has been divided into three separate sub-divisions. The first consists of the languages of the wild Semang and Sakai who live in the Malay Peninsula. The second contains the languages of the Khasi hillmen of Assam, the inhabitants of the Nicobar Islands, and some of the isolated inhabitants of Burma, such as the Palaung, the Riang and the Wa. The third sub-division consists of the Munda or Kolian languages of Central India and the group of languages called the Mon-Khmer, which are spoken in Lower Burma and Cambodia.

The Neolithic Age.

Scholars connect the invasion of India by the Austric people with the age of weapons of polished stone or the Neolithic Age. In this age men learnt to throw missiles, such as arrows and darts, and improved their weapons of stone very greatly by polishing them. The discovery of the potter's wheel also belongs to this age.

Traces of Austro-Asiatic Languages in Kashmir and Nepal.

While the traces of the people of the Palæolithic Age are confined to the hilly region of Central India and the eastern part of the Deccan plateau, the remains of the Neolithic Age are spread all over India. Traces of the habitation of Neolithic men in the flat alluvial plains in the basins of the great northern rivers are still apparent. The use of the Austric languages is supposed to have extended at one time from the north of Kashmir to Annam in Further India. It is supposed that when the Austric-(Kol)-speaking neolithic people were driven out of the fertile lands of the second region, some of them took shelter in the inaccessible valleys of the Himalayas. The little-known language of the people of the Yasin valley, called Burushaski, is regarded by some scholars as being allied to the Austric group of languages; and Austric influence is apparent in some of the languages spoken in certain inaccessible valleys of Nepal.

The Kolian Tribes.

The largest group of Austric languages in Central India is the Kolian or the Munda group. People who speak these languages live in the hilly jungle tracts on both sides of the Vindhyan range. They are the Santals, Mundas, Bhumijes, Birhors, Kodas, Larka Kols, Turs, Asurs, Agars, and Korwas. These people live in the eastern part of the Vindhyan chain, extending from Rajmahal in the east to certain parts of Chota-

Nagpur. This group of languages extends as far west as the Mahadeo Hills in the Central Provinces, where Kurku is spoken. In the hilly tracts of Orissa, a small wild tribe, called the Juangs, and in the Oriya-speaking districts of Madras two other wild tribes, called the Savaras and the Gadabas, speak similar languages. This group of languages, which is commonly called the Munda languages, is supposed to represent the language of the first group of the Austric people, who came to India from the north-east.

The Second Invasion of the Austric People.

The second wave of the Austric race, which invaded India some time after the first, used polished stone weapons with "shoulders".[1] This new type of weapon is to be found in Burma and Assam and very rarely in Chota-Nagpur. The languages of the second group do not extend westwards beyond Bengal. The present remnants of these languages are to be found in Assam, Burma, and the Nicobar Islands. Certain Mongoloid tribes who invaded Assam in historical times, such as the Angami Nagas, continued the use of "shouldered" stone implements up to recent times.

The Aborigines of the West and the South.

The aboriginal tribes, who live in the western portion of the Vindhyas, in the Aravalli range and the Western Ghats, are allied to the Kolians or the Austric people, though they have ceased to speak Austric languages. These are the Bhils, the Minas, the Mairs, and the Kolis of Rajputana and Western India. The wild tribes of Southern India, such as the Yanadis of the Telugu country, the Kurumbas, the Irulas, the Paniyans, and the Kadirs, have adopted Dravidian languages, though they seem to be of Negrito origin or the result of a mixture of the Negrito and the Austric races. Some of these tribes have become partially civilized and Hinduized. The Kurubas of the Madras Presidency belong ethnically to the same stock as the wilder Kurumbas, but they have taken to agriculture and turned Hindu.[2]

Ancient Cities.

The Neolithic phase of culture in the Indus valley was a complex one. Remarkable evidence has been brought to light by the discovery of brick-built, well-planned and highly-organized cities of agriculturists and traders at

[1] A shouldered weapon possesses a small area on each side of the tenon which fits it into the handle. They are mostly adzes or axes.

[2] E. Thurston, *Castes and Tribes of the Madras Presidency*, Vol. IV, pp. 155–9.

Harappa, in the Montgomery area of the Punjab and Mohenjo-daro, in the Larkana area of Sindh. Although copper was in use, stone implements were very freely used, and a wonderful craftsmanship was displayed in the production of ornaments of gold, silver, ivory, semi-precious stones and even faience. Trading relations with other centres of civilization have been established by finds of Indus valley "seals" in Sumeria (Lower Mesopotamia) and Elam (Western Persia). These cities were built by Dravidians, or proto-Dravidians. The scanty human remains so far forthcoming indicate that representatives of the Mediterranean race were, during the late city period, mixing with "roundheads" of the Alpine race and, perhaps, proto-Mongols.

Trade with Sumeria and Elam.

The Dravidian languages are divided into four broad groups: Tamil, Telugu, Kannada, and Malayalam. Telugu is spoken in the northern part of the Madras Presidency and the eastern part of the dominions of the Nizam of Haidarabad. Tamil is spoken along the eastern coast from near Madras to the end of the Indian Peninsula as well as in the northern part of Ceylon. It is the richest of Dravidian languages, and its literature is of extraordinary merit and goes back to the early centuries of the Christian era. Old Tamil literature enables us to form some idea of the civilization of the Dravidians of the south at an early date. The Kannada language is spoken in the south-western part of India, consisting of the southern districts of the Bombay Presidency, the western districts of the dominions of the Nizam of Haidarabad, the Bellary and South Kanara districts of Madras, and the state of Mysore. This, too, is an old language which possesses a considerable literature of its own, and can be divided into two different strata, old and new. Along the south-western coast, Malayalam, which is regarded by scholars as a branch of Old Tamil, is spoken from Cannanore to Cape Comorin. Kodagu, the language of Coorg, is regarded by some as a dialect of the Kannada language. The northernmost of the Dravidian languages is Brahui, the language of Central Baluchistan. Other northern Dravidian speeches are the language of the Malers of the Rajmahal Hills, and that of the Oraons of Chota-Nagpur. These two

The Dravidians: their Languages.

The Southern Dravidian Languages.

Ruins of Mahenjodaro; Buddhist stupa built on ruins of the Copper Age

tribes migrated to the north in historical times, after adopting Dravidian languages, manners, and customs. In the eastern part of the jungle tract, which lies to the south of the Vindhya Hills, live the Gonds, another aboriginal tribe, who for a time destroyed the Aryan kingdoms in this area. Many of these Gond kings became Hindus and ruled over the country extending from Orissa in the east to Saugor, in the Central Provinces, on the west. The Hinduized Gonds call themselves Nāgavaṁśī Rajputs and have given up speaking the Dravidian dialects, which the wilder Gonds still use.

The Northern Dravidian Languages

The language of the Oraons is called Kurukh and that of the Gonds, Gondi. Gondi, Kurukh, Malto (the language of the Malers of Rajmahal), Kandh (the language of a small tribe in the hill tracts of Orissa), Kollami (spoken by a very primitive tribe in Berar), and Telugu together form the northern group of the Indian Dravidian languages.

To the south of the Narmada, all wild aboriginal tribes adopted Dravidian languages, religions, and customs; and later on, some of them migrated to the north. The Bhils, the Minas, and the Mairs of Rajputana at present speak dialects of the Aryan language.

The Dravidians possessed a distinctive culture of their own, and, perhaps, brought the knowledge of the use of metals with them. They practised burial without cremation, and followed the same customs regarding the disposal of the dead as the ancient inhabitants of the islands of Crete and Rhodes, and the cities of Troy and Babylon.

Dravidian Burial Customs.

They placed the dead bodies in a crouching position inside terracotta sarcophagi or placed the disintegrated bones in an earthenware vessel. These earthenware vessels containing dead bodies or bones have been found along the northern coast of the Mediterranean Sea, in Mesopotamia, Babylonia, Persia, Baluchistan, Sindh, and Southern India. When they came in touch with the Indo-Aryans, who cremated their dead instead of burying them, the Dravidians started burning their dead also, but continued their ancient custom of placing some of the bones in an earthenware jar, which was placed in the family vault. Along with the dead, food, clothing, the personal ornaments of the deceased, his arms, and other favourite objects were placed in the same burial urn, terra-cotta sarcophagus, or stone burial chamber. The tombs of the Dravidians in Baluchistan and Sindh show the exclusive use of copper and bronze weapons and ornaments. But the tombs discovered to the south of the Godavari show the use of iron, along with ornaments and vessels of bronze and copper. Some of the bronze vessels are of exquisite beauty, and show that the people who made them had advanced considerably in the use of metals. The Dravidians also knew the use of gold and silver and used golden crowns and armlets. Some of these golden crowns have been discovered in Dravidian tombs of the Iron Age at Adittanallur, in the extreme south of the Indian Peninsula. The terra-cotta sarcophagi found at Pallavaram and Perumbur in the Chingleput District, Dadampatti in the Madura District, and certain places in the Salem District are exactly like the bath-tub-shaped sarcophagi discovered at Brahmanabad and Mohenjo-daro in Sindh, at Gehareh near Bagdad, and other places in Babylonia. The multiple-legged cists found at Perumbur and numerous other places in the Madras Presidency resemble the terra-cotta chests (*larnakes*) found at different places in the Island of Crete. Herodotus has recorded that the Lycians in Asia Minor were descended from the ancient Cretans and they brought their national name, Termilai, from Crete, and the ancient inscriptions of the Lycians tell us that they call themselves *Trimmili*, which is the same as the Greek form used by Herodotus.[1] The method of cist-burials and urn-burials, the similarity of names, and the identity of certain pictograms or ideograms discovered in South-western Panjab and Upper Sindh with the pictograms and the linear script of Crete, indicate that the ancient Dravidians were a branch of the same race as the ancient Cretans, and they brought the picture-writing and the burial customs with them from South-eastern Europe. The Indian Dravidians discovered the use of money and were the first people to build dams across rivers for the purpose of irrigation. The dams built by them in rivers which dried up long ago still exist in different parts of Baluchistan. They also improved their pottery

Use of Metals.

Copper and Iron

Gold and Silver.

Dravidian Earthenware Coffins.

Certain Affinities of the Dravidians

[1] S. K. Chatterji, *Modern Review*, 1924, pp. 675–6.

and made very fine thin jars and vases like egg-shell china, some of which were decorated with paintings in many colours. Most of their pottery is wheel-turned and kiln-burnt. Beautiful vases with magnificent polychrome decorations have been discovered in Baluchistan and Sindh.

Poly-throm Pottery.

The pottery discovered in the Dravidian tombs of Southern India is not painted. This pottery is very well made and is in two colours only, red and black. Some of the tribes of Austric origin, such as the Mundas and the Oraons of Chota-Nagpur, adopted the system of burying the bones of the dead in earthenware urns and jars. These jars have round bottoms and resemble the jars discovered in Sindh. Similar round-bottomed jars have been discovered in Pegu, which was colonized by the Dravidians long before the birth of Christ.

Dravidian Burial Customs in Central India and Burma.

The Dravidians were driven out of the fertile plains of Northern India by a round-headed race about whom we know nothing. They form a belt of round-heads between the Dravidians of the south and the long-headed Aryans of the north at the present day. These round-headed people are supposed to have come from the Pamirs.[1] We do not know anything about their manners and customs or their language. Most probably they adopted the language, religion, manners, and customs of the more civilized Dravidians, and mixed with them.

The Pamirian Round-heads.

The Aryans or Indo-Aryans invaded Persia and Babylonia more than two thousand years before the birth of Christ. They were nomads living somewhere to the north-east of Babylon, who came to sell horses in Babylon and Asia Minor, and the oldest inscriptions found at Boghaz-Köi in Northern Asia Minor gave some words of Indo-Aryan origin, such as *Panz-āvartanna*, i.e. five rounds, or *Satt-āvartanna*, i.e. seven rounds, to a horse at the time of breaking. Later on, the Aryans founded a powerful kingdom in Asia Minor and Babylon. The Aryan kings of Babylon were called the *Kash-shu* or the Kassites, and they ruled over that country for many centuries. The Aryan kingdom of Asia Minor was called the kingdom of Mitanni, and we possess a very interesting series of documents of the Aryan rulers of Mitanni discovered at

The Aryans in Asia Minor.

Aryan Kings of Babylon and the Mitanni.

[1] Chanda, *Indo-Aryan Races* Part I, pp. 37–78.

Tell-el-Amarna in Egypt and at Boghaz-Köi in Asia Minor. From the Boghaz-Köi inscriptions we know that the kings of the Mitanni worshipped the same gods (Mitra, Indra, Varuṇa, and the Nāsatyas or Aśvins) as the early Indo-Aryans of India, and their names, like Dashratta, Artatama, Yash-data, Shaush-shattar, also were of the same origin.[1]

After 1714 B.C. the Kassites occupied Babylon and destroyed the independence of the early Semitic kings of that country. The Kassites are supposed to have been a people of the same origin as the Indo-Aryans, but when they conquered Babylon they were certainly barbarians. After settling down in Babylon they adopted the worship of the local gods and gradually became united with the Semitic population of that country. Evidence has been discovered of the existence of another Aryan colony on the eastern bank of Lake Urumiah in Persia. These people are called the Manda in the inscription of Naram-Sin, one of the kings of Babylon, who lived two thousand six hundred years before the birth of Christ, and the Amadai in the inscriptions of the first millennium B.C. found in Assyria. The Greek writers called them Mantiane or Matiene. They existed as a separate tribe even at the time of Alexander's conquest of the ancient Persian Empire in 331 B.C., and were called the Matiani. The Manda were horse-dealers and they came to Asia Minor to sell horses. The introduction of horses into Babylonia was due to the Aryan barbarians who came from the steppes of Central Asia under different names, such as the Kassites or the Kash-shu, the Mitanni, the Matiani or the Medes.

The Kassites.

The Manda.

Aryans introduce the horse into Asia Minor.

The Kassite kings ruled in Babylon for more than six centuries. Their language was quite different from the language of Akkad or old Semitic Babylonian. The ancient Babylonians compiled dictionaries of the Kassite language which now enable us to fix the Aryan affinities of the old Kassite language. The name of the Sun-god was *Shuriyash* (Sanskrit *Sūryas*), but the Semitic or Babylonian form is *Shamash* (Arabic *Shams*). Similarly, another god was called *Maruttash*, which is a very close approach to the name of the Indian Wind-god *Marut*. The Kassites were mountaineers who started plun-

Aryan Gods of the Kassites.

[1] *Cambridge Ancient History*, Vol. I, pp. 311 12.

dering the rich and fertile land on the banks of the Tigris and the Euphrates about 2072 B.C. Gandash, the first Kassite king of Babylonia, conquered Babylon in 1746 B.C. Very little is known of the Kassite kings, but we get more light about the early Indo-Aryan invaders of Asia Minor from the records discovered at Boghaz-Köi and Tell-el-Amarna.

From these records we learn that the Mitanni were people of Aryan descent; their kings were at first independent, but later on they had to become feudatories of the Egyptian Empire. The earliest and most interesting of the records is the correspondence of the kings of the Mitanni with the Pharaohs of Egypt of the eighteenth dynasty. Thutmosis III of Egypt defeated the king of the Mitanni in Asia Minor and recorded this event in hieroglyphics on the pylons of the great temple at Karnak in Egypt. Thutmosis III was obliged to invade the kingdom of the Mitanni, which lay to the east of the River Euphrates, in order to punish its king for the part he had taken in encouraging the rebels of Syria. The king of the Mitanni was heavily punished, and the Egyptian Pharaoh crossed the Euphrates and set up his boundary pillar. These events happened in the first half of the fifteenth century before the birth of Christ. After the conquest of the Mitanni, the princes of that country were not removed but were allowed to remain as feudatories of the Egyptian Empire. Amenhotep II of this dynasty received the submission of the princes of the Mitanni during his Syrian campaign of 1447 B.C. His son, Thutmosis IV, married a daughter of King Artatama I, named Mutemuya. Thutmosis is said to have demanded the daughter of Artatama, to which demand the latter acceded and the lady was sent to Egypt. The alliance between the Mitannian royal house and the Pharaohs strengthened the power of Egypt in Asia Minor, and was productive of great benefit to the kings of the Mitanni also. Mutemuya became the mother of the next Pharaoh, Amenhotep III. In the Mitannian kingdom Artatama I was succeeded by his son, Shutarna, who was the contemporary of Amenhotep III, and married his daughter Gilukhipa to Amenhotep. Shutarna's son and successor, Dushratta, continued to be the favourite of Amenhotep. Dushratta married his daughter Tadukhipa to Pharaoh

Pharaoh Thutmosis III

Subdues the Kings of Mitanni.

Marriages between the Aryan Kings of the Mitanni and the Egyptian Pharaohs.

Amenhotep IV, the son of Amenhotep III. The letters from Dushratta to Amenhotep III reveal the position of the Mitannian kings. They were ambitious enough to desire a daughter of the royal house of Egypt for their harems, and their demands for Egyptian gold were incessant. During the last illness of Amenhotep, Dushratta sent the image of the goddess Ishtar to Egypt in the hope that the goddess might drive away the evil spirits which were causing the illness.

Dushratta.

Dushratta reigned for a long time. In his reign the Mitannian kingdom was invaded by the Hittites. These were defeated at first, but after the death of Amenhotep III they returned in large numbers. Dushratta renewed the alliance with the Pharaoh Akhenaten. At this time Shubbiluliuma, the young and energetic king of the Hittites, invaded the territories of Egypt and the Mitanni in Asia Minor. King Dushratta was one of the three sons of Shutarna, and had gained the kingdom after the death of his brother Artashumara. His other brother, Artatama, remained his rival throughout. Artatama had taken refuge in Naharin, a place beyond the reach of Dushratta, and here Artatama II, his son Shutarna II, or Shutatara, and his grandson Itakama lived as semi-independent kings. They intrigued with the Hittite kings and remained a thorn in the side of the kings of the Mitanni. Shubbiluliuma supported Itakama, and after some time crossed the Euphrates, but Dushratta somehow or other avoided open war. Shutatara, or Shutarna II, and Itakama fought with the Hittite king on account of his neglect of their interests, but both were defeated and carried off to Khati, the capital of the Hittites.

Invasion of the Hittites.

In 1369 B.C. Shubbiluliuma placed Mattiuaza, the son of Dushratta, on the throne of his father. The latter is said to have been murdered by his son. Shutarna II and his son Itakama now seized the kingdom, and the power of the Mitanni came to an end. The kingdom was divided between the Hittites and the Assyrian kings of Nineveh. Shubbiluliuma married his daughter to Mattiuaza and drove out Shutarna II and his son. Mattiuaza is the last known Aryan king of the Mitanni. The names of these kings of the Mitanni are distinctly Indo-Aryan. Artatama, Shutarna, and Dushratta

Murder of Dushratta

Hittite supremac in Asia Minor.

(which stands for Sanskrit *Daśaratha*) are certainly Sanskritic, and the names of the gods of the Mitannian kings show that they worshipped some of the gods whom the Indo-Aryans of India worshipped. It is therefore evident that the Mitannian kingdom existed at a time when the Indian Aryans had not separated from the Aryans living in Persia. Some of these gods are mentioned in the sacred literature of the ancient Persians, but there the forms of their names have changed. The name *Nāsatya* is common to the Mitanni and the Aryans of India, but in ancient Persian literature these two gods, who are called the Aśvins or the Aśvinī-kumāras in later Indian literature, are called the *Naonhaithya*. It is also quite possible that the affinity between ancient Mitannians and the Aryans of India was greater than that with the Aryans of Persia.

The Gods of the Kings of Mitanni.

The Aryans invaded India through Afghanistan and the Khaibar Pass. At one time scholars supposed that they invaded India on two different occasions. They were supposed to have come in two waves, the first of which came by the usual route, through Afghanistan and the Khaibar Pass, and the second through the more difficult route along the Pamirs and Dardistan to the north of Kashmir. This theory, based on linguistic evidence, has now been abandoned by the majority of scholars, because the Pamirs are so arid and barren that it must have been absolutely impossible for large masses of men to traverse that route.

The Route of the Indo-Aryans.

Some time before the Aryan invasion, the Dravidians of Northern India had fused with the Pamirians or the round-headed people who had come through North-eastern Afghanistan and the Indus valley to Northern India. Evidently these people had not colonized the Panjab, which had been left to dark-skinned, flat-nosed aboriginals. The Indo-Aryans, when they reached the fertile plains of the Panjab, found these dark-skinned people in occupation.

The Indo-Aryans in the Panjab.

The Indo-Aryans had enemies of two different classes, the Vṛitras, i.e. civilized foes, and Dāsas or Dasyus, i.e. enemies of non-Aryan origin. The Italian anthropologist Giuffrida Ruggieri agrees with Ramaprasad Chanda in thinking that the first inhabitants of India whom the Indo-Aryans met in the

Vṛitras and Dasyus.

basins of the five rivers of the Panjab were aboriginals. Side by side with these aboriginals appeared the Vṛitras, who were civilized. In many cases, in later literature, reference is to be found to a cultured race called the Asuras. These Asuras are recognized as having been a civilized people, but were looked down upon as they did not worship the deities whom the Indo-Aryans revered. Some scholars thought that the Asuras were the Medes or the Aryans of Assyria; but one fact has not been considered by such writers, namely, the existence of an aboriginal tribe called the Asuras in Chota-Nagpur, and the repeated mention of the Asuras in Vedic and post-Vedic literature.

Asuras.

The Asuras are generally represented in the epics as a cultured race of demons who possessed considerable skill in building and were formidable enemies even to the gods. Vedic literature contains numerous references to the Dāsas also, and it appears that after conquering the flat plains of the Panjab the Indo-Aryans encountered a more civilized people. These people are also called Dāsas. Indra is said to have shattered the hundred castles of Śambara. He is also said to have occupied the seven cities of the enemies of Purukutsa and plundered the wealth of the Anus. He destroyed the cities of another non-Aryan chief named Pipru and plundered Śushṇa. From this account it is evident that the terms Asura and Dāsa were used indiscriminately. The Nishādas, who are described as noseless beings, were the first people whom the Indo-Aryans met in the plains of the Panjab. But in the fertile country between the Satlej and the Yamunā they came across a more cultured people who possessed castles, cities, and considerable wealth. Śambara was a Dāsa and a formidable enemy of the Indo-Aryan king Divodāsa; his father's name was Kulitara, the structure of which shows that the name at least was non-Aryan. The name Anu, of the tribe whose seven cities were conquered by the Aryan chief Purukutsa, also appears to be of non-Aryan origin. The Dānavas or the Asuras formed a belt around the small Indo-Aryan colony. They were probably the descendants of the Pamirians and the Dravidians, who were certainly far more civilized than the Indo-Aryan invaders. Gradually they were conquered by the

Their Forts and Cities.

The Asura or Dravidian Kingdom in North India.

newcomers, and mixed with them. Some of them belonged to the mysterious people whom the Indo-Aryans called Nāgas or snakes, and whose representations are to be seen in paintings and bas-reliefs of the historical period. Thus Vṛitra, the Asura chief, is called a snake in the Śatapatha Brāhmaṇa, but in Mahābhārata he is regarded as a prince among the Daityas. The Kālakeyas, the Kāleyas, or the Kālakhañjas are another Dānava tribe who worshipped the Sun, from whom they were supposed to be descended. It thus appears that the term Dāsa or Dasyu was indiscriminately applied to all enemies of the Indo-Aryans and that the latter, after crossing the Panjab, encountered another race or people called Asuras, Daityas, or Dānavas. The Nāgas formed a part of this civilized race. When the Indo-Aryans had conquered and colonized the basin of the Indus and its tributaries and that of the Ganges as far as Benares, the Asuras surrounded them on all sides. They were certainly in possession of Magadha or South Bihar and modern Rajputana at the time of the tribal war between the Pāṇḍavas and the Kurus. These Asuras were great builders, and their building operations were regarded with awe and reverence by the Aryans. In Vedic literature mention is made of castles of the Dāsas built of stone. Cities belonging to the Asuras are called Pātāla, Saubha, Prāgjyotisha, Hiraṇyapura, and Takshaśilā. In the eastern countries Girivraja, the capital of the Asura chief Jarāsandha, and its defences excited the admiration of the Pāṇḍava chief Bhīma. When Yudhishṭhira, the eldest of the Pāṇḍavas, performed the Rājasūya ceremony, the Asura architect Maya was called to design and build the buildings required for the sacrifice. The Asuras were thus a people who gradually succumbed to the virility of the new invaders and ultimately merged among them. A portion of them found refuge in the Chota-Nagpur Hills, where they lapsed into barbarism. Such lapses of a more civilized people have been recorded, as in the case of the Red Indians of North America. These Asuras are generally regarded as worshippers of the Phallus with obscene rites. The epic literature refers to the Asura kings as worshippers of Mahādeva in the majority of cases, and the prevalence of phallic worship in the south is a clear indication of the fact that before the Asuras had adopted

The Identity of Nāgas and Asuras. *The Asuras of Chota-Nagpur.* *The Religion of the Asuras.*

the outward form of worship of the Aryans, they were worshippers of the phallic emblem.

In the extreme north-east the kings of Prāgjyotisha or Assam claim to be descended from an Asura named Naraka. References in the Vedic literature very clearly indicate that the Indo-Aryans regarded that part of Northern India only to be fit for the occupation of Indo-Aryans where their peculiar manners and customs and mode of worship had obtained prevalence.

The Indo-Aryan Fire-worshippers.

The Indo-Aryans had brought with them the cult of the worship of Fire, a practice which they and the ancient Iranians had adopted after the downfall of the Mitannian kingdom and the Hittite conquest of Asia Minor. In the Aitareya Brāhmaṇa it is mentioned that Bharata Dauḥshyantī, the king of the Kaurava clan, performed one hundred and thirty-three horse sacrifices, out of which seventy-eight were performed on the banks of the River Yamunā and fifty-five on those of the Ganges. This indicates that in the middle Vedic period, when the Brāhmaṇas were being compiled, the land between the Ganges and the Yamunā was the centre of Indo-Aryan activities. The Śatapatha Brāhmaṇa mentions that from the banks of the River Sarasvatī the sacred fire travelled along

The Legend of the Migration of the Sacrificial Fire.

the northern bank of the Ganges and crossed the Sarayu, Gandak, and Kosi rivers, and reached the western bank of the River Sadānīrā, i.e. the modern Rapti. There is no mention of the entrance of the sacrificial fire into Magadha or South Bihar and Bengal. A number of Indian law-books expressly mention that such Indo-Aryans as went to the countries of Bengal, Kaliṅga, and Sauvīra (Kathiawad-Cutch) had to perform a special ceremony of purification. These references show that the Indo-Aryans did not colonize any other part of India except the Panjab and parts of the United Provinces. Their immigration into the east and the south was barred by the powerful Asura kingdoms.

The process of fusion of the Indo-Aryans and the earlier inhabitants of India of Dravidian origin was very slow. The

The Limits of Indo-Aryan Conquest.

Aryans never succeeded in conquering or colonizing any part of India which lay to the south of the Yamunā and to the east of N. Bihar. Their settlement in the modern provinces of Sindh and Rajputana is also problematical, and it is certain that they never succeeded in penetrating the country to the south of the Vindhyan range and the River Narmada.

The immigrations into India through the more difficult passes of the north-east are less familiar to us. It is certain that the Austric people came to India in two different waves in the Neolithic period, but later waves of immigration through these passes must be referred to the historical period. The wild tribes living in Assam and the Indo-Burman frontier must have entered India long after the Aryan colonization of the north-west. The earliest of these are the Tibeto-Burmans, represented by the Boda, Koch, Tipra, &c., tribes of Northern Bengal, the Khyen, and the Chutiyas of Assam. The Tibeto-Burmans came into the Brahmaputra valley in several different waves, and it is now impossible to classify their invasions in any reliable chronological order. The latest of these newcomers are the Sino-Siamese, such as the Shans or the Ahoms of Assam and the Khamtis of the border. These tribes rarely intermarried, and, with the exception of the Ahoms, they retain their barbaric habits and primitive forms of worship to the present day.

The Tibeto-Burman Invasion.

The Sino-Siamese.

BIBLIOGRAPHY

H. H. Risley, *The People of India*, chap. i.
E. Thurston, *Castes and Tribes of the Madras Presidency.*
Imperial Gazetteer of India, Vol II.
Cambridge History of India, Vol. I, chaps. ii–iii.

CHAPTER III

THE EARLIER INDO-ARYANS AND THE MARITIME EMPIRE OF THE DRAVIDIANS

The Date of Indo-Aryan Invasion.

The date of the Indo-Aryan settlement in India remains shrouded in mystery. The affinity between the names of the Indo-Aryan deities in the tablets of treaties between the kings of the Mitanni and the Hittites and the forms of the names of the same deities in the Vedic literature of India shows that the Indo-Aryan settlement in India must have taken place about the same date as the Aryan invasion of Asia Minor. Scholars are divided in opinion about the date of the immigration of the Indo-Aryans into India. The majority of European scholars hold that they came in the second millennium B.C., sometime between 1500 and 1200 B.C. Others, including Jacobi, are inclined to place the date of the Indo-Aryan conquest or immigration in the fourth millennium B.C. The existence of a powerful Indo-Aryan empire in Asia Minor from the beginning of the second millennium B.C., and the long process required for the Aryanization of Dravidian culture, show that the date of the Indo-Aryan conquest must be pushed back into the third millennium B.C., and that the separation of the Indo-Aryans and Indo-Iranians probably took place long after the settlement of the Indo-Aryans in India.

The Separation of the Indian and Iranian Groups

The Indo-Aryans were divided into a number of small tribes, each ruled by a king, or tribal chief, when they colonized Afghanistan and the Panjab. There was no caste system among the Indo-Aryan tribes at the time of their immigration, but a priesthood had already grown up. Before the immigration, the functions of the tribal priest and the ruler seem to have been united, but the long wars which took place between the Indo-Aryans and the earlier settlers in Afghanistan and the Panjab must have forced the members of an Indo-Aryan tribe to divide themselves into different groups according to their vocations in life. Magic rites being regarded as equally important with the conquest of the enemy, the functions of the tribal magician or priest appear to have become different from those of the tribal chief or the leader in war, at a very early date. But even after the settlement of the Indo-Aryans in India, the priestly functions were not confined to a particular class, or in other words, division of labour had not yet degenerated into a rigid caste system.

The Constitution of the Indo-Aryan Tribes.

The Magicians and the Priests.

Opinion is yet divided about the state of culture of the Indo-Aryans at the time of their irruption into Afghanistan or the Panjab. Even if agriculture was known to these people, their skill in it appears to have been of a very low order. After their settlement in the Panjab their progress seems to have been very rapid. The fertile plains on the banks

Indo-Aryan Civilization.

Agriculture.

of the five rivers made agricultural operations very easy. At this time the Indo-Aryans were carrying on a ceaseless war with the earlier and more civilized inhabitants of the country, and very often it became impossible for the warriors of a tribe to return to their villages in time for the sowing of corn. The adults of the tribe appear to have been divided into two groups, the tillers of the soil and the warriors. As in the case of the priests, the functions of the agriculturists and the warriors appear to have been interchangeable at the beginning.

The Division between the Fighters and the Cultivators.

Later on, when more skill was required for the cultivation of the field, as well as for fighting a more civilized enemy, the division of labour in each tribe became fixed. Gradually the warriors obtained the upper hand, and the agriculturists became the members of a lower stratum of the tribal society.

The Origin of the Indo-Aryan Priesthood.

The Indo-Aryans came to India in very small numbers, and they did not make any attempt at preserving the purity of their stock. From the very beginning they admitted tribes of foreign or mixed origin into their communities, and the statements of the present-day Brahmanical writers about the racial purity of the Indo-Aryans and the rigidity of their marriage regulations are inaccurate. When the Ṛigveda was compiled, the priestly caste had already been separated. Among the priests, however, two of the warrior clans had forced their way. The Aṅgirasas, the Vaśishṭhas, the Agastyas, and the Bhārgavas are stated to have been of divine origin, but the Viśvāmitras and the Kāṇvas belonged to the warrior

The Sages of Divine Origin,

class. The Aṅgirasas are called the sons of heaven, or of the Fire. The Bhārgavas claim descent from Varuṇa, the god of the Sky. The Vaśishṭhas are called the descendants of Mitra or the Sun-god. But the Kuśikas or the Viśvāmitras belonged to the Bhārata group of the warrior caste.

and of the Warrior Caste.

Kaṇva is the son of Nṛishad, who according to the *Purāṇas* was a Kshatriya. According to the Śrauta-sūtra of Āśvalāyana, Viśvāmitra, Jamadagni, Bharadvāja, Gotama, Atri, Vaśishṭha, and Kaśyapa with Agastya are regarded as progenitors of all Brāhmaṇas. Out of these eight clans four are regarded as the original sources of the Brahmanic clans (*gotras*). In the Mahābhārata it is stated that Aṅgiras, Kaśyapa, Vaśishṭha, and Bhṛigu were the sages from whom the earliest priests of the Indo-Aryans were descended. Vedic literature shows very clearly that those early priests began to resent the assumption of the priestly functions by men of other classes. The quarrel between Viśvāmitra and Vaśishṭha is clearly an indication of the earlier struggles for supremacy and power between the warrior and the priestly classes of the Indo-Aryan tribes. The various sections of the priestly castes appear to have been of different origin. Some of them were white-skinned while others were dark. Even in the time of the grammarian Patañjali the tradition about the white-skinned and yellow-haired priests lingered in India. The priests or Brāhmaṇas were of two classes, of which the first or the earliest belonged to the pure Indo-Aryan stock, while the second, or the adopted priests, appear to have belonged to some other ethnic stock.[1]

Adoption of Priests of other Races among Brāhmaṇas.

Similarly, the warrior caste was also composed of different ethnic elements. Some of them belonged to the Indo-Aryan stock, like the first group of priests or Brāhmaṇas, while others were adopted into the Indo-Aryan tribes or clans from the earlier settlers in the country. Vedic literature shows that the Indo-Aryans were obliged to admit certain tribes into their community from the very beginning. Indra, the god of Thunder, is said to have crossed the sea and brought the Turvasas and the Yadus with him. Chanda's view about the original habitat of these two tribes is generally accepted. They are supposed to have emigrated from Mesopotamia, where they had mixed with the Semitic inhabitants, into Saurāshṭra, or Kathiawad, whence they spread towards the north-east as far as Mathura. The idea generally accepted in India about the ethnic purity of the earlier Indo-Aryan settlers is thus proved to be fallacious.

The Mixture of Races among the Kshatriyas.

Mesopotamian Elements among the Warrior Tribes.

The earliest Indo-Aryan settlers in Afghanistan and the Panjab were divided into a number of small tribes and clans. The earliest event in the history of these settlers known to us is the war between the Bharatas and ten other tribes. At this time the Bharatas were ruled over by a king or chief named Sudās, who belonged to the Tṛitsu clan. Viśvāmitra was the priest of this tribe. Later on, he was superseded in the

The War of the Ten Tribes.

[1] Chanda, *Indo-Aryan Races*, Pt. I, pp. 24–5.

priestly office by the sage Vaśishṭha. Viśvāmitra was a man of revengeful disposition, and he led a confederacy of ten tribes against the Bharatas. The sage was also a general and had led the Bharatas to victory against their enemies on the banks of the rivers Beas and Satlej. The ten tribes allied against the Bharatas were the Anus, who dwelt on the River Parushṇī (modern Ravi), the Druhyus, the Yadus, the Turvasas, the Purus, the Alīnas, who most probably lived in Kafiristan, the Śivas, who lived on the Indus, the Vishāṇins, the Pakthas, and the Bhalānases. Sudās defeated the ten tribes, whose warriors were swallowed by the waters of the River Parushṇī, while the chiefs of the Anus and the Druhyus were killed. Immediately after the battle Sudās had to return to the eastern frontier to meet three other tribes called the Ajas or the goats, the Śigrus or the horse radishes, and the Yakshus or dwarfs. These three tribes appear to have been of non-Aryan origin.

The War with the Dravidians.

Among these earlier tribes the Purus were a great people. We possess the names of a large number of their chiefs. One, Trasadasyu, had often led them to victory against the Dravidians or the Dasyus. The Purus in part continued to exist as a separate tribe till the end of the fourth century B.C., when two of their chiefs met Alexander the Great. But quite early they mixed with their enemies, the Bharatas, and thus became the most powerful tribe in the Panjab. The united tribe became known as Kurus. A section of them, known as the Northern Kurus, dwelt in Afghanistan or Kashmir.

The Purus.

The Constitution of the Tribe.

The Indo-Aryan tribes consisted of loosely grouped families or clans. The father was the head of the family, and his descendants, both male and female, lived under his authority. The patriarchate was the earliest form of tribal government. There are clear indications of the survival of matriarchy, and the institution of marriage appears to have been very recent. The Indo-Aryan was a monogamist, though polygamy was not unknown. The husband was the master of the household, and the wife, though the mistress, was dependent on the husband. The standard of female morality was very high. The existence of polyandry cannot be proved, though it is known to have existed among the earlier Dravidian settlers. The later re-

The Patriarchate.

Marriages.

strictions placed on marriage were almost entirely unknown to the early Indo-Aryans, but marriage between father and daughter and between brother and sister, so very common in Egypt and the Near East, was not allowed. Child marriage was unknown, and great latitude was allowed in the choice of mates. Women enjoyed considerable independence and were fairly well educated. Before their marriage they lived under the protection of their fathers, and if they remained unmarried at the time of their father's death, they passed on to the protection of their brothers. Dowries and bride-prices had to be paid, and ugly men had to purchase their wives at a high price. Divorces were practically unknown, and the Vedic marriage was indissoluble. The marriage of widows was permitted, and generally a widow was expected to marry her late husband's younger brother.

The Position of Women.

The rights of the father or *paterfamilias* were very extensive. He had a certain amount of control over the marriage of his sons and daughters, and the son lived with his parents or grandparents in a joint family. The head of the family was regarded as the owner of the joint-family property, though individual members of the clan were allowed to possess separate movable property. The fields were divided into two classes, the cultivated area and the pasture land. The groups of huts or dwellings of the early Indo-Aryans formed the nucleus of the *grāma* or village. Several villages were combined into one *Viś* or district, and a group of districts was called *janapada* or tribal territory.

Patriarchal Rights.

Originally the Indo-Aryans were divided into three classes or castes. The Brāhmaṇa or priest, the Kshatriya or warrior, and the Vaiśya, i.e. the trader or cultivator, all claimed Indo-Aryan origin. The growth of the fourth caste belongs to a later stage of the history of the Indo-Aryan settlements in India. The Indo-Aryans made a large number of captives during their wars with the aboriginal Nishādas and the Dravidian Dasyus. These captives were enslaved, and with the increase in their numbers a rank had to be provided for them in the tribal constitution. But even after their manumission, they were regarded as serfs whose principal function was to minister to the wants of the three higher castes.

The Early Indo-Aryan Castes.

Śūdras.

The political constitution of the Indo-Aryan communities was monarchical. The king was the head of the state, and his power appears to have been uncontrolled. The office was normally hereditary, but in some cases elections took place. The king is called alternately *Rājan* or *Viśpati*, "the leader of the district". He was expected to maintain a large number of priests to perform sacrifices and magical rites. His income consisted of tribute paid by the conquered tribes and gifts from his people. It is not known whether he was regarded as the owner of the soil.

The King.

The principal officers mentioned in the Vedic literature are: (1) the *Senānī*, "the leader of the army", who was appointed by the king to command minor expeditions; (2) the *Grāmaṇī*, or "the head of the village"; (3) the *Vrajapati*, "the leader of the pastoral population"; and (4) the *Purohita* or "the priest", who was not merely the tribal priest or magician, but also a diplomat, and accompanied the tribe during wars, and was expected to aid the tribal army by spells or incantations at the time of battle. The power of the king was limited by the expression of the will of the people at the assembly which was called the *Sabhā* or the *Samiti*. Some scholars think that these two terms denote two different assemblies. The king was often present at these meetings. The election of a new king, after the deposition of a tyrant, or upon the failure of issue of the hereditary dynasty, was made by this tribal assembly.

The Principal Officers of the State.

The Tribal Assembly.

The king was the fountain of justice and administered civil as well as criminal law. The system of wergild, or blood-money, was very well known. Blood-money was paid in cattle, and ransom, called *Vaira-deya*, is mentioned. The principal crimes were cattle-lifting, burglary, house-breaking, and highway robbery. The punishment of the thief rested with the aggrieved persons, and the custom of tying up the culprit in stocks was well known.

Justice

Our knowledge of civil law is confined to barter and transfer of property. Movable property was bartered openly in the market, and any metallic currency or medium of exchange was probably unknown. The Dravidians, whom the Indo-Aryans displaced in Northern India, had introduced the use of coins

Currency.

in trade relations, but the Indo-Aryans had not advanced beyond fixing heads of cattle as the recognized standard of value. The term *nishka* was used to denote a certain weight of gold. Property passed by inheritance, and could be acquired by a man's personal exertion. The legal remedy for the recovery of debts was very well known. Rates of interest were unknown, but the debtor had to pay a fixed amount at the time of repayment as the price of the use of the money. The debtor was liable to be imprisoned for non-payment and to be reduced to slavery. Arbitration was very usual. **Usury.**

The Aryans had introduced the horse into Babylonia, and in war the Indo-Aryans relied principally on their war-chariots drawn by horses. The king and the principal nobles used chariots, while the army consisted of two other arms, infantry and cavalry. The principal weapons were bows and arrows, lances, spears, swords, and axes. **The Army.** **Chariots.**

The chief occupations of the people were agriculture and cattle-rearing. The land was ploughed, and the plough was drawn by oxen instead of horses. Irrigation was known, and, as at present, the fields were watered either from canals or from wells. The unit for the measurement of corn was called *Khāri*. Lotus ponds and fruit gardens are often mentioned. Cattle consisted mostly of kine and sheep. The cattle were kept in stables and pens. Milking was done by the members of the household as well as by professional milkers. Dogs were used for guarding cattle and houses. Meat was freely used by all classes of Indo-Aryans, and the use of strong drink was not prohibited. A special kind of liquor, called *Soma*, was offered in the form of libations to the gods. Weaving in cotton and wool was done by both sexes. Chariot-making was one of the principal industries. Images were made from wood. Boats and ships are also mentioned, though we do not know whether the Indo-Aryans were able to navigate the open seas. The blacksmiths used a metal called *ayas*, a term applied both to copper and iron. The term used by the early Indo-Aryans for a blacksmith (*karmāra*) appears to have been derived from a Dravidian word. The use of gold was very well known but silver was rare, though it was known to the earlier settlers, the Dravidians. Mixed metal, bell-metal, tin, and lead were **Occupations of the People.** **Meat-eating and Drinking.** **Weaving.** **Industries.**

also used, and articles made of leather are often mentioned. The practice of medicine was yet mixed with magic, but we find that even at that early date the Indo-Aryans were able to

Medicine. recognize a number of diseases, such as jaundice, fever, phthisis, rheumatism, scrofula, dysentery, venereal diseases, heart diseases, elephantiasis, and smallpox. The purchase of drugs from the people of the Himalayan regions, which has developed into an extensive trade at the present day, is also mentioned. The ancient Hindu surgeons had a better knowledge of anatomy than their successors of the present day, and they used ligatures for stopping hæmorrhage. Other professions mentioned are those of the barber, the spy, the dancer, the vintner, the currier, the fisher, the potter, the dyer, and the tanner.

While the Indo-Aryans were settling in increasing numbers in the Panjab, the Dravidians were divided into a number of small and large kingdoms. The principal Dravidian kingdoms were those of Magadha and Kāmarūpa in the north, and Kaliṅga, Kerala, Choḷa, and Pāṇḍya in the south. The

Dravidian Colonies. Dravidians had developed their navy very early, and had spread their colonies over Southern India, Ceylon, and the Indian Archipelago. They had spread their civilization over South-eastern Asia. In Pegu and Arakan they mixed with the local people of Austric origin, and this mixed tribe, now speaking the Austric Mōn language, is now known as the Talaings, "the people from the country of the Three Kaliṅgas". In other places in the Malay Peninsula they are called *Klings*, which is a contracted form of the Dravidian term "*Kaliṅga*". The local chronicles of the Talaings claim that the capital of Upper Burma, Tagaung or *Ḍavāka*, was founded as early as 2600 B.C. For a long time it was a fashion of scholars to sneer at these local histories, but opinion is gradually veering round. It is now recognized that Northern India played but a small part in the colonization of the Indian Archipelago. Kern recognized long ago that the earliest Indian colonists in Sumatra were of Dravidian origin. Before the spread of the Malays in different parts of the archipelago, the Dravidian element was supreme.

Cambodia. The Austric people of Cambodia mixed with the Dravidians and founded a powerful kingdom long before the birth of

Christ. The Dravidians spread to the neighbouring island of Ceylon and occupied the northern half of it. Everywhere they carried their distinctive culture, and after they became Hinduized, they maintained the Hindu or Aryo-Dravidian culture until recent times. It was long after the first colonization that these Dravidian colonists accepted Brahmanism and Buddhism and abandoned or modified their original national faith. After they had been settled for a long time in Indo-China and Insulindia, or the Indian Archipelago (Sumatra, Java, Bali, &c.), the Indian colonists were assimilated by the original Austric peoples, and gradually merged among them; but for a long time they retained the Sanskrit language, and the South Indian alphabets, which they brought from India, are the source of the Mōn and Burmese, Siamese and Cambodian, Javanese, Bugese, and other alphabets of Indo-China and Malaya still current from Arakan to the Celebes. **Ceylon.**

BIBLIOGRAPHY

Cambridge History of India, Vol. I, chaps. iii–iv.
CHILDE, *Aryans.*
Cambridge Ancient History, Vol. II, chaps. i–iii.

CHAPTER IV

THE SPREAD OF INDO-ARYAN CIVILIZATION AND THE CONVERSION OF THE DRAVIDIAN PEOPLE TO HINDUISM

Long after the period when the hymns of the *Ṛigveda* were composed, the Indo-Aryans spread towards the east and the south. The centre of culture also shifted towards the east, and when the *Brāhmaṇas* were being compiled, Kurukshetra had already become the most important centre. The tribes of the Panjab were rarely mentioned. The regions to the east of the Kuru kingdom became more prominent. Kośala or Oudh, Magadha or South Bihar, and Aṅga or South-eastern Bihar began to be mentioned. We now hear for the first time of the Andhras, and of the tribes living **The shifting Centre of Aryan Culture.**

to the east and the south of Aṅga, such as the Puṇḍras of Bengal, the Śabaras of Orissa and the Central Provinces, and the Pulindas of South-western India. The country to the south of the Yamunā was gradually becoming known. The kingdom of Berar, the ancient Vidarbha, is mentioned in the Aitareya and Jaiminiya *Brāhmaṇas*. The northern part of Rajputana became known, and the Indo-Aryans learned that the River Sarasvatī lost itself in the Indian Desert. The tribe of Kāśis founded the city of Benares in the east. The Bharatas disappeared from the field; their place was taken by the Kurus, who combined with the Pañchālas and obtained supremacy over the Indo-Aryan tribes for some time. The Matsyas, a tribe of Indo-Aryans who adopted the fish as their totem, colonized Northern Rajputana. To the north of the Ganges, Kośala or Oudh and Videha or North Bihar became independent centres of Indo-Aryan civilization.

To the south of the Ganges, Magadha or South Bihar resisted all attempts of the Indo-Aryans to conquer it, and the flat plains of Bihar and Bengal remained independent under local kings. The country was still unknown to the Indo-Aryans. Minstrels from this country spread throughout Indo-Aryan colonies, and the word *Māgadha* came to be used as a synonym for a minstrel or bard by the Indo-Aryans. The latter did **Magadha.** not like Magadha because the manners and the customs of the inhabitants of that country were strange to them. The civilization of Magadha was utterly different from their own. The gods were foreign to the Indo-Aryans; the Indo-Aryan priests and gods were not tolerated by the people of Magadha. The Māgadhas and the Andhras were at first regarded as outcasts, but later on, when the Indo-Aryan priests came to realize that it was not possible for them to conquer or convert these people, they accepted some of the gods of the Dravidians, gave them Indo-Aryan names, and began to worship them. This common worship aroused the sympathy of the Dravidians and gradually brought them within the pale of the transformed religion of the Indo-Aryans. The conversion of Magadha took place long before the birth of Buddha, but even at that time the Brāhmaṇas had not attained there the supremacy which they possessed in the Indo-Aryan territories.

The later Vedic literature recognizes the position of the Śūdras as a distinct order of society, though it denies them the right of taking part in the sacrifices. Śūdras were allowed to exercise any trade. Some of them appear to have combined themselves in tribes, such tribal names as the Baindas, Parṇakas, and the Paulkasas having been preserved in the later Vedic literature. **The Śūdras.**

During this period, the power of the Indo-Aryan tribal chief, or king, increased, and we hear very seldom of the tribal assembly or *samiti*. The king had obtained the power of depriving any commoner of his private property. The nobles obtained the position of landlords, or intermediaries between the cultivator and the king. Slaves and serfs became very common. The Vaishyas were divided into various sub-castes according to profession. The cultivator regarded himself as belonging to a higher caste than the carpenter, the smith, and the tanner. The Śūdras also were increasing in power and wealth, and with their increase in number they approached the position of the Vaishyas of the lowest orders. **The King.** **The Lower Castes.**

In later Vedic literature the superior position of the Brāhmaṇa was assured, and he was given a distinct preference in law, both criminal and civil. A father had the right of dividing property among his sons according to his will. The position of women deteriorated and they were denied the right of inheriting property. On the death of her husband a widow passed on to his family like his property. Her earnings belonged either to her father or her husband. With the increase in the royal power the Indo-Aryan chiefs became polygamous. **The position of Brāhmaṇas and Women.**

The occupation of the fertile plains of the regions of the seven rivers of the Panjab and the Ganges and the Yamunā increased the material prosperity of the Indo-Aryan tribes. Society was divided into a large number of castes or classes. Among the servile castes we hear of several classes, such as fishermen, shepherds, fire-rangers, charioteers, workers in jewels, basket-makers, washermen, rope-makers, dyers, chariot-makers, weavers, slaughterers, cooks, sellers of dried fish, gatherers of wood, professional acrobats and musicians. The boatman was assisted by oarsmen and polemen. The Brāh- **Artisans.**

maṇas were subdivided into several classes and the life of the priest came to be more rigidly regulated. In the first stage of his life, he was to be apprenticed to another priest, and at this stage he used to be called the *Brahmachārin*. He was taught by his master, for whom he begged and did all sorts of menial work. In the next stage of his life (*gārhastha*), the apprentice married and became a full-fledged priest. In the third stage of his life, when he grew old, he used to leave his home and retire with his wife or alone to some holy place for meditation. The third stage is called *Vānaprastha* and the fourth that of a *Yati*. In the former, however, he was not to give up Vedic sacrifices completely, which he used to perform in his home-life. But even this ceased in the latest stage when, freed from all ties, he gave himself up entirely to meditation.

The Four Stages of the Brāhmaṇa's Life.

It was about this time that increasing commerce compelled the Indo-Aryans to adopt a currency. In its earlier stage the Indo-Aryan currency consisted simply of certain weights of gold, silver, and copper. The red and black seed of the *Krishṇāla* or the *Guñjā* berry was adopted as the unit of weight. In the Brāhmaṇas we hear of the *Śatamāna*, or gold weighing a hundred Krishṇālas. The cow was superseded by coins as the standard of value. The methods of weighing gold, silver, and copper were different. In weighing gold, five *Guñjā* seeds were taken to be equal to one *Māsaka*, while only two seeds were required to form a *Māsaka* in the case of silver. Eighty *Guñjā* seeds weight of gold formed the standard of gold currency, the earliest name for which is *Suvarṇa*, i.e. gold. This simple name shows that the Aryans had not yet started minting coins, but, like all primitive communities, used a certain weight of unminted gold for exchange. Similarly, in the case of silver, thirty-two *Guñjā* berries formed a Dharaṇa, which is the oldest name of a silver coin in India. In fact, this weight of silver, which later on became the standard weight of silver coins, is called "antique" or "old" (*purāṇa*) by later writers. The standard weight of copper was quite different from that of gold or silver, and eighty *Guñjā* berries or one hundred and forty grains of copper became the unit of copper coinage,

The Coinage.

"Purāṇas."

which was called the *Kārshāpaṇa* in Sanskrit and *Kāhāpaṇa* in Pali. **Kārshāpaṇas.**

The Indo-Aryans remained confined to the basins of the Indus and the Ganges and do not appear to have colonized any part of India which lay to the south of the River Narmadā and to the east of Mithilá. The great non-Aryan kingdoms of the East, e.g. those of Magadha and Kāmarūpa (*Prāgjyotisha*), never submitted to the Indo-Aryan invaders and kept them at bay for centuries. The Indo-Aryan conquest of North-eastern and Southern India was cultural, not physical. **Dravidian Kingdoms.**

We do not know what the religious ideas and cults of the Dravidians were in the days of their greatest glory, but can make a very near approach to the actual facts by comparing the deities of modern Hinduism with the deities of the earlier Indo-Aryans. The Indo-Aryans worshipped the powers of nature. We have seen earlier that the Aryans of Asia Minor worshipped the Sun, which they called *Mitra* or *Shuriyash*, the Wind, called *Maruttash*, the Sky, called *Varuṇa*, and the *Nāsatyas* or the *Aśvins*, who were regarded as divine magicians. To this group of gods they added the Moon and Fire later on. Compared with this simple pantheon, the multitude of gods and goddesses worshipped by the Hindus at the present day seems bewildering. The original Vedic gods have now been thrust into the background. Indra, Varuṇa, the Nāsatyas, and even the Sun, are seldom worshipped. Their place was once taken by the divine trinity, Brahmā, Vishṇu, and Śiva. But at the present day Brahmā possesses only a very few followers. The majority of Hindus belong to three different groups, the followers of Vishṇu, the followers of Śiva, and the worshippers of the Śakti or Female Energy. Vishṇu and Śiva are seldom mentioned in the Vedic literature. Some scholars think that Vishṇu has been evolved out of the Sun-god, while Śiva is a development of the minor Vedic deity, Rudra. The Vedic literature contains no reference to any female deity to which the Durgā or the Devī of the present day might even approximate. Even Śiva and Vishṇu, as they are represented in worship at the present day, contain certain elements of non-Aryan origin. Śiva, with his emblem the phallus, is evidently a non-Aryan deity whose admission into the Indo-Aryan

The Gods of the Primitive Indo-Aryan Religion. **The Trinity of Modern Hinduism.** **The Entry of Śiva.**

pantheon caused bitter strife. The story of the sacrifice which Daksha, the son of Brahmā, wanted to celebrate by excluding Śiva and who was destroyed by Śiva, is only an allegorical way of representing the final triumph of the phallic god and the formal inclusion of Śiva and his emblem in the Indo-Aryan pantheon. A similar allegorical representation hides the true story of the worship of the snake goddess Manasā by the Dravidians of Bengal.

Siva-worship by the Asuras.

Numerous references in post-Vedic literature clearly indicate that the earlier Dravidian settlers were worshippers of Śiva. Durgā was originally the goddess of vegetation, and her worship was celebrated at the end of the winter, when the melting of the snows brought down floods in the rivers and fertilized the land. The earliest legend about her worship in post-Vedic literature is to be found in connexion with the slaughter of the buffalo-demon. In many cases this primitive goddess retained her original shape even after her glorification by the Indo-Aryans. The images of Yogamāyā at Vindhyachala, of Kirīṭeśvarī near Murshidabad, and of Kāmākhyā near Gauhati still retain their original primitive forms.

The Origin of Durga.

Transformation of Local Goddess.

The Conversion of the Priesthood.

Gradually the Dravidian priests obtained a place in the Indo-Aryan caste system. The old gods and goddesses of the Dravidian people underwent slight changes, but their worshippers accepted these. In Rajputana and Gujarat the old goddesses were worshipped alike by the aboriginal Minas, Mairs, Bhils, and the Aryanized Gujars. Even after the conversion of the kings and the richer people to Jainism, the worship of Durgā, which required bloodshed every day, survived in all parts of Gujarat. The shrines of the Mother on a peak of Girnar Hill close to one of the holiest places of the Jains in Kathiawad, at Khodiarmata and at Pavagadh in Northern Gujarat, testify to the popularity which this non-Aryan goddess had attained in Western India. In Sindh the worship of the Mother is still carried on, at Hinglaj, more than one hundred miles to the west of Karachi, and a form of suppressed Mother-worship is practised by the Musalmans at Satyan-jo-than near Sukkur.

When Śiva and the Female Energy, Durgā, Devī, or Śakti,

found a place among the older gods of the Indo-Aryans, many Dravidian priests of this sect became Brāhmaṇas. Very few Brāhmaṇas of Bengal, Bihar and Orissa are really of Indo-Aryan origin. South Indian tradition records numerous instances of their Brāhmaṇas taking wives from the lower castes. In many cases non-Brāhmaṇas were admitted into the Brāhmaṇa caste as sufficient Brāhmaṇas were not available, when the reformed Indo-Aryan religion obtained preference.[1]

Origin of Northern, Central, and Southern Brāhmaṇas.

The Brāhmaṇas of the post-Vedic period became more liberal, and some of them became the priests of the Śūdras, for which they lost their rank among the more orthodox conservative Brāhmaṇas. These priests worshipped the older gods and goddesses of the Dravidian settlers, as the village gods (*Grāma-devatā*), the goddess of fecundity (*Shashṭhi*), the snake goddess (*Manasā*), and a host of others who now claim to be members of the Indo-Aryan pantheon. South of the Narmadā, the Brāhmaṇa declines to worship certain non-Aryan deities who are worshipped by the Śūdra priests, called *Guravas* in the Maratha country. Some shrines of such gods are celebrated all over the country, and the chief of them is that of Khāṇḍobā, the hereditary deity of the Holkars of Indore. In the Madras Presidency, the worship of non-Aryan deities is still continued in various forms. Chief among such deities are the seven sisters, whose worship still prevails in the north also, where they are called the seven mothers (*Saptamātṛikā*).

The Degeneration of the Brāhmaṇas.

Non-Brāhmaṇa Priests. Village Dieties.

The Śiva-worship of India had one element in common with the primitive worship of the early Dravidian people, which is the worship of the phallus and the dedication of virgins to the worship of the god. The second element was, probably, brought by the Dravidians from their original home in South-western Asia. Some scholars have found references to the worship of the phallus in the Vedic age in a particular passage of the Ṛig-Veda; but the word on which this theory is based may mean something else.

The Dedication of Virgins.

References to Śiva-worship.

With the change in the form of the religion of the early Dravidian settlers and the Indo-Aryan invaders, the fusion of the different races became easy. The Dravidian deities

[1] E. Thurston, *Castes and Tribes of Southern India*, Vol. I, p. 54.

now obtained worship both from the Indo-Aryan and the Dravidian, but the ritual changed. The lower orders of society retained their primitive form of worship and their own priests, who gradually began to claim Indo-Aryan origin and became low-caste Brāhmaṇas in the long run. People of non-Aryan origin gradually began to claim descent from one or other of the Indo-Aryan castes. The non-Aryan magicians and the Dravidian priests became Brāhmaṇas. Indo-Aryan Brāhmaṇas married aboriginal and Dravidian women, and their children came to be regarded as pure-born Indo-Aryans. Warriors of all classes, aboriginals, pre-Dravidians, Dravidians, and Indo-Aryans claimed to be Kshatriyas, while traders, artisans, and cultivators, irrespective of their racial origin, became Vaiśyas. The fusion of races and claims of Indo-Aryan descent were encouraged by the Brāhmaṇas as they were sure means of eradicating primary racial differences. Gradually the Dravidians forgot that they could claim a civilization much older than that of the new invaders and that their ancestors did not worship the rude primitive gods of the Aryans.

The Fusion of Races.

The Dravidian hatred for the Indo-Aryan is still preserved in the earliest Tamil poetry. Even after their Aryanization, the Dravidians preserved their independence, and while the Indo-Aryans of Northern India remained divided into small principalities, four great kingdoms sprang up in the south. They are the kingdoms of Kaliṅga, Chera or Śera, Choḷa or Śoḷa, and Pāṇḍya. The Dravidian kingdoms formed a cluster along the edge of the peninsula, while the earlier inhabitants of the western coast fell under the steady advance of the Indo-Aryans of the north and of the barbarians from across the sea. The western coast of the Indian Peninsula is very rich in ports, and the natives of this coast-land have been expert sailors from the earliest times. These ports obtained independence on account of their great wealth, and remained independent even in modern times. Such were the ports of Cutch and Southern Sindh, which region the Indians called *Sauvīra* and the Greeks Ophir; Saurāshṭra, now called Verawal, in Kathiawad; Cambay or Khambāyat; Bhṛigukachchha or Bharukachchha, which the Greeks called Bary-

The Dravidian Kingdoms.

The Ports of the Western Coast.

gaza and which is now called Broach by the English; and Muziris or Muyiri, which lay south of Mangalore. The western coast of India is rich in large and small creeks and lagoons which formed schools of navigation for the sailor boys of the locality and made them better sailors than the people of the eastern coast.

The Ports of the Eastern Coast.

On the eastern coast of the peninsula, on the other hand, the sea is shallow and its bed slopes gently, which makes it difficult for ships to ride at anchor or to find a safe harbourage. The ships of the eastern coast are therefore far less seaworthy, while the coast itself is liable to violent storms. In spite of these disadvantages, the sailors of Kaliṅga became the pioneers of Indian colonization. But while Kaliṅga grew into a powerful empire, the ports on the western coast developed into small city-states.

The Traders of Western India.

They were entirely devoted to the trade with western lands. Later, on the downfall of Kaliṅga, they started trading with China and the eastern archipelago. But up to the historical period they were divided into small states, seldom acknowledging the supremacy of the great empires of the Deccan plateau. The plateau remained for the most part very sparsely inhabited and the last resort of the aborigines, who refused to come under the domination of the Dravidian or the Indo-Aryan.

The State of the Deccan Plateau.

Such were the Kunbis and the Marathas of Western India, the Kolis and the Bhils of Gujarat and Rajputana, and the Gonds, the Mundas, and other minor aboriginal tribes, who lived in the secluded valleys of the Vindhya range.

BIBLIOGRAPHY

Cambridge History of India, Vol. I, chap. v.

CHAPTER V

VEDIC LITERATURE

The sacred literature of the old Indo-Aryans is the Veda. For a long time it was not reduced to writing.

The Vedas.

The Vedas consist of odes and hymns addressed to the various gods, such as Agni (Fire), Varuṇa (the Sky), Mitra (the Sun),

Indra (the Thunder), &c. Each collection of verses was composed by a particular priest or a particular clan of priests, who are now regarded as sages (*Ṛishis*). The Hindus of India now think that Ṛishis were not the actual composers of these verses; but that the verses were of divine origin and revealed to these priests. The Kshattriya priest Viśvāmitra composed a good many verses of the Vedas. The earlier hymns of the Vedas contain a pre-Indian element, and it is quite possible that some of them were composed long before the Indo-Aryans settled in India proper. At a much later date, the verses of the Vedas were divided into four different classes. These four divisions are called the Four Vedas: Ṛik, Sāman, Yajus, and Atharvan.[1]

The pre-Indian Element.

The Ṛig-veda.

The Ṛigveda contains ten *maṇḍalas* or great divisions, which are arranged either according to the names of the Ṛishis or according to subject-matter. The literature contains a good deal of material for the history of the period which has already been considered in Chapter III. Most of the hymns of the Ṛigveda, as it stands at present, are intended for the use of that division of the Indo-Aryan priesthood which recited these verses or formulæ at the time of throwing oblations into the Fire. This particular division of the Indo-Aryan priesthood is termed the *Hotṛi*-priests. The Sāmaveda consists of hymns which were chanted or sung. The particular class of priests who used to chant, played a part of secondary importance at the sacrifices and were regarded as the assistants of the *Hotṛis*. They were called the singers (*Udgātṛis*). A third division of the Vedas is called the Yajurveda and contains the earliest prose in the Indo-Aryan languages, or perhaps in the Indo-Germanic languages. This division is devoted to the details of the ritual to be followed in the sacrifices and contains the prayers and formulæ of the *Adhvaryu* priest, whose duty it was to arrange the offerings (*charu*) and the sacrifices (*bali*), with the small and large oblations (*āhūti*) in proper position and order, on and around the altar of the sacrificial Fire. The Yajurveda is divided into two different schools, the Black and the White. The position of the fourth group is

The Sāma-veda.

The Yajur-veda.

[1] In combination with *Veda*, Ṛik and Yajus become Ṛigveda and Yajurveda.

difficult to determine. Scholars used to think that the Atharvaveda was a later compilation, but this supposition has now been proved entirely false. This group contains some of the oldest verses of the Ṛigveda. Technically the hymns in this Veda are regarded as being the verses for the fourth priest, the *Brahman*, who in the later stage of the evolution of the Vedic ritual was appointed to superintend and harmonize the functions of the three groups mentioned above. The Atharvaveda contains much earlier matter for which Vyāsa, the classifier, could find no place in the first three Vedas. It is a repository of the magical charms and incantations which were used by the Indo-Aryan people before they became civilized by contact with the Dravidians and which, in a later stage of culture, they were ashamed to recognize as a part of their holy ritual. The late Bal Gangadhar Tilak traced some Sumerian names in the Atharvaveda; such as *Taimata*, who is a black serpent in Indian literature and a snake-goddess in the Sumerian religion, and *Urugula*, the word for a great city in the non-Semitic Sumerian language of Babylon.[1]

The Atharvaveda.

Sumerian Elements in it.

Scholars are of opinion that the redaction of the Saṁhitā of the Ṛigveda took place long before the compilation of other Saṁhitās. The *Saṁhitā* of the Sāmaveda depends a good deal on the Saṁhitā of the Ṛigveda. The Black Yajurveda contains at least three different texts—the *Saṁhitās* of the Maitrāyaṇīya, the Taittirīya, and the Kāṭhaka schools. There exists a large number of fragments of another *Saṁhitā*, called the *Kāpishṭhala*, which is closely allied to the Kāṭhaka school. The white school of the Yajurveda possesses the Vājasaneyī *Saṁhitā*, and the Atharvaveda has only one *Saṁhitā*. The Yajurveda contains more prose than verse. Thus in the Black Yajurveda verses or formulæ for recitation are followed by prose explanations and commentaries combined into a single whole.

The Saṁhitās.

Each Veda is again divided into four parts: (i) the *Saṁhitā* or the texts for recitation, (ii) the *Brāhmaṇa*, (iii) the *Āraṇyaka*, and (iv) the *Upanishad*. The *Brāhmaṇa* is a prose commentary on the *Saṁhitā*. The *Āraṇyakas* are a class of

Sub-divisions of Vedic Literature.

[1] *Bhandarkar Commemoration Volume*, pp. 29–92.

expositions which were so novel and important that knowledge of them had to be imparted in the *Araṇya* or the forest. The *Upanishads* are philosophical doctrines which were to be kept very secret and to be imparted to students in secrecy. Among the *Brāhmaṇas* of the Ṛigveda, the Aitareya and Kauśitakī are the only ones known. The Pañchaviṁśa *Brāhmaṇa* of the Sāmaveda is regarded as earlier than the *Brāhmaṇas* of the Ṛigveda. The Śatapatha *Brāhmaṇa* of the White Yajurveda is one of the most important works of the Vedic literature. Of the Black Yajurveda, the Taittirīya *Brāhmaṇa* is really a supplementary work which contains details not taken up in the *Saṁhitā*. The Gopatha *Brāhmaṇa* appertains to the Atharvaveda. It contains portions of other texts, such as the Śatapatha *Brāhmaṇa*. Special portions from the *Brāhmaṇas* have been called *Āraṇyakas*, or texts which had to be studied in forests where other students could not overhear. The texts of the *Āraṇyakas* which we know, are the Aitareya and Kauśitakī of the Ṛigveda and the Taittirīya of the Black Yajurveda.

The Brāhmaṇas.

The Araṇyakas.

The Upanishads, or the esoteric portions, consist entirely of philosophical writings. They are of later origin than the texts of the *Brāhmaṇas* and the *Āraṇyakas*, and their composition was carried on till the historical period. The secrecy maintained in teaching these philosophical doctrines was necessary; because, at first, these pure innovations in the primitive faith of the Aryans must have excited popular opposition. Each of the three *Āraṇyakas* has an *Upanishad*, but the most important among this class of literature are the *Bṛihad-āraṇyaka*, which is attached to the Śatapatha *Brāhmaṇa*, and the *Chhāndogya*, attached to the Sāmaveda. These two are regarded as the oldest of the Upanishad class of literature. The Jaiminīya Brāhmaṇa of the Sāmaveda contains one chapter which is an Upanishad of the same name, but in reality is an *Āraṇyaka* and contains the brief Kena *Upanishad*. Many of the Upanishads date from a period not much more remote than the time of Buddha.

The Upanishads.

The Date of the Upanishads.

The *Sūtras* are brief rules giving directions for the performances of various duties and fall into three great classes. The *Gṛihya-Sūtras* deal with small domestic sacrifices, and the *Śrauta-Sūtras* describe great sacrifices at which it was necessary to employ a large number of priests. A third class of Sūtras, called *Dharma-Sūtras*, enunciate ordinary law and practice. The *Sūtras* throw a great deal of light upon certain practices which are expressed in doubtful terms in the *Brāhmaṇas*. **The Sūtras.**

With the increase in literature referring solely to religion, the Indo-Aryans progressed in other directions of thought. In the Brāhmaṇa period, which is the name given by scholars to the latter part of the Vedic period, the Indo-Aryans made a distinct advance in astronomy. In the Ṛigveda we come to know the year of three hundred and sixty days, divided into twelve months, which is six days longer than the synodic lunar and nearly six days short of the solar year. To bring this imaginary year to the level of the solar year, the intercalation of one month was begun early. The *Saṁhitās* show knowledge of the lunar mansions, roughly corresponding to the position of the Moon in the different regions of the horizon, during the lunar month. The number of these lunar mansions or Nakshatras is given as twenty-seven in the Taittirīya Saṁhitā and twenty-eight in the Atharvaveda. The names of twelve of the Nakshatras were selected as names of the months. **Astronomy.**

The ritual was developed a great deal. Animal sacrifices became much more elaborate. In addition to the simple sacrifice, with an oblation of the Sóma juice, elaborate performances lasting months or even years came to be celebrated. Some of the well-known sacrifices were associated with popular customs. Thus, the *Rājasūya* was the sacrifice for the anointing of the king; the *Vājapeya* was the sacrifice in which a popular chariot-race was the most important feature; the *Gavāmayana* sacrifice, lasting a whole year, was a celebration of the winter solstice. **Sacrifices.**

During the Brāhmaṇa period we notice the beginning of the regular worship of Śiva. Rudra becomes a popular god, and we find verses addressed to him in the *Saṁhitā* of the Yajurveda. In this period, Śiva or Rudra gradually came to be one of the most important figures of the reformed Indo-Aryan pantheon. Though Śiva had obtained a place in the **Worship of Śiva.**

pantheon, Vishṇu had not in this period; but the constant association of Vishṇu with the sacrifices shows that he held, probably, a very strong position among the lower classes, who were mostly descended from the Dravidians and the aborigines, and consequently the Indo-Aryan priests found it very difficult to ignore him.

The Position of Vishṇu.

The Date of the Vedic Period.

The date of the Vedic literature cannot be fixed with accuracy. An attempt has been made to fix this date from the position of the equinoxes; but the view of Jacobi has not been universally accepted. Tilak and Jacobi held that the year began with the summer solstice, but Keith holds that the verses do not state that at that time the year really began with the summer solstice. There is another assumption which does not seem to be based on reliable evidence. Its chief factor is the date of the death of Buddha. Scholars assume that Buddha died *c.* 486 B.C., and, calculating backward, think that the Brāhmaṇa period began a little earlier than 800 B.C., and that therefore the oldest hymns of the Ṛigveda cannot be earlier than 1200 B.C.

There is another traditional date, which has not been properly discussed by scholars. According to the *Purāṇas*, the Kuru king Parīkshit was born 1050 years before Mahāpadma, the first king of Magadha. According to the Vāyu *Purāṇa*, Mahāpadma began to reign forty years before the accession of Chandragupta the Maurya. If Chandragupta's accession is placed in 322 B.C., then the accession of Parīkshit has to be placed in 1412 B.C. There may be very slight discrepancies in this, but the evidence of the Purāṇas shows clearly that in the middle of the fifth century A.D. it was believed in India that Parīkshit lived at the end of the fifteenth century before Christ. Now Parīkshit is a king of the Vedic period. One of his descendants, Janmejaya, is stated to have performed a horse-sacrifice. According to the Purāṇas, this king performed two horse-sacrifices. One of these sacrifices was performed by the priest Indrota Daivāpi Śaunaka. According to the Aitareya *Brāhmaṇa*, the other horse-sacrifice was performed by Tura Kāvasheya. The Vedic literature does not mention the later hero-god Kṛishṇa nor any of the hundred Kuru brothers, nor again the Pāṇḍavas. But Parīkshit is known and so is Dhṛitarāshṭra Vaichitravīrya. There is ample evidence

The Date of Parīkshit.

for believing that Parīkshit was a real king and not the mere shadowy creation of a poet. The traditional date of this king, which was accepted by Indian scholars at the time when the earliest *Purāṇas* were composed, can therefore be accepted as a basis for the approximate calculation of the date of the Ṛigveda. If a king mentioned in the Śatapatha and the Aitareya *Brāhmaṇas* was living in the last decade of the fifteenth century before the birth of Christ, then the composition of the Indian verses of the Ṛigveda cannot be placed at a date later than 2000 B.C. In other words, it is very likely that the irruptions of the Aryan barbarians took place simultaneously into the valleys of the Euphrates and the Indus.

BIBLIOGRAPHY

Cambridge History of India, Vol. I, chaps. iv, v, ix, and x.
WINTERNITZ, *History of Indian Literature*, Vol. I.
H. C. RAYCHANDHURI, *Political History of Ancient India*, pp. 5–24.

CHAPTER VI

THE EPIC LITERATURE OF INDIA

The Mahābhārata is the earliest epic of the Indo-Aryans. It is mentioned in the Sūtra literature of the later Vedic period. Indian epic poetry is divided into the two parts: (*a*) *Itihāsas* and *Purāṇas* and (*b*) *Kāvyas*. The Mahābhārata is a combination of both the classes. The Itihāsas and Purāṇas are mentioned in literature from the time of the Atharvaveda. Originally the great epic must have been a popular ballad about the war between the Kurus and the Pāṇḍus. It is closely connected with the White Yajurveda and its *Brāhmaṇa*, the Śatapatha. The heroes of the epic are mentioned in that *Brāhmaṇa*, and Janamejaya is mentioned as a recent personage.

The Origin of the Mahābhārata.

Though the Kurus are known to the later Vedic literature, the Pāṇḍus are entirely unknown. They are sons of the wife of one of the Kuru princes. Some scholars think that the Pāṇḍus were immigrants into India who were entirely unconnected with the Kurus. It is quite possible that Kunti, a daughter

The Origin of the Pāṇḍus.

of the Yādava clan, was carried away by a barbarian named Pāṇḍu and the five Pāṇḍava brothers were born of this illicit connexion. The mythical origin of the five Pāṇḍava brothers and the story of the birth of Dhṛitarāshṭra and Pāṇḍu indicate possible illegitimacy. Dhṛitarāshṭra is recognized in Vedic literature as the son of Vichitravīrya, but Pāṇḍu is not mentioned, and the epics seek to justify the birth of these two princes according to the law of *niyoga*. Ambā and Ambikā, the wives of a Kuru prince, are mentioned in the Śatapatha *Brāhmaṇa*. The Pāṇḍus are called a mountain clan in Buddhist literature. They are generally regarded as a polyandrous tribe on account of the marriage of the five brothers with one daughter of Drupada. The Mahābhārata describes them as being unmannerly and unruly and not polished courtiers like the Kurus. These facts indicate that the Pāṇḍus had very little in common with the Kurus.

The Different Texts of the Mahābhārata.

Three different texts of the Mahābhārata are known: (*a*) the northern or the Kashmīrian, (*b*) the southern, and (*c*) the Javanese. The northern text differs from the southern text a good deal. A study of the interpolations in the so-called southern text shows that thousands of verses of narrative and didactic material have been added to the epic text, and that the redaction comprises an incorporation of materials drawn from the Purāṇas and the Harivaṁśa (a sort of appendix, which was added to the Mahābhārata), as well as elaborations of the original text, sometimes by the insertion of a dozen or so of verses, or by the addition to a section of half-dozen new chapters narrating feats of the heroes or insisting on the divine character of some demi-god. The Javanese version, however, shows a much purer text of this epic.

The Southern Version.

The Purity of the Javanese Text.

The "Hero-lauds".

The epics are supposed to have originated from "*gāthās*" or verses, sung in honour of great men at certain ceremonies. The Gṛihya-Sūtras mention another kind of "*hero-lauds*". These *Gāthās* and *Nārāśaṁsis* are generally supposed to have developed into epic poems like the Mahābhārata. At the year-long celebration, preparatory to the horse-sacrifices, ten days were devoted to the singing of a series of lauds of gods and heroes wherein the great and noble deeds of kings were sung by priests and warrior musicians in *gāthās* of an extemporaneous character; while the recitation of legends in verse accompanied other events of life.

The Mahābhārata could not have been the work of any single person, and in order to be brought up to its present size the process of interpolation must have gone on for several centuries. It cannot therefore be said that the Mahābhārata depicts the state of India at any particular period. The verses of the Mahābhārata are less polished than those of the Rāmāyaṇa. There are many tales in both the epics which depict similar economic conditions, and the social usages recorded are identical; but the Rāmāyaṇa betrays a later or a more advanced stage of civilization. The Rāmāyaṇa is therefore regarded as a much later poem than the Mahābhārata. The Rāmāyaṇa is the outcome of a hero-laud describing the triumph of a chief of the Kośala clan, whose wife was carried away by a Dravidian chief. Later on, the Kośala chief, Rāma, and the shepherd chief, Kṛishṇa, were deified and considered to be the incarnations of Vishṇu. The outlines of the Rāmāyaṇa and the Mahābhārata are mentioned among the Buddhist stories, where we can recognize the normal forms of these heroes, because there we see them without their divine attributes. The Rāmāyaṇa is also the product of ages and was not the composition of any single author. The identity of Rāma with the rival chief of the Kośalas was a later thought.[1]

The Mahābhārata an Earlier Poem than the Rāmāyaṇa.

Earlier forms of the Stories.

The majority of writers on the history of India have been obsessed with the idea of an epic age following the later Vedic age. It is now quite clear that there was no epic age proper in India. The Mahābhārata is a story or a hero-laud belonging to the later Vedic period. Janamejaya and Parīkshit were real kings who belong to the *Brāhmaṇa* period and whose ancestry was probably non-Aryan. While the Rāmāyaṇa is solely the

The so-called Epic Age.

[1] "But the Rāmāyaṇa differs essentially from the Mahābhārata not only in time but in spirit. Its most spirited scenes occur before the epic plot begins. After the introduction in the history of Sītā, Rāma, and Rāvaṇa, turgidity replaces tragedy and the description of scenery and sentimentality take the place of genuine passion. The didactic overload is indeed lacking, and the Rāmāyaṇa gains thereby; but in this epic the note of savage lust and passion, which is the charm of the Mahābhārata, as it reveals genuine feeling of real men, is replaced by the childish laments and pious reflections of Rāma, whose foes are demoniac spirits, while his allies and confidants are apes. It is a polished fantasia, the finest example of the Kāvya or artificial poetry, which appeals to Hindu taste much more than does the rough genuineness of the great epic. The Rāmāyaṇa is in truth artificial in both senses, for one cannot possibly believe the tale; whereas the Mahābhārata makes its tales real." (*Cambridge History of India*, Vol. I, p. 264.)

production of a poet's brain, the Mahābhārata possesses a solid substratum of historical truth. Most of its heroes were real men, and much of the framework of the story is historically correct. In the Mahābhārata we find that the king had not yet become an autocrat. If he was born defective then he was not allowed to succeed, even though the next heir to the throne. He was controlled by his clansmen and ministers. At times he was elected to be the leader of his tribe in battle. The assembly is mentioned, but it had already become merely a body for military consultation. The king's city, or the capital, was defended by battlemented towers and moats, and had squares and streets which were watered and were lighted by lamps. The king's palace contained a hall of justice, a hall of gambling, and a place for the contests of wild animals. The royal army included the nobles as well as the common Aryan soldiers, and consisted of archers, slingers, rock-throwers, chariot-men, elephants, and cavalry. The king pensioned the widows of his fallen soldiers, and his captives became slaves. Dancing girls and prostitutes formed a part of the royal retinue. Meat-eating and the drinking of strong liquor were common, and in the epics we read of a crowd standing around the meat shops. A large part of the population was pastoral, and cattle-raiding was one of the principal occupations of the kings and the nobles. Cattle-branding, too, was well understood, as was the use of ear-marks, for identifying the cattle of different proprietors. The people were settled in small villages around the fort, in which they took refuge in time of war, and in time some of these forts expanded into towns. The villages were largely autonomous and managed their own affairs, though the king frequently administered justice and gathered the taxes. The taxes were paid in kind, but people in towns paid their fines in copper coins. Merchants bringing goods from a distance paid customs duties. They were addicted to the use of false weights, and a supervision of the market place was considered necessary. The guilds of merchants and artisans were very powerful, and heads of guilds are mentioned as objects of special solicitude on the part of the kings.

The State of Society in the Mahābhārata.

The People.

The eighteen Purāṇas, with a similar number of Upa-Purāṇas,

contain the traditional history of the Indo-Aryan kings so far as they were handed down from bard to bard and recorded in the *gāthās* and *nārāśaṁsis*. The term *Purāṇa* ought in strictness to be applied to any work which contained the following five sections:

"(1) *Sarga*, the evolution of the universe from its material cause; (2) *Pratisarga*, the re-creation of the universe from the constituent elements into which it is merged at the close of each æon (*kalpa*) or day in the life of the creator, Brahmā; (3) *Vaṁça*, the genealogies of gods and rishis; (4) *Manvantara*, the groups of "great ages" (*mahāyuga*) included in an æon, in each of which mankind is supposed to be produced anew from a first father, Manu; (5) *Vaṁçánucharita*, the history of the royal families who rule over the earth during the four ages (*yuga*) which make up one great age."[1]

General Plan of the Purāṇas.

None of the existing Purāṇas, however, has been written in accordance with this scheme, but they profess generally to conform to this definition. Only seven Purāṇas retain the fifth division, which contains an account of kings. All of these works are regarded by orthodox Hindus as of divine origin. Each purports to be spoken by Vyāsa, who heard it from the creator. At first the Purāṇas were narrated by a class of bards, the Sūtas. Gradually these Sūtas of Kshatriya origin were supplanted by the Brāhmaṇas. The records of the lineage of the princes gradually disappeared, and their place was taken by legends about holy places or hymns to deities. Thus, like the Mahābhārata, all the Purāṇas have undergone a radical change. The Mahābhārata, originally the story of a local feud between two clans of the Kurus, or between one Kuru clan and some foreigners, has now developed into a manual of religious exercises and civil law. So also each Purāṇa, originally a dynastic list and a religious manual, has become an elaborate treatise for the glorification of the new Indo-Aryan gods, Vishṇu or Śiva.

Origin of the Purāṇas.

Each Purāṇa consists of two parts, old and new. The old part contains portions of ancient historical tradition and genealogy of kings, while the new part, which varies in date, contains various *Tīrtha-māhātmyas* or descriptions of Hindu

[1] *Ibid.*, p. 296.

holy places. The majority of them have been tampered with by the Brāhmaṇas at various periods of their ascendancy. The earliest additions and alterations are generally supposed to have taken place during the rule of the Śuṅga and Kāṇva kings, who were Brāhmaṇas by descent. The majority of the Purāṇas, which contain genealogies of kings, were compiled in their present form during the rule or after the fall of the Gupta dynasty, which subsisted in India from 319 to 525 A.D.

Gradual Development of Purāṇas.

In addition to the eighteen Purāṇas there are eighteen other works called the Upa-Purāṇas. These are very narrow sectarian works dilating upon the merit of worshipping a particular deity and are of purely local interest. The majority of these appendages are based on local traditions, while the Purāṇas are based on genuine records which in many cases were misunderstood by the Brāhmaṇas when they redacted the entire work. These records carry us back to the period of the *Brāhmaṇas*, and they contain materials which no longer exist in their original form. They have preserved, though in a very distorted form, an independent tradition of the Kshatriyas, which supplements the later traditions of the priests. Contemporary dynasties which ruled in different parts of India have been taken by the misguided Brāhmaṇa compilers as successive. In many cases the lists of the same dynasties given by the Purāṇas do not agree, but such mistakes may be due to copyists. The Purāṇas ignore non-Hindu kings, and the foreigners are generally mentioned by their tribal names, while the names of the Hindu kings are given in detail.

The Upa-Purāṇas.

Importance of the Purāṇas.

Indications of the Age of Final Redactions.

The majority of the genealogical lists start from the great war between the Kurus and the Pāṇḍus, and after that event three royal lines come into prominence. These are the Purus, the Ikshvākus, and the kings of Magadha. The kings of other countries are mentioned in vague terms. In the Purāṇas, the Kurus and the Bhāratas of the Vedic literature have become merged with the Purus. Twenty-nine Puru kings lived after the great war and reigned at Hastināpura. The ancient capital of the Purus, called Asandīvanta in the Vedic literature, is seldom mentioned. During the reign of Nīchakshu, Hastināpura was destroyed, and the Puru capital was removed to Kauśāmbī, modern Kosam, in the Allahabad

The Purus.

District. The Ikshvākus were originally a branch of the Solar Race and ruled over Kośala, which lay to the west of the Videha or Mithilā and to the east of Oudh, the chief cities of which were Ayodhyā or Sāketa and Śrāvastī. In historic times, i.e. when Buddha was born, Kośala became the paramount power in Northern India, and its position was being contested by the semi-Aryanized kingdom of Magadha. The name Magadha was not known to the Indo-Aryans in the age of the Ṛigveda, and even in later times they regarded that province with scorn. The inhabitants of Magadha, i.e. of the modern districts of Patna and Gaya, and of Aṅga, i.e. of the modern districts of Munger and Bhagalpur, are mentioned in the Atharvaveda as living on the borders of the Indo-Aryan kingdoms. Though their kings claimed to be Purus, they were most probably of mixed origin. During the period of the great war between the Kurus and the Pāṇḍavas, Magadha was ruled by the Asura (Dravidian) chief Jarāsandha. Even in later times the Aryanization of this province was of doubtful completeness. The earliest opposition to the reformed religion of the Indo-Aryans arose in Magadha. Both Buddhism and Jainism were first promulgated in this province, and a king of Magadha, Aśoka, gave prominence to Buddhism by making it his state religion. The development of Buddhism and its widespread acceptance in Asia gave a very severe blow to the religion of the Indo-Aryans.

The Ikshvākus.

BIBLIOGRAPHY

Cambridge History of India, Vol. I, chaps. xi and xiii.
PARGITER, *Ancient Indian Historical Tradition*.

CHAPTER VII

JAINISM: ITS ORIGIN AND DEVELOPMENT

The religious literatures of the Jains and Buddhists, as far as they are known at present, reveal quite a different state of society from that depicted in the epics or the later Vedic literature. From these we learn that a large number of different sects which did not recognize the orthodox tenets of the Indo-Aryan religion existed in Northern India in the seventh and sixth centuries before the birth of Christ. All of them gradually died out or were merged in other sects, except the Jains and Buddhists. We know the names of some which exercised an influence on the political history of the country; among them were the Ājīvikas, who were powerful at the time of the birth of Gautama Buddha and who existed up to, at least, the third century B.C.

Existence of various Religious Sects.

Sixty-three different philosophical schools, most of which were unorthodox in nature, existed in the sixth century B.C., proving thereby that the revolt against the orthodox Indo-Aryan religion began long before that date. Magadha, or South-western Bihar, which had long resisted the advance of the Indo-Aryans, was the home of these religious movements, which orthodox Hindus still regard as heretical. Many of these schools of thought appear to have been influenced by the religious tenets of the earlier inhabitants of Magadha. It seems now, that though the priests of the Indo-Aryans made the admission of non-Aryan races into Indo-Aryan society easier by regarding them as of Indo-Aryan origin but fallen from the status of purity demanded by strict Brāhmaṇas, yet a large number of people of Dravidian origin clung to the older religions. Their priests and their trend of thought influenced or even brought into existence many of these heterodox schools.

Origin of the New Religions.

Mahāvīra Varddhamāna.

Mahāvīra Varddhamāna is now recognized to have been the founder of the Jain religion. The Jains regard him as the twenty-fourth and last patriarch or prophet. His predecessor Pārśva is said to have died two hundred and fifty years before the death of Mahāvīra, and therefore he appears to have lived in the eighth century B.C. Twenty-two other patriarchs (called *Tīrthaṅkaras*) are said to have lived and preached the Jain religion before these two.

Previous Patriarchs.

Pārśva.

There are reasons to believe that Pārśva was a historical personage and not a mythical being like the earlier twenty-two Tīrthaṅkaras. Like all of them, Pārśva belonged to the Kshatriya caste. His father Aśvasena was King of Benares, and he lived for thirty years in royal style with his family.

Then he quitted his regal state and became a mendicant. After eighty-four days of meditation Pārśva obtained supreme knowledge and lived for seventy years more. He taught his followers the four supreme commands: (1) not to injure life,

Mahāvīra Varddhamāna, the founder of Jainism (12th century A.D.), from Tripurī, the ancient Chedī capital; Tewar, near Jubbulpur

(2) not to tell lies, (3) not to steal, and (4) not to possess any property. To these four rules Mahāvīra added a fifth which insists upon chastity. Pārśva allowed his disciples to wear the ascetic's robes, but Mahāvīra enjoined complete nudity.

Many scholars think that the division of the modern Jains

into two sects, the white-clothed one (*Śvetāmbara*) and sky-clothed or naked one (*Digambara*), is due to the difference of opinion between Mahāvīra and the followers of Pārśva. This, however, is denied by others, who believe that the main points of difference between the two sects originated after the return of the Jains from Southern India. A Life of Pārśva was compiled by the Jain saint Bhadrabāhu, who lived in the time of the Maurya emperor Chandragupta. We do not know how far the tenets of the Jain religion were accepted by the people of India at the time of Pārśva's death or afterwards; but it is certain that the religion was placed on a firm basis by the next patriarch, Mahāvīra.

Schism in the Jain Religion.

Varddhamāna was born at Vaiśālī, the capital of the Vajji tribe, a place now situated in the Muzaffarpur District of Bihar. His parents belonged to the wealthier classes. His father Siddhārtha was the head of the Jñātṛika clan of Kshatriyas and his mother Triśalā was the sister of Cheṭaka, one of the foremost men in the oligarchical government of the Lichchhavi tribe. King Bimbisāra Śreṇika of Magadha had married Chellanā, the daughter of Mahāvīra's maternal uncle and the mother of the next king of Magadha, Ajātaśatru Kuṇika. The Life of Mahāvīra, as told by the Jains, bears a considerable resemblance to that told by the Buddhists about the conception and the birth of Buddha. In due time Mahāvīra was married to a lady named Yaśodā, by whom he had a daughter, who married Jamālī, who became a disciple of his father-in-law. In his thirtieth year Mahāvīra left his home with the permission of his elder brother Nandivardhana, after the death of his parents, and became a homeless mendicant.

Family of Varddhamāna.

Legends about his Birth.

During the succeeding thirteen months Mahāvīra did not change his robes; on the expiry of that period he discarded clothing entirely. He succeeded in subduing his senses by continual meditation, chastity, and a very strict observance of the rules concerning food. He wandered over a large area and visited Rājagṛiha, modern Rajgir, on several occasions. After twelve years spent in meditation and penance, he attained supreme knowledge and became free from the bonds of pleasure and pain. It was at this time, when forty-two years old, that he ceased to be called Varddhamāna and became

The Mendicant Life of Varddhamāna.

known as Mahāvīra. As head of the *Nirgranthas* (" free from fetters ") or *Jains* (" the followers of the Jina ") he then began to teach his new knowledge. Buddhists refer to him as *Nigganṭho Nātaputto* in Pali or *Nirgranthaḥ Jñātṛiputraḥ* in Sanskrit.

During the next thirty years Mahāvīra travelled over Northern and Southern Bihar and spent most of his time in the provinces of Magadha and Aṅga. In the rainy season he spent his time at Champā, the capital of Aṅga, Mithilā in Videha, Śrāvastī, the capital of Kośala, and Vaiśālī, his native place. From Buddhist literature we learn that Mahāvīra met Gautama Buddha frequently and that he was worsted at each encounter.

Varddhamāna as a Teacher.

His Connexion with Buddha.

The relations between the Jains and the Buddhists were by no means cordial. The Jains represent in their fundamental tenets the oldest modes of thought. In their system even the inanimate objects of nature are regarded as endowed with life. There is no resemblance between their system of thought and the Buddhist faith, though the partial similarity of the views of each on monachism has often given rise to incorrect conclusions regarding a common origin. Gautama at first thought that freedom from the bondage of work (*Karman*) would lie in self-torture, but afterwards gave up this idea and did not enforce penance upon his followers. He enjoined them to follow a middle course. Mahāvīra, on the other hand, had found that the road to deliverance lay in severe self-torture and advised death by starvation. Buddha always warned his disciples not to hurt any living thing, but Mahāvīra exaggerated this idea to an impracticable extent.

Relation between Jainism and Buddhism.

Gośāla, a former disciple of Mahāvīra, was a more dangerous rival, as many of his tenets were borrowed from his former spiritual guide. He had many followers in the city of Śrāvastī, and the two leaders fought bitterly till the sixteenth year of Mahāvīra's career as a prophet, when Gośāla died. The death of Gośāla took place shortly after the accession of Ajātaśatru as the king of Magadha. In the fourteenth year of Mahāvīra's career as a prophet his son-in-law Jamālī founded a rival sect, and two years later another member of Mahāvīra's community raised further opposition. Mahāvīra survived Gośāla by sixteen years and died at the age of seventy-two in the house

Rivalry between the Ājīṅkas and the Jains.

of a scribe employed by King Hastipāla at Apāpapurī, near Rājagṛiha.

After the death of Mahāvīra, his principal disciple Sudharman became pontiff of the new religion. On the extinction of the Śaiśunāga dynasty the empire of Magadha fell to the Nandas, who were probably Jains. One of the kings of this dynasty removed an image of a Jina, or *Tīrthaṅkara*, from Kaliṅga, and this was taken back by Khāravela when he conquered Magadha. Udayin, the last king of the Śaiśunāga dynasty, was also a staunch Jain. It is therefore evident that Buddhism failed to become a popular religion in Northern India till its advocacy by the Emperor Aśoka. The emperors of the Maurya family appear to have been Jains before the accession of Aśoka, and even Aśoka's descendants were not faithful followers of Buddhism. It may now be accepted that side by side with the orthodox Indo-Aryan faith the religion of Mahāvīra prevailed in Northern India up to the fourth century B.C.

Subsequent History of Jainism.

The great schism among the Jains took place in the beginning of the third century B.C. During a great famine in Bihar, Bhadrabāhu, one of the two high priests, headed an exodus of the monks of the community to Southern India. He took up his abode in the province of Karṇāṭa. Returning later to Magadha, he appears to have gone to Nepal after an interval, though the Digambaras say that he was murdered by his disciples. When his companions returned from Karṇāṭa, they found that their brethren who had remained in Magadha under the guidance of the second pontiff, Sthulabhadra, had become lax in discipline. A great council was convened at Pāṭaliputra, the modern Patna, in order to collect and revise their sacred writings. As the *Pūrvas*, or the older works, were known only to Bhadrabāhu, Sthulabhadra was sent to Nepal to learn them, but though he learnt fourteen of them he was forbidden to teach more than ten. The monks who had gone to Karṇāṭa took no part in this council. They became the predecessors of the Digambaras, who hold that the canonical texts of the Śvetāmbaras are unorthodox and that the real canon was lost. In their opinion the Śvetāmbara texts were compiled by a monk named Jinachandra at Valabhi at a much later date.

Cause of the Schism.

The Digambaras.

From this time, i.e. the beginning of the third century B.C.,

Jainism lost ground in Magadha. Samprati, one of the grandsons of Aśoka, is regarded as a patron of the Jain religion; but later on, the revival of Brahmanism and the adoption of the Buddhist faith by the majority of the Scythians led to the gradual decline of the religion of Mahāvīra. The Śvetāmbaras flourished in Mathurā during the Scythian period, but the Digambaras also were not absent. The Śvetāmbara sect remained confined to Rajputana and Western India, while Bengal, South Bihar, Chota - Nagpur, and the whole of Central India, Mahārāshṭra, and Southern India, contained thousands of followers of the Digambara sect, and in these countries the followers of the Śvetāmbaras are very rare. Numerous Śvetāmbara images have been found in different parts of the United Provinces and the Panjab, but in Bengal and Central India they are rare. The Jain caves of Mahārāshṭra, such as those at Ellora and Maungya Tungiya, belong to the Digambara sect. In Southern India, i.e. the country to the south of the River Godāvarī, the Jains and their temples and monuments belong entirely to the Digambara sect. In the countries to the north of the Narmadā, Jainism has almost disappeared except in Mālava and Rajputana. A degraded variety is prevalent in Orissa, where members are called *Sarākas*, a corruption of the Sanskrit term *Śrāvaka*. Jain ruins and images abound in Western Bengal, South Bihar, and the states of Rewa, Maihar, Panna, Nagod, Bijawar, and the whole of Bundelkhand as far as the eastern part of Malava.

The Śvetāmbaras.

BIBLIOGRAPHY

Cambridge History of India, Vol. I, chap. vi.
BÜHLER, *The Indian Sect of the Jains.*
MRS. STEVENSON, *The Heart of Jainism.*

CHAPTER VIII

BUDDHISM: EARLIER PHASE OF ITS DEVELOPMENT, AND THE LIFE OF GAUTAMA BUDDHA

Gautama Siddhārtha, the founder of the Buddhist religion, was born at Kapilavastu, a village now lying near the southern frontier of Nepal. He came of a clan of mountaineers who, in the sixth century B.C., ruled over the western part of the jungle area lying at the foot of the Himalayas and now called the Nepal Tarai. His father, whose name was Śuddhodana, was king of the Śākyas, as they are called in the Pali literature. Buddha's mother is called Māyā. Gautama Siddhārtha was born in a park or garden attached to the village of Lumbinī or Lummini, which lay close to the capital of the Śākyas, when his mother was journeying from her father's house to Kapilavastu. Suddenly seized with the pains of childbirth, Māyā stood under a Śāla tree in the park of Lumbinī, and there the child was born.

Family of Gautama.

Buddhism of a later age has surrounded the birth of the divine child with romance and mystery. We are now told that before the birth of Gautama, his mother, Māyā, dreamt that a white elephant had entered her womb. When the child was born, the gods from Heaven came down and Brahmā held the new-born child on a cloth of gold. Immediately after his birth, the child was bathed in the water of a spring which suddenly gushed forth from the earth attended by serpents or Nāgas, and the infant took seven steps and recited seven verses. These are stories which, though believed by the Buddhists for more than two thousand years, have no place in history. Māyā's dream, the bathing of the child in the water of the mysterious spring, and the wonderful seven steps taken by the new-born child, have been the subjects of bas-reliefs and paintings in India from the second century B.C. to the twelfth century A.D. The great Buddhist emperor, Aśoka, went on a pilgrimage after his conversion to Buddhism. He set up a pillar on the site where Buddha was born, and in the inscription on that pillar he states "here Buddha was

Legends about the Mysterious Birth.

born, the sage of the Śākya race ". The name of the village is given as Lumminī and it was made revenue free. From this pillar we learn that the modern village of Rumin-dei was believed to be the site of ancient *Lumminī Grāma*, in the twentieth year of the reign of Aśoka, when the pillar was set up.

Birthplace of Gautama.

Buddhist tradition has introduced a good deal of romance into the early life of Gautama Siddhārtha. It is said that he learnt the sixty-four letters of the alphabet in a single day, and that, when he learnt shooting, his arrow went to a miraculous distance, stories which have found no credence outside Buddhist countries. It is said that he was married early, but we do not know how many wives he had. We are told of three different ladies who were married to him, but it is surmised that the three names may have belonged to one and the same person. These names are Gopā, Yaśodharā, and Mṛigajā.

Early Life of Gautama.

Śuddhodana became afraid that Gautama Siddhārtha might leave his home, and therefore he is said to have kept his son virtually a prisoner in a pleasure garden, where he was surrounded by musicians, beautiful dancing girls, and all sorts of pleasures. The gods then conspired against the king, and soon after, when the young prince went out in his chariot, he saw certain things which affected him very greatly. First of all he saw an old man who was walking with great difficulty with the aid of his stick. The prince's charioteer, on being questioned, told him in reply that the man had been forsaken by his relations on account of his infirmity, and that all men grow old. On another day he saw a sick man who had been abandoned on the roadside. The charioteer told the prince that the man was very sick and about to depart this life, and that all men would become ill when the term of their lives came to an end. On another day the prince saw a dead body surrounded by weeping relatives, and in answer to the prince's question the charioteer replied that life had departed from this body; that this man would never see his father, mother, or wife any more, and that it was the common fate of all living beings. On another day the prince was powerfully moved by seeing a mendicant, and when he was told

Causes of Gautama's Departure from his Home.

that he had abandoned the pleasures of life, the prince himself determined to do so. It is said that the prince, on seeing a man ploughing his field, asked his charioteer the reason of this great labour, and was told in reply that all men had to keep themselves alive, for which food was needed, and that food could only be produced by hard labour. The Lives of Gautama Siddhārtha depict these scenes as due to the conspiracy of the gods Indra and Brahmā to divert the attention of the young prince from the pleasures of life. But the real truth is that the prince was moved by these scenes of distress, and determined to find a way for the removal of all human affliction. One day the prince left his home at midnight and, mounting his favourite horse Kaṇṭhaka, and accompanied by his favourite groom Chhandaka, left the city of his birth when everybody was asleep. Buddhist writers, sculptors, and painters have magnified this event in poetry, bas-reliefs, and painting. It is rightly called the "great renunciation" (*Mahābhinishkramaṇa*).

After journeying for some time the prince left his horse and bade his groom return. He then changed his costly robes and cut his long hair. The prince exchanged raiment with a hunter and journeyed to the city of Vaiśālī in North Bihar. There he became the disciple of a sage named Ālāḍa Kālāma, but he was not satisfied with the course prescribed by his first spiritual guide and left for Magadha or South Bihar.

Earlier Period of Gautama's Mendicant Life.

From Rājagṛiha he journeyed to Gaya, and practised austerities on the banks of the River Nairañjanā, now called the Phalgu. In the Lives of Buddha this part of the narrative is dealt with more fully than any other part, because Buddha's conquest of temptations, which appear personified in Buddhist sacred literature as Māra (Satan) and his daughters, is regarded as the supreme moment of his life. On the banks of the Nairañjanā, Gautama Siddhārtha became emaciated by continual fasting, and when his body became very thin he found that mortification of the body is not the proper road to perfect knowledge. He is said to have journeyed to the foot of a

The Buddhist Satan.

Pipal tree (*Aśvattha*), and when he had seated himself in meditation under the branches of that tree, which became noted afterwards as the tree of knowledge (*Bodhidruma*),

Māra came with his thousand sons and thousand daughters to tempt the mendicant prince. At this point of the narrative romance once more takes the place of sober fact, and the story told is impossible to believe. Māra is said to have attacked the prince with his demoniacal army, but is vanquished. When he had failed in his attack, he returned home. There his daughters, named Rati, Tṛishṇā, and Ārati, comforted him and undertook to seduce Gautama from the true path of perfect enlightenment (*Samyak-sambodhi*). Their blandishments also failed to move Gautama.

His Fight with the Prince.

Temptation by his Daughters.

After the defeat of Māra, Gautama obtained perfect knowledge by constant meditation, and became known as the Buddha. The theory promulgated by him is that the root cause of all human affliction is ignorance and desire. Ignorance leads men ultimately to rebirth, and birth brings in its train all the afflictions of human kind. The Bodhisattva thus determined that ignorance lies at the root of all our afflictions, and he set himself to remove it and effect the stoppage of rebirth.

Principles of the New Faith.

He went to Benares and met five of his former disciples outside that city in the Deer park (*Mṛigadāva*). At one time King Śuddhodana had sent five noble Śākya youths to his son to bear him company. When Buddha gave up the austerities enjoined by the rules of orthodox mendicants, these five Śākya youths left him in disgust and went to Benares. Buddha preached his first sermon in the Deer park, to these five men. This first sermon, which was the beginning of Buddha's preaching of his religion or "Law", became known as the "Turning of the wheel of Law" (*Dharmma-chakra-pravartanā*). The event, together with the birth of Buddha at Kapilavastu, his perfect enlightenment at Bodh-Gaya, and his death at Kuśināra, are regarded by the Buddhists as the four principal events of the Master's career. The places where these events took place are regarded as the holiest places of pilgrimage.

First Sermon at Benares.

Buddhist Holy Places.

The rest of Buddha's life was spent in preaching his faith. He had a rival in his own cousin Devadatta, who became the favourite of Ajātaśatru Kuṇika, the son of Bimbisāra, King of Magadha, and who tried to kill Buddha on two different

Attempt on Buddha's Life.

occasions in the streets of Rājagṛiha, but Buddha escaped miraculously. The rest of the history of Buddha's life is also full of miracles. At Śrāvastī, Buddha appeared simultaneously at ten points in order to vanquish his opponents in a discussion, because they held that such a thing was impossible in nature. This event is known as the miracle of Śrāvastī. The Buddhists believe that Buddha went to Heaven to preach his religion to his mother, who had died shortly after giving him birth. When Buddha started on the return journey, three ladders leading from Heaven to the Earth appeared. Buddha descended by the central ladder, attended by Indra and Brahma. The accepted gods of Indo-Aryan faith are always shown as attending Buddha in some menial capacity. On this occasion Indra is said to have held an umbrella over Buddha's head, while Brahma fanned the Master with a fly-whisk. Buddha made his descent on the Earth at Saṅkāśya, a place in the Allahabad district now called Sankisa. On another occasion, when the Master was seated by the side of a tank at Vaiśālī, modern Besarh in the Muzaffurpur District of North Bihar, a monkey came and presented a bowl of honey to him. Afterwards the monkey danced with joy and committed suicide by drowning itself in a well. The monkey was reborn as a god, and the tank became known as the tank of the monkey. This event became known as the incident of Vaiśālī. The incidents of Rājagṛiha, Śrāvastī, Saṅkāśya, and Vaiśālī are known as the four minor great events of the life of Buddha. The places at which the four major and the four minor great events happened became known as the eight great places (*Ashṭa-mahāsthāna*).

Miracle of Śrāvastī. **Sankisa, and Vaiśālī.**

Buddha's teaching was much simpler than that of the Jains, and his religion was more acceptable to the lower classes. The sage Gautama, the author of the *Dharmasûtra*, had promulgated five general rules for the conduct of orthodox mendicants in India: (1) they were not to covet others' property; (2) they were not to intoxicate themselves with wines or drugs; (3) they were not to destroy life; (4) they were not to associate with women; and (5) they were not to tell lies. To these rules the Buddha added five more. He ordered that: (6) the monks of his order were not to eat at

Rules of the Order.

Stele with the principal events of the life of Buddha: birth, conception, enlightenment, first sermon at Benares, descent from heaven and the miracle of Srāvastī; from Sarnath near Benares (5th century A.D.).

forbidden times; (7) they were not to dance, sing, or take part in theatricals; (8) they were not to use flowers, scents, or ornaments; (9) they were not to sleep on high spacious beds; and (10) they were not to retain or accept gold or silver. Buddha preached that in order to obtain salvation men should follow the eightfold path: (1) right belief, (2) right thought, (3) right speech, (4) right action, (5) right means of livelihood, (6) right exertion, (7) right remembrance, and (8) right meditation. This path was described as the middle path, because it lay between gross sensualism and strict asceticism. Ordinary men and women could obtain success by following the middle path, but success was assured by joining the community of monks. Women were also admitted into the order. Buddha founded a moral system based on certain abstruse doctrines of metaphysics. He always avoided discussions about God or the nature of the soul. His system ignores the existence of God. Though he denied the authority of the Vedas, he did not interfere with the popular beliefs, and therefore his followers always made the accepted gods of the Indo-Aryan religion appear in a menial capacity in his presence. The new religion became more acceptable to the masses than the intricate religion of the orthodox Indo-Aryans.

The Eightfold Path.

Nuns.

The religion of Buddha does not appear to have made much impression on the educated people or the powerful nobles during his lifetime. Kings, like Bimbisāra of Magadha or Prasenajit of Kośala, paid reverence to mendicants of all sects, and their reverence to Buddha is no sign of their acceptance of his religion. Many powerful merchants, like Anāthapiṇḍika of Śrāvastī, patronized the new order, but Buddhism remained a minor faith till the rise of Aśoka. The principal disciples of Buddha were Brāhmaṇas like Mahākāśyapa or his kinsmen like Ānanda. Among others, Sārīputra and Moggallāyana were distinguished by their zeal for the Master.

State of Buddhism in the Lifetime of the Buddha.

Buddha's Death.

Buddha died at the age of eighty at Kuśīnāra. His body was burned and his ashes divided into eight parts by his principal disciple Mahākāśyapa, who became the head of the order. Mahākāśyapa convened the first great assembly of monks at Rājagṛiha in order to collect the sayings of Buddha. The kingdom of Kapilavastu and the clan of Śākyas were destroyed by Viḍuḍabha, the son of Prasenajit, during the lifetime of Buddha. Some relics of these Śākyas were found in a crystal casket in a mound at Piprahwa in the Basti District. **Relics of the Śākyas.**

BIBLIOGRAPHY

KERN, *Manual of Buddhism.*
OLDENBERG, *Buddha.*
RHYS DAVIDS, *Buddhist India.*

BOOK II

Ancient India

CHAPTER I

THE SIXTEEN KINGDOMS OF THE NORTH

The rise of Buddhism marks the beginning of the historical period in India. We obtain for the first time a generally reliable chronology of events and a glimpse into the social and economic life of ancient India. Kings and dynasties become more real, and in spite of short gaps in the sequence of events, the history of the country can be treated as a continuous narrative. It is a mistake to call this age the Buddhist period, merely on the ground that most of the material on which the history of this period is based is taken from Buddhist birth stories (*Jātakas*) or from story books connected with Buddhism. We ought to bear in mind that the entire country never accepted Buddhism, and society remained unchanged till the irruption of the Greeks and of Scythian barbarians from the north-west. The reformed Indo-Aryan religion remained strong until the reign of Aśoka. It was revived again by the Śuṅgas and did not lose its hold on the educated middle classes till the period of Kushan domination in Northern India. Buddhism, at the height of its glory, never succeeded in stamping out Hinduism, or the orthodox Indo-Aryan faith as it is now known. Jainism existed side by side with numerous other religions. Even under the Kushans, Buddhism did not remain the state religion for long. Vāsudeva I gave up Buddhism and accepted Hinduism. Buddhism never again succeeded in becoming the state religion after the time of Huvishka, except for a quarter of a century under Harshavardhana of Thanesar.

So-called Buddhist Period.

In the beginning of the sixth century before the birth of

Christ we find that Northern India was divided into the following sixteen kingdoms:

The Sixteen Kingdoms.

1. Aṅga (the Bhagalpur and Munger (?) Districts of Bihar and Orissa).

2. Magadha (the Patna and Gaya Districts of the same provinces).

3. Vajjī (the Muzaffarpur, Saran, and Champaran Districts of North Bihar).

4. Kāśī (the Benares, Ghazipur, and Mirzapur Districts).

5. Kośala (? the Lucknow and Fyzabad Districts).

6. Malla (? the Gorakhpur District).

7. Vaṁśa (the Allahabad and Banda Districts).

8. Cheṭī (? the Cawnpur and Unao Districts).

9. Pañchāla (modern Rohilkhand).

10. Kuru (the Aligarh, Meerut, Delhi and Thaneswar Districts).

11. Machchha or Matsya (? the Rewari and Gurgaon Districts, with portions of Alwar and Jaipur States).

12. Śūrasena (? the Mathura District, Bharatpur State, and the northern part of the Jaipur State).

13. Aśmaka on the Godavari (Sutta nipāta).

14. Avantī (? Mālava or Malwa).

15. Gandhāra (? the north-western frontier districts of the Panjab as far as Peshawar and adjoining districts).

16. Kāmboja (? the modern districts of Kabul and Jalalabad).

Authorities, however, are not strictly in accord regarding those areas before which a mark of interrogation appears.

In the lifetime of Buddha Northern India was divided into a number of small kingdoms and republics. The more notable of these kingdoms were Magadha, with its capital at Rājagṛiha, Kośala, with its capital at Śrāvastī, and Vatsa or Vaṁśa, with its capital at Kauśāmbī. Among the republics and the smaller kingdoms the following names are prominent:

Republics and Tribal Territories.

1. The Śākyas of Kapilavastu.
2. The Bulis of Allakappa.
3. The Kālāmas of Kesaputta.
4. The Bhaggas of Suṁsumāra.

5. The Koliyas of Rāmagāma.
6. The Mallas of Pāvā.
7. The Mallas of Kuśinārа.
8. The Moriyas of Pipphalivana.
9. The Videhas of Mithilā.
10. The Lichchhavīs of Vaiśālī.

Supremacy of Magadha. During the lifetime of Buddha, the kingdom of Magadha rose to be the paramount power in Northern India and triumphed over its rival of Kośala. It had already absorbed the neighbouring kingdom of Aṅga. In the Vedic literature the people of Magadha are always spoken of with contempt. They are called Vrātyas, i.e. Indians who were still living outside the pale of Indo-Aryan civilization. During the period of the Sūtras the Vrātyas were admitted into Indo-Aryan society. The Brāhmaṇas of Magadha are spoken of with open contempt, and this is a clear indication that the people of Magadha were not entirely Aryanized.[1] The earliest dynasty of Magadha is mentioned in the Mahābhārata as a dynasty of Asuras. We hear of Bṛihadratha, the son of Vasu and the father of Jarāsandha, the reputed conqueror of the hero-god Kṛishṇa. The Purāṇas contain the names of

Early Kings. Jarāsandha's son and grandson. The race of Jarāsandha became extinct in the time of Buddha.

The second dynasty of Magadha was founded by a king named Śiśunāga. Bimbisāra, a contemporary of Buddha, belonged to this dynasty, according to Purāṇas, but the Ceylonese chronicle, Mahāvaṁśa, makes Śiśunāga the successor of Bimbisāra's dynasty. There are two different views about the Śiśunāga dynasty and that of Bimbisāra. One

Bimbisāra. group of scholars regards Śiśunāga as the founder of the dynasty which followed that of Bimbisāra, while the second group follows the Purāṇas in thinking that Bimbisāra was a descendant of Śiśunāga. Bimbisāra conquered Aṅga and occupied Benares after defeating the King of Kośala. He married three wives, one of whom was the daughter of the King Kośala and sister of Prasenajit; the second was Chellanā, the daughter of the Lichchhavi prince Chetaka and first

[1] *Cambridge History of India*, Vol. I, p. 123.

cousin of Mahāvīra Varddhamāna. The third was a daughter of the chief of the Madra clan of the Panjab. At this time Rājagṛiha (modern Rajgir in the Patna District) was the capital of the kingdom. It is also called the Girivraja or "the fort surrounded by hills". Old Rājagṛiha was situated in a well-watered valley surrounded by a chain of hills. It was defended by a high stone wall which ran along the top of the hills and was protected by stone towers at regular intervals. In the valley there were other stone walls, built of very heavy stones, which remind one of the Cyclopean walls of Mycenæ and Tiryns in Greece. These walls exist at the present day, and the masonry is the oldest known in India. The city was approached by two ways, one on the south, which led to the southern part of Magadha, i.e. the Gaya District, and one on the north, which led to northern Magadha and the Lichchhavi country. Both passes were protected by heavy stone walls with towers. After some time, evidently during the period of the Śiśunāgas, the old city was abandoned and a new one built outside the northern gate. The new city was protected by a square fort with brick walls and towers. This city was visited by Buddha, but the holy places inside the old city continued to be visited by pilgrims, both Jain and Buddhist, up to the twelfth century A.D. Mahākāśyapa, the principal disciple of Buddha, held the first great assembly of Buddhist monks under the Vaibhāra Hill, close to the rampart of the old city, at a place which became known as the Sattapanni Hall. The site of the first great council is now marked by a stone platform reached by a sloping causeway of stone. In the centre of the old city the shrine of the Nāga Maṇibhadra was rebuilt on several occasions, the latest being in the sixth century A.D. In the new city Bimbisāra gave a grove of bamboos for the use of Buddha, and this became famous in Buddhist literature as the *Karaṇḍa-veṇu-vana*. Bimbisāra was murdered by his son Ajātaśatru, who succeeded him in the Empire.

Rājagṛiha or Girivraja.

New Rājagṛiha

Sattapanni Hall.

Karaṇḍa-veṇu-vana.

Ajātaśatru was distinctly hostile to Buddha. He invaded the kingdom of Kośala, and as the first step of the conquest of Videha, he built a strong fort at the village of Pāṭali, situated at the junction of the rivers Śoṇ and Ganges, and which

Ajātaśatru builds Pāṭali Fort.

became celebrated in later history as Pāṭaliputra, the capital of the Maurya and Gupta empires of Magadha. Ajātaśatru defeated his aged uncle, King Prasenajit of Kośala, and forced him to fall back upon his capital, Śrāvastī. But Ajātaśatru was led into an ambush and captured by Prasenajit. The king of Kośala liberated his nephew and gave him his daughter Vajirā in marriage. During the absence of Prasenajit from his capital his son Viḍuḍabha captured the throne. Prasenajit sought refuge in Magadha, but died outside the city of Rājagṛiha. Ajātaśatru invaded the republic of the Lichchhavīs of Vaiśālī on account of a breach of faith by the latter. The Lichchhavīs were the allies of the kings of Kośala, and Ajātaśatru's wars with these two powers were probably due to an effort on the part of the former to curb the growing power of the kingdom of Magadha. The war was protracted for more than sixteen years, and finally Vaiśālī was conquered by Ajātaśatru and remained a part of the Magadhan Empire for centuries. Ajātaśatru had another rival in King Pradyota of Avantī or Mālava, and at one time he was afraid of an attack on his capital, Rājagṛiha. He was succeeded by his son Udayībhadra, who is mentioned in the lists of the Purāṇas as well as in the canonical literature of the Jains and the Buddhists.

War with Kośala.

War with the Lichchhavīs.

Conquest of Vaiśālī.

The successors of Ajātaśatru are shadowy figures. Geiger holds, on the authority of Buddhist Chronicles, that Udaya or Udayībhadra was the successor of Ajātaśatru, but Smith and others, relying on the Purāṇas, make a king named Darśaka (who is probably the same as Nāgadāsaka of the Ceylonese Chronicle and who is mentioned in a play of Bhāsa called the *Svapna-Vāsavadattā*) the successor of Ajātaśatru. Udaya is credited with the building of the city of Pāṭaliputra, which was also called Kusumapura. He was the viceroy of his father in the province of Aṅga. The kings of Avantī or Mālava were the rivals of the later kings of the Śiśunāga dynasty. Pālaka, the successor of Pradyota, conquered the kingdom of Kauśāmbī, and the two great kingdoms of Magadha and Mālava were brought into contact. According to the Purāṇas, Udaya was succeeded by Nandivarddhana and Mahānanda, but the Ceylonese Chronicles state that Munda and Anuruddha

Udaya.

The building of Pāṭaliputra.

succeeded Udaya. The same Chronicles make Śiśunāga, a minister of Magadha, succeed the dynasty of Bimbisāra. Śiśunāga is credited with the destruction of the kingdom of

Bas-relief from Munger district: Penance of Arjuna, a scene from the *Mahābhārata*, Pataliputra school (5th century A.D.)

Avantī or Mālava. The capital was transferred from Rājagṛiha to Pāṭaliputra by Śiśunāga, according to the Buddhist authorities, after the fall of the dynasty of Bimbisāra. According to the Purāṇas, the transfer was made by the Nandas in order to avoid the hatred of the Brāhmaṇas of Rājagṛiha on

Transfer of the Capital.

The Nandas.

account of their humble origin. The Nandas were born of the union of a Śūdra woman with one of the Śiśunāga kings. They therefore form a separate branch of the Śiśunāgas and not a separate dynasty.

Effect of the Rule of Śiśu-nāgas.

The dynasty of Bimbisāra made Magadha great in Eastern India. Aṅga was incorporated into the kingdom, Benares was conquered, and the republic of Vaiśālī destroyed. Ajātaśatru conquered the kingdom of Kauśāmbī, and Mālava soon also succumbed. The conquest of Kaliṅga is attributed to Nandivarddhana by Mr. K. P. Jayaswal. In the Purāṇas Mahāpadma is stated to have been born of a Śūdra woman, but in Jain literature he is called the son of a courtesan by a barber. According to Q. Curtius, the King of Magadha, contemporary with Alexander the Great, was the son of a barber who had become the paramour of the queen of the last king and who afterwards murdered the king. The murder of one of the kings named Kākavarṇa is mentioned in the Harshacharita of Bāṇa-bhaṭṭa. According to the Ceylonese Chronicles, the name of the first king of the Nanda dynasty was Ugrasena. The conquest of Kaliṅga by one of the Nandas is referred to in the Hāthigumphā inscription of Khāravela. From this inscription we learn that a canal was excavated by one of the Nanda kings in the year one hundred and three of the era of the Nandas, and that this king had brought away an image of a Jain patriarch from the country of Kaliṅga. According to the Purāṇas, the first Nanda king was the destroyer of all Kshatriyas and the sole monarch of the earth. This term most probably means that all small kingdoms in Northern India had at that time been absorbed in the Empire of Magadha. Mahāpadma Nanda was succeeded by eight other kings of his family, the last of whom was overthrown by Chandragupta the Maurya. The Nanda kings were regarded as the possessors of great wealth. The historians of Alexander state that they maintained 80,000 cavalry, 200,000 infantry, and 8000 four-horsed chariots, with 6000 war elephants. The enormous wealth of the Nandas is mentioned in a Tamil poem, by the Chinese traveller Yuan Chwang, and in a passage of the *Kathāsarit-sāgara*. According to Pāṇini, the Nanda kings invented a peculiar system of weights. The fall of the

Origin of the Nandas.

Reference to the Nandas in the Hāthi-gumphā Inscription of Khāravela.

Mahā-padma Nanda.

Nandas took place after the invasion of India by Alexander the Great, some time between 321 and 312 B.C. **Fall of the Nandas.**

BIBLIOGRAPHY

D. R. BHANDARLEAR, *The Carmichael Lectures*, 1918, chap. ii.
H. C. RAYCHAUDHURI, *Political History of India*, 3rd edition.
Cambridge History of India, Vol. I, chap. xiii.

CHAPTER II

THE PERSIAN CONQUEST OF NORTH-WESTERN INDIA AND THE INVASION OF ALEXANDER THE GREAT

Long after the separation of the Indo-Aryans and the Aryo-Iranians the connexion between the two branches remained very intimate. The Indo-Iranians possessed an intimate knowledge of the province of Afghanistan, and there are reasons for believing that no definite line of demarcation existed between the two branches. It has been noticed in the previous chapters that the Kāmbojas were included in the sixteen great nations of Northern India and that they lived to the west of Gandhāra, i.e. Peshawar. They spoke a language which is allied more to the Iranian group of languages than to the Indian. The country which lies on both banks of the River Oxus (Sanskrit *Vakshu*) is regarded as a part of India in Sanskrit literature and as a part of Iran in Old Persian literature. Bactria was probably Iranian in speech even in the sixth and seventh centuries B.C., but it is called Bāhlika, and the people are regarded as Kshatriyas in Indo-Aryan literature. No boundary line between India and Iran was known in Afghanistan, but to the south of that country the borderland which divided the Indo-Aryan from the remnants of the Dravidians in Baluchistan is called *Zranka* in Persian and *Draṅga* in Sanskrit, both of which mean a boundary. The Indian term *Draṅgānī*, which means "frontiers" or "boundaries", was corrupted by the Greeks into **Intercourse between the Aryo-Iranians and the Indo-Aryans.**

The Boundary, Drangiana. Drangiana and applied to the hilly country which separates the fertile basin of the River Indus from the deserts of Baluchistan lying to the south of the valley of Kandahar.

In the middle of the sixth century B.C. the Indo-Iranian *Hakhamanishiya* dynasty of Persia, called the Achæmenian or the Achæmenidæ by the Greeks, became supreme in the near east. Cyrus or Kurush of this dynasty conquered Afghanistan, Bactria, and Gandhāra some time between 558 and 530 B.C. The dynasty to which Kurush belonged was founded by Chishpish (Greek Teispes), the son of Hakhamanish (or Achaimenes). Chishpish appears to have been reigning in the last quarter of the seventh century B.C. and was the first king to conquer Babylon. Kurush extended the empire of Persia towards the west as far as the Mediterranean. The Ionian Greeks were subdued, and the kingdom of Babylon was finally overthrown. The city was stormed in the month of March in 538 B.C., and the whole of the Babylonian Empire fell under the Persians. We do not know how the Indian provinces were conquered. The earliest allusions to the Indian provinces of the Persian Empire are to be found in the historical work of Herodotus, which refers their conquest to the reigns of Darayavaush (Darius) and Kshayārsha (Xerxes). But it is certain that the conquest of Bactria, Drangiana, and Gandhāra was the work of Kurush I. According to Ktesias, Kurush I died of a wound inflicted by an Indian in a battle, when the Indians were fighting for the Darbikes, a people of unknown origin, whom they had supplied with elephants. According to Xenophon, Kurush brought under his rule the Bactrians and the Indians, and he records the arrival of an embassy from an Indian king to the court of Kurush I.

The Hakhamanishiya Dynasty of Persia.

Conquest of North-western India.

When the Greeks came into direct contact with India, the Persian conquest of the North-western Frontier Provinces had become traditional and hazy, and therefore the account of Nearchos differed from that of Megasthenes. According to Pliny, Kurush destroyed the city of Kapiśā near modern Kabul. There cannot be any doubt about the fact that Kurush I conquered those provinces of India which lay between the western bank of the River Indus and the Persian frontier. We do not possess any evidence from Persian sources about Persian domination in India during the reigns of Kāmbujīya I (Cambyses), Kurush II, and Kāmbujīya II. With the accession of Darayavaush, or Darius I, we obtain fresh light. It appears that before the accession of Darayavaush in 522 B.C., the Indian provinces of the Persian Empire had shaken off the yoke of Persia. The Bahistan or Bisitun inscription of Darayavaush I does not mention India among the twenty-three provinces which obeyed that king, and from this fact scholars infer that the Indus region did not form a part of the Persian Empire at that time (520–518 B.C.). Later on, India is specially mentioned in the Old Persian block tablets on the platform of the palace at Persepolis and in the inscriptions on the tomb of Darayavaush at Naqsh-i-Rustam. Both of these inscriptions mention India, i.e. the Panjab, as part of the Persian Empire. The term employed in these inscriptions is *Hidu*, a corruption of *Hindu*, which is the Old Persian form of the name *Sindhu*. The older Persian dominion most probably did not include the whole of the Panjab and was restricted to the Indus region, i.e. as far as the western bank of the River Chenab.

Successors of Kurush I.

Reconquest of the Indian Provinces by Darayavaush I.

Extent of the Persian Domination in India.

Herodotus places India in the twentieth satrapy or province of the empire of Darayavaush. India paid the enormous tribute of three hundred and sixty talents of gold into the Persian treasury, an amount which is equivalent to one million pounds sterling. Upper and Lower Sindh formed a part of the Persian Empire, and in 517 B.C. Darayavaush sent Skylax, a native of Karyanda in Karia, to explore the River Indus. This squadron started from some place in the Gandhāra country, sailed down the Indus, and finally reached the Indian Ocean.

Expedition along the Indus under Skylax.

The Persian Empire in India was bounded on the east by the Thar or the Indian Desert, as Herodotus states that to the east of India the country is sandy. Herodotus never refers to the Ganges valley or to the kingdom of Magadha, which strongly suggests that the knowledge of the Persians about India was limited to the provinces of the Persian Empire. The inscriptions on the platform at Persepolis and the tomb at Naksh-i-Rustam mention the following three provinces:

Indian Provinces of Persian Empire.

(1) *Bakhtri* (Bactria), (2) *Haraiva* (Herat), and (3) *Zaranka* or *Zranka* (Drangiana). These three provinces together constitute modern Afghanistan and Baluchistan. To the east of them lay the provinces of India proper, consisting of (1) *Gandara* (Gandhāra), the Kabul valley as far as Peshawar;[1] (2) *Thatagu*; (3) *Harahuvati* (the Kandahar district); (4) *Sakā* (Seistan); and (5) *Maka* (Mekran).

Indian Soldiers in the Persian Army.

During the reign of Kshayārsha (Xerxes) an Indian contingent went with the Persian army to invade Greece. Herodotus describes the equipment of the Indians in the following words. "The Indian foot soldiers were clad in garments of cotton and carried bows and arrows of cane, the latter tipped with iron. The cavalry was armed in the same manner but they brought riding horses and chariots, the latter drawn by horses and 'wild asses'." The decadence of the Persian Empire began after the defeat of Kshayārsha in Greece. Even in the time of the last Persian emperor of the Hakhamanishiya dynasty an Indian contingent formed a part of the Persian army with which Darayavaush III met Alexander the Great for the last time on the battlefield of Arbela.

State of North-western India after the battle of Arbela.

After Alexander's victory at Arbela (331 B.C.), the small states in Afghanistan and the Western Panjab, which had so long obeyed the commands of the Persian emperors, became helpless because they were suddenly confronted by the Greeks. The Indian princes of the North-western Frontier had no time to organize themselves. They were divided in opinion, and some of them, instead of resisting Alexander, actually invited him and thus turned traitors to their country. After the destruction of the Persian army at Arbela and the death of Darayavaush III, Alexander moved towards Afghanistan. In the winter of 330 B.C. the Greek army was camped in Seistan, and in the same year it moved eastwards towards modern Kandahar. Many scholars think that the city of Kandahar was founded by Alexander the Great. In the summer of 329 B.C., the Greek army was camped in the Kandahar valley, and in the winter of the same year it crossed the mountains and reached the valley of the Kabul River—in the winter of 329–328 B.C. Alexander passed that winter in Kabul

Alexander in Afghanistan.

[1] *Cambridge History of India*, Vol. I, p. 338.

preparing for the invasion of Bactria, where a prince of the Persian imperial family was still holding out. Leaving a Persian satrap and a Macedonian general to hold the Kabul valley, Alexander crossed the Hindu-Kush and advanced as far as the bank of the River Jaxartes in Eastern Turkistan. He was absent in Bactria up to the summer of 327 B.C.

Alexander in Bactria.

At this time there were two rival kings in the Western Panjab, the king of Taxila or Takshaśilā and the king of the ancient Puru tribe. The king of Taxila possessed the country from the eastern bank of the River Indus to the western bank of the River Jhelum, but the king of the Purus had extended his kingdom towards Kashmir and the east. He was the most formidable monarch in the whole of the Panjab, and the king of Takshaśilā was afraid of him. Long before the advance of Alexander towards the banks of the River Indus, jealousy and fear of his rival made the king of Takshaśilā send envoys to the former in Bactria. The king of Takshaśilā was growing old and at first hesitated to adopt the Greek side, but his son Āmbhi was a thorough traitor, and even in his father's lifetime this prince sent messengers to Alexander on his own account, informing him that he was ready to march with the Greek army against his own countrymen.

Kings of the Panjab.

Treachery of Āmbhi.

The Greek army, formed into two divisions, descended to the plains of the Panjab by two different roads. Alexander himself marched to the north and reached the banks of the Indus through the country now called the Indus Kohistan; while the second Greek army, under the command of the proudest noble of the Macedonian king, named Perdikkas, marched upon Peshawar by the direct route, which probably lay through the Khaibar Pass. The hillmen of what is still the north-western frontier fought stubbornly as they do even now. They were, however, punished very heavily for their resistance to the advance of the Macedonian king. Entire towns were destroyed and thousands of people massacred. The king of Takshaśilā accompanied the second Greek army commanded by Perdikkas, and they reached Peshawar in 326 B.C. In this region the Greeks were opposed by a small chief whose capital was Pushkalāvatī, but he was shut up in his own town and his principality was given to an adherent of the king

Alexander's march to the Indus.

Conquest of Pushkalāvatī.

of Takshaśilā. The Lower Kabul valley was constituted a separate province, which was placed under the rule of a Greek named Nikanor, while the Upper Kabul valley was ruled by a Persian named Turyaspa (Tyriespes). During the winter of 326 the Greeks captured the strong fort of Aornos (? modern Ūṇa), which stood on a high mountain on the banks of the River Indus. This fort was placed in the charge of a garrison under an Indian traitor named Śaśigupta. A bridge was built over the River Indus at Ohind, about sixteen miles above Attock, and the entire army crossed into the Panjab.

Capture of Aornos.

Āmbhi had by this time succeeded his father in the kingdom of Taxila. He sent a message of homage to Alexander and informed him that he wanted to take his kingdom back from the Macedonian king as his vassal. At the head of his army Alexander marched into the city of Taxila and was received with royal honours by his new Indian vassal. He held a grand Durbar in that city, when there were Greek sacrifices and games. A crowd of chiefs of Eastern Afghanistan and the Panjab were present. The gold and silver vessels of the Persian emperors, the embroideries of Babylonia and Persia, had come to Takshaśilā with Alexander who now distributed them to the Indian chiefs. Indians who had turned traitor and submitted to the European invader had their territories increased, and those who had not submitted lost most of their possessions. Thus, without fighting, Alexander became the master of the Western Panjab.

Alexander's Entry into Taxila.

The king of the Purus watched the progress of events anxiously. He heard of the alliance between the foreigners and his hereditary enemies, the kings of Takshaśilā, and that the princes of other provinces were submitting without fighting. One of his kinsmen also submitted. The innate pride of the Purus and the tradition of centuries compelled him to resist the invasion of his own country by a foreign army. The Greek historians have preserved his tribal designation, but his name they have not recorded for us. In India we have forgotten the name of almost every defender of faith and motherland. The Greek historians call the chief of the Purus "Poros", which is equivalent to *Paurava* in Sanskrit, and from this fact we learn that even in the fourth century B.C.

King of the Purus.

kings were yet known by their tribal designations, as we see in the epics.

An open defiance was sent by the Paurava king to Alexander the Great. Somewhere near the modern town of Jhelum, in the spring of 326 B.C., the Paurava king mustered his army to oppose the foreigners. Alexander marched with the main army, which was supplemented by five thousand men under Āmbhi. A small part of the Greek army crossed in boats and a skirmish was fought, but the main army eluded the vigilance of the Indians and crossed the Jhelum elsewhere unopposed. In the battle which followed the Indian army was ranged to receive the attack of the Greeks. The Indian cavalry could not resist the Greek cavalry, and the elephants of the Indian king fled in terror. All the great captains of the Indian side, and thousands of soldiers, laid down their lives in the first battle. The Paurava king was wounded and captured. Alexander came galloping to meet him and asked him, through an interpreter, to indicate what treatment he wished to receive. "Act as a king," said the proud Paurava king, but when the interpreter explained that the Greek king wanted a more definite statement, the Paurava replied, "When I said 'as a king', everything was contained in that." The romantic vein in Alexander was touched. He reinstated the Paurava king in his kingdom. A city was built on the field of battle and was named "Bukephala", after the favourite horse of Alexander the Great which had fallen in the fight.

Skirmish on the Jhelum.

Battle of the Jhelum.

Foundation of Bukephala.

After the battle of the Jhelum no power which could oppose Alexander was left in North-western India. The Raja of Abhisāra (the Punch valley) sent presents with his brother. Alexander then moved to the banks of the Chenab, beyond which lay the territories of the King of Abhisāra, who was also a Paurava. He fled at the approach of the Greek army. Alexander crossed the Ravi and marched along the foot of the Southern Kashmir Hills, through a district ruled by a number of small chieftains who were called Kshatriyas. The town of Sangala was sacked and the other Kshatriyas submitted. Among them was a king named Saubhūti, who entertained the Macedonian king with great splendour, and later on struck coins with his name written in Greek as "Sophytes". The

Greek army marched to the banks of the River Beas, and here Alexander heard of the power and riches of the empire of Magadha. But on the banks of the Beas the great conqueror received a check from his own army. The Macedonians refused to advance any farther, and the proud world-conqueror was obliged to pass orders for return. On the banks of the river the Greek army built twelve gigantic altars and then turned back. The return march began in July, 326 B.C. Alexander returned by the route over which he had advanced, and reached the Jhelum. Here a fleet was built by a Cretan named Nearchos, and in November, 326, the main portion of the army embarked for the south. Two divisions, under Hephæstion and Krateros, marched along the banks of the river. The Sibæ offered their submission. They were the same as the Śiva Kshatriyas of the Vedic period. But two tribes called the Malloi and Oxydrakoi by the Greeks, who are the Mālavas and the Kshudrakas of Indian literature, resisted the Greeks at the junction of the Jhelum and the Chenab. The Mālavas lived on the borders of the Indian Desert, and their city was surprised and sacked. Alexander very nearly lost his life at the sack of the Mālava capital, but the Mālavas and the Kshudrakas submitted at last. Other tribes, whose names we cannot recognize, were defeated, and Alexander reached the junction of the Indus and the Chenab. At this time Oxyartes, an Iranian noble who had given his daughter to Alexander, was made governor of the Kabul valley.

Alexander in the Eastern Panjab. **The Greeks Retreat.** **The Sibæ.** **Malloi and Oxydrakoi.**

The most powerful tribe in the basin of the Indus was the Mushikas (called Mousikanos by the Greeks). The Śāmba Kshatriyas, belonging to the Yādava tribe, were at war with the Mushikas, and they allied themselves with Alexander against the latter. The king of the Mushikas submitted, as he was surprised by Alexander's rapid movements. The Śāmbas next opposed Alexander but were defeated. The people of Middle Sindh now opposed him. Their capital was called the city of the Brāhmaṇas, and is very probably the same as the Brāhmaṇābād of the Arab geographers and historians, the site of which now lies eight miles east of Shahdadpur station in the Nawab Shah District of Sindh. The king of the Mushikas rebelled once more, and a national movement against the

Mushikas and Śāmbas. **Brāhmaṇābād.**

aggression of the Greeks was begun by the Brāhmaṇas of Sindh. Pithon, the Greek governor of Sindh, defeated the Mushikas and brought their king as prisoner to Alexander. The Brāhmaṇas of Sindh were massacred and their bodies exposed on the roadside without cremation.

In Lower Sindh the city of Pattalā lay at the point where the delta of the Indus began. Greek historians state that, like Sparta, it was ruled by two kings and a council of elders. One of these kings came to pay homage to Alexander; but when the Greeks approached the city the kings and the people fled. Before that city was reached the elephants and one division of the Macedonian army began to march towards Babylon under the command of Krateros. Alexander continued his advance down-stream and reached Pattalā in July, 325 B.C. Near the great port of Deval, which has now disappeared, the Greek fleet reached the sea. Alexander then marched with the rest of his army along the southern coast of Baluchistan. The fleet returned to Pattalā and remained there till the end of October. The inhabitants of Makran, the Arava, who were of Dravidian stock and were called Arabitæ by the Greeks, deserted their villages in terror. Alexander crossed the River Hab and passed on to the country of another Dravidian people called the Oritæ. Their principal city, Rhambacia, was occupied, and Alexander passed on, leaving Apollophanes as Satrap in the country of the Oritæ. He then marched to Gedrosia and, keeping near the wells, reached the desert. Sixty days after his departure from the country of the Oritæ, Alexander passed out of India after enduring great privations. The fleet under Nearchos left India from a place near Karachi, which the Greeks called "the wooden town". It reached the good harbour at the mouth of the River Hab, where it obtained fresh stores deposited by the order of Alexander at a place called Kokala near the coast. At the mouth of the River Hingol the Greeks saw the aboriginal inhabitants of Makran, and then the fleet sailed on past the promontory of Malan, which was the limit of India.

Pattalā or Patalene.

Alexander's march through Baluchistan.

Voyage of Nearchos.

At the time of Alexander's departure from India his Indian dominions were divided into three provinces. The first province was placed under Philip, son of Machatas, who remained at Taxila; the second province, consisting of the province of Sindh, was placed in the charge of Pithon, son of Agenor; the third province was the easternmost division of Alexander's empire and extended from the River Jhelum to the River Beas. It was placed under a Paurava prince. Afghanistan was placed under the rule of Alexander's father-in-law, the Persian Oxyartes. A number of Macedonian soldiers, with Grecian and Thracian auxiliaries, remained as the army of occupation. Within a few months after Alexander's departure the Greek mercenaries under Philip mutinied. Philip was killed, and Alexander ordered that his province was to be ruled jointly by the king of Taxila and Eudamos, the commander of the Thracian contingent. This provisional arrangement continued till the death of Alexander, in the summer of 323 B.C., at Babylon.

Indian Provinces of Alexander's Empire.

Death of Alexander.

Many Greek coins, bearing Alexander's name, are found in India. The coins of Athens, bearing an owl, are found in the Panjab and were imitated there, most probably during the occupation of the Macedonian army. It is now supposed that a squarish bronze coin of Alexander was minted in India. On a group of silver coins Alexander's name is to be found in full, but none of these pieces bears the king's title. In the district in which Alexander's coins are found, the coins of the Hakhamanishiya emperors are also met with in small numbers. The gold daric, which was the standard coin of Persia, and a gold coin of Crœssus have been found in the Kohat district. Persian silver coins called *Sigloi* or *Shekels* have been found in small numbers in Western Panjab and Afghanistan. They bear small punch-marks like the oldest Indian coins, but some scholars are of opinion that these punch-marked *Sigloi* were current in Lycia, Cilicia, and other parts of Asia Minor and the Island of Cyprus, but not in India.

Greek Coins in India.

Persian Coins.

While Alexander's invasion left very little impression on India, the long occupation of the north-western provinces by the Persians left a permanent mark. Persian clerks introduced the use of the Aramaic script, and an inscription in that script has been discovered at Taxila. The Aramaic script was partly changed and adapted for the writing of Indian dialects, and this new script is called Kharoshṭhī. It is derived entirely from

Effects of the Persian Occupation.

The Kharoshṭhī Script.

the Aramaic prototype and contains aspirated consonants, which are required in Indian languages. The Kharoshṭhī script became the principal script of Turkistan, Bactria, Afghanistan, the Panjab, and Sindh. It remained in use in these countries till the third century A.D., when it was finally driven out by the Indian Brāhmī. Persian architecture was introduced by the Persian governors, and was used by the Indian emperors of the Maurya dynasty. The pillars of Aśoka, with round bell-shaped *abaci* and bull or lion capitals, are of pure Persian origin. The use of winged animals as capitals of pillars and pilasters was introduced by Persian architects and remained in use till the end of the first century B.C. Persian noblemen were employed by the Mauryan emperors, and one of them, Tushāspha, was the governor of Kathiawad, and is called a *Yavana* or Greek in the Junagadh rock inscription of the Scythian king Rudradāman I. **Persian Architecture.**

BIBLIOGRAPHY

Cambridge Ancient History, Vol. VI, chap. viii, xii, xiii.
Cambridge History of India, Vol. I, chap. xiv, xv.
SIR AUREL STEIN, *On Alexander's Track to the Indus*.
V. A. SMITH, *Early History of India* (4th ed.), chaps. iii–iv.

CHAPTER III

THE MAURYA EMPIRE

At the time of Alexander's invasion of India, the Greek writers speak of a king named Agrammes or Xandrames as ruling in Eastern India. This king has been identified with Dhanananda of the Purāṇas. He was overthrown by Chandragupta, who is represented as a relation of that king. Chandragupta appears to have been the commander-in-chief of the last Nanda king, and he is said to have attempted to overthrow his master with the help of the Brāhmaṇa Vishṇugupta or Chāṇakya. The attempt failed and the principal conspirators were forced to flee the country. The events of the period are narrated in a drama called *Mudrārākshasa* by **Dhanananda.** **Mudrārākshasa.**

Viśākhadatta, which is probably based on reliable contemporary accounts. With the help of a king of the Himalayan regions, named Parvataka, Chandragupta invaded Magadha and overthrew Dhanananda. Most probably Chandragupta obtained possession of Magadha in 321 B.C., two years after the death of Alexander the Great. After the overthrow of the Nandas, Chāṇakya contrived to kill Parvataka, the chief ally of Chandragupta. Parvataka's son, Malayaketu, withdrew to a distance with the remaining allies. Rākshasa, the faithful minister of the Nandas, joined Malayaketu against Chandragupta, but Chāṇakya contrived to make Malayaketu suspicious of his allies, who were put to death. Malayaketu now accepted an offer of peace from Chandragupta and retired.

Chandragupta.

Invasion of Seleukos.

In 305 B.C. Seleukos, who had succeeded in occupying the eastern provinces of Alexander's empire, invaded India. He found that Chandragupta, now master of all Hindustan, was ready to confront him with an immense army. Seleukos was overawed by the power of the Indian emperor. He was either defeated or compelled to purchase peace by cession of the easternmost provinces of Alexander's empire. He received five hundred elephants in exchange for Aria, Arachosia, Gedrosia, and Paropanisadæ. The Greek historians mention a matrimonial alliance, but we do not know whether a Greek princess was given to Chandragupta or an Indian princess was sent to Seleukos. After the departure of Seleukos from India he sent an envoy named Megasthenes, who arrived at Pāṭaliputra, the capital of Northern India, some time between 305 and 297 B.C.

Treaty between Seleukos and Chandragupta.

The empire of Chandragupta, at the time of his death, extended over almost the whole of India. But his authority could not have been exercised everywhere in the same manner or the same measure. After the defeat of Seleukos, the empire of Magadha included the provinces of Aria, Arachosia, Gedrosia, and the Paropanisadæ, i.e. Herat, Kandahar, Baluchistan, and the Kabul valley. Kathiawad was conquered at some later date and was ruled by the viceroy Pushyagupta of the Vaishya caste. Pushyagupta was called a Rāshṭrīya, or viceroy, and became famous as the originator of the Sudarśana Lake near Mount Girnar. South Indian tradition has preserved the record of the Mauryan invasion of the far south. According

Empire of Chandragupta.

to an ancient Tamil poet named Mamulanar, the Mauryas advanced as far as Podiyil Hill in the Tinnevelly District. The statements of Mamulanar are supported by Paranar and other Tamil authors. The Mauryas conquered Southern India through Konkan, or the coastal region to the west, and not from Pāṭaliputra along the eastern coast. The Maurya conquest of Southern India was fresh in the memory of men in Mysore in mediæval times, and one Mysore inscription records that Nāgakhaṇḍa in the Shikarpur Taluka was included in the kingdom of Chandragupta. The conquest of Kaliṅga by Aśoka proves that the eastern coast of the Peninsula was not included in the kingdom of his grandfather.

Conquest of Southern India.

The most valuable account of India in the third century B.C. was written by Megasthenes, the ambassador sent by Seleukos of Asia Minor and Babylonia to the court of the Emperor Chandragupta. The original work of Megasthenes is missing, but fragments survive in quotations made by later authors, such as Strabo, Arrian, &c. Megasthenes appears to have possessed very little critical acumen and was often misled by his informants. He describes Pāṭaliputra, which he calls Palimbothra, as the largest city in India, and states that it was situated in the land of the *Prasii*, i.e. the easterners (*Prāchyas*), at the confluence of the Ganges and the Erannoboas (Hiranyavahu, i.e. the Son). The city was surrounded by a ditch six hundred feet wide and thirty cubits deep. There were five hundred and seventy towers and sixty-four gates in the wall of the city. The most important cities in the empire after Pāṭaliputra were Taxila and Ujjain.

Megasthenes.

His Description of Pāṭaliputra.

An account of the palace of Chandragupta is to be found in the work of Ælian: "In the Indian Royal Palace where the greatest of all the kings of the country resides, besides much else which is calculated to excite admiration, and with which neither Susa nor Ekbatana can vie, there are other wonders besides. In the Parks tame Peacocks are kept, and Pheasants which have been domesticated; there are shady groves and pasture grounds planted with trees, and branches of trees which the art of the woodsman has deftly interwoven; while some trees are native to the soil, others are brought from other parts, and with their beauty enhance the charms of the landscape.

The Palace of Chandragupta.

Parrots are natives of the country, and keep hovering about the king and wheeling round him, and vast though their numbers be, no Indian ever eats a parrot. The Brachmanes honour them highly above all other birds—because the parrot alone can imitate human speech. Within the palace grounds are artificial ponds in which they keep fish of enormous size but quite tame. No one has permission to fish for these except the king's sons while yet in their boyhood. These youngsters amuse themselves by fishing in the unruffled sheet of water and learning how to sail their boats."[1]

Its Ruins. The ancient Mauryan palace discovered by Dr. D. B. Spooner at Kumarhar near Patna appears to belong to the period of Chandragupta. The ruins indicate that there was a large hall supported by tall columns of stone, the foundations of which were laid on large platforms of wood closely packed together. According to Dr. Spooner, the general outlines of the ground indicate that the plan of the palace at Pāṭaliputra agreed in many details with that of the Hakhamanishiya palace at Persepolis, " but," as V. A. Smith observes, " the resemblance is not yet definitely established."[2]

Megasthenes on Indian Castes. "The most interesting part of Megasthenes' account is that relating to contemporary India, so far as he could learn about it at Pāṭaliputra. . . . The *first* class of Megasthenes consisted of 'philosophers', under which term, as has just been said, Brahmans and ascetics were confused. It was numerically the smallest class, but the highest in honour, immune from labour and taxation. Its only business was to perform public sacrifice, to direct the sacrifice of private individuals, and to divine. . . . The *second* class consisted of the cultivators, and included the majority of the Indian people. They never took any part in war, their whole business being to cultivate the soil and pay taxes—to the kings or to the free cities, as the case might be. . . . All the land belonged to the King, and the cultivators paid one-fourth of the produce in addition to rent. The *third* class Megasthenes described as herdsmen and hunters. . . . The *fourth* class consisted of the traders, artisans, and boatmen. They paid a tax on the produce

[1] *The Political History of Ancient India*, Second Edition, pp. 172–3.
[2] *Oxford History of India*, p. 77.

of their industry, except those who manufactured implements of war and built ships. . . . The *fifth* class was that of the fighters, the most numerous class after the cultivators. They performed no work in the community except that of fighting. Members of the other classes supplied them with weapons and waited upon them and kept their horses and elephants. They received regular pay even in times of peace, so that when not fighting they could live a life of ease and maintain numbers of dependents. . . . The *sixth* consisted of the government secret inspectors, whose business it was to report to the king, or, among the free tribes, to the headmen, what went on among the people, and the *seventh* of those constituting the Council of the King or the tribal authorities." [1]

Megasthenes travelled through the country and saw it for himself. The Indian towns, built on the banks of the rivers, contained houses made of wood, but other towns, built on elevations, were made of brick and clay. Nearchos describes the arms of the Indians. The foot-soldiers carried bows as long as the body. To shoot, they rested one end of the bow on the ground and set their left foot against it. They had to draw the string far back, since the arrows in use were six feet long. In their left hands they carried long narrow shields of raw hide, nearly coextensive with the body. Some had javelins instead of bows. All carried long two-handed swords with broad blades. The horsemen had two javelins and a shield smaller than the foot-soldiers'.[2] According to the same writer, the laws were preserved by oral tradition and not in books. According to Megasthenes, many of the laws were sufficiently severe. The latter observed that the Indians were polygamous and that brides were purchased from their parents. According to the same writer, officials were divided into three classes: (1) the *Agronomoi* or the district officials, (2) the *Astynomoi* or town officials [3], and (3) the members of the War Office.

[1] *Cambridge History of India*, Vol. I, pp. 409–11.

[2] *The Cambridge History of India*, Vol. I, p. 412.

[3] The town officials were divided into six Boards of Five. "Their respective functions were: (1) supervision of factories; (2) care of strangers, including control of the inns, provision of assistance, taking charge of sick persons, burying the dead; (3) the registration of births and deaths; (4) the control of the market, inspection of weights and measures; (5) the inspection of manufactured goods, provision for their sale with accurate distinction of new and second-hand articles; (6) collection

The district officials supervised the irrigation and land measurements, the various industries connected with agriculture, the maintenance of the roads, and hunting.

Constitution of the Maurya Empire. An accurate idea of Chandragupta's administration of the vast empire founded by him can be gleaned from the *Artha-śāstra* of Kauṭilya and the account of Megasthenes. **The Emperor.** The Emperor was the supreme head of the government. He exercised military, judicial, and legislative as well as executive functions. He left his palace on military expeditions and considered plans of campaigns with his commander-in-chief. He sat in court to administer justice and receive petitions. Kauṭilya states that he was the fountain-head of legislation. His highest ministers were the Mantrins. They received the largest salaries, and all administrative measures were prepared in consultation with three or four of them. **Executive Council.** The Executive Council, called the *Mantri-parishad*, included ministers of all classes. It contained many inferior officers who were consulted on occasions of emergency. Besides the chief ministers and the assembly of ministers, there was a third kind of officials, called **Civil Service.** the *Amātyas*, who held high administrative and judicial appointments. They were appointed to superintend the pleasure gardens, mines, timber, and elephant forests. More experienced *Amātyas* were employed as diplomatic agents or ambassadors, ministers of correspondence, and superintendents. The Magistrates in charge of the civil administration of the cities were called Superintendents of cities (*Nagarādhyakshas*). The officers in charge of the military affairs were called *Balādhyakshas*. Neither the *Arthaśāstra* of Kauṭalya nor the account of **Viceroys.** Megasthenes mentions the Viceroys, who are called *Rāshṭrīyas* in the Junagadh inscription of the Scythian king Rudradāman I. They were probably the same as the *Rāshṭrapālas*, who were equal in rank with the *Kumāras* or the princes of the blood royal, and who received a salary of 12,000 *paṇas* per annum. Inspection and espionage were regarded as the

of the tax of 10 per cent, charged on sales. The six Boards acting together exercised a general superintendence over public works, prices, harbours, and temples. The third kind of officials constituted the War Office, and were also divided into six Boards of Five. The departments of the six were: (1) the admiralty, (2) transport and commissariat, (3) the infantry, (4) the cavalry, (5) the chariots, (6) the elephants. Connected with the army were the royal stables for horses and elephants, and the royal arsenal." *The Cambridge History of India*, Vol. I, pp. 417-8.)

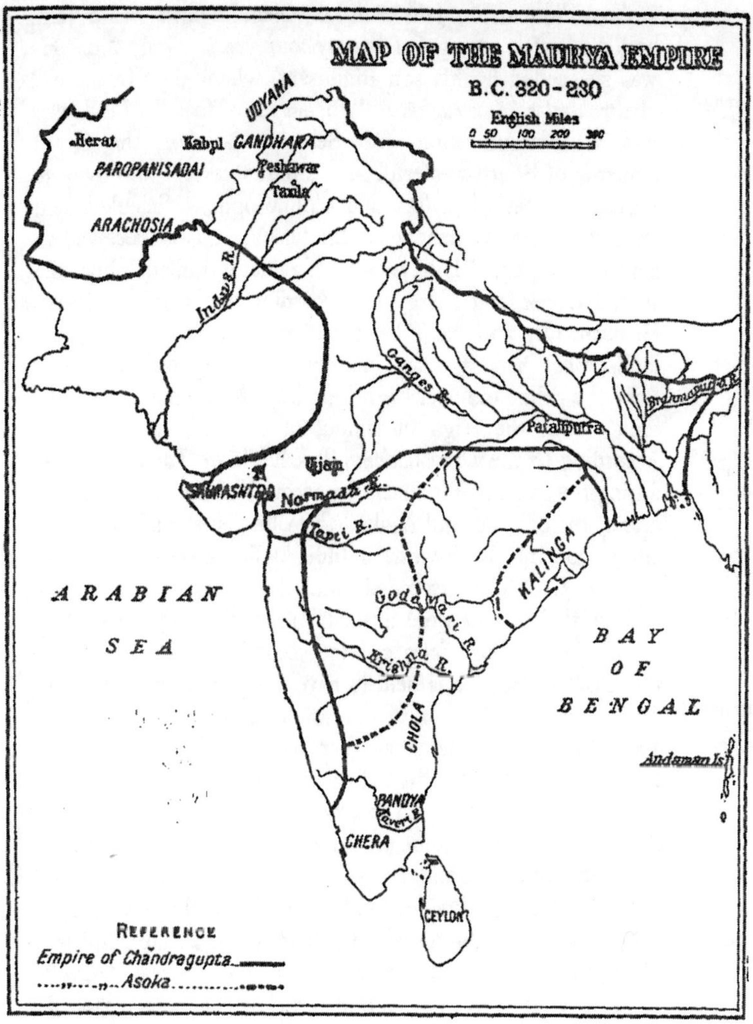

principal methods of government. It is probable that the villages were administered by *Grāmikas* with the aid of the village elders or Gramavridhas, who were not paid officers. A chief of five or ten villages was called the *Gopa*; over him was the "*Sthānika*", who ruled over one-fourth of a district (*Janapada*). **District Officers.**

According to the Jain tradition, Chandragupta was a Jain, and died, after a reign of twenty-four years, *c.* 297 B.C. He was succeeded by his son Bindusāra, whom the Greeks call

Bindusāra. *Amitrokhates* (*Amitraghāta*), " the slayer of foes ". Bindusāra was in communication with Seleukos Nikator, the Greek emperor of South-western Asia. Bindusāra sent an envoy to purchase sweet wine, figs, and a philosopher. Seleukos sent an envoy named Daïmachus to Bindusāra, who also received an ambassador named Dionysios from Ptolemy Philadelphus, the second Greek king of Egypt. According to the Jain historian Hemachandra and the Tibetan historian Tārānātha, the great minister of Chandragupta, Chāṇakya-Vishṇnugupta, continued to be the prime minister of the empire. We do not know anything about the reign of Bindusāra except from tradition.

Revolution in Taxila. According to the *Divyāvadāna*, Takshaśilā or Taxila revolted during the reign of Bindusāra on account of the high-handedness of the officials, and Aśoka had to be dispatched as governor to control North-western India. Bindusāra had at least three sons. Aśoka succeeded him. According to the *Divyāvadāna*, their names were Susīma, Aśoka, and Vigatāśoka, but the Ceylonese Chronicles call the second and third Sumana and Tishya. Susīma is held to have been the step-brother of

Bindusāra's Sons. Aśoka and the eldest son of Bindusāra. The Chinese traveller Yuan Chwang mentions another brother of Aśoka named Mahendra. Bindusāra died after a reign of twenty-five years, according to the Purāṇas, and twenty-eight years, according to the Ceylonese Chronicles. His death took place at some time between *c.* 273 and 270 B.C.

A war of succession followed the death of Bindusāra, and

Aśoka. Aśoka gained the throne with the help of the Prime Minister Rādhagupta. The formal consecration of Aśoka was delayed for three or four years, and this period is generally regarded by scholars as the period of the civil war. Aśoka is said to

Slaughter of his Brothers. have slaughtered all his male relations. Many scholars, however, do not believe this story, told by the Ceylonese Chronicles, and think that his brothers were alive in the seventeenth or eighteenth year of his reign. The fifth rock edict mentions the female establishments of his brothers, but the existence of the female establishments does not necessarily indicate that his brothers were alive. Aśoka assumed the title of "*Devānāṁpiya Piyadasi*", "the favourite of the gods, the beautiful one". His real name, Aśoka, has been used in addition to his titles in the Maski rock edict. In the Junagadh rock inscriptions of Rudradāman I and in the Sarnath inscription (twelfth century A.D.) of the Queen Kumāradevi, Aśoka is called by his personal name. During the first thirteen years of his reign Aśoka seems to have carried on the traditional policy of the empire. At the time of his accession the Maurya Empire consisted of the whole of Northern India, from the hills which separate Bengal from Burma to Herat in the west, and from Kashmir to the River Pennar near Nellore in the south. The Konkan and a portion of the Deccan plateau were also added to it, but the eastern coast, beginning with Orissa, was entirely unsubdued.

Extent of the Empire at the Time of Aśoka's Accession.

Aśoka's attention was turned in the first instance to the powerful kingdom of Kaliṅga, which lay between his empire and the great Dravidian kingdoms of the south. Kaliṅga itself was a Dravidian kingdom, where the Jain religion flourished. Its people had grown enormously rich by the overseas trade, and its colonies extended over the whole of Farther India and the northern islands of the Indian Archipelago. Some time after the fall of the Śiśunagas or the Nandas, Kaliṅga had regained its independence. If Pliny is to be believed, Kaliṅga was an independent kingdom during the reign of Chandragupta. It maintained sixty thousand infantry, one thousand cavalry, and seven hundred elephants as its peace strength. The Maurya invasion of this kingdom and its conquest constitute a landmark in the political history of India. The war with Kaliṅga was carried on with exceptional severity. Aśoka himself records that nearly one hundred thousand men were slain and many times that number died, evidently of privation. One hundred and fifty thousand souls from Kaliṅga were carried away as captives. The country was placed under a viceroy of the royal family stationed at Tosalī, and two subordinate governors were placed in charge of the northern and southern divisions of the country.

Kingdom of Kaliṅga

Its Conquest by Aśoka.

The conquest of Kaliṅga marks the beginning of the decline of the political power of the Mauryas. The change produced in the mind of Aśoka by the slaughter and bloodshed of the Kaliṅga war led to a revolution in the policy of the Maurya Empire. Like all other kings who abandoned statecraft for religion, Aśoka paved the way for the conquest of India by foreigners. Outwardly the empire remained as great as ever. The great viceroys ruled over the provinces and the ministers controlled the revenue, the army, and trade, but a change had come imperceptibly over all of them.

Subsequent Change in the Policy of the State.

The changes came in quick succession. Aśoka joined the Buddhist Church soon after the conquest of Kaliṅga. He next entered the order of monks and began missionary work for the propagation of Buddhism. The minor rock edict was issued *c.* 259 B.C. Thirteen years after his coronation Aśoka appointed a new class of officers called *Dharma-Mahāmātras*, whose duty it was to inculcate piety, to overcome misfortune, to redress wrong, and to organize charitable endowments. In the previous year he had instituted a quinquennial circuit by his leading officials for the purpose of proclaiming moral law. We can imagine stern viceroys and old generals going about the country and preaching the latest fad of the emperor. Buddhism was yet a faith of minor importance, and its adoption as a state religion must have given great offence to the Jains as well as to the Brāhmaṇas. The regulations introduced by Aśoka in his edicts gave great offence to the votaries of the orthodox Indo-Aryan religion. The cessation of popular processions and festivals must have offended the common people, who were used to much pomp and circumstance in such functions. In these respects Aśoka resembled the bigoted Mughal emperor Aurangzeb, who forbade singing and who persecuted Musalmans of other sects as well as Hindus.[1] Aśoka's adoption of the Buddhist faith and his intolerance of the orthodox Indo-Aryan religious practices must have produced great disaffection throughout the entire empire, just as the bigotry of Aurangzeb caused the Rajput war and subsequently paralysed the Mughals.

Aśoka becomes a Monk.

Religious Officers.

Popular Dissatisfaction caused by the change in the State Religion.

Aśoka and Aurangzeb.

The peace which ensued after the conquest of Kaliṅga caused

[1] A directly contrary opinion of Aśoka's character has been expressed by Dr. D. R. Bhandarkar in his *Aśoka*, and by Dr. H. C. Raychandhuri, *Political History of Ancient India.*

a change in the foreign policy of the empire. The great Dravidian kingdoms of the south: the Choḷas, the Pāṇḍyas, and the Cheras, across the River Tāmraparṇī, escaped destruction. In the internal policy, an improvement was visible for a short time. Wells were dug at regular intervals along the highways, trees were planted to provide shade for travellers. Hospitals were built for men as well as animals. Medicinal herbs were cultivated, but the adoption of the administrative machine for the propagation of the new faith must have caused a severe dislocation. The emperor himself went about preaching the religion and on pilgrimage to the new Holy Places. We know that he went to Bodh Gaya and commenced what are called the tours of piety. We know from the position of the uninscribed pillars that he went to Vaiśālī and to Kauśāmbī. The position of the inscribed pillar at Rumin-dei indicates the actual place of Buddha's birth, and another pillar in the same neighbourhood records the repairs to the reputed *stūpa* of the previous Buddha *Kanaka-muni*. The other edict-inscribed pillars mark other holy places of Buddhism. These are the pillars of Sarnath and Sanchi.

Aśoka's Public Works.

Aśoka's Tours and Pilgrimages.

Aśoka was reputed to be the builder of eighty-four thousand religious edifices. In the thirteenth as well as the twentieth year after his coronation he excavated cave dwellings in the Barabar Hills of the Gaya District for the use of the monks of the Ājīvika sect. In the nineteenth year after his coronation, according to the Buddhist Chronicle, *Mahāvaṁsa*, Aśoka convened the third Council of Buddhist monks at Pāṭaliputra. The first of these Councils was convened by Mahākāśyapa, the eldest disciple of Buddha at Rājagṛiha. The second Council was convened at some later date in the city of Vaiśālī, because the monks of the Lichchhavi country had started unorthodox practices, such as the acceptance of money. The Council had to be assembled for the third time by Aśoka to settle the differences between the different sects of Buddhism, of which as many as eighteen are mentioned. Buddhist monks from the different countries met in the Aśokārāma at Pāṭaliputra, under the presidency of a famous monk called Moggaliputta Tissa according to the Ceylonese Chronicles, and Upagupta according

Aśoka's Buildings.

The Third Great Buddhist Council.

Façade of Lomas-rishi Cave, Barabar hills, Gaya district (3rd century B.C.)

Its President. to Sanskrit Buddhist literature. They deliberated for nine months and finally decided in favour of the *Sthaviras*, which school afterwards prevailed in Ceylon. For this reason this Council is ignored by the northern Buddhists.

Propagation of the Buddhist Religion. At the close of the Council, Aśoka began to send missionaries to countries outside of India. The names of these Buddhist missionaries have been carefully preserved. Mādhyantika was sent to Kashmir and Gandhāra; Mahārakshita was sent to the Greek countries, i.e. the Greek kingdom of the Seleucidæ in South-western Asia. Mahādeva was sent to the

Mahishamaṇḍala or the country lying to the immediate south of the River Narmadā; a Greek named Dharmarakshita was sent to Gujarat, Mahādharmarakshita to the Mahārashṭra country or the north-western Deccan, and Rakshita to Vanavāsi or the north Kanara District. Majjhima was sent to the Himalayan regions, and the brothers Sona and Uttara went to Burma. Two of Aśoka's own children, his son Mahendra and his daughter Saṅghamitrā,[1] embraced monastic life and, accompanied by the Buddhist elders Rishṭriya, Utriya, Sambala, and Bhadrasāra, went to preach the Buddhist religion in Ceylon. Tissa, the King of Ceylon, welcomed them, and the king was converted with his people.

Aśoka's Missionaries.

Mission to Ceylon.

According to the concurrent testimony of the Purāṇas and the Buddhist histories, Aśoka reigned for thirty-six or thirty-seven years, and he died as a Buddhist monk near Rājagṛiha *c.* 231 B.C. His empire consisted of the whole of Northern India, beginning with Afghanistan in the west. We are not in a position to judge whether any of the provinces ceded by Seleukos Nikator to Chandragupta had been lost during the reign of his son or grandson. The north-western provinces of the empire included the vassal states of Kāmboja and Gandhāra. The country of the Greeks, i.e. the Seleucid empire, lay to the west and is referred to in the inscriptions as the *Yona* country. The Kāmboja country lay in approximately the north-central part of modern Afghanistan, while the Gandhāras lived to the east of them. The capital of the north-western provinces was Taxila. There is no direct contemporary evidence of the inclusion of Kashmir in the empire of Aśoka, but Kalhaṇa in his *Rājataraṅginī*, and the Chinese traveller Yuan Chwang, mention that Kāśmīra formed a part of the Maurya Empire. Aśoka is said to have built the town of Srinagar and numerous Buddhist edifices. Among these may be mentioned a *stūpa* inside the Vihāra of Dharmāraṇya, and the temple of Vijayeśvara. In the east, Bengal formed the easternmost province, and there is no direct evidence to prove that Assam was ever included in the empire of Aśoka. In the south, Central India was ruled by the Viceroy of Ujjain. There were many vassal tribes, among whom may be men-

Extent of Aśoka's Empire.

[1] Some writers consider that Mahendra was Aśoka's brother, Saṅghamitrā his sister.

tioned the Andhras of the eastern coast, the Pulindas of the Central Provinces, and the Bhojas and the Rāshṭrikas of the northern Deccan. In the south-west, Aparānta was included in the empire of Aśoka, and Surāshṭra or Kathiawad was ruled by the Yavani viceroy Tushāspha.

Aśoka's Officers. The principal officers of Aśoka's empire were: (1) The *Kumaras* or *Āryaputras*, who acted as viceroys. (2) The *Mahāmātras*, who are mentioned in the *Arthaśāstra* of Kauṭilya and existed even in the twelfth century, when one of them dedicated an image in South Bihar or Magadha. (3) The *Rājukas*, executive officers, whose duty it was to survey land and collect revenue. (4) The *Prādeśikas*, who are generally taken to be provincial governors. Scholars, however, differ in opinion about the translation of this term. Senart, Kern, and Bühler translate it as "local governors or chiefs"; Smith takes it to mean District officers, while Thomas translates it as "Reporters or News Agents", identifying them with the *Pradeshṭris* of the *Arthaśāstra*. Their principal functions appear to have been the collection of taxes and the administration of criminal justice. They are also supposed to have acted as intermediaries between the divisional commissioners or *Samāhatṛis* and village, *pargana*, and district officials (*Gopa*, *Sthānika*, and *Adhyakshas*). (5) The *Yutas* appear to be the same as the *Yuktas* of the *Arthaśāstra*. They are mentioned in the third rock edict of Aśoka along with the *Rājukas*. According to Manu they were police officers, whose duty it was to trace lost property. Three other classes of officers, the *Pulisas* or the *Purushas*, the *Prativedakas*, and the *Vachabhumikas*, were evidently officials of the lowest orders. (6) The *Dharma-mahamatras*, a class of officers created to act as superintendents of morality.

Names of his Ministers. The northern Sanskrit texts mention Rādhagupta as the chief minister of Bindusāra and Aśoka, and a Khotanese legend mentions another minister named Yaśas who is also mentioned in the *Sūtrālaṅkāra* of Aśvaghosha.

Aśoka is famous for his religious activities and the propagation of Buddhism. The Kaliṅga war awoke humanitarian instincts in his mind, and he was gradually drawn towards Buddhism. Three years later he became active in the propagation of his new faith. He directed his energy to the spread of Buddhism, and he engaged the entire force of the empire for the attainment of this single object. It has been generally held by scholars that he tolerated all creeds. The dedication of caves in the Barabar Hills for the use of the monks of the Ājīvika sect, and the mention of the Brāhmaṇas, conjointly with the Śramaṇas, in his inscriptions, are generally taken to be indications of his religious toleration, but we must take into account the hindrance to the religious practices of orthodox Hinduism caused by his prohibition of sacrifices and of convivial assemblies. The introduction of the new religion must have diverted to its propagation a good deal of revenue which, before that date, appears to have been spent on the Jain and Brahmanical religions. Later on, when he became a monk and nominally renounced the world, offence must have been given to other sects, while their members must have suffered considerably from the preference shown to Buddhists. In spite of these facts Aśoka was a great king and a great man. Like Aurangzeb, he was a man of tireless energy. He made himself accessible at all hours and was ready to transact business with his officers even in private seclusion. He restricted the extravagances of the palace and at the same time infused a great deal of his personal energy into the officers of the empire, both high and low. He was one of the great monarchs of the world who came to realize that they had moral and religious responsibilities in addition to the ordinary cares of a ruler; but religious fervour always produces evil results in a kingdom where different sects prevail, and Aśoka's religious activities, though highly beneficial to the Buddhist sect, produced evil results.

Aśoka's Character.

His Treatment of Other Sects.

Acts of Intolerance.

His Personality.

The inscriptions of Aśoka fall into three principal groups:

I. The group of fourteen rock edicts found at Girnar near Junagadh in Kathiawad, Shahbazgadhi and Mansera in the North-western Frontier Provinces, Kalsi near Mussouri, Dhauli near Cuttack, and Jaugada near Berhampur-Ganjam.

II. The minor rock edicts of Rupnath, Sassaram, Bairat, Brahmagiri, Siddhapur, and Maski. These minor

Inscriptions of Aśoka.

edicts have been found in Central India and the Deccan. Sassaram is in Bihar, Rupnath near Jubbulpur in the Central Provinces, and Bairat in the Jaipur State. Brahmagiri and Siddhapur lie in the Mysore State, while Maski is in the territories of the Nizam of Haidarabad.

III. The pillar edicts in two subdivisions: (1) the general edicts and (2) the minor edicts. The general edicts consist of moral exhortations and are divided into seven parts; hence they are known as the Seven Pillar Edicts. Such edicts have been found on the pillars discovered at Meerut and Sivalik, both of which are now at Delhi, the pillar inside the fort at Allahabad, and the three pillars standing *in situ* at Araraj, Nandangarh, and Rampurwa in North Bihar. The minor pillar edicts are five in number and have been found at Sarnath and Sanchi and on the Allahabad pillar. Besides these there are two other pillar edicts, one marking the birthplace of Buddha at *Lumbini-grāma* or Rumin-dei, and the *stūpa* of the mythical Buddha *Kanaka-muni*, both of which have been found in Nepal Terai. In addition to these inscriptions there are three votive inscriptions of Aśoka in the caves at Barabar.

Contents of the Edicts.

The rock edicts and the seven pillar edicts contain moral exhortations and recommendations about the practice of simple virtues, viz. proper treatment of slaves and servants, obedience to parents, generosity and respect to friends, companions, relations, ascetics, and Brāhmaṇas, as well as abstention from cruelty to living beings. All the edicts insistently refer their readers to *Dharma*, a word very difficult to translate, but which may generally be taken to mean "the sacred law" or "the law of piety". With the advance of age the religious feeling grew stronger in Aśoka, and in the later edicts we find exhortations to a special self-examination and to adherence to one's faith. Scholars have remarked, "in a country where, during later ages, the ecstatic, metaphysical, and fanciful aspects of religion have predominated, the sober Buddhist piety revealed in the edicts deserves remark".[1]

[1] *The Cambridge History of India*, Vol. I, p 508.

Evidently there was a good deal of difference of opinion between the different Buddhist sects during the lifetime of Aśoka. The Sarnath pillar edict refers to a schism in the Buddhist Church, a schism which the emperor was anxious to terminate. This edict is repeated on the Allahabad pillar and on that at Sanchi. Aśoka succeeded in transforming Buddhism from a minor sect to a world-wide religion. The movement set on foot by him continued for centuries, and the disciples of the monks sent out by him as missionaries succeeded in converting entire nations to the religion of Buddha. Two hundred years after his death this movement succeeded in Indianizing a large number of Greeks, Scythians, and Turks, and thus saved Indian civilization from total extinction.

Schism in the Buddhist Church.

Buddhism becomes a World-religion.

Aśoka had many children. His sons by his queens represented the Imperial authority at Taxila, Ujjain, and Kaliṅga. Kunāla or Suyaśas, Jalauka, and Mahendra are mentioned in literature. Tīvara, the son of the queen Kāruvākī, does not appear to have ascended the throne. We do not know who succeeded Aśoka or the events which immediately followed his death.

Aśoka's Family

Indian art of the Mauryan period was generally regarded by older writers, like Fergusson, as being the nearest approach to perfection, but the latest authorities differ from this view. Instead of regarding the history of Indian art as a narrative of general decay, the best authorities are now of opinion that it is a record of continual progress. Sir John Marshall says: "In reality, as we shall presently see, its history is one of continuous forward progress, and, when the works of extraneous schools have been recognized and eliminated, it is found to follow a clear and logical sequence, in obedience to the fixed and immutable principles which govern the artistic efforts of all primitive peoples."[1] The same authority considers that the dignified and massive simplicity of the pillars of Aśoka is common to all other architectural remains of the Maurya epoch. The Monolithic rail at Sarnath and the throne under the Bodhi tree at Bodh-Gaya are "devoid of ornament, but each is cut with exquisite precision from a

Maurya Art.

Its Massive Simplicity.

[1] *Cambridge History of India*, Vol. I, p. 618.

single block of stone". The dwellings and chapels excavated for the Ājīvika ascetics in the Barabar Hills of the Gaya District are equally chaste and severe. The ornamental façade of the Lomas Rishi cave at Barabar is an accurate replica of a wooden building. This particular cave is not inscribed and may not belong to the reign of Aśoka. The skill with which

Its Peculiar Polish.

these monuments were chiselled is hardly less striking than the brilliancy with which they were polished. Sir John Marshall is of opinion that two different classes of sculpture are met with during the Mauryan period. The first of these is the older school of Indian sculpture, of which the statue from Parkham in the Mathura Museum can be regarded as the "type specimen". "The second class of Indian sculpture is represented by the Sarnath capital, which evinces a striking disparity in the style of sculptural ornamentation. This disparity is well exemplified by comparing the primitive treatment of the statue from Parkham in the Mathura Museum with the highly developed modelling of the Sarnath capital. The former represents a stage of art not yet emancipated from

Primitive Indian Art; the Parkham Image.

the binding law of frontality or from the trammels imposed by the prepossessions of the artist. The head and torso are so posed that, were they bisected vertically, the two halves would be found to be almost symmetrical; while the flattened sides and back of the figure, connected only by a slight chamfering of the edges, are conclusive proof that the sculptor failed to grasp more than one aspect of his subject at a time, or to co-ordinate its parts harmoniously together as an organic whole. These features are not mere superficial details of technique, due to the caprice of the artist. They are the fundamental characteristics of the nascent sculpture of all countries, and the primitiveness of the art which they signify is borne out in this particular statue by other traits, namely, by the subordination of the side and back to the front aspect, by the inorganic attachment of the ear, by the uncouth proportions of the neck, by the intentional rotundity of the abdomen, and the absence of modelling in the feet.

"The Sarnath capital, on the other hand, though by no means a masterpiece, is the product of the most developed art of which the world was cognizant in the third century B.C.—

the handiwork of one who had generations of artistic effort and experience behind him. In the masterful strength of the crowning lions, with their swelling veins and tense muscular development, and in the spirited realism of the reliefs below, there is no trace whatever of the limitations of primitive art. So far as naturalism was his aim, the sculptor has modelled his figures from nature, and has delineated their forms with bold faithful touch; but he has done more than this; he has consciously and of set purpose infused a tectonic conventional spirit into the four lions, so as to bring them into harmony with the architectural character of the monument, and in the case of the horse on the abacus he has availed himself of a type well known and approved in western art. Equally matured is the technique of his relief work."[1]

Advanced Mauryan Art; the Sarnath Lion-capital.

According to the same authority, the difference between the artists of the two schools is due to the training of Aśoka's men under Persian artists. At this time Greek influence alone could have influenced the modelling of the Sarnath capital. The artists of Aśoka learnt to impart the wonderful polish from the artists of the Achæmenide Empire, but they learnt modelling from the Greek artists of Bactria. "While the Sarnath capital is thus an exotic alien to Indian ideas in expression and in execution, the statue of Parkham falls naturally into line with other products of indigenous art and affords a valuable starting point for the study of its evolution. These two works represent the alpha and omega of early Indian art, between which all the sculptures known to us take their place, approximating to the one or the other extreme according as the Indian or the Perso-Hellenic spirit prevailed in them."[2]

Persian Influence on Mauryan Art.

The same authority holds that this difference in style is noticeable in the indigenous punch-marked coins, which are very ugly and crude, and the beautiful coins struck by the Indian king Saubhūti, who adopted the Greek model. The Mauryan craftsmen had attained a good deal of proficiency in the jeweller's and lapidary's art. Their special aptitude lay "not in the plastic treatment of form, but in the high technical skill with which they cut and polished refractory stones or

Mauryan Coins and Jewellery.

[1] *The Cambridge History of India*, Vol. I, pp. 620–1. [2] *Ibid*, p. 622.

applied delicate filigree or granular designs to metal objects ".[1] The same authority attributes the rock-crystal bowl from Piprahwa and the beryl relic caskets found in the Bhattiprolu *stūpa* to the Mauryan period.

BIBLIOGRAPHY

Cambridge History of India, Vol. I.
D. R. BHANDARKAR, *Asoka*, 2nd ed.
E. HULTZSCH, *Corpus Inscriptionum Indicarum*, Vol. I, 2nd edition.
H. C. RAYCHANDHURI, *Political History of Ancient India*, 3rd ed.

CHAPTER IV

THE DECLINE OF THE POWER OF MAGADHA, AND THE GREEK INVASIONS

I. The Later Mauryas

Authorities differ about the history of the successors of Aśoka. According to the Purāṇas and the Buddhist literature, **Kunāla.** Aśoka was succeeded by Kunāla, to whom the former assign a reign of eight years. The Purāṇas interpose three kings between Kunāla and Samprati, who was the next king, according to the Buddhists, and whose name is found in both the Pauranic and the Buddhistic lists. These kings are: Bandhupālita, the son of Kunāla, who reigned for eight years; Indrapālita, and the latter's son Daśona, who reigned for seven years. This Daśona's son was Samprati or Saṅgata, who **Daśaratha.** reigned for eight years. Daśaratha is, however, known, from three contemporary records, as one of the Maurya emperors who succeeded Aśoka, because, after his coronation, he dedicated three caves in the Nagarjuni Hill, close to the Barabar Hills, for the residence of the monks of the Ājīvika sect. We are therefore obliged to accept the Purāṇas as more authoritative than the *Divyāvadāna*, which makes Samprati the son **Samprati** and successor of Kunāla. Samprati was the son and successor

[1] *Ibid.*, p. 623.

of Daśaratha. Both these kings were inimical to Buddhism, and Samprati is famous in Jain tradition as a Jain and the dedicator of thousands of Jain images. After Samprati the lists of Maurya kings given in the Purāṇas and the Divyāvadāna do not agree. Even the lists of different Purāṇas vary, and the attempts made by different scholars to evolve a reliable sequence of reigns have failed utterly. Samprati was succeeded, according to the Purāṇas, by his son Śāliśuka, who is said to have reigned for thirteen years. Śāliśuka's son Devavarman or Devadharman or Somaśarman is said to have reigned for seven years, and his grandson Śatadhanvan or Śaśadharman for eight years. The last Maurya king was named Bṛihadratha, and he is mentioned in the Harsha-charita of Bāṇabhaṭṭa. After a reign of seven years Bṛihadratha was assassinated, during a military review, by his general Pushyamitra. According to the Purāṇas, the successors of Aśoka reigned for seventy-five years, but some of the later Maurya kings are not mentioned in all of the Purāṇas. These are: (1) Bandhupālita, who reigned for eight years; (2) Indrapālita; (3) Daśona, who reigned for seven years; and (4) Śāliśuka, who reigned for thirteen years. After deducting twenty-eight years for the doubtful reigns of the Maurya dynasty, the majority of scholars have fixed the year 184 B.C. as the date of the death of the last Maurya emperor, Bṛihadratha, and the accession of the first Śuṅga emperor, Pushyamitra.

Difference among the Purāṇas.

Bṛihadratha.

The later Maurya emperors came one by one to the throne in rapid succession. Eight generations are stated by the Purāṇas to have occupied the throne for about half a century. We do not know anything about their reigns, but the ease with which the last king, Bṛihadratha, was slain, shows that, like the later Mughals, the later Mauryas had become mere puppets in the hands of their ministers and generals.

Condition of the later Mauryas.

The Mauryan Empire reached the zenith of its glory when Aśoka annexed Kaliṅga, extending as it did then from the foot-hills of the Hindu-Kush to the borders of the Tamil country in the extreme south. But there are good reasons to believe that soon after the death of Aśoka disintegration set in. The great emperor himself cannot be completely exonerated from the charge that he himself was one of the causes

Why the Empire fell. of this downfall. His idealism and religious fervour must have considerably damped the morale of his army. When he propounded the theory that the chief conquest was that by *dhamma*, and told his subjects that in his time *bherighoso* had become *dhammaghoso*, he sounded the death-knell of the Mauryan Empire. To this must be added the fact that the provincial officers were oppressive. We find ample evidence of it in literature and Aśokan edicts. But the main cause seems to be that none of Aśoka's successors was worthy to bear the great burden. While one by one the provinces fell off, and through the unguarded passes of the north-west the *Yavanas* fell upon the hapless provinces, the descendants of Chandragupta and Aśoka were either thinking of *dhammavijaya* or indulging in shameful debauchery. It is therefore quite probable that when Pushyamitra drew the final curtain over these *rois fainéants* the people breathed a deep sigh of relief.

II. The Śuṅga Dynasty

Pushyamitra, the successful general of the last Maurya emperor, was a Brāhmaṇa of the family of Bharadvāja. The Śuṅga Brāhmaṇas are well known as teachers in the *Śrauta-sūtra* of Āśvalāyana.

Origin of the Śuṅgas.

The rise of the Śuṅgas and the weakness of the later Mauryas gave a fitting opportunity to the Greeks of Bactria and the Dravidian kingdoms of Kaliṅga and southern India to reassert their power. Kaliṅga regained its independence shortly after the death of Aśoka. "In the coastal region of the Madras Presidency, between the rivers Godāvarī and Kṛishṇā,"[1] arose a new power—the Sātavāhanas, who are generally called Andhras. Khāravela of Kaliṅga conquered Magadha and overran practically the whole of Northern India during the lifetime of Pushyamitra, and the Sātavāhanas very soon deprived the descendants of Pushyamitra of the province of Mālava. The invasion of the Greeks of Bactria was far more serious. Diodotos I, a Seleucid governor of Bactria, asserted his independence. Under Euthydemos

Independence of Kaliṅga and the Deccan.

Greek Invasions.

[1] *Cambridge History of India*, Vol. I, p. 529.

the Greeks overran Afghanistan. Under Demetrios and Menander they conquered the whole of the Panjab, and the latter fixed his capital at Sangala or Sialkot. The Greek kings led regular forays into Northern India.

Mention in Sanskrit Literature.

The *Yuga Purāṇa* of the *Gārgī Saṁhitā* records the invasion of Sāketa or Ayodhyā, Pāñchāla or Rohilkhand, Mathurā, and finally Kusumapura or the capital, Pāṭaliputra, by powerful Greek kings, and records that the different districts of the empire became disorganized. It is more probable that the occupation of Afghanistan and the Western Panjab by the Greeks took place during the rule of the later Mauryas; but the Greek kingdom in the Panjab was founded during the lifetime of Pushyamitra.

The Empire to which Pushyamitra succeeded.

According to the majority of scholars, the Yavana or Greek invasion of the midland countries must have taken place after the foundation of the Greek kingdom of the Panjab. We may conclude safely that the empire of Magadha, which Pushyamitra secured after the murder of Bṛihadratha, included the modern provinces of Bengal, Bihar, United Provinces, Rajputana, Mālava, and the eastern portion of the Panjab. Out of these provinces the Panjab and Northern Rajputana were soon lost. The grammarian Patañjali, who was a contemporary of Pushyamitra, has recorded the invasion of Southern Rajputana by a Greek king. The city of Madhyamikā, near Chitor, was invaded by the Greeks at this time.

Simuka.

We do not know how the southern provinces of the Maurya Empire were lost, but the first king of the Śātavāhana dynasty, Simuka, founded a kingdom in the Bellary district, which is called the *Sātavāhanī-hāra* in a later Śātavāhana inscription, and in the time of his son Kṛishṇa this kingdom included the whole of the Deccan between the Godāvarī and the Kṛishṇā. Some of the events of Pushyamitra's reign are recorded in the historical drama of Kālidāsa, called the *Mālavikāgnimitra*.

The "Mālavikāgnimitra".

From it we learn that during the reign of Pushyamitra, his son Agnimitra was the viceroy at Ujjain.

Pushyamitra's Aśvamedha.

Pushyamitra performed the *Aśvamedha* sacrifice twice, after defeating the king of Vidarbha and repelling the Greeks from the United Provinces. His grandson Vasumitra fought with the Greeks on the banks of the River Sindhu. Some scholars are of opinion that this Sindhu is the River Kali Sindh of

Mālava (a tributary of the River Yamunā), and not the Indus.

Though Pushyamitra repelled the Greeks from the midland countries he suffered serious reverses at their hands. The Greeks were fighting among themselves at this time, and their withdrawal from the middle countries was due more to their internal dissensions than to the prowess of the army of Magadha.

Khāravela's Invasion of Magadha.

More serious results were effected by Khāravela, king of Kaliṅga. In the eighth year of his reign Khāravela invaded the southern frontier of the province of Magadha. He defeated the army of Pushyamitra at Gorathagiri or Barabar Hill, in the Gayā District, and raided the old capital, Rājagṛiha. At this time a Greek king, whose name is not clearly legible, but who was probably the same as Demetrios, invaded Pushyamitra's dominions from the west, and Khāravela's advance from the south-east compelled the former to fall back upon Mathurā. For the next two years the empire of Magadha enjoyed peace on its south-east frontier. In the tenth year of his reign Khāravela invaded Northern India or Bhāratavarsha. In the twelfth year Khāravela invaded Magadha once more and caused the King of Magadha, Bahasatimitra, to acknowledge defeat. Mr. K. P. Jayaswal identifies this Bahasatimitra with Pushyamitra, but most probably he was a governor of the province of Magadha, with the title of *Rājan*. At this time Khāravela brought away the image of a Jain patriarch which had been taken away by one of the Nanda kings from Kaliṅga. The repeated incursions of the army of Kaliṅga into the metropolitan district of the empire caused very great panic, and Pushyamitra seems to have withdrawn permanently from Magadha. These incursions of Khāravela in Magadha weakened the hold of the Śuṅgas over the middle country, and they ceased to be a power in Magadha or the eastern country.

Battle of Gorathagiri.

Second Invasion of Northern India.

Bahasatimitra.

Agnimitra.

Pushyamitra died at a very great age after a chequered reign of thirty-six years and was succeeded by his son Agnimitra, who was also an old man at the time of his accession. He must not be confused with Agnimitra, the King of Pañchāla, whose coins have been discovered in Rohilkhand. Agnimitra was succeeded, after a reign of eight years, by his son Vasujyeshṭha.

Vasujyeshṭha, in turn, was succeeded by his brother Vasumitra, after a reign of seven years. This Vasumitra reigned for ten years, and is probably the Vasumitra who escorted the sacrificial horse of Pushyamitra and fought with the Greeks on the banks of the Sindhu. His successor was Oḍraka or Bhadraka, who is assigned a reign of two years or seven years in the Purāṇas. Oḍraka is mentioned in an inscription in the cave at Pabhosa, near the ruins of Kauśāmbī, in which it is stated that this king ruled for at least ten years. **Vasumitra.** **Oḍraka.**

At this time the kingdom of the Śuṅgas had become divided into a number of semi-independent states, the rulers of which merely acknowledged the suzerainty of the Śuṅga emperor. The principal feudatories of the Śuṅga Empire were the rulers of Ḍāhala. A king named Dhanabhūti ruled over Northern Ḍāhala (the western part of the Rewa State), and during his reign the *stūpa* of Bharhut was erected. Three generations of the kings of Ḍāhala are enumerated in the inscription on two of the gates of the Bharhut *stūpa*. In this inscription the Śuṅgas are mentioned as overlords. Dhanabhūti's father Agarāju and his grandfather Visadeva are mentioned in the same inscription, while we learn the name of Dhanabhūti's son Vādhapāla from a Mathurā inscription. **Feudatories of Ḍāhala.** **Stūpa of Bharhut.**

In the tenth year of Oḍraka, the cave at Pabhosa was excavated by Āshāḍhasena, the maternal uncle of King Bahasatimitra. This Bahasatimitra may be the same governor of Magadha who was defeated by Khāravela in the twelfth year of the latter's reign. Āshāḍhasena appears to have been a contemporary of Oḍraka, but he must have been a very old man when the cave was dedicated by him at Pabhosa. Bahasatimitra is also known from his coins. From this time Indian kings started to use their names on their coins, in imitation of the coinage of the Greek kings of India. Many scholars think that in the second century B.C. the feudatory chiefs of Ahichchhatra and Kauśāmbī belonged to the Śuṅga family. In Mathurā there was another line of subordinate kings who, like the feudatory kings of Ahichchhatra, issued coins. The eastern part of Oudh contained another feudatory kingdom. The kings of this country also issued coins, from which we know their names, such as Āryamitra and Mūladeva. **Āshāḍhasena.** **Kings of Mathurā** **Kings of Kośala**

Henceforth Magadha becomes an obscure province and the centre of political activities is transferred to the west.

According to the Purāṇas, five kings of the Śuṅga dynasty followed Oḍraka and reigned for fifty-seven years. The last but one king is called Bhāgavata, and he is said to have reigned for thirty-two years. An inscription, incised in the twelfth year of his reign, has been discovered at Besnagar in Mālava. Bhāgavata was succeeded by the last king, Devabhūti, who reigned for ten years and was murdered by his Brāhmaṇa minister Vāsudeva, of the Kāṇva family. Devabhūti was a dissolute prince and was done to death by his chief minister with the aid of his slave-woman's daughter. According to the computation of scholars, Śuṅga rule came to an end in Magadha in 72 B.C., but there is warrant for believing that the Śuṅgas continued to rule over a small kingdom till the conquest of Northern India by the Andhras or Sātavāhanas. A king named Bhāgabhadra is mentioned in the inscription on a pillar discovered at Besnagar near Sanchi in Central India. This pillar was really a standard of Vishṇu, surmounted by a figure of the mythical bird Garuḍa. It was dedicated by a Greek named Heliodora (Heliodoros), son of Diya (Dion), a native of Taxila, who came as an ambassador from King Aṁtālikita (Antialkidas II) of Taxila to King Bhāgabhadra Kāśīputra (i.e. the son of a princess of Benares). This Bhāgabhadra is taken by some scholars to be the same as the Śuṅga king Bhāgavata of the second pillar inscription at Besnagar.

Bhāgavata.

Devabhūti.

The Garuda Standard of the Greek Ambassador Heliodoros at Besnagar.

III. The Greek Kings of Bactria and India

When Afghanistan and Baluchistan were ceded by Seleukos Nikator, Bactria remained a province of the Greek empire of Western Asia. During the reigns of Seleukos and his son Antiokhos I, Bactria remained quiet. But under Antiokhos II the Greeks of Bactria became independent under their governor Diodotos. The inhabitants of the hilly regions of Parthia revolted at the same time. Under Seleukos II (246–226 B.C.) and Seleukos III (226–223), the successors of Antiokhos II, the Seleucid emperors lost their hold on their

Revolution in Parthia.

eastern provinces. The creation of an independent buffer state in Parthia between him and the empire of the Seleucidæ emboldened Diodotos to revolt. Seleukos II led an expedition to the East after the battle of Ancyra in 240 B.C. At this time Diodotos I had been succeeded by Diodotos II. Later on, Antiokhos III invaded Bactria about 212 B.C., but at that time Diodotos II had been defeated and killed by another Greek named Euthydemos. We do not know who this king was, and the only glimpse which we obtain of the state of affairs in Bactria is during the campaign of Antiokhos III—surnamed Magnus or "the Great". He invaded the kingdom of Parthia and compelled its king, Arsakes III, to come to terms. In 208 B.C. Antiokhos invaded Bactria. He crossed the River Arius (Hari Rud) by outmanœuvring Euthydemos. A fierce battle was fought between the Bactrian and the other Greeks in which Antiokhos displayed great personal courage. Euthydemos was frightened by the defeat and at once retreated to his capital, Zariaspa or Balkh. Antiokhos III besieged Balkh for nearly two years, but at last he was obliged to raise the siege owing to a threatened Scythian invasion of his dominions. A treaty was concluded, and Antiokhos III appears to have given one of his daughters in marriage to Demetrios, the son and successor of Euthydemos. Antiokhos received provisions for his army and war elephants from Euthydemos, and crossed the Hindu-Kush to invade India. At this time the valley of the Kabul River was ruled by a petty chief named Sophagasenos (*Saubhāgyasena*), who submitted to Antiokhos and gave him some war elephants. The latter now returned hastily to Mesopotamia through Arachosia, Drangiana, and Karmania.

Independence of Bactria.

Bactria invaded by Antiokhos III.

Battle of Arius.

Siege of Balkh.

Antiokhos invades India.

Saubhāgyasena.

Under Euthydemos, Afghanistan was very soon conquered. His son Demetrios conquered a portion of Chinese Turkistan in the north, and also the Western Panjab. He was the first Greek king who used the Indian language, written in Kharoshṭhī characters, along with the Greek language, on his coins. From this time onwards Greek coins usually bore inscriptions in two languages, Greek and Indian Prakrit. Demetrios is said to have founded a new city, or renamed the city of Sangala, Euthydemia, in honour of his father. During his absence in India, the Greeks in Bactria revolted under an able general

Euthydemos.

Demetrios.

Bactrian Rebellion under Eukratides. named Eukratides. The Greeks of Eastern Asia thus became divided, and Eukratides remained in possession of Bactria while Demetrios became king of the Panjab. There was a good deal of fighting between Demetrios and Eukratides, and after the former's death Eukratides conquered the Panjab. **Euthydemos II.** Demetrios was succeeded by his son Euthydemos II. From this time the Western historians of the period do not mention much about the history of the eastern Greeks. Parthia became a powerful rival of the Seleucidæ, and the eastern Greeks of Asia lost all touch with the western Greeks. This division led to the final downfall of the Greek power in Bactria and India. Three other Greek kings, who are known from their coins only, are associated by their coin-types with the dynasty **Later Kings of the dynasty of Euthydemos I.** founded by Euthydemos I. These are Agathocles and Pantaleon. Both of these kings used Brāhmī or the pure Indian alphabet on their coins, instead of Kharoshṭhī. The third king is named Antimakhos, who used Greek only. Another king named Demetrios II is also known from his coins. Euthydemos II and Demetrios II are regarded as the sons of Antimakhos I.

Some time during the reign of Eukratides barbarian tribes invaded Bactria. They conquered the country lying to the north of the River Oxus. Soon afterwards they occupied the **Scythians and Parthians invade Bactria.** whole of Bactria. Eukratides was murdered by his son, who is said to have driven his chariot through his father's blood. At this time the Parthians also invaded Bactria and defeated Eukratides. The provinces of Aria and Arachosia were ceded to them. The invasions of the barbarians from the north and of the Parthians from the west obliged the Greeks of Bactria to ask for help from the Seleucid king Demetrios II (146–140 B.C.). Tribe after tribe of barbarians now invaded Northern **Scythian Tribes in Bactria.** Bactria. Some of them, such as the Sakæ and the Sogdiani, were driven to the south of the Oxus by the Asii, the Pasiani, the Tokhari, and the Sakarauli, according to Strabo. The Chinese historians have recorded that about the year 165 B.C. the Hiungnu or the Huns drove the Yueh-chi westward, **The Greeks retire from Bactria.** and they displaced the Sse or the Sakas. The latter, driven out from the northern bank of the Jaxartes, fell upon the Greek cities of Bactria and conquered the whole of Sogdiana. Bactria was abandoned by the Greeks, who fell back upon Afghanistan and the Panjab.

Eukratides was succeeded by his son Heliokles, who is regarded by all scholars as the last Greek king of Bactria; at least he is the last ruler whose coins have been found to the north of the Hindu-Kush. He is also the last Greek king who struck coins on the Attic standard like Apollodotos and Antialkidas. The bronze coins of Heliokles and the silver coins of Euthydemos were copied in large number by the Scythian barbarians, who had no coinage of their own. **Heliokles.** **Scythians copy Greek Coins.**

Heliokles was succeeded by Apollodotos, who is mentioned on two occasions, jointly with Menander, by Western historians For this reason some scholars think that they belong to the same family, i.e. the family of Euthydemos. The coins of Apollodotos have been carried over long distances, and when the Greek author of the *Periplus of the Red Sea* came to India, he found them in circulation in the bazaars of Broach in the first century A.D. The province of Sindh and the peninsula of Kathiawad were conquered by the Greeks early in the second century B.C. **Apollodotos.** **Greek Conquest of Sindh and Kathiawad.**

Menander was a king of the Western Panjab, and his coins are not found in Ghazni, Kandahar, and Seistan, where the coins of Apollodotos are found in large numbers. After the conquest of the Western Panjab by the kings of the house of Eukratides, the kings of the dynasty of Euthydemos ruled over the Eastern Panjab. They are known from their coins only. Strato I, Dionysios, Zoilos, Hippostratos, Apollophanes belong to this dynasty. Among these coins some bear the name of a Greek queen named Agathokleia, from which it is evident that she was a princess by birth and was the mother of Strato I. The coins of Strato I at first bore his name jointly with that of his mother Agathokleia; but later on he struck coins for himself, and finally he issued coins jointly with his grandson, Strato II Philopator. To the same period belong the coins of Apollodotos II Philopator, Dionysios, and Zoilos. **Greek Kings of the Panjab.**

Eukratides was to some extent the contemporary of Apollodotos I, because the former restruck the coins of the latter, thus proving that the territory once occupied by Apollodotos I was later on conquered by Eukratides. In the conquered territory was the city of Kapiśā, which lay between Kabul and Peshawar. By far the greatest king of the house of Euthydemos was Menander, who left a deeper mark on Indian tradition than any other Greek king. He overran the whole of Northern and Western India, and, according to some, carried his raids as far east as Pāṭaliputra. The Indian conquests of Greek kings are attributed by Apollodorus to Demetrios and Menander, but they are ascribed to Apollodotos and Menander by Trogus Pompeius. It was Menander who carried the Greek arms as far south as Pattala near Karachi in the south-west and Pāṭaliputra in the south-east. He has been identified with the "Milinda" mentioned in the *Milinda-pañho* as a contemporary of the Buddhist sage Nāgasena. The coins of Menander belong to various types and are to be found all over North-western and Central India.

Menander.

The *Milinda-pañho*, "the questions of Milinda", is a Pali work dealing with the fundamental principles of Buddhist philosophy. It is written in the form of a dialogue between the king Milinda and the Buddhist teacher Nāgasena. King Milinda is represented as harassing the Buddhist monks by putting religious puzzles to them. But Nāgasena solves those puzzles. Milinda is said to have been attended by five hundred Greek (*Yonaka*) courtiers, the names of some of whom can still be recognized. Thus *Devamantrīya* is *Demetrios* and *Anantakāya* is *Antiokhos*. Milinda is said to have been born in the village of *Kalasi*, in the dvipa of *Alasanda*. The site of *Kalasi* is unknown, but *Alasanda* is one of the towns founded by Alexander and named "Alexandria" after him. This Alasanda was two hundred *Yojanas* distant from Sakala. Plutarch says that Menander was a just and great king, and that after his death the cities of his kingdom contended with each other for the honour of preserving his ashes.

The Milinda-pañho.

Details about Menander

Pushkalāvatī.

In the kingdom founded by Eukratides, Pushkalāvatī (Gr. Peukelaotis) was an important city. The coins of Diomedes, Epander, Philoxenos, Artemidoros, and Peukelaos were struck in this city. The Greek dynasties of India very shortly divided their kingdom into a number of city states, in imitation of the city states of Greece proper, and this division shortly led to downfall. The barbarians, called *Sakai* by the Greeks and *Śakas* by the Indians, soon conquered Afghanistan. The cities of Kapiśā and Pushkalāvatī were occupied by them, but the descendants of Euthydemos continued to rule over the Eastern Panjab, and those of Eukratides in the Upper Kabul valley. Of the latter dynasty Heliokles was succeeded by Antialkidas, Amyntas, and Hermeus. Hermeus was the last Greek king who ruled over Afghanistan. In some of his silver coins this king is associated with his queen Calliope, who, like Agathokleia, appears to have been a princess by birth. Hermeus was hemmed in on all sides by barbarians. The Śakas occupied Southern Afghanistan; Western Afghanistan was in the possession of the Pahlavas, while the northern frontier was threatened by the Yueh-chi. The coins of this king were imitated by the first Yueh-chi king, Kujula Kadaphisa. For this reason some scholars supposed at one time that Hermeus was the contemporary of Kujula Kadaphisa, but it is now recognized that Hermeus ceased to rule about forty years before the birth of Christ.

Last Greek Kings.

IV. The Kāṇvas or the Kāṇvāyanas

According to the Purāṇas, the ten Śuṅga kings were succeeded by four Brāhmaṇa kings of the Kāṇva *gotra*. These four kings ruled for forty-five years, when the last of them, Suśarman, was overthrown by the first Sātavāhana king, Simuka, after a reign of ten years. The Kāṇvas are spoken of as "the servants of the Śuṅgas", and their first king, Vāsudeva, is said to have ruled for nine years, his son Bhūmimitra for fourteen years, his grandson Nārāyaṇa for twelve years. The Purāṇas distinctly state that the entire Śuṅga Empire did not pass into the hands of the Kāṇvas. Some of the Śuṅgas continued to rule over portions of Northern India till the final conquest of Northern India by the Śātavāhanas. Scholars think that the Kāṇva dynasty came to an end about 28 B.C., when portions of Northern India were included in the empire of the Śātavāhanas.

The Servants of the Śuṅgas.

Remains of the Śuṅga Empire.

The Śātavāhana Conquest.

BIBLIOGRAPHY

K. P. JAYASWAL, "Revised note on the Brahmin Empire" in the *Journal of the Bihar and Orissa Research Society*, Vol. IV (1918), pp. 257–65.
F. E. PARGITER, *Dynasties of the Kali Age*.
V. A. SMITH, *Early History of India* (4th ed.), chaps. viii–ix.
Cambridge History of India, Vol. I, chaps. xvii–xxii.

CHAPTER V

THE DRAVIDIAN DYNASTIES OF THE SOUTH

I. The Chetis of Kaliṅga

Some time after Aśoka's death Kaliṅga regained its independence. The only reliable account of Kaliṅga which we possess is derived from the Hāthigumphā inscription of the great

Extent of Kaliṅga. conqueror Khāravela, of the Cheti dynasty. The boundary of Kaliṅga varied at different times. At the time of its greatest extent it included the whole of the province of Orissa and the northern Sarkars, as well as the district of Midnapur in Bengal. Ordinarily it included the low land below the Eastern Ghats, between the mouths of the rivers Mahanadi and Godāvarī.

Hāthigumphā Inscription of Khāravela. The Hāthigumphā inscription is a record of the first thirteen years of Khāravela's reign, and appears to have been incised in the fourteenth year. Some scholars believe, and others deny, that the sixteenth line of this inscription contains a date in the Maurya era.

Khāravela's Accession. The accession of Khāravela, according to Mr. K. P. Jayaswal, took place in 183 B.C. As Khāravela ascended the throne when he was twenty-four years old, he appears to have been born in 207 B.C.

The record supplies us with many important facts about the history of India. In the first place we get a glimpse into the life and training of Indian princes in the second century B.C., or, as others hold, in the first century B.C. Khāravela was installed as heir-apparent in his fifteenth year. After nine years he ascended the throne. While heir-apparent he was trained in writing, mathematics, law, and finance. **[Khāravela's Training.]** In the second year of his reign Khāravela sent an army consisting of infantry, cavalry, chariots, and elephants to the west. **[Invasion of the Deccan.]** This army reached the Western Deccan, where the River Kṛishṇā rises, and attacked the town of Mushika. The third year was spent in rejoicings, and in the fourth he caused the Raṭhikas and Bhojakas of the Central and Northern Deccan to submit to him. In the fifth year of his reign he **[Public Works.]** re-excavated a canal excavated by a king of the Nanda dynasty one hundred and three years earlier, and extended it as far as his capital city. He is also said to have performed the Rājasūya ceremony in the same year. During the eighth year of his reign King Khāravela began his series of campaigns in Northern India. In that year, he crossed the jungle country lying between Orissa and South Bihar and defeated the army of Magadha in the battle of Gorathagiri, or the Barabar Hills, in the Gayā District, and harassed Rājagṛiha, the old capital of Magadha. **[First Campaign in Magadha.]** Demetrios had advanced as far as Pāṭaliputra after occupying Mādhyamika (near Chitor) and Sāketa (or Ayodhyā), but Khāravela's invasion compelled him to retire to Mathurā. After the campaign of the ninth year Khāravela became rich enough to give away horses, elephants, and chariots, and to build a palace called *Mahāvijaya*, " the great conquest ". Three million eight hundred thousand coins, evidently of copper, were required for the building of this palace. **[Invasion of Northern India.]** In the tenth year Khāravela invaded Northern India, or *Bhāratavarsha*, once more and obtained great wealth. The next year saw the army of Kaliṅga in the north-eastern provinces of India under the command of Khāravela. He terrorized the inhabitants of Magadha. The governor of Magadha, who is called Bahasatimita, was obliged to sue for peace, and Khāravela carried away in triumph the image of a Jain *Tīrthaṅkara* which had been removed by a Nanda king from Kaliṅga to Magadha. **[Fall of Pātaliputra.]** In the thirteenth year of his reign Khāravela subdued the king of the Pāṇḍyas of the south and obtained great wealth from him. In the same year he built caves for the residence of Jain ascetics on the *Kumārī Parvata*, i.e. Udayagiri Hill. The dwelling-place of the Jain ascetics excavated by Khāravela is the biggest excavation on Udayagiri

Rock-cut Jain Monastery—excavated by Khāravela, King of Kaliṅga, in the 2nd century B.C.—on Khandagiri hill, Puri district

Hill and is now popularly known as "the cave of the Queen's Light", "*Rānī-nur-gumphā*". Khāravela was a Jain and a great patron of Jainism. He was a man of Kaliṅga, of pure Dravidian origin, who succeeded in destroying the remnants of the power left to the Śuṅgas in Magadha, and who compelled Pushyamitra to seek refuge in the middle country.

We do not know anything about Kaliṅga after the death of Khāravela. Magadha most probably remained unmolested for more than a century after that event, and continued to be ruled by the viceroys of the Śuṅgas and, later on, by the Kāṇvas. Kaliṅga itself fell under the power of the Sātavāhanas, and the southern part of it, near the mouth of the Godāvarī, became a part of the Sātavāhana Empire. **Later History of Kaliṅga**

II. The Sātavāhanas of the Kanarese Country

Some time in the beginning of the second century before the birth of Christ, Simuka, an inhabitant of the modern district of Bellary, in the Madras Presidency, founded a kingdom which was destined to become one of the most important empires of India. The chronologies given in the Purāṇas state that Simuka was the contemporary of the last Kāṇva king, Suśarman. But the script of the inscriptions of his brother Kṛishṇa and his nephew Śrī-Śātakarṇī at Nanaghat prove beyond doubt that Simuka could not have dethroned the last Kāṇva king in the last quarter of the first century before the birth of Christ. The kingdom of Simuka lay in the district of Bellary, but very soon he conquered the wild Maratha tribes of the Western Deccan. During the reign of Simuka's brother Kṛishṇa, the Nasik district formed a part of the Sātavāhana kingdom, and during the next reign the kings had occupied the fertile western coast land, called the Konkan, and were regarded as lords of the entire Deccan plateau. **Original Kingdom of the Sātavāhanas.**

In their inscriptions the Sātavāhanas claim to be Brāhmaṇas, but evidently they were of Dravidian origin, and later on they intermarried with the non-Indian satraps of Kathiawad and Gujarat. In spite of the adherence of the Sātavāhana kings to the orthodox Indo-Aryan faith, the account of them given in **Origin of the Sātavāhanas.**

the Purāṇas is very unreliable, and during the earlier period the Sātavāhanas or the Andhras, as they are called in the Purāṇas, could not have ruled over Magadha or any part of Northern India. The Sātavāhana occupation of Northern India could not have lasted for more than three-quarters of a century, and must have ended with the Scythian conquest of Northern India. Chronologies which accept 28 B.C. as the date of the conquest of Magadha by Simuka go directly against the evidence of the Nanaghat and Nasik inscriptions. The period of rule assigned in the Purāṇas to the Sātavāhanas (three or four centuries) includes all the kings of this dynasty, even those who reigned in the Kuntala country, i.e. the Vanavāsi District of Northern Mysore. One of the later Sātavāhana kings, Gautamīputra Śātakarṇī, claims to be "the unique Brāhmaṇa" and the destroyer of the pride of the Kshatriyas. This dynasty of the Dravidian kings was therefore regarded as hostile to such kings as claimed Kshatriya descent.

The Sātavāhanas and the Kshatriya Kings.

Nothing is known about the first king, Simuka. He was succeeded by his brother Kaṇha or Kṛishṇa, in whose reign one of the caves of the Pāṇḍu-Leṇā group (near Nasik) was excavated. Kaṇha was succeeded by his nephew Śrī-Śātakarṇī, the son of Simuka. Śrī-Śātakarṇī was a follower of the orthodox Indo-Aryan faith. His queen, Nāyanikā, performed many sacrifices and gave away large sums of money and many cattle. She inscribed a record of her deeds in a cave at the top of the Nana Pass, which was one of the principal passes of the Western Ghats, and led to the more fertile coast lands of the Konkan. In this cave statues of the three kings, Queen Nāyanikā, her father the Marāṭhā chief Traṇakayira, the princes Hakusiri and Sātavāhana were carved out of the solid rock. These statues disappeared long ago, but the inscriptions, which served as labels, have survived to our times. The names in these inscriptions and those given in the Purāṇas serve to identify the dynasty to which Simuka and Kaṇha belonged. In the Purāṇas these kings are called Andhras, and as the Andhra country lies on the eastern coast, for a long time it was supposed that the Sātavāhanas conquered Western India from the eastern coast. The discovery of two

The Nanaghat Records.

Original Home of the Sātavāhanas.

inscriptions in the Bellary District has proved that there was in that district a province called the *Sātavāhanī-hāra*, which must have been the original home of the Sātavāhanas. The inscriptions of the earliest kings also prove that the centre of Sātavāhana power was confined to the Western Deccan and Eastern Mālava up to the birth of Christ. The Purāṇas called the Sātavāhana kings Andhras because they conquered Magadha marching from the Andhra or Telugu country.

Śrī-Śātakarṇī, the third king of the dynasty, was the real founder of the greatness of his line. He was the contemporary, to some extent, of Pushyamitra of the Śuṅga dynasty and of Khāravela of Kaliṅga. He performed the horse-sacrifice twice and defeated the Śuṅgas. He conquered a portion of Mālava and issued coins in his own name. It appears that from this time Western Mālava, with its capital Ujjayinī or Ujain, passed away from the hands of the Śuṅgas. Upon the downfall of the Śuṅgas, Eastern Mālava, with its capital Vidiśā or Bhilsa, was also conquered by the Sātavāhanas. Half a century later the Sātavāhanas occupied some parts of Northern India by overthrowing the last Kāṇva king, Suśarman.

Conquests of Śrī-Śātakarṇī.

At this time the Sātavāhanas were at the apex of their power. But their northern dominions were soon to be conquered by an alien race. Early in the first century B.C. the Śakas drove them out of Mālava, and in the latter part of that century out of Mahārāshṭra. A Scythian governor ruled over Rajputana and Mālava, while a second governor was placed in charge of Northern Konkan and the Western Deccan. The Sātavāhanas were driven to the south of the Bhīmā and became once more rulers of a southern kingdom, which, however, extended from the Arabian Sea to the Bay of Bengal. The revival of their power in the first century A.D. and their long wars with the western satraps belong to a later period of Indian history.

Scythian Conquest of the Northern Deccan.

III. The Tamil Kingdom

In the dawn of history, the Tamil kingdom extended over the greater part of the Madras Presidency. On the north it extended as far as Tirupati, and on the south as far as Cape

Comorin. Towards the west it extended as far as Mahé, near Cannanore. The Malayālam language had not yet become separate. This country was divided into three kingdoms.

The Pāṇḍyas. The Pāṇḍyas ruled over the greater part of the modern districts of Madurā and Tinnevelly. Their first capital was Kolkai, on the Tāmraparṇī River; later on it was removed to Madurā. The Choḷa kingdom lay on the eastern coast, to the **The Choḷas.** north of the Pāṇḍya kingdom, and contained the districts from Trichinopoly to Tanjore. Its capital was Uraiyur or old Trichinopoly, and the great port of the kingdom lay at the mouth of the Kāverī. Another of its principal towns was **The Chera Kingdom.** Kāñchī or Conjeeveram. The Chera or Kerala kingdom consisted of the modern district of Malabar, and the states of Cochin and Travancore. Its capital was at Vanji near Cochin, and the principal ports were Tondi near Quilon, Muchiri or Muziris, Palaiyur near Chowghat, and Vaikkarai near Kottayam. The different races of people living in this country were a mixture of the descendants of Negrito fishermen, the Austric bowmen, and the Dravidians. The Pāṇḍya king claimed to be descended from a tribe called the Māṛar; the Choḷa kings are said to have belonged to the tribe called " the men of the sea " (Tiraiyar). In the time of the Choḷa king Karikāla, another Tiraiyan dynasty was ruling at Conjeeveram. The Chera kings claimed to be descended from the Vanavar tribe. Nothing is known about these tribes. Later on Indo-Aryan genealogies were provided for the kings of all three provinces.

Brāhmaṇa Colonies. Even in the first century B.C. very little Indo-Aryan influence had penetrated to the extreme south. Some Brāhmaṇa colonists settled in the Dravidian countries and intermarried with the priest-caste of the natives, but on the whole they made very little impression on the masses. Their teachings were counterbalanced by the influence of the Jains and the Buddhists, who gained more devotees on account of the resemblance of their tenets to the now lost Dravidian religion.

The Dravidian Monarchy. Dravidian society was well organized and was divided according to intelligence and wealth. The system of government was monarchical, but the kings were very greatly influenced by the " Five Great Assemblies, bodies representa-

Maritime Activity.

tive of the five classes of society". The unit of the state was the village community, and representatives of villages met in a district assembly which possessed considerable power over the management of local affairs. The Pāṇḍyas and the Choḷas were maritime peoples, and the first Roman emperor, Augustus Cæsar, is said to have received an embassy from a Pāṇḍya king. In the beginning of the Christian era we find Peru-naṛ-kiḷḷi as the king of the Cheras and Neḍuñ-jéral-ádan as the ruler of the Choḷas. They fought with each other and were killed. Peru-naṛ-kiḷḷi was succeeded by his son Ilañ-jeṭ-śenni, and Neḍuñ-jéral-ádan by his son Karikāla. At this time the Choḷas became the leading power in the south, and Karikāla defeated an allied army of the Cheras and the Pāṇḍyas.

Struggles for Supremacy.

He made his capital at Kāverī-pattana and protected it from the floods by a high embankment. After his death the Choḷa power declined; but after some time Karikāla's grandson, Neḍu-muḍu-kiḷḷi, gained victory over the Pāṇḍyas and the Cheras. In his time the capital, Kāverī-pattana, was destroyed by a flood, and the great Choḷa landlords rose in rebellion. The Chera king Ādan II had married a daughter of Karikāla, and their son Śeṅguṭṭuvan came to the aid of his kinsmen, with the result that the Choḷa rebels were twice defeated in battle.

Rebellion in the Choḷa Kingdom.

Under Śeṅguṭṭuvan, the Cheras became the supreme power in the south. His successor, Śey, was defeated by the Pāṇḍya king Neḍuñ-śeḷiyan II, and the Pāṇḍyas became the premier power in Southern India and remained so until the rise of the Pallava foreigners in the third or fourth century A.D.

Origin of the Marāṭhās.

The western part of the Indian Peninsula, which is now known by the name of Deccan, remained inhabited by uncivilized Dravidian tribes and aboriginals. The modern Marāṭhās are the product of this racial interfusion and still retain many Dravidian characteristics in their social system and their primitive worship. The Brāhmaṇas of this country as well as the western coast-land incorporated the priestly classes of many foreigners.

Origin of the Western Brāhmaṇas.

The *Gujarati* Brāhmaṇas, according to some scholars, contain a very large Mesopotamian element, while the *Konkanastha* or *Chittapāvana* Brāhmaṇas of the southern Konkan appear to be an alien race. Whatever be the truth of these theories, there cannot be any doubt about the fact that colonies of northern Brāhmaṇas assimilated into their caste the magicians and priests of the local inhabitants. The Marāṭhās appear to be the same as the *Bhojakas* and the *Raṭhikas* of the inscriptions, and were very much behind the pure Dravidians of the extreme south in civilization and culture. They fell an easy prey to the invasion of the Dravidians under the Sātavāhanas and remained subject to them for several centuries.

The Marāṭhās under Dravidian Rule.

BIBLIOGRAPHY

"The Hathigumpha Inscription of Kharavela" in the *Epigraphia Indica*, Vol. XX.

D. R. Bhandarkar, "The Dekkan of the Satavahanas" in the *Indian Antiquary*, Vols. XLVII and XLVIII, 1918 and 1919.

Cambridge History of India, Vol. I, chaps. xxi and xxiv.

R. D. Banerji, *History of Orissa*, Vol. I, chap. vi.

CHAPTER VI

THE IRRUPTION OF THE BARBARIANS INTO NORTHERN INDIA

I. The Śakas

The Śakas.

The Śakas, whom the Greek writers call *Sakai* or *Sakarauli*, were perhaps the same people as the Soghdi or the original inhabitants of Trans-Oxiana in the second century B.C. Some time after 165 B.C. the country to the north of the Oxus was conquered by the Yueh-chi. The Śakas thus dislodged gradually migrated to the south of the Oxus and settled down in the Greek provinces of Aria (Herat), Arachosia (Kabul), Gedrosia (Kandahar), and Drangiana (Seistan). The last two, together with Sindh, gradually became known as the *Sakastana* to the Iranians and the *Śakadvīpa* to the Aryans. The Śakas, who are called Sse by the Chinese historians, gradually acquired a veneer of polish by closer contact with the Indo-Aryans and Indo-Greeks of Afghanistan. Their kings assumed the Indian title of *Mahārāja* and the corresponding Greek title "*Basileus*".

Maues.

One of the earliest Śaka kings, Maues or Moa, struck coins in exact imitation of Demetrius a Greek king of Bactria and India. His coins are found all over Afghanistan and the Western Panjab. In his time the Western Panjab was governed by a governor or satrap. Western India was conquered early in his reign and was governed by a separate satrap. Four other Śaka kings are known from their coins. They are named Azes I, Azilises, Azes II, and Aspavarman the Strategos. Liaka-Kuśulaka was the satrap of Moa at Taxila. **The Satrap of Taxila.** From the fact that he was succeeded by his son Patika, it appears that the rule of the Scythian emperors in India was neither lasting nor very effective. At the same time another family of satraps was ruling over Mathurā and the adjoining districts. **The Satraps of Mathurā and the Deccan.** Rañjubula, the great satrap of Mathurā, was succeeded by his son Śoḍāsa, who was a contemporary of Patika. Rañjubula of Mathurā, and Nahapāna, the satrap of Mahārāshṭra, assumed royal titles along with the title of satrap, and were therefore independent monarchs. Certain other satraps of Taxila, such as Zeionises, struck coins and most probably became independent. The rule of the early Scythian monarchs came to an end shortly after their conquest of the Panjab. Their dominions in India proper were divided among the satraps or governors of the provinces, and in Afghanistan proper they were dispossessed by a Parthian dynasty. Maues reigned in the last quarter of the second century B.C. **Azes I.** One of his successors, Azes I, founded an era, probably beginning with the date of his coronation, in the beginning of the first century B.C. The coins of Azilises are the finest ever struck by Śaka monarchs. Azes II was associated in his coins with a general (*strategos*) named Aspavarman and a king named Sasas. These two princes were the last independent kings of the Śaka tribe. **The Era of Azes.** The era of Azes was current in the Western Panjab in the third quarter of the first century A.D., when the chiefs of the Kushan tribe of the Yueh-chi had already conquered the whole of Afghanistan and the Panjab.

The Śakas were overthrown by the combined pressure of the Yueh-chi from the north and the Parthians from the west. In the middle of the second century B.C. the Parthian kings Phraates II (138–128 B.C.) and Artabanus I (128–123 B.C.) were defeated by the Scythians, but the Persians succeeded in defeating the Śaka invasions of Persia proper under Mithradates II (123–88 B.C.). In the middle of the first century B.C. the Parthians under Vonones succeeded in driving the Śaka kings out of Afghanistan and the Western Panjab, but the Śaka satraps of Mathurā and Western India continued to rule uninterruptedly till their overthrow by the Kushans in the north and the Sātavāhanas in the south. The narrative of the events of their rule belongs properly to the chapter on the Kushans and the revival of Sātavāhana power.

Overthrow of the Śakas.

The Parthians.

II. The Indo-Parthians

The earlier kings of the Indo-Parthian dynasty are known from their coins only. Modern writers call them Indo-Parthians on account of the Iranian form of their names and the Iranian appearance of their kings in their coin portraits. It is also possible that the Indo-Parthians were really Śakas who had been Persianized by long contact with the Iranians.

Origin of the Term Indo-Parthian.

The history of the Indo-Parthian kings is still imperfectly known. They are usually divided into two groups. The first group begins with Vonones, whom some regard as a king of pure Parthian extraction. Vonones assumed the title of "The great king of kings", which remained in abeyance in Parthia itself. The dynasty of Vonones consisted of two of his brothers and a nephew. The brothers, Spalahores and Spalyrises, and the nephew, Spalagadames, were associated with him in the coinage of his dynasty. While the name Vonones is Persian, the other names have a Scythian sound. The most important coins of this dynasty are those which bear the name of the suzerain on one side and the subordinate chief on the other side. One of the coins of Spalyrises is struck with the name of a king named Azes. Some scholars think that this Azes is a king of the Parthian dynasty, but it is more

Vonones.

Azes II and Spalyrises.

probable that the last king of the dynasty of Maues was obliged to acknowledge the suzerainty of the Indo-Parthian king. Azes II is thought by certain scholars to have been ruling towards the close of the first century B.C.

The kings of the second Indo-Parthian group are believed to have succeeded the satraps of the first dynasty. The first of their number was Gondopharnes or Vindapharṇa. It is now generally recognized that this king ruled from A.D. 19 to 45. One of his inscriptions is dated in the year 103 of an unknown era which corresponded with the year 26 of his reign. Gondopharnes succeeded to the dominions of the Śakas and Indo-Parthians in Eastern Persia and in North-western India. From his coins we know that he was also associated with the same *strategos* or general, Aspavarman, as Azes II. Gondopharnes was at one time the subordinate of a king named Orthagnes, and he was associated with another king named Gudana. The name Orthagnes is Persian, its real form being "Verethragna", "the victorious" or "the slayer of enemies". Gondopharnes struck coins either alone or with his nephew Abdagases, and with his general Aspavarman and his nephew Sasas. He is associated in Christian legends with the Apostle St. Thomas. According to this story, St. Thomas was sold by Jesus Christ to a merchant named Habban and travelled with him to the court of King Gondopharnes, who ordered him to build a palace. Instead of spending the king's money on the palace, St. Thomas spent it on acts of charity, for which he and the merchant Habban were cast into prison. While they were in prison, the king's brother Gad died, and was shown the heavenly palace by the angels. Gad was restored to life, and finally both King Gondopharnes and his brother Gad were converted to Christianity. Gondopharnes was succeeded by Pakores, and then the dynasty was overthrown by the Kushans or the Yueh-chi.

Gondopharnes.

His Coinage.

Saint Thomas in India.

Legend of Saint Thomas.

III. The Great Kushans

In or about the year 165 B.C. a war broke out between two nomad tribes living on the borders of the Chinese Empire, the Yueh-chi and the Hiung-nu (Huns). In this war the Yueh-chi were defeated and forced to march westward. On the way they met another nomad tribe named the Wu-sun. In the fight which followed, the Wu-sun were defeated and their chief Nan-teou-mi was killed. The Yueh-chi, marching westwards, defeated the Śakas or the Sok of Trans-Oxiana and drove them into Bactria. But in the meantime Kwen-mo, the son of Nan-teou-mi, had grown up, and under him the Wu-sun defeated the Yueh-chi and drove them out of Ta-hia or Bactria. This account of the migrations of the Yueh-chi is derived from the writings of the Chinese ambassador, Chang-kien, who visited Bactria in or about 125 B.C.

Migration of the Yueh-chi.

The next mention of the Yueh-chi is to be found in Pan-ku's history of the first Han dynasty of China. At this time the Yueh-chi had given up their nomadic habits and settled down in Bactria. They had become divided into five tribes: (1) the Hieu-mi, (2) the Chouang-mo, (3) the Kouei-chouang, (4) the Hi-thun, and (5) the Kao-fu. We find in the history of the second Han dynasty of China, that nearly a century after the division of the Yueh-chi into the five tribes, the chief of the Kouei-chouang tribe, Kiu-tsiou-kio, attacked and subjugated the four other tribes and made himself the master of the kingdom, which was called Kouei-chouang, after his tribal designation. We know now from coins that the real name of the Kouei-chouang was Khushana or Kushan, and that the chief who united the five tribes was named Kujula Kadaphisa, which was written Kozoulo Kadphises in Greek. The tribes of the Yueh-chi are called *Yavuga* (*Jabgou*) on their coins.

The Five Yueh-chi Tribes.

Union of the Yueh-chi.

Kujula Kadaphisa.

Kujula Kadaphisa died at the age of eighty and was succeeded by his son Yen-kao-ching, also called Vima Kadaphisa, who conquered India. From the accounts preserved by the Chinese historians, we learn that the Yueh-chi tribes were united into a single kingdom in the last decades of the first century B.C. Kujula Kadaphisa was to some extent the contemporary of Gondopharnes and his successor. The Kushan power appears to have been extended into Afghanistan and Baluchistan in the first half of the first century A.D., and into the Panjab in the third quarter of that century. At first

Vima Kadaphisa.

Kushan Conquest of India.

the Kushans remained unknown to the Indian peoples. Their names and titles were not understood in India proper, and consequently, even after their conquest of Northern India, the Indians could not mention their names and titles in their inscriptions. In a Kharoshṭhī inscription discovered at Panjtar, in the North-western Frontier Provinces, the name of the king is omitted, but he is called " the great king of the Kushaṇa family ". Similarly, in the year 136 of the era founded by Azes, an inscription was incised on a silver plate at Taxila, in which also the reigning king is not named, but is simply mentioned as "the great king, king of kings, the son of the gods, of the Kushaṇa family ".

The Kushans or Khushaṇas are mentioned in later inscriptions as well as on the coins of a group of kings who are now known as " the great Kushan " emperors. They begin with Vima Kadaphisa and end with Vāsudeva I. The coins of Vima Kadaphisa are found all over Northern India, and it is certain that his kingdom extended as far as the United Provinces. Most probably he ruled India by his generals and viceroys. The coins of this king were struck in gold and copper. He had most probably become a Hindu, as on his coins we find a figure of Śiva standing by the side of his bull. Vima Kadaphisa used the title " The great king, king of kings, the Lord of all people, the Great Lord ". He used the Greek language and script on one side and the Indian language and script on the other side of his coins. His father or predecessor did not use any royal title. In his coins he is called simply " Kozoulo Kadphises of the Kushaṇas ", or " Kujula Kasa of the Kushaṇa tribe ". The assumption of imperial titles by Vima Kadaphisa indicates that after his accession he made an end of the Śaka and Parthian kingdoms in Afghanistan and the Panjab.

Vima Kadaphisa a Hindu.

His Titles.

The most important person among the great Kushans was the Emperor Kaṇishka I, who was the successor of Vima Kadaphisa. We do not know the relationship between these two kings, but most probably Kaṇishka was not the son of Vima Kadaphisa. Kaṇishka I was the founder of the greatness of the Kushan empire in Asia. He defeated the Parthian kings and also occupied the whole of Central Asia by defeating the Chinese. An era was counted from the day of his coronation

Kaṇishka.

His Foundation of the Śaka Era. in A.D. 78, which subsequently became known as the Saka era. During his reign the whole of Northern India as far as Pāṭaliputra and Bodh-Gaya was included in the Kushan Empire. A great satrap or viceroy (*Mahākshatrapa*) ruled over Northern India from Mathurā. We know the name of one such satrap who ruled in the year A.D. 81. He was Kharapallāna. **His Satraps.** Together with his subordinate, the satrap Vanaspara, he dedicated an image of the Bodhisattva Gautama at Benares in the third year of the reign of Kaṇishka. We do not know as yet who ruled over Mālava as the satrap of Kaṇishka I, but it is quite possible that one of the satraps of that country was Chashṭana, whom the Greeks called Tiastanes, and who was a contemporary of the Sātavāhana king Puḷumāvi.

Kaṇishka I is regarded by the northern Buddhists as one of the greatest patrons of Buddhism. He is said to have convened the fourth or last great council of the Buddhist theologians, to settle the disputed points of their religion. This conference is said to have met in Kashmir or Jullundur. **The Fourth Great Buddhist Council.** The Buddhist elder who presided over this congregation is called Pārśva in the books of the Northern Buddhists. The decrees of the council were written on sheets of copper and placed in a stone chest inside a Buddhist *stūpa*. These writings have not been discovered as yet. Though Kaṇishka I is claimed as a great patron of Buddhism, it has been proved by modern research that he venerated the gods of many religions. **Kaṇishka's Religious Beliefs.** On his coins we find images of Greek gods, Zoroastrian deities, and some of the Babylonian gods. Images of Buddha and Śiva appear very rarely on them. It is quite possible that Kaṇishka I adopted Buddhism late in life; but it is certain that he did not succeed in making it the state religion permanently, because Zoroastrian deities also appear on the coins of Huvishka, one of his successors.

Kaṇishka was a great warrior. He had to fight hard to keep together the dominions to which he had succeeded. His principal struggles were with the Chinese. **Chinese Wars of Kaṇishka I.** The Chinese conquered Kashgar and Khotan in the middle of the second century B.C. Later on, when the Yueh-chi became powerful, they lost their western dominions. In the beginning of the Christian era, in A.D. 8, Chinese communication with Central Asia had ceased. In A.D. 23 Chinese influence in Kashgar and Khotan had been reduced to nothing, and for the next fifty years China was deprived of her newly conquered territories in Central Asia. In A.D. 73, five years before the accession of Kaṇishka I, the Chinese viceroy Pan-chao attacked Central Asia once more and fought with the Kushans up to A.D. 102. He carried the Chinese flag right up to the borders of Persia. In A.D. 87 the great Kushan emperor assumed the title of "The son of Heaven" (*Devaputra*), which the Chinese emperors regarded as their exclusive monopoly. Kaṇishka I demanded a Chinese princess in marriage. This proposal was regarded as an insult, and Pan-chao arrested the Kushan envoy. After the year 22 of the Śaka era, i.e. A.D. 100, Kaṇishka I made Vāsishka king of India in his stead, and crossed the Pamirs to fight the Chinese. The result of Kaṇishka's expedition against China was disastrous. He was completely defeated and purchased peace by agreeing to pay tribute to "*The Son of Heaven*".

Chinese Dominion in Central Asia.

Conquests of Pan-chao.

Vāsishka did not issue any coins in his own name, but he was regarded by the Indians as the reigning emperor. In the year 24 of the Kushan era a stone post of the horse-sacrifice (*Aśvamedha*) was dedicated in Mathurā. On this stone post Vāsishka is mentioned as the reigning emperor. In the year 28 of the Kushan era, i.e. A.D. 106, Vāsishka is mentioned as the reigning emperor in an inscription on a Buddhist image dedicated in that year at Sanchi in Northern Mālava. In the year 41 of the Kushan era, i.e. A.D. 119, Kaṇishka I returned to India, and is mentioned as the reigning emperor in an inscription discovered in the Peshawar District. After Vāsishka, Huvishka was made the Viceroy of India, but on the return of Kaṇishka I he seems to have resigned his position. After the year 41, and up to the year 60 of the Kushan era, Huvishka ruled alone, and appears to have succeeded Kaṇishka I after his death.

Vāsishka.

The Kushan Empire in Central India.

Huvishka as Viceroy.

Some scholars regard Vima Kadaphisa as the founder of the Kushan era and as the Kushan king who was defeated by the Chinese. Others consider that Kaṇishka's reign ended in the year 28 of the Kushan era, and regard the Kaṇishka mentioned in the inscription of the year 41 as Kaṇishka II. Ac-

Different Theories about Kaṇishka.

cording to this theory, Kaṇishka I came to the throne in A.D. 120 and the Kushan empire in Central Asia was re-established in A.D. 124. Kaṇishka I was succeeded, according to this theory, by Vāsishka, Huvishka, Kaṇishka II, and again by Huvishka. There is, however, no valid reason for supposing that the Kaṇishka of the inscription of the year 41 is a different king from Kaṇishka I.

Some time after his return from Central Asia, Kaṇishka found it necessary to engage in a further expedition to that district, and this time he defeated Pan-Yang, the son of Pan-chao. The campaign was carried on by Huvishka, and Central

Final Conquest of Central Asia by the Kushans.

Asia was finally lost to the Chinese Empire. According to tradition, Kaṇishka I was murdered by one of his generals or ministers during his second campaign in Central Asia.

Extent of Kaṇishka's Empire.

Kaṇishka's empire included the whole of Northern India from Persia to the borders of Bengal. It included the northern part of Western India, such as Mālava and Sindh. Outside India his empire included Kashgar, Khotan, and Yarkand, and he spent the best years of his life in the conquest and reconquest of these regions. After the final conquest of Central Asia he kept some hostages of the kings of these countries in Afghanistan and the Panjab. He was finally succeeded by Huvishka, who is generally regarded as his son.

Kaṇishka's Public Works.

Buddha's Relics.

Kaṇishka I founded the city of Kaṇishkapura near Baramula in Kashmir, and this town is still called Kanispor. He built outside the gate of the city of Peshawar a huge *stūpa* and monastery in which he placed the relics of Buddha. The ruins of this *stūpa* were excavated in 1910, when fragments of Buddha's bones and a relic casket of bronze were discovered.

The Mathurā,

and the Gāndhāra School of Art.

In Mathurā the Jain religion flourished during the reign of Kaṇishka I, and many Buddhist and Jain images were made by the local artists. Kaṇishka employed Indian Greeks as architects, and his *stūpa* at Peshawar was built by a Greek named Agesilaos. Like Vima Kadaphisa, Kaṇishka I used the Greek and Persian language in the Greek script on his coins.

Kaṇishka's Patronage of Buddhism, &c.

Kaṇishka's claim to be remembered by posterity rests not so much on his military expeditions and conquests as on his patronage of learning and of Buddhism. The stories told about the king's conversion and his subsequent zeal for Buddhism have so much resemblance to the Aśoka legends that it is difficult to decide how far they are records of actual fact.[1] Whatever may be the value of these stories, the testimony of coins and epigraphs undoubtedly shows that at some time during his long career Kaṇishka was converted to Buddhism, and that he soon showed the zeal of a convert. He built at Purushpura (modern Peshawar) the celebrated *vihāra* which in succeeding centuries inspired the awe and admiration of all. He convoked the last great council of the Buddhist ecclesiastics. The council met in Kashmir, about 500 delegates attending. The great barbarian king was a patron of learning also. His Imperial court was adorned by Pārśva, Aśvaghosha, Vasumitra, Charaka, and various other distinguished scholars.

Huvishka. Huvishka is known from his inscriptions to have ruled, with interruptions, from the year 33 to the year 60 of the Kushan era (A.D. 111 to 138). Within this period he appears to have retired to the background for three or four years, when Kaṇishka I returned to India. His empire included North India from Afghanistan in the west to Bodh-Gaya in the east. We do not know anything about the history of Central Asia during his reign, but from the silence of the Chinese historians about the provinces of Kashgar, Yarkand, and Khotan after the year A.D. 124, we can easily infer that the Chinese armies had been driven out of Central Asia. **Extent of his Empire.** Similarly, in India proper, we do not know whether Mālava formed a part of his dominion. In A.D. 130 Cutch was being ruled by an independent king, Rudradāman I, the grandson of Chashṭana. Rudradāman I had conquered the whole of Mālava and Western India before the year 72 of the Kushan era, i.e. A.D. 150. **Dissolution of the Kushan Empire.** From this fact it can be gleaned that during the last years of Huvishka's reign the Kushan empire in India was convulsed by civil wars and revolution. After A.D. 138 we do not know anything about the successors of Huvishka till A.D. 155, when we find a king named Vāsudeva I on the throne.

Huvishka's Public Works. Huvishka was a great patron of Buddhism, and he built a Buddhist monastery and temple at Mathurā. In Kashmir he built a city called, after himself, Huvishkapura, which still

[1] V. A. Smith, *Early History of India*, (4th ed.), p. 280.

His Coins. exists as Hushkur or Ushkur. His coins are known in two metals only, and on them he used the Persian language and the Greek script exclusively. On his coins we find the images of a large number of gods, among whom may be mentioned Babylonian, Greek, Zoroastrian, and Indian deities.

The Gap. Huvishka was succeeded by Vāsudeva I after an interval of nearly fourteen years. Nothing is known of this period. Most probably there was a war of succession, which ended in

Vāsudeva I. the triumph of Vāsudeva I. In the year 74 of the Kushan era Vāsudeva I was reigning in Mathurā, over which he seems to have ruled continuously for at least twenty-two years. The last known date of Vāsudeva I is the year 99 of the Kushan era, or A.D. 177. During the reign of Vāsudeva the Kushans appear to have lost their northern dominions and Western India. His coins have been discovered in large numbers in the Panjab and Northern Sindh as well as in the United Provinces. No inscriptions of Vāsudeva I have been found outside Mathurā, and that city appears to have become the capital of the Kushans

Vāsudeva a Hindu. from this time. Vāsudeva I appears to have abjured Buddhism and reverted to the Śaiva faith, of which Vima Kadaphisa had been a devout follower.

Division of the Kushan Empire. After Vāsudeva's death the Kushan Empire seems to have been divided into small principalities. Afghanistan and Central Asia continued under local chiefs of the Kushan family for some time. In India proper the empire of Kaṇishka was divided into two parts, the kingdom of the Kushans and the

The later Great Kushans. kingdom of the Western Satraps. The later Great Kushans ruled over small fragments of the kingdom left to them by Vāsudeva I, for several generations. They are known solely from their coins. We know that Kaṇishka II, Vāsudeva II, and Vāsudeva III ruled over the Indian kingdom after

The later Kushan Kingdoms of the North. Vāsudeva I. In India proper these later Great Kushans continued to issue gold coins of the type introduced by Vima Kadaphisa, but only the first syllable of their names is given on their coins. These chieftains were defeated by Samudragupta and finally overthrown by Chandragupta II. A king named Vāsudeva ruled in the third century A.D. in Seistan,

Kushano-Sassanians. and his successors acknowledged the suzerainty of the Sassanian kings Hormazd II and Varāhrān I. In Afghanistan the Kidāra Kushans ruled for nearly two centuries after the downfall of the Great Kushans, and were overthrown by the Hūṇas.

BIBLIOGRAPHY

R. D. BANERJI, "The Scythian Period of Indian History" in the *Indian Antiquary*, Vol. XXXVII.

"The Date of Kanishka", *Journal of the Royal Asiatic Society*, 1913 and 1914.

Cambridge History of India, Vol. I, chap. xxiii.

H. C. RAYCHANDHURI, *Political History of Ancient India* (2nd ed.), pp. 272–303.

V. A. SMITH, *Early History of India* (4th ed.), chap. x.

CHAPTER VII

GENERAL CULTURE OF NORTHERN INDIA (235 B.C.–A.D. 280)

I. Indian Literature of the post-Mauryan Period

The fifty years of decadence which followed the death of Aśoka are not remarkable for activity in any direction. The overthrow of the Mauryan Empire and the foundation of the Brāhmaṇa kingdom by Pushyamitra mark the beginning of the revival of the orthodox Indo-Aryan religion and Sanskrit literature. The Śuṅgas were Brāhmaṇas by caste and revived many Vedic practices. Pushyamitra performed the Aśvamedha ceremony twice, though he continued to use the modest title of "*Senāpati*" throughout his life. Under the Śuṅgas and even the Kāṇvas, royal patronage was once more extended to the Brāhmaṇas, and the priestly caste once more turned their attention to their own literature and ritual. The majority of the works on philosophy were re-cast during the supremacy of the Śuṅgas. The *Gāthās* and *Nārāśaṁsis* were rewritten in verse and included as *Itihāsas* in the *Purāṇas*. Foundations were laid of the later elaborate grammatical system by Kātyāyana and Patañjali, who wrote extensive glosses on the grammar

Brahmanic Revival.

Philosophy.

Genealogy.

Grammar.

of Pāṇini. These glosses formed the bases of later provincial grammatical literature. Many of the old law books (*Smṛitis*) were recast and the older writers gradually abandoned in favour of the *Mānava-Maitrāyaṇīya* school. Rhetoric and prosody also revived.

Law.

Shortly afterwards this literary revival received a rude shock in Northern India. Harassed by repeated Greek and Scythian invasions, the Śuṅgas and Kāṇvas became very weak, and the centre of Brāhmaṇical activity was transferred to the south. The Southern Pratishṭhāna (Paithan on the Godāvarī) became the refuge of Brāhmaṇical lore. The Sātavāhanas claimed to be Brāhmaṇas and were great patrons of the Indo-Aryan religion. The Nanaghat inscription records immense donations to Brāhmaṇas and the performance of many Vedic sacrifices by the Sātavāhana kings and nobles. Upon the destruction of the Śuṅga and Kāṇva monarchies in Northern India, the capital of the Sātavāhanas became the sole refuge of the Brāhmaṇical religion. In Northern India the irruption of the Greeks and the Scythians caused a great upheaval which changed the character of the old Indo-Aryan religion. To this period belong the older dramas of Bhāsa, which betray more antique characteristics than the dramas of Kalidāsa.

Transfer of Brāhmaṇical Activity to Southern India.

The Sātavāhanas patronize Brāhmaṇical Religion and Literature.

Drama.

II. Religion and Society

The influx of the barbarians into Afghanistan and the Panjab in the last centuries before the birth of Christ caused a social and religious upheaval, traces of which are only too apparent in contemporary lithic records. The Brāhmaṇical religion of the period appears to have become slightly conservative in comparison with Buddhism, while Jainism does not appear to have succeeded in making any fresh converts. Earlier Greek settlers are known to have adopted the Hindu religion. But in the first century B.C. or A.D. Buddhism succeeded in making a larger number of converts among the barbarian invaders than Hinduism or Jainism. Inscriptions mention Greek and Scythian converts to Buddhism, but converts to the Hindu or Brāhmaṇical religion were very few in

Brāhmaṇical Conservatism.

Conversion of Barbarians.

number. The large number of Jain records discovered in Mathurā during this period contain hardly any names of Scythian or Greek converts. It is true that the Great Kushan emperors Vima Kadaphisa (Wema Kadphises) and Vāsudeva I used the image of Śiva exclusively on their coins, but there is no reason to suppose that the Hindu religion had become the state religion even in their time, while Kaṇishka I and Huvishka were eclectic worshippers of gods of many different faiths. Buddhism thus gained a great impetus during the Scythian period, while the Hindu and Jain religions declined on account of their conservatism.

Conversion of Great Kushan Emperors to Hinduism.

Spread of Buddhism.

Gradually a great change had come over the simple religion of Gautama Buddha. Early in the first century A.D. we find that the Indian Buddhists were divided into two great parties, who are now known as the followers of the Mahāyāna (northern Buddhism) and of the Hīnayāna (southern Buddhism) respectively. With the beginning of the worship of the image of Buddha, numerous minor deities had crept in, and gradually Mahāyāna had become an elaborate religion with a separate ritual and a pantheon of its own. The followers of the Hīnayāna differed widely from the followers of the Mahāyāna, and the fourth Great Council of Buddhists convened by Kaṇishka was not recognized by them. It is not known how far the two sects of Buddhists were distributed, but this much is certain, that the followers of the Mahāyāna system preponderated in Northern and Central India. This schism in the Buddhist Church gradually spread to the Indian colonies in Farther India and the Indian Archipelago. The Brāhmaṇical religion and Hīnayāna went on declining, and their place was taken by Mahāyāna everywhere except in Southern India and Ceylon. In Burma, Siam, Cambodia, Java, and Sumatra the half-breed Indian kings gradually adopted and became great patrons of the Mahāyāna system, while Hīnayāna was confined to the extreme south of the Indian Peninsula, where it existed side by side with Jainism.

Schism in Buddhism.

Mahāyāna or Northern Buddhism.

Hīnayāna or Southern Buddhism.

Spread of Mahāyāna Doctrine into Farther India and the Indian Archipelago.

The period of the Scythian irruptions gave a very severe blow to the Brāhmaṇical caste system. During this period the original divisions of Indo-Aryan society became largely merged into each other. New castes and sub-castes

Change in the Caste System.

arose. With the help of Buddhism, the great leveller, the three lower castes practically became merged into one another, while only some families of Brāhmaṇas succeeded in secluding themselves. These new castes and sub-castes were formally recognized upon the reconstruction of Hindu society during the domination of the Guptas.

Disappearance of the Three Lower Castes.

In place of the language of Magadha and other local dialects, classical Sanskrit gradually came to be recognized as the literary language of Northern and Central India. The canonical texts of the northern Buddhists were composed in this language, as also were many of the lithic records. The use of the local dialects or Prakrits gradually died out, and they survived only in certain portions of dramas. The great leaders of northern Buddhism, such as Aśvaghosha, Nāgārjuna, and Pārśva—mostly contemporaries of Kaṇishka I—wrote in classical Sanskrit. Only a few of their works survive in their original form; but the majority of them, as preserved in Tibetan or Chinese translations, prove definitely that they were written originally in classical Sanskrit and not in the Prakrits.

Rise of Classical Sanskrit.

Decline of Prakrits.

Language of Northern Buddhism.

III. The Coinage

The establishment of Greek kingdoms in Afghanistan and the Panjab led to important changes in the coinage. The older Indian coins, both silver and copper, were of two different types, both of which were uninscribed. The silver coins called *Purāṇas* were made by cutting sheets of silver into round or square discs. Each province or city through which a coin passed for circulation punched its distinctive mark on one side of it in token of its genuineness. Such silver coins were used from Afghanistan in the west to Bengal in the east, and from the sub-Himalayan tracts in the north to the south of the Vindhyas. The older copper coins can be divided into three different varieties, the first of which was in all respects similar to the silver *purāṇa*. The second variety consisted of the required weight of copper molten and cast in a special mould bearing particular devices. These two varieties are the oldest specimens of copper coins in India,

Initial Coinage of India.

Punch-marked Silver,

and Copper Coins.

The Die-struck Copper Coins of the North-west.

The third variety was current in the Panjab and Sindh, and was a die-struck oblong or square coin bearing a single device.

Long contact with the Greeks gradually led to a change in the form of the coinage. Some Indian kings issued coins in imitation of Greek coins, e.g. Saubhūti of the Panjab, who used the Greek script to write his name. The feudatories of the Śuṅgas at Kauśāmbī, Ahichchhatra, and Mathurā issued copper coins bearing their names. These are the oldest Indian coins bearing the name of a king, and the majority of these coins are of copper.

The King's Name on Coins.

The Indo-Greeks first of all struck coins in gold, silver, and copper, the weight of which corresponded to the Greek or Attic standard. Later on they also adopted the Indian standard. Greek coins in gold are very rare, but their silver and copper coins are still very common all over Northern and Western India. To the period of the Scythian occupation belong the majority of silver and copper coins based on Greek types, but the earlier Scythian monarchs do not appear to have coined gold at all. To the same period belong the earliest tribal coins issued by the Rājanya, Kuninda, Audumbara, Mālava, Yaudheya, and Arjunāyana tribes, who used both silver and copper, and employed Kharoshṭhī and Brāhmī characters in the legends of their coins.

Greek and Indian Standards.

Scythian and Tribal Coins.

The Great Kushans coined very largely in gold. Vima Kadaphisa issued double staters of heavy gold, as well as staters, on the model of the Roman coinage. Kaṇishka I, Huvishka, and Vāsudeva I issued gold and copper coins only. The majority of the Great Kushans struck abundantly in gold and copper, but they do not appear to have used silver for currency purposes. The later Kushans struck exclusively in gold. Sporadic copper issues prove that tribal copper coins had become current all over Northern India in the second and the third century A.D. Among the latter should be mentioned the long series of tribal coins of the Mālavas and the Yaudheyas, who struck coins from the first century B.C. to the beginning of the fourth century A.D.

The Kushan Gold Coinage

Later Kushan Coins.

Coinage of the Mālava and the Yaudheya Tribes.

IV. Sculpture

The later Mauryan sculpture shows a blending of the best practice of early Mauryan sculpture with the primitive sculpture of Northern India. The retention of the Mauryan polish is evident in the Barabar caves of Daśaratha and the Patna statues, supposed to be either Śaiśunāga statues or Yaksha figures. The Parkham image does not bear any polish, but the same characteristic is observed in the female statue from Dedarganj near Patna. In the Śuṅga period we find the introduction of bas-reliefs in Buddhist structures. The great *stūpas* of Sanchi and Bharhut belong to this period, and their ornamentations are purely Indian. To the same period belongs the ancient railing around the great mediæval temple at Bodh-Gaya. Sir John Marshall, the greatest authority on the subject, is of opinion that the Bharhut *stūpa* is the oldest monument of the Śuṅga period. It was built at the junction of the roads from Magadha and Allahabad to Mālava and the Deccan. It was constructed of brick and stone, but the cost of the elaborately carved circular railing around it, with its four gateways, was met from private subscriptions. Each pious Buddhist lay worshipper or monk or nun contributed to the cost of a pillar, a cross-bar, or a portion of the great architrave. The *stūpa* was dismantled by the neighbouring villagers after the disappearance of Buddhism. The remains were found by Cunningham, when portions of the eastern gateway and of the railings were removed to the Museum at Calcutta. The eastern gateway was twenty-three feet in height, and the pillars, cross-bars, and the architrave of the *stūpa* are decorated with numerous bas-reliefs representing scenes from the life of Buddha or those illustrative of his previous births (*Jātakas*).

Barabar Caves. **Śaiśunāga Statues.** **Sanchi and Bharhut.** **Position of Bharhut.** **Stūpa built from Donations.** **Its Bas-reliefs.**

"The style of the carvings on the ground rail is by no means uniform. Some show little advance on the indigenous work of the previous century, the defects of rudimentary technique being almost as striking in these reliefs as they were in indigenous sculpture in the round."[1]

[1] *Cambridge History of India* Vol. I, pp. 624–5.

Part of Corner Pillar of Railing, Bharhut stupa, Nagod State, now in the Indian Museum, Calcutta (2nd century B.C.)

The Bodh-Gaya Railing. The same authority is of opinion that the oblong railing around the great temple of Bodh-Gaya comes next in chronological order. "This railing was disposed in a quadrangle measuring 145 feet by 108 feet, but in other respects was designed and adorned much in the same way as the rail at Bharhut. On the outside of the coping was a continuous band of flowers; on the inside, a frieze of animal or mythical monsters; on the cross-bars, lotus medallions centred with busts or other devices; and on the upright pillars, standing figures in high relief or medallions and panels containing a variety of miscellaneous scenes." [1]

Great Stūpa of Sanchi. The great *stūpa* at Sanchi near Bhilsa in Northern Mālava was originally a brick structure erected by Aśoka; the present stone-built one belongs to a much later date. The great railings around this *stūpa* were constructed long after the death of Aśoka. According to Sir John Marshall, the earliest of the gateways of the *stūpa* at Sanchi was erected on the south side, the northern, the eastern, and the western being erected later. "Each gateway was composed of two square pillars surmounted by capitals, which in their turn supported a superstructure of three architraves with volute ends, ranged one above the other at intervals slightly in excess of their own height. The capitals were adorned with standing dwarfs or with the fore-fronts of lions or elephants set back to back in the Persepolitan fashion; and, springing from the same abacus and acting as supports to the projecting ends of the lowest architrave, were Caryatid figures of graceful and pleasing outline. Other images of men and women, horsemen, elephants, and lions were disposed between and above the architraves, while crowning and dominating all was the sacred wheel, so inseparably connected with Buddhism, flanked on either side by attendants and *Triśūla* emblems. For the rest, both pillars and superstructure were elaborately enriched with bas-reliefs illustrative of the *Jātaka* legends or scenes from the life of the Buddha or important events in the subsequent history of the Buddhist religion. Besides which, there were representations of the sacred trees and *stūpas* symbolical of

Gateways of the Sanchi Stūpa.

The Sanchi Bas-reliefs.

[1] *Ibid*., p. 626.

Śākyamuni and the preceding Buddhas; of real or fabulous beasts and birds; and many heraldic and floral devices of rich and varied conception."[1]

To the same school belong the oldest bas-reliefs from Mathurā, which can be divided into three groups. The earliest of them belongs to the middle of the second century B.C., the second to the first century B.C., and the third to the first century A.D. Of these three groups the first two are very closely related to the sculptures of Sanchi and Bharhut. The style of the third group is that of the first and second, but in a late and more decadent stage. "In all works of the Mathurā school of this period the same tendency towards schematic treatment is apparent, but it appears to have affected the Jain sculpture more than the Buddhist. The dramatic vigour and warmth of feeling, which characterized the reliefs of the Sanchi

The old School of Sculpture at Mathurā.

The School in the Saka Period, c. A.D. 50.

[1] *Ibid.*, pp. 628–9.

Ancient Railing around the great temple of Mahabodhi, Bodh-Gaya, Gaya district (2nd century B.C.)

gateways, is now vanishing; the composition is becoming weak and mechanical, the postures formal and stilted."[1]

The Indo-Greek School of Gāndhāra

With the rise of a Greek kingdom in Bactria and the conquest of Afghanistan by the Indo-Greeks, a new school of art, which derived its inspiration solely from Hellenistic ideals, rose in the North-western provinces of India. Greek sculptors were employed in carving scenes from the life of Buddha and in the production of statues generally. This school of art held sway for nearly five centuries, and gradually influenced all other schools of India proper and the countries within its zone of influence. The relics of Indian art found in Central Asia and the Buddhist relics at Amarāvati in the Krishna District all betray the far-reaching influence of the Indo-Greek school of art.

The Buddha Image.

The most important contribution of this school to Indian sculpture is the fashioning of images of the Buddha and the Bodhisattvas. The idea of depth was introduced by them into bas-reliefs. The Scythian monarchs continued these ideals and motifs, and the Buddhist structures of Central Asia and North-western India were all decorated with sculptures, painting, and terra-cotta, which prove the very deep hold which this school of art had obtained over Northern India. The style introduced by the Indo-Greeks in bas-reliefs, depicting scenes from the life of Buddha, persisted in Northern India till the twelfth century A.D. The pure Indo-Greek style deteriorated with the irruption of the Scythian barbarians, but the school lingered on in Gāndhāra and in Eastern Turkistan till the fifth or sixth century A.D.

The School of Gāndhāra under the Scythians.

Influence of the Gāndhāra School on Indian Sculpture.

Kaṇishka I was a great patron of art, and during his reign the schools of sculpture in Gāndhāra and the middle country received lavish support. The relic casket made for him and discovered in the *stūpa* at Peshawar shows that Indo-Greek art was on the decline, but the support given by him and his officers to Buddhism, coupled with the great prosperity of Mathurā, caused a revival of plastic art and architecture in that city. The Mathurā school received fresh impetus from the Gāndhāra school and changed its technique soon after the fourth year of the reign of Kaṇishka I. Subsequently it

Revival of the Mathurā School.

[1] *Ibid.*, p. 633

became famous throughout Northern India. Images made in Mathurā were carried to distant countries. Early in the reign of Kaṇishka, a monastery full of images made in Mathurā was dedicated at Sarnath near Benares. Images in the red sandstone for which Mathurā is famous were carried as far as Sanchi in Mālava, Rājagriha in Eastern Magadha, Śrāvastī in the north, and Sindh in the extreme west. The Mathurā school flourished exceedingly during the reigns of the Kushans. It showed a mixture of Indian and Greek ideas, which could be recognized separately in their motifs. The remains discovered at Mathurā indicate a period of feverish building activity and the production of new features both in bas-reliefs and images. A large number of statues of important historical persons were carved by the local sculptors; such as those of Kaṇishka I, Chashṭana, the satrap of Ujjain, and several other Kushan emperors. Numerous Jain images and Jain *stūpas* were dedicated and built. The inscriptions on them enable students of art to fix their chronology with greater precision than in the case of the products of any other school.

Its Influence on Indian Art.

The Statues of the Mathurā School.

No complete building of the Mathurā school has survived to our time, but we can judge of their nature and size from the fragments that have been discovered at Mathurā. The great Huvishka *Vihāra*, or the Buddhist temple and monastery built by that great Kushan emperor, was surrounded by a colonnade of massive redstone columns. The Kaṅkālī Tilā Mound at Mathurā yielded the remains of an immense Jain *stūpa*. Jain *stūpas* are rather uncommon in mediæval and modern shrines, but from the remains at Kaṅkālī Tilā and certain older bas-reliefs discovered at Mathurā we know that they were very common in Northern India in the first century B.C. In form they were exactly like the great Buddhist *stūpas* of Sanchi, Mankiala, or Bharhut, being huge hemispheres decorated on the exterior and surrounded by railings with lofty gateways on the cardinal points. The Buddhist and Jain remains at Mathurā were destroyed by Sultan Mahmud of Ghazni in 1018 A.D., and the great iconoclast was very forcibly struck by the beauty of the sacred and profane edifices.

Buildings at Mathurā.

Huvishka Vihāra.

Jain Stūpas; their Form.

Destruction of Buildings at Mathurā.

Death of Buddha—Indo-Greek or Gandhara School of Sculpture—from Loriyan Tangai, Swat Valley, N.W. Frontier Province—now in the Indian Museum, Calcutta (1st century B.C.)

V. Trade and Commerce

The rise of the Greek power in Egypt and Asia Minor was a great hindrance to the commercial enterprise of the inhabitants of the western coast of India. Like the European traders of the sixteenth century, the early Greek navigators of the Indian Ocean were more or less pirates, and their nefarious activities on the western coast of India, combined with the apathy and lack of protection of Indian commerce on the part of the Indian monarchs, very nearly destroyed that commerce. Up to the end of the first century B.C. there were very few Greek merchant ships in the Indian Ocean, and Strabo has recorded that Indian merchandise reached Europe by way of the Red Sea and Alexandria. The overland route being long and hazardous, only a very small quantity of merchandise from India and China reached European markets through Persia and Asia Minor. The Indian and Chinese overseas trade with Europe revived with the foundation of the Roman and Kushan Empires. Under the great Kushans, Northern and Central India enjoyed a much-needed respite from foreign invasions and internal turmoil. Merchandise could be sent with comparative safety from the distant parts of the Kushan Empire to the great ports on the western coast, and after the conquest of Egypt by the Romans, and the discovery of the monsoon winds by Greek and Roman sailors, the sea-borne commerce of India increased very rapidly. Ships could come from the Egyptian ports on the Red Sea to the Indian ports on the western coast in July and August in forty days, and return, after the completion of the commercial transactions, in December or January. Before the discovery of the course of the monsoons, Greek and Roman ships were obliged to follow the outline of the southern coasts of Arabia, Persia, and Baluchistan, which were even then infested with pirates. The course of the monsoons was known to Indian navigators, who imparted the knowledge to Arab sailors, who in their turn informed the Greeks and thus enabled the European vessels to sail directly across the Indian Ocean. The discovery of the monsoons gave a very great

Greek Pirates.

The Overland Route.

Monsoons and Commerce.

Impetus to Trade.

impetus to European trade, which is indicated by the very large number of Roman coins of all metals discovered in different parts of India. It is also believed that Roman merchants lived in many of the ports on our western coast. The goods exported from India consisted of pearls, precious stones and spices, such as pepper, cinnamon, &c., along with sandal-wood and fine cotton cloth. The effect of this trade was very marked on the Indian gold currency of the period, Kushan and Gupta coins being close copies of the Roman gold coinage of the time.

Roman Coins in India.

Trade Goods.

VI. Greek and Roman Influence on Indian Civilization

Considering the length and extent of the Greek occupation of India, traces of Hellenic influence on Indian civilization are very scanty. No inscription in the Greek language has been discovered in India or Afghanistan, and even in the time of the Great Kushans the use of the Greek language had become obsolete, though the use of the script continued. Inscriptions prove that the Greeks readily intermarried with the natives of the country, and even as early as the fourth century A.D. all traces of the Greek settlers in India had vanished. The influence of Greek civilization and culture is, however, more marked on the plastic art and literature of the period. The influence of Greek writers on astronomy can still be traced in the works of Indian authors, who still quote Yavaneśvara or Yavanāchārya with respect. Greek influence can also be traced to some extent in Indian works on mathematics, but with the exception of Indo-Greek sculpture in Afghanistan and the Western Panjab, and the coinage of the Greek kings of India, all traces of Hellenic rule in India have vanished completely. During the rule of Greek kings in India and Afghanistan, many Indians must have learnt Greek and become familiar with Greek literature and thought. But with the exception of Greek influence on Indian philosophy and drama, subjects which are still matters of controversy, little else in India can be traced to Hellenic influence. On the other hand, traces of Greek intercourse with India can be

Scanty Traces of Greek Occupation.

Greeks Intermarry with Indians.

Greek Influence on Indian Astronomy and Mathematics.

readily traced in modern and mediæval fables of Europe.

The influence of Roman civilization on contemporary Indian culture was still more slight. The Romans never occupied any part of India, and during the Roman rule in Egypt and Asia Minor their merchant vessels were mostly manned by Asiatic Greek and Arab sailors. The Roman influence on Indian culture can be traced to some extent in certain works on mathematics and astronomy, such as the Romaka-Siddhānta and in certain classes of later Indian sculpture which are still imperfectly known to us, such as those of the Telugu country. The Roman influence on Indian coinage was more lasting. Roman gold coins influenced the gold issues of Indian princes from the first century A.D. to the end of the fourth. It is supposed by some writers that Roman gold coins were current in Western and Southern India, but no definite evidence has yet been discovered to support this view. With the rise of the Arabs and the decline of the Eastern Roman Empire, direct connexion between Europe and India ceased.

Roman Influence on Astronomy, Sculpture, and Currency.

BIBLIOGRAPHY

WINTERNITZ, *History of Sanskrit Literature.*

A. B. KEITH, *History of Sanskrit Literature.*

V. A. SMITH, *Catalogue of Coins in the Indian Museum, Calcutta,* Vol. I.

CUNNINGHAM, *Coins of Ancient India.*

COOMARASWAMY, *A History of Art in India and Indonesia.*

V. A. SMITH, *A History of Art in India and Ceylon.*

MARSHALL, *A Guide to Taxila.*

L. BACHHOFER, *Early Indian Sculptures,* 2 Vols.

CHAPTER VIII

THE DRAVIDIAN AND SCYTHIAN KINGDOMS OF SOUTHERN AND WESTERN INDIA

I. Early Satraps, Western India

The downfall of the first Sātavāhana Empire was caused by the invasion of the Scythians. Soon after their conquest

Scythian Conquest of Western India. of Northern India, the Śakas conquered Mālava and then poured into Western India from two different points, namely the delta of the Indus and the banks of the Narmadā. Early in the first century B.C., we find that the whole of the Northern Deccan had passed into the hands of the Śakas. These Śakas did not long recognize the suzerainty of their overlords in Northern India. The Scythian or Śaka satraps became independent in Taxila, Mathurā, and Western India at the same time. The earliest known satrap of Western India who struck

Bhūmaka and Nahapāna. coins in his own name was Bhūmaka. Another independent Scythian satrap, Nahapāna or Nambanos, was contemporary with the great satrap Śoḍāsa of Mathurā, and the inscriptions of his son-in-law Ushavadāta, discovered at Nasik and Kārlā in the Northern Deccan, show the use either of regnal years or of some era, which may be the same as that to be found in the Mathurā inscriptions of Śoḍāsa. This era is quite different from that used by Liaka Kuśulaka in the Taxila copper-plate inscription.

His Coins. Nahapāna struck silver coins in imitation of the small silver coins of Menander. On his coins he uses the title *Rājan*, which is written in Greek characters. The Kharoshṭhī script is also used by him, proving his northern origin. The type of coins issued by him was continued by his successors in Mālava and Western India till the conquest of these two provinces by the Guptas at the end of the fourth century A.D. The successors of Nahapāna also struck coins in his name and were most probably known as Nahapānas, just as the successors of the first Ptolemy of Egypt adopted that monarch's name.

Nahapāna belonged to the Khakharāta family, which originally hailed from Mathurā. He is known from his coins as well as from the inscriptions of his son-in-law, Ushavadāta, at Nasik and Kārlā, and those of his minister Āryaman, in the

Cave Temple of Ushavadāta. cave at Junnar. Ushavadāta's inscriptions in the caves near the city of Nasik (Pāṇḍu-Leṇā) are dated, Cave No. 10 bearing the year 42 of an unspecified era, during the reign of Nahapāna. It is a chaitya-hall, like those at Kārlā and Ajanta.

His campaign in Mālava. From these inscriptions we learn that the kingdom of Nahapāna extended over the whole of Mālava, because they state that Ushavadāta had gone with an army to Mālava to help the chief of the Uttamabhadras, who was besieged by the chief of the Malayas, i.e. the Mālavas of the coins and the "Malloi" of the Greek historians. After defeating the Malayas, Ushavadāta went on pilgrimage to Poshkara, i.e. modern Pushkara near Ajmer, which lies immediately to the north of the province of Mālava. Most of the places mentioned in these inscriptions lie between Bombay and Ajmer, and were included in the kingdom of Nahapāna. Ushavadāta paid the marriage expenses of eight Brāhmaṇas at Prabhāsa, i.e. Verawal in Kathiawad, Bharukachha, i.e. modern Bharochh (Broach), Daśapura (modern Mandasor in Central Mālava), Govardhana (a town of the same name in the North Kanara District of the Bombay Presidency), and Sorparāga (modern Sopārā, north of Bassein island). The rivers mentioned by him over which he established ferries are the Damanā, the Tāpī (Tapti), the Dahaṇukā (Dāhānu), the Ibā (Revā or Narmadā), the Pāradā (the Wardha), and the Karabeṇā (Kṛishṇā).

His Pilgrimage to Pushkara.

Extent of Nahapāna's Kingdom.

The caves at Junnar are situated in the northern part of the Poona District and have been excavated out of four hills which surround the central rock fort at Junnar. On the Manmodi Hill, Āyama or Āryaman, the minister of Nahapāna, excavated a shelter and a chaitya hall in the year 46 of the same era as that used in the Nasik cave. At Kārlā, in the western part of the Poona District, Ushavadāta gave the village of Kārājika for the expenses of the monks living in the caves of Vāluraka, which was the old name of Karla.

The Caves at Junnar and Karla.

Nahapāna lived to a great age, but his son-in-law Ushavadāta survived him. The coins issued in the name of Nahapāna bear the face of that king in his youth, middle age, and old age, as well as the portraits of many of his successors.

Dynasty of Nahapāna.

II. The Sātavāhanas

With the rise of the Kushan power in Northern India the different Śaka kingdoms became weak, and at this time the power of the Sātavāhanas revived under Gautamīputra

Revival of Sātavāhana Power

Śātakarṇī. In the eighteenth year of the reign of that king the Northern Deccan passed away from the family of Nahapāna. In the inscription of his son it is stated that Gautamīputra Śātakarṇī destroyed the power of the Khakhārāta family and re-established the power of the Sātavāhana dynasty. From the same inscription we learn that Gautamīputra Śātakarṇī's kingdom included the provinces of Asmaka (Mahārāshṭra), Mūlaka (the district round Paithan), Suraṭha (Kathiawad), Kukura (West Rajputana), Aparānta (North Konkan), Vidabha (Berar), Anupa (Central Gujarat) and Ākarāvantī (Eastern and Western Mālava). The list of these provinces shows clearly that Gautamīputra Śātakarṇī conquered all the provinces which had once formed the kingdom of Nahapāna. He reigned for at least twenty-four years, and in the eighteenth year of his reign dedicated a small cave at Pāṇḍu-Leṇā near Nasik. From this inscription we learn that he gave away to some ascetics a field which was previously enjoyed by Ushavadāta. Another inscription, incised below the first, records that the same king, in the twenty-fourth year of his reign, gave another field to the ascetics living in the cave dedicated by him, because the first one could not be cultivated.

Conquest of Gautamīputra Śātakarṇī.

His Kingdom.

The Cave of Gautamīputra Śātakarṇī near Nasik.

He was succeeded by his son Vāśishṭhīputra Puḷumāvi. In the nineteenth year of Puḷumāvi's reign, his grandmother Bālaśrī enlarged the cave dedicated by her son Gautamīputra Śātakarṇī. This cave is Cave No. 3 in the Pāṇḍu-Leṇā group. We can gather from these inscriptions that Northern Deccan or Mahārāshṭra, consisting of the modern districts of Nasik and Poona, had passed out of the hands of the Khakhārātas before the eighteenth year of the reign of Gautamīputra Śātakarṇī.

Cave Temple No. 3 near Nasik.

When this king and his son re-established the power of the Sātavāhanas to the north of the Kṛishṇā, the Kushan emperors were gradually reducing the whole of Northern and Central India to obedience. Nothing is known definitely about the successor of Vāśishṭhīputra Puḷumāvi; but a king named Yajña Śrī-Śātakarṇī ruled some time afterwards over the whole of the Deccan and a portion of the Northern Konkan. One of his inscriptions has been found in the caves of Kanheri

Yajña Śrī-Śātakarṇī.

in the Thana District of Bombay, and is dated in the sixteenth year of his reign; another in one of the Pāṇḍu-Leṇā caves near Nasik; and a third at Chinnā in the Kṛishṇā District of Madras Presidency, on the eastern coast of the Indian Peninsula. The last inscription was incised on a pillar in the twenty-seventh year of his reign, and proves that the Sātavāhana dominions extended west to east from the Arabian Sea to the Bay of Bengal, and north to south from the Godāvarī to the Tuṅgabhadrā, and at times as far north as the Narmadā.

There is no evidence to prove that Vaśishṭhīputra Puḷumāvi or Yajña Śrī-Śātakarṇī ruled over Mālava, which was certainly in the possession of the Great Kushans as early as the year 28 of the Kushan era (106 A.D.). Puḷumāvi was the undisputed master of the whole of the Deccan, as his inscriptions have been found at Kārlā in the Poona District, at Pāṇḍu-Leṇā in the Nasik District, and at Amarāvatī in the Kṛishṇā district. It may therefore be supposed that Puḷumāvi and Yajña Śrī ruled over the whole of the Indian Peninsula, between the rivers Narmadā and Kṛishṇā; but the provinces to the north of the Narmadā had passed into the hands of the Great Kushans. Shortly after the death of Yajña Śrī-Śātakarṇī a new power arose in Western India under Rudradāman and very soon reduced the Sātavāhanas to the position of petty chiefs. Minor branches of this dynasty continued to rule at Vanavāsi in the North Kanara District and at other places in the Deccan till the beginning of the third century A.D.

Kushan Conquest of Mālava.

Minor Sātavāhana Dynasties.

III. The Later Western Satraps *—The Dynasty of Chashṭana

Chashṭana or Tiastanes was satrap of Mālava under the Great Kushans. Chashṭana attempted to found an independent kingdom in Mālava, but appears to have been defeated either by the Sātavāhanas or the Kushans. In imitation of the coins of Nahapāna, he struck coins on which we find his bust and his name in Greek, Kharoshṭhī, and Brāhmī characters. His father's name was Zamotika. Chashṭana's son, Jayadāman, probably succeeded his father, as he also struck coins in silver.

Chashṭana in Mālava.

* See p. 307.

The coins of Chashṭana and Jayadāman are very rare and are only found in Kathiawad and Gujarat. Chashṭana was a person of sufficient importance in the Kushan Empire to have his statue placed in the Imperial gallery, where it has been discovered in recent times.

The Empire of Rudradāman I.

Rudradāman I, the son of Jayadāman, founded a new kingdom in Kathiawad and Cutch. As early as A.D. 130 Rudradāman I was in possession of Cutch, and within twenty years of that date he had mastered the whole of Western India, including Mālava. His empire included Eastern and Western Mālava, Anarta and Anupa (Central Gujarat), Saurāshṭra (Kathiawad), Maru (Marwar), Kachchha (Cutch), Sindhu-sauvīra (Upper and Lower Sindh), Kukura (West Rajputana) and Nishāda, and Aparānta (North Konkan). Before the year 72 of the Śaka-Kushan era, the dam of the Sudarśana Lake gave way during a storm. This lake had been constructed during the reign of the Emperor Chandragupta of the Maurya dynasty, when Pushyagupta was the governor of Kathiawad. During the reign of Aśoka the Persian governor Tushāspha led out irrigation canals from this lake. During the reign of Rudradāman I the damage to the embankment of this lake was repaired by Suviśākha, son of Kulaipa, a Pahlava by descent, governor of Anarta and Saurāshṭra. The inscription recording these repairs was incised at the mouth of the pass through which the waters of the lake flowed into the level country to the north of Mount Girnar, by the side of the rock edicts of the Maurya emperor Aśoka. In this inscription, Rudradāman I claims to have defeated the Sātavāhana king, who was the lord of the south (*Dakshiṇāpatha-pati-Śātakarṇi*), on two different occasions, but to have spared him on account of the close relationship which existed between them. He also claims to have defeated the Yaudheyas, who were living in South-western Panjab and Northern Sindh at this time. Rudradāman I struck coins in imitation of the silver coins of Nahapāna. In a damaged inscription in the caves at Kanheri it is stated that a great satrap, whose name begins with the word Rudra, married his daughter to a Sātavāhana king.

History of the Sudarśana Lake.

Rudradāman's Wars in the North and the South.

Rudradāman I was succeeded by two of his sons and two of

his grandsons. His immediate successor was Damaysada, i.e. Damazada I (A.D. 150–178), who is known from his silver coins only. We do not know anything about the dates of the death of Rudradāman I or his son Damazada I. With Jīvadāman I, the son and successor of Damazada I, begins the series of dated coins for which the dynasty of Chashṭana is remarkable. The date is usually found in the silver coins on the obverse, behind the head of the king. Jīvadāman I struck coins in silver as well as in the compound metal called potin. He ruled from A.D. 178 to 198 with interruptions; during his reign his uncle Rudrasiṁha I, the second son of Rudradāman I, appears to have made several attempts to dethrone him.

Damazada I. **Dated Coins of the Western Satraps.** **Jīvadāman I.**

After the death of Rudrasiṁha I three of his sons ascended the throne in succession. Rudrasiṁha I is also known from an inscription discovered inside a well at Gunda in the Halar District of Northern Kathiawad. It records the excavation of a well in the village of Rasopadra by the general Rudrabhūti, son of the general Bāpaka of the Ābhīra clan, in the year 181, during the reign of Rudrasiṁha I.

The Gunda Inscription of Rudrasiṁha.

The immediate successor of Rudrasiṁha I was his son Rudrasena I, who struck coins in silver and potin. The potin coins do not bear any name, but they are dated and are to be found in the province of Mālava. Rudrasena I reigned from 198 to 222. In 199 an inscription was incised at Mulwasar, near Dwarka in Kathiawad, in which Rudrasena I is mentioned as a ruling sovereign. In another inscription discovered at Gadha, near Jasdan in Kathiawad, it is stated that during the reign of Rudrasena I a refectory was erected in 205 by a man named Kharapattha. Rudrasena I was succeeded by his brother Saṅghadāman I, who ruled for two years only (222–223) and was succeeded by his brother Dāmasena, who was the third son of Rudrasiṁha I to ascend the throne. Dāmasena ruled for fourteen years (223–236).

Rudrasena I. **The Mulwasar Inscription.** **The Gadha Inscription.** **Saṅghadāman I.** **Dāmasena.**

After Dāmasena the kings of the dynasty of Chashṭana appear to have been driven from Kathiawad and their kingdom usurped by another king named Īśvaradatta. This king did not use the Śaka era on his coins; but the dates are given in his regnal years in words, while the dates on the coins of the kings of the family of Chashṭana are always given in numerals.

Īśvaradatta.

Īśvaradatta appears to have reigned for two years only, and during his reign Vīradāman, the eldest son of Dāmasena, ruled and struck coins as a subordinate chief, from 234 to 238.

The independence of the dynasty was restored by Yaśodāman I, another son of Dāmasena, who ruled for two years only (238–239). After Yaśodāman I, two other sons of Dāmasena occupied the throne in succession. Vijayasena ruled for twelve years (238–250), and his brother Damajadaśrī III from 251 to 254. The last named prince was succeeded by his nephew Rudrasena II, son of Vīradāman, who ruled from 256 to 274. Rudrasena II was succeeded by two of his sons, Viśvasiṁha and Bhartṛidāman. The former ruled for two years only (277–278), and the latter for sixteen years (279–295). During the last years of the reign of Bhartṛidāman, his son Viśvasena ruled as a subordinate chief. He was the last king of the dynasty of Rudrasiṁha I, and he struck coins as a subordinate chief till 304.

Yaśodāman I. Vijayasena. Damajadaśrī III. Rudrasena II. Bhatṛidāman.

With the death of Viśvasena I the family of Rudrasiṁha I appears to have become extinct. The succession then devolved upon Rudrasiṁha II, the son of Svāmī Jīvadāman II, who was King of Mālava in 279. An inscription of Svāmī Jīvadāman II was discovered at Sanchi in Northern Mālava, from which we learn that this prince ascended the throne of Mālava in 265, and that the thirteenth year of his reign fell in the Śaka year 201, i.e. 279, when a well was excavated at Sanchi by the general or magistrate Śrīdharavarman, of the Scythian family, who was the son of a Scythian named Nanda. The Sanchi inscription proves that some time in the beginning of the second half of the third century the Scythian kingdom of Western India had become divided. The division most probably began during the reign of Vijayasena, when we find the beginning of the deterioration of the Western Kshatrapa coinage. The descendants of Svāmī Jīvadāman II ruled in Kathiawad for two generations only. Svāmī Rudrasiṁha II, the son of Svāmī Jīvadāman II, ruled for about eight or ten years and was succeeded by his son Yaśodāman II, who ruled from 317 to 322. Yaśodāman II was succeeded by a king named Svāmī Rudrasena III after a gap of nearly sixteen years. On his coins he calls himself the son of a *Mahākshatrapa* named

Svāmī Jīvadāman II in Mālava. The Sanchi Inscription of 279. Svāmī Rudrasiṁha II. Yaśodāman II. Rudrasena III.

Rudradāman II, but this prince is not known to us from any other source. Rudrasena III revived the title of *Mahākshatrapa*, which had remained in abeyance after 295. He reigned from 348 to 378. His coins were struck both in silver and in lead. He was succeeded by his sister's son Svāmī Siṁhasena, who ruled from 382 to 384. Siṁhasena was succeeded by his son Rudrasena IV, who struck coins in the lifetime of his father and ruled up to 388. The succession then devolved upon Svāmī Satyasiṁha, whose coins have not yet been discovered. He was succeeded by his son Svāmī Rudrasiṁha III, who is the last known prince to have ruled in Kathiawad. His rule began in 388, and he appears to have ruled over Kathiawad till the conquest of that province by Chandragupta II of the Gupta dynasty of Northern India.

Rudradāman II.

Svāmī Siṁhasena.

Rudrasena IV.

Svāmī Satyasiṁha.

Rudrasiṁha III.

The dynasty of Chashṭana is the earliest Indian dynasty whose entire genealogy can be reconstructed from coins and inscriptions, and in this sense it resembles the mediæval dynasties of Northern and Southern India, whose history and chronology have been reconstructed from similar materials discovered in recent times.

BIBLIOGRAPHY

JOUVEAU DUBREUIL, *A History of the Deccan.*
JOUVEAU DUBREUIL, *Pallavas.*
D. R. BHANDARKAR, "The Dekkan of the Sātavāhanas" in the *Indian Antiquary*, Vols. XLVII and XLVIII, 1918 and 1919.
E. J. RAPSON, *Catalogue of Coins in the British Museum*, Andhras and W. Ksatrapas, &c.

CHAPTER IX

THE CIVILIZATION OF SOUTHERN INDIA UP TO THE END OF THE SIXTH CENTURY

I. Sculpture and Architecture

Cave Temple of the Jain Royal Family of Kaliṅga.

The earliest examples of southern art and architecture are the caves excavated by Khāravela, King of Kaliṅga, and by his relations, in the Udayagiri Hill in the Puri District of Orissa, which are also the earliest known examples of Jain temple architecture. The biggest cave at Udayagiri was excavated in the middle of the second century B.C. for the residence of Jain monks. It consists of a big central courtyard with buildings on three sides. The central wing is two storeyed and contains a veranda with a row of cells behind it. Another two-storeyed cave, now called the Svargapurī and the Mañchapurī, belongs to the same period, and was excavated by Khāravela's principal queen and a prince named Vaḍukha. Most of the caves in Udayagiri Hill belong to the second and the first centuries B.C.

Sir John Marshall on the Udayagiri Caves.

Sir John Marshall says of the sculptured reliefs of the cave of Khāravela: "In the upper the composition is relatively free, each group forming a coherent whole, in which the relation of the various figures to one another is well expressed; the figures themselves are posed in natural attitudes; their movement is vigorous and convincing; and from a plastic and anatomical point of view the modelling is tolerably correct. In the lower, on the other hand, the reliefs are distinctly elementary and crude. . . . At first sight it might appear that in proportion as these carvings are more primitive-looking, so they are anterior to those of the upper storey; but examined more closely they betray traces here and there of comparatively mature art, which suggest that their defects are due rather to the clumsiness and inexperience of the particular sculptors responsible for them than to the primitive character of plastic art at the time when they were produced. Accordingly, it seems probable that in this case, as in the Mañchapurī, the upper of the two floors was the first to be excavated, though the interval of time between the two was not necessarily a long one. . . ."[1]

The Ananta Cave.

Sir John Marshall is of opinion that the Svargapurī and the Mañchapurī are the oldest caves in the Udayagiri Hill; next to them comes the Ananta cave in the neighbouring hill, Khandagiri. The same authority takes the Ananta cave to be the prototype of all the more important caves excavated on this site. The third in order is the biggest cave, the Rāṇī-

[1] *The Cambridge History of India*, Vol. I, p. 641.

gumphā, and after it comes the Gaṇeśa cave on the Udayagiri, which lies close to the Rāṇīgumphā. The Jayāvijayā, the Alakāpurī, and the other caves come last in chronological order. Sir John Marshall says: "the truth appears to be that the art of Orissa, unlike the art of Central and Western India, possessed little independent vitality, and flourished only so long as it was stimulated by other schools, but became retrograde the moment that that inspiration was withdrawn."[1]

The Later Caves on the Udayagiri and the Khandagiri Hills.

Artistic Inspiration of Orissa.

In Western India the artists followed the custom common in Egypt and Persia of hollowing out buildings from the living rock. From Persia the idea was taken by Aśoka and Daśaratha when they excavated the plain cells in the hills of Barabar and Nagarjuni near Gaya. In Western India the artists became more ambitious in the first century B.C., when they carved out large and high halls with *Chaityas*, two- or three-storeyed dormitories for the use of the monks during the rainy season, and separate chapels and dormitories combined for the use of the monks of a higher order. Among the earliest establishments of this kind are the caves at Bhaja, Kondane, Pitalkhora, Ajanta, Bedsa, Nasik, and Karla. Sir John Marshall says about them:

The Buddhist Cave Temples of Western India.

"The plan and general design of these halls is approximately the same, and the description of one will suffice for all. The finest example, undoubtedly, is the hall at Karla, which is at once the largest, the best preserved, and most perfect of its type. It measures 124 feet 3 inches long by 45 feet 6 inches wide and is of the same apsidal plan as the contemporary structural *Chaityas*. . . . Between the nave and the aisles is a single row of thirty-seven columns, of which those round the apse are of plain octagonal form, while the remainder, to the number of fifteen on either side of the nave, are provided with heavy bases and capitals of the bell-shaped type surmounted by kneeling elephants, horses, and tigers, with riders or attendants standing between. Above these figures, and rising to a height of 45 feet at its apex, springs the vaulted roof, beneath the soffit of which is a series of projecting ribs, not carved out of the stone itself, but constructed of wood and attached to the roof. At the apsidal end of the hall

The Great Buddhist Cathedral of Karla.

[1] *Ibid.*, p. 642.

the vault terminates in a semi-dome, beneath which, and hewn, like the rest of the hall, out of the solid rock, is a *stūpa* of familiar shape with a crowning umbrella of wood above. At the entrance to the hall is a screen pierced by three doorways, one leading to the nave, the others to the side aisles; this screen rose no higher than the tops of the pillars within the hall, and the whole of the open space above it was occupied by a great horse-shoe window, within which there still remains part of its original wooden centring. It was through this window that all light was admitted into the hall, the nave and the *stūpa* being thus effectively illuminated, but the side aisles left in comparative darkness. In front of the entrance to the hall was a porch 15 feet deep by about 58 feet high, and as wide as it was high, closed in turn by a second screen consisting of two tiers of octagonal columns, with a solid mass of rock between, once apparently decorated with wooden carvings attached to its façade."[1]

Ancient Wooden Structures in the Cathedral.

Dates of the Karla and Nasik Caves.

The Nasik cave should be referred to the middle of the second century B.C., and the caves of Bhaja and Karla to the opening decades of the first century B.C. Cave No. 3 at Kānherī was excavated during the reign of the Sātavāhana king Yajña Śri-Śātakarṇī, and the rest of the caves are later in date. Some of the caves were excavated in the mediæval period in the ninth century, and the Buddhist monks inhabited them till the sixteenth century, when they were forcibly converted by the Portuguese. The caves of Ajaṇtā fall into two broad groups, the earlier of which belongs to the same date as the caves at Karla and Bhaja, but the paintings in the later group belong to a much later time.

The Kānheri Caves.

The Early Caves of Ajaṇtā.

II. The Coinage

The Śātavāhana Coinage.

The earliest Sātavāhana coins can be divided into many varieties. The coins of the Andhra or the Telugu country bear figures of horses, lions, and elephants, and the symbol of Mount Meru, which is called the *Chaitya*-symbol by numismatists. The metal used is what is known as potin. The

Potin.

[1] *Ibid.*, pp. 635–6.

Sātavāhanas also used lead for coining, and on such coins we find a ship, which comes from the Coromandel coast. Large lead coins are found in Mysore and the N. Kanara district in the southern part of the western coast. The Sātavāhanas also coined in silver and copper, and Gautamīputra Śātakarṇī restruck his own name on a large number of the silver coins of Nahapāna and his descendants. Yajña Śri-Śātakarṇī imitated the silver coins of the satraps, but these silver coins are very rare. The Sātavāhanas struck coins both in lead and in potin in Mālava. The Sātavāhana coinage was quite distinct in standard and type from the southern coinage, and the issue of potin and lead coins appears to have been influenced solely by the demands of the overseas trade.

Ship Coins of Lead.

Gautamīputra Śātakarṇī restrikes the Silver Coins of Nahapāna

The Mālava Coins of the Śātavāhanas.

The earliest coins of Southern India were simple weights of gold and silver. Instead of cutting out thin sheets of gold, silver, and copper, the Dravidian races of the south used pellets of gold or other metals, of a certain weight. Later on these pellets were flattened, and in order to prevent dishonesty they were stamped with a granular surface. The southern coinage thus remained quite distinct from the northern coinage. The *Purāṇa* and the *Kārshāpaṇa* were cut out from sheets of silver and copper, and the latter were at times cast in moulds, but the southern coins were simply round flattish pellets resembling the seeds of certain berries. Later on symbols used to be struck on these pellets, the oldest of which are the ship coins of the Choḷas or the bow-and-arrow coins of the western coast.

Primitive Southern Coinage.

The Flat Pellets.

Southern Ship Coins.

III. Literature

Very little is known of the literature, manners, and customs of the south during this period. A king named Hāla composed a book of verses called the *Sapta-Śatī*, but scholars are divided in opinion about the true date of the present form of this work. The western Kshatrapas have left no literary monuments, and nothing is known of the state of culture in Western India under their rule.

The Sapta-Śatī Hāla.

The earliest poems in Ancient Tamil belong to this period.

Early Tamil Literature. They contain many references to Choḷa, Pāṇḍya and Chera kings, and whatever knowledge we possess of the Dravidian kings of the first and second centuries before and after the birth of Christ, is derived from the writings of the early Tamil poets. The earliest Tamil literature is preserved in a class of work, partly fragmentary and partly in quotations, which was approved by an assembly of literary men, principally in the Pāṇḍya country. In Tamil this assembly is called *Śaṅgam* (from Sanskrit *Saṅgha*). According to certain authorities this class of Tamil literature, which was approved by these assemblies, is called "*Śangam* works", and are assigned to the period before the rise of the Pallavas in Southern India, but others differ with regard to their date. Tradition in Southern India regards three different periods in the life of this literary assembly as being the most glorious. The works approved by this assembly contain references to many Pāṇḍya kings and their contemporary rulers in the Choḷa and Chera kingdoms. Many of the works approved by this assembly are hero-lauds, but the majority of them are poems about a particular emotion. Many of them are of the type of Sanskrit *Mahākāvyas*, and all of them betray the stamp of classical Sanskrit literature and rhetoric on them, and therefore, even if they are as old as certain writers make them to be, they must have been compiled and re-classified at a very late date.

BIBLIOGRAPHY

Cambridge History of India, Vol. I, chap. xxvi.

COOMARASWAMY, *A History of Art in India and Indonesia.*

E. J. RAPSON, *Catalogue of Coins in the British Museum*, Andhras, W. Ksatrapas, &c.

ELLIOTT, *South Indian Coins.*

S. K. AIYANGAR, *Some Contributions of South India to Indian Culture*, Calcutta, 1923, chap. i.

S. K. AIYANGAR, *The Beginnings of South Indian History*, Madras, 1918, chap. ii.

S. K. AIYANGAR, *Mani-Mekhalai in its Historical Setting*, London, Luzac & Co.

BOOK III

History of Mediæval India

CHAPTER I

THE GUPTA EMPIRE OF NORTHERN INDIA

I. Chandragupta I *

Early in the fourth century Chandragupta I, the son of a petty landholder of Bihar, succeeded in founding an independent kingdom, and threw off the authority of the Scythian kings. He was the son of Ghaṭotkachagupta and the grandson of Śrīgupta. The names of his father and grandfather are unknown in history, and most probably they were men of very little importance. Chandragupta I married Kumāradevī, the daughter of a Lichchhavi noble. This marriage enabled him to combine the people of Magadha, i.e. Southern Bihar, against the Scythian foreigners and to make Magadha independent once more. The new king was a Hindu and a Vaishṇava, and the struggle between the people of Magadha and the Scythian kings was one between the followers of Hinduism and Buddhism. Chandragupta I died after a short reign, having established the independence of Magadha; but the real foundation of the empire of the Guptas was laid by his son and successor, Samudragupta.

The Independence of Magadha.

Chandragupta's Marriage with Kumāradevī.

Chandragupta I liberates Magadha.

For the next two hundred years dates are given in a new era, called the Gupta era, which was founded in 320. At first scholars used to think that the Gupta era began from the

The Gupta Era.

* See p. 308.

Its Origin. date of the coronation of Chandragupta I; but some scholars now think that this era was founded by the Lichchhavis and adopted by the Gupta emperors. The earliest dates in it are found in the inscriptions of Chandragupta II, the son and successor of Samudragupta. Most of the dates in the inscriptions and the coins of the Gupta emperors are given in this era and after the decline and fall of the Gupta Empire it was used in Assam till 829 and in Kathiawad till 1264. The Gupta Empire was dismembered in the beginning of the sixth century of the Christian era, but the dynasty founded by Bhaṭārka in Kathiawad continued to use this era till the reign of their last king, Śilāditya VII, in 766. The capital of this dynasty was at Valabhi, modern Wala near Bhavnagar. From their capital this dynasty came to be known as the kings of Valabhi and the era of the Guptas as the era of Valabhi. Hence the name given to it by modern scholars, viz. Gupta-Valabhi era.

Use of the Era till the Muhammadan Conquest.

Its Use in Kathiawad.

Change in its Name.

II. Samudragupta *

Samudragupta, the second king of the Gupta dynasty, was one of the many sons of Chandragupta I. He had an elder brother, named Kācha, who was most probably killed during the war of independence. We do not know much about the reign of Samudragupta except the summarized record which was prepared according to his order by one of his principal officers, named Harisheṇa. It was inscribed on Aśoka's pillar at Allahabad. From this inscription we learn that the capital remained at Pushpapura or Pāṭaliputra, and that Samudragupta defeated two kings named Achyuta and Nāgasena of Northern India, as well as the kings of the Kota family. Achyuta is known from his coins as probably being a king of Central India, and the Kota kings probably belonged to Northern Rajputana. This summary further informs us that in Āryāvartta, or Northern India, Samudragupta defeated kings named Rudradeva, Matila, Nāgadatta, Chandravarman, Gaṇapatināga, Nāgasena, Achyuta, Nandi, and Balavarman. Of these kings, only three, besides Achyuta already mentioned, are known to us from other sources. Matila was probably a

Kācha.

Record of Samudragupta's Conquest.

The Kings of Northern India.

* See p. 308.

Inscribed Iron Pillar of King Chandra, courtyard of the Masjid of Qutbuddin Aibak, old Delhi (4th century A.D.)

king of the United Provinces, and one of his clay seals was discovered in the Bulandshahr District. **Chandravarman of Pushkaraṇā.** Chandravarman was the king of Pushkaraṇā, probably modern Pokaran in the Jodhpur State. He is also known from two other records. Before the rise of Samudragupta, this Chandravarman invaded Western Bengal **His Inscription on the Susunia Hill.** and left a record of his conquest there on the Susunia Hill in the Bankura District. From this inscription we know that he was a king of Pushkaraṇā and that his father's name was Siṁhavarman. Chandravarman was a Vaishṇava; he carved the wheel or discus of Vishṇu on the Susunia Hill, and calls himself "the foremost of the slaves of the wielder of the discus" in that inscription. Subsequently Chandravarman set up an iron standard of Vishṇu we do not know where, which is now placed in the courtyard of the Masjid attached to the Qutb-Minar. In the inscription on this iron pillar he claims to have defeated the people of Bengal and overrun the whole **His Campaigns in the Panjab and Afghanistan.** of the Panjab and Afghanistan, as far as Balkh. Chandravarman was defeated by Samudragupta after his campaigns in Bengal, the Panjab, and Afghanistan. **His Brother Naravarman.** His brother Naravarman retired to Northern Mālava and was reigning there in 404. **Gaṇapatināga.** Gaṇapatināga was the king of Narwar, near Gwalior, where several kings of the Nāga family ruled. He issued coins in copper, and his dynasty appears to have been exterminated by Samudragupta. In the summary of the conquests of Samudragupta, he claims to have subjugated the forest countries and **Samataṭa.** made the kings of Samataṭa or South-eastern Bengal, **Ḍavāka.** Ḍavāka, Kāmarūpa, Nepāl, and Kartṛipura his feudatories. Ḍavāka is generally regarded as the old name of North-eastern Bengal, but it is more probable that this is the name of a Hindu kingdom of Northern Burma, the capital of which was at Tagaung. Kāmarūpa is the name of South-western Assam. Kartṛipura is the ancient name of the Kangra valley. **The Conquest of the Tribal Chiefs and Republics.** In Northern India Samudragupta claims to have also subjugated the Mālava, Arjunāyana, Yaudheya, Madraka, Abhīra, Prārjuna, Śanakānīka, Kāka, and Kharaparika tribes. Among these tribes the Mālavas are the same as the Malloi of the historians of Alex- **The Mālavas.** ander the Great and the Malayas of the time of Nahapāna. These tribes lived in the Panjab and in Rajputana. They issued coins in copper. Later on, some of them settled in the

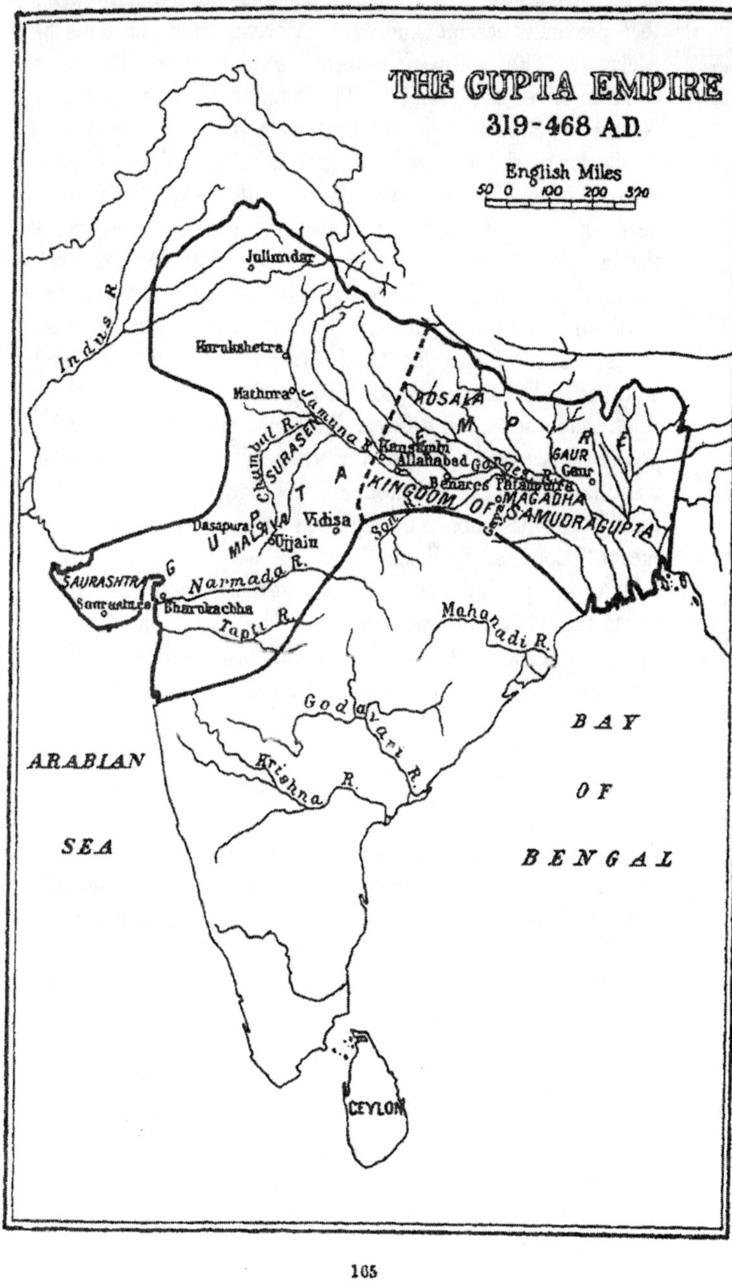
THE GUPTA EMPIRE
319-468 A.D.
English Miles
50 0 100 200 300
Jullundar
Indus R.
Kurukshetra
Mathura
Jamuna R.
Chambul R.
SURASENA
KOSALA
Kausambi
Allahabad
Ganges R.
Benares
Pataliputra
GAUR
Gaur
MAGADHA
KINGDOM OF SAMUDRAGUPTA
Son R.
Dasapura
Vidisa
MALAVA
Ujjain
SAURASHTRA
Narmada R.
Bharukachha
Tapti R.
Mahanadi R.
Godavari R.
Krishna R.
ARABIAN
SEA
BAY
OF
BENGAL
CEYLON

fertile plains watered by the Narmada and its tributaries, and that province became known as Mālava, from the tribe of Mālavas. **The Arjunāyanas.** The Arjunāyanas were a Panjabi tribe who issued coins in silver and copper. The Yaudheyas were a tribe of Northern Rajputana, where they were found living in 371. A district of the Bahawalpur State is called Johiyawar after them. Portions of the tribe still live in the delta of the Indus near Karachi. Not much is known of the other tribes except that a chief of the Sanakānīka tribe served under Chandragupta II in Mālava. **Defeat of the Later Kushans.** Samudragupta specially mentions the Scythian king as being defeated by him, as also were two other tribes, viz. the Śakas and the Muruṇḍas. The Kushan king is called "Devaputra-Shāhī-Shāhānushāhī". All of these titles were used by the Great Kushans. The Śakas were no doubt the western satraps of Kathiawad, but the Muruṇḍas are unknown. Some scholars have thought, however, that Śaka-Muruṇḍas should be regarded as one word, and that it meant "Lords of the Śakas".

Southern Campaign of Samudragupta. After conquering the whole of Northern India, Samudragupta turned his attention to the south. He defeated a king named Mahendra of Mahākośala (Raipur and Bilaspur Districts in the valley of the Mahanadi) and then entered Mahakantara (probably the Gondwana forests), where he defeated a chief named Vyāghrarāja. **Defeat of the Kings of the Eastern Coast.** Emerging from the forests, he defeated Maṇṭarāja of Korala (the region near the Colair Lake), and thereafter the kings of Pishṭapura (Pittapuram), Mahendragiri (Ganjam District), and Koṭṭura. Another authority translates this passage in a different way. According to Professor Jouveau-Dubreuil, Samudragupta, after crossing the forest, defeated Maṇṭarāja, king of Korala, Mahendra of Pishṭapura, and Svāmidatta of Koṭṭura, a citadel on the top of a hill. When the kings of Southern India saw him advancing to the south of the Godāvarī, they formed a **Coalition of Southern Kings.** coalition to stop him. Damana of Eraṇḍapalla (Eraṇḍapali near Chicacole), Vishṇugopa, the Pallava king of Kāñchī, Nīlarāja of Avamukta, Hastivarman of Veṅgī, Ugrasena of Palakka, Kuvera of Devarāshṭra (Vizagapatam District), and Dhanañjaya of Kosthalapura joined this coalition. Samudragupta claims to have defeated all of them, but most probably he felt that it would be much safer not to go farther south. The current view about the route of Samudragupta in the south and his conquest of the Palghat, the Mahārāshṭra, and Khandesh is quite wrong. He penetrated to the south as far as the country between the mouth of the rivers Kṛishṇā and Godāvarī, but never went to any part of Western India or even as far south as Veṅgī or Kāñchī.

Mistaken Notions of the Southern Campaign.

After his return from the southern campaign he revived the Aśvamedha sacrifice, which he performed with great splendour. He issued special gold coins, with the horse of the sacrifice on one side and the figure of his queen Dattadevī, with a sacrificial ladle, on the other side. This coin was used for distribution to the Brāhmaṇas who attended or took part in the sacrifice.

The Aśvamedha, and special Gold Coins issued for it.

At the conclusion of the sacrifice Samudragupta became the recognized emperor of Northern India. He issued coins of various types. First of all he issued a series of gold coins in memory of his father and mother, and another in memory of his eldest brother, Kācha. The Aśvamedha gold coins are very rare. Among the other types may be mentioned the "standard" type, in which the emperor is seen standing in front of an altar, wearing trousers, a coat, and a close-fitting cap. In front of the emperor is the celebrated standard of the Gupta Empire, *Garuḍa-dhvaja*, "the standard surmounted by Garuḍa", the vehicle of the God Vishṇu, who was the tutelary deity of the Guptas. Among other types may be mentioned the "archer" and "battle-axe" types, in which the king's dress resembles that of the figure in the "standard" type. The special types of Samudragupta's gold coinage are the "lyrist" and the "tiger-slayer" types. The "lyrist" type represents the king as seated on a high-backed couch, playing on a lyre. The "tiger" type shows the king wearing the ordinary waist-cloth and slaying a tiger with bow and arrows. Samudragupta was one of the greatest kings of India. He united the eastern portion of Northern India under his rule, and gave peace and prosperity to the country. He reformed the currency and stopped the issue of the base gold coins of the later Kushana kings. Large numbers of his coins are discovered every year, and this proves that under him the material prosperity of the people had increased very much. During the

Samudragupta's Memorial Medals in Gold.

The "Standard" Coins.

Other Types of Samudragupta's Gold Coinage.

reign of Samudragupta a king of Ceylon named Meghavarna sent an embassy to him for permission to build a monastery at Bodh-Gaya. Such embassies were sent from time to time to many kings of Magadha by other kings who desired to build temples in the holy land of Buddhism.

III. Rāmagupta *

Samudragupta was probably succeeded by his son Rāmagupta. This king is known to us from the fragments of a now lost drama by the poet Viśākhadatta, preserved in a recently discovered work on dramaturgy, entitled the *Nātya-darpaṇa*.

"Devī-Chandragupta" of Viśākhadatta.

The name of the drama is *Devī-Chandragupta*. According to this drama, the Scythian king, evidently of Mathurā, demanded that Dhruvadevī, the wife of Rāmagupta, should be sent to his court. The people of Pāṭaliputra were panic-stricken and asked the king to send his queen to the Scythian monarch. The craven Rāmagupta agreed, but the queen was saved from the disgrace by his brother, Prince Chandragupta, who decided to go to the Scythian capital in the guise of Dhruvadevī.

Romantic Story of Chandragupta.

Surrounded by a band of faithful attendants, all disguised as women, Chandragupta went to the Scythian king. The story ends there. Evidently Chandragupta succeeded in defeating the Scythians and on his return was hailed as the king. This statement of the drama by Viśākhadatta is supported by the *Harsha-charita* of Bāṇabhatta, according to which Chandragupta killed the king of the Scythians in the guise of a woman.

Reference in the Harsha-charita.

The reference in the *Harsha-charita* is made more explicit in the commentary on that work, according to which "Chandragupta in the guise of Dhruvadevī killed in privacy the king of the Scythians, who wanted his brother's wife". Later on Chandragupta married his brother's widow Dhruvadevī, this being the first recorded instance of a widow-marriage among kings of the mediæval period. Rāmagupta is not known to us from any other source and does not appear to have struck any coins. The actual dates of his succession and death are not known to us, but the discovery of his name fills up a long gap between the reigns of Samudragupta and Chandragupta II.

* See p. 308.

IV. Chandragupta II (380–414)*

According to Indian tradition as current in the ninth century, Chandragupta II is said to have killed his brother (Rāmagupta) and married his wife. This statement is to be found in a grant of the Rāshtrakūta king Amoghavarsha I dated A.D. 871, discovered at Sanjan in the Thana District of Bombay.

Chandragupta II seems to have enjoyed a long reign, as is testified by the long range of his coins in all metals. It is therefore probable that he ascended the throne some time before 380 A.D. Most of his inscriptions have been discovered in Mālava, and the only inscriptions of this king discovered in Northern India are two fragmentary records found in Mathurā and one at Gadhwa in the Allahabad District. An inscription newly discovered at Mathurā proves that Chandragupta II was already on the throne in A.D. 380. Early in the fifth century we find Chandragupta II in possession of the province of Mālava. In a cave at Udayagiri in Northern Mālava, a place very close to the railway station of Bhilsa in the Gwalior State, there is an inscription which mentions Chandragupta II as the reigning sovereign and records the excavation of the cave by a chief of the Sanakānīka clan, in the year 82 of the Gupta era. This inscription proves that in 401 Northern Mālava had passed out of the control of the Scythian kings. The last known date of the Scythian satraps of Kathiawad is the year 388 on the coins of Svāmi Rudrasiṁha III. The stoppage of the coins of the Scythian satraps indicates that either Kathiawad also was conquered or that the satraps had ceased to be independent kings. The Gupta hold over Mālava was continuous, and an inscription found on the ancient railing of *Stūpa* No. 1 at Sanchi, near Bhilsa, records the gift of a village by one Āmrakārdava for the feeding of five Buddhist monks and the lighting of a lamp. In this inscription Chandragupta II is called Devarāja, a name by which he is also known in the inscriptions of his relations, the Vākāṭakas. This record is dated 412 and is the last known inscription of this emperor.

The Udayagiri Inscription of the year 82.

The Sanchi Inscription of the year 93.

* See p. 308.

The annexation of Mālava and Kathiawad brought the empire of the Guptas to the western coast. There is direct

Cave-temple of Vishnu—excavated in the time of the emperor Chandragupta II near Bhilsa in Northern Mālava (Gwalior State)

Egyptian and Roman Trade of Northern India.

evidence to prove that the ports of Kathiawad were included in the Gupta Empire and that trade with the western world brought vast wealth to it. The merchants who landed their goods at Verawal or Porbandar could easily transport them by the land route from Saurāshṭra, which would go straight to Ujjain and thence to Mathurā and Pāṭaliputra, while the silks and muslins of Eastern India could be brought straight from Bengal to the ports of Kathiawad without paying internal customs duties. Previously, each petty chief through whose territory the goods of the merchants passed levied a contribution on them, thus raising the price and diminishing the profits of manufacturers, merchants, caravan leaders, and importers of the goods at the ports. The unification of Northern India under one ruler gave a very great impetus to inland trade as well as to overseas commerce. We do not know whether the great western ports of Surat, Broach, Cambay, and Sopara were included in the Gupta Empire. Even if they remained under independent rulers their trade must have been drawn off to the Kathiawad ports in coasting schooners, and thereby evaded the vexatious customs duties.

The Gold Coins of Chandragupta II.

The coins of Chandragupta II are not so varied in type as those of his father, but they are found in very large numbers all over Northern India, the principal types being the "archer" type, which resembles that of his father; the "couch" type, in which the king is seated on a couch; and the "umbrella" type, which is rather rare. Much rarer are the "lion-slayer" and the "horseman" types of Chandragupta II's gold coinage. After the conquest of Mālava and Kathiawad he issued a silver coinage in imitation of the coins of the Western Satraps. Many of these coins are dated, and their dates have enabled scholars to fix 409 as the year of the final conquest of Kathiawad. Unlike his father, Chandragupta II struck copper coins of many different types: (1) with the bust of the king, as on the silver coins; (2) with the standing figure of the king, as on many of the gold coins; (3) without any figure. On his coins Chandragupta II assumed many titles, such as *Vikramāditya*, *Vikramāṅka*, and *Siṁhavikrama*. For this reason writers on the literary history of India consider him to be the same as the mythical king *Vikramāditya* of Ujjain, who was a great patron of literature.

His Silver and Copper Coins.

Vikramāditya.

Chandragupta II married his brother's widow, Dhruvadevī or Dhruvasvāminī, who is mentioned as the empress-consort in the inscriptions. Her seal, discovered at Vaiśālī, shows a lion-couchant as her emblem. She bore at least two sons, Kumāragupta and Govindagupta. Kumāragupta succeeded Chandragupta II, and Govindagupta remained the viceroy of the Western Provinces. By another queen named Kuberanāgā, Chandragupta II had a daughter named Prabhāvatī, who married the Vākāṭaka king Rudrasena II. The date of the death of Chandragupta II is not exactly known, but that event must have happened some time between the years 93 and 96 of the Gupta era (413 and 415).

Fa-Hsien. The Chinese pilgrim Fa-Hsien spent fifteen years on his journey (399–414) from China to India and back. He came by the land route from China, across the Gobi Desert and Khotan. He then crossed the Pamirs into the Swat valley and passed on to Taxila. **At Pāṭaliputra and Tamluk.** He spent three years at Pāṭaliputra, the capital of the empire, and two years more at Tāmralipti, modern Tamluk in the Midnapur District of Bengal, which was then one of the most important ports on the eastern coast. The sea has now receded more than sixty miles from its site. Fa-Hsien spent nine years in India proper. He described the Indian towns as large and prosperous. **Charitable Institutions.** They possessed numerous charitable institutions as well as rest houses for travellers. Inns were provided for travellers on the great highways, and the larger towns contained hospitals. There was a very big free hospital in the city of Pāṭaliputra. **Pāṭaliputra.** The capital of the Mauryas was still fairly prosperous, though two centuries later Yuan Chwang found it deserted. **Mathurā.** Mathurā and its big Buddhist monasteries amazed the simple Chinese pilgrim. The great temples and monasteries built by the Great Kushan emperors were still standing, and Mathurā seemed to Fa-Hsien the most beautiful city in India. He states that the people were free to go about without passports. **Condition of the People.** Offences were punished by fines only, and capital punishment was never inflicted. Persistent political offenders were mutilated for rebellion. The revenue of the crown was derived mostly from the produce of the royal demesne lands. The officers and the soldiers were paid regular salaries. Throughout the country the people did not kill any living beings; they did not eat onion or garlic, nor did they drink wine. The outcastes were obliged to live apart in towns and villages.

Fa-Hsien notes that the Gupta Empire was well governed. The government was very moderate and tolerant. The pilgrim returned to China with many manuscripts, images, and paintings.

V. Kumāragupta I (414-455)*

Kumāragupta I, the eldest son of Chandragupta II by the empress Dhruvadevī, succeeded to an empire which extended from Eastern Bengal to the borders of the Western Panjab and from the Himalayas to the banks of the River Narmadā. During the earlier part of his reign the empire was at peace and the country fairly prosperous. The emperor resided for the most part at the capital, Pāṭaliputra. The government of the Scythian provinces of the western frontier was entrusted to the emperor's younger brother Govindagupta, whose descendants ruled as the local kings of Mālava and Magadha after the decline and fall of the Gupta Empire. The last years of the reign of Kumāragupta I were disturbed by the inroads of northern barbarians, called the Hūṇas, who were the same people as the Huns of Roman history and the Hiung-nu of Chinese history. The first invasion of the Hūṇas was driven back by the valour of the crown prince, Skandagupta. This prince was born of an unknown consort of Kumāragupta I. In his old age Kumāragupta I married another lady, Anantā or Anantadevī, who bore him a second son, called Puragupta. Under Kumāragupta, Bengal was governed by the viceroy Chirātadatta. Another viceroy named Ghaṭotkachagupta ruled over Northern Mālava. In Western Mālava, Bandhuvarman, the grandson of Naravarman of Pushkaraṇā, acknowledged his suzerainty. A chief named Pṛithivīsheṇa was the minister of Kumāragupta I and afterwards became his commander-in-chief. After the defeat of the first Hūṇa army, Kumāragupta I celebrated the horse-sacrifice and struck a special type of gold coins for distribution among the priests and the Brāhmaṇas who officiated or were present on the occasion.

Extent of the Gupta Empire.

The Viceroy of the West.

First Hūṇa Invasion.

Second Marriage of Kumāragupta I.

Principal Officers of the Empire.

The Aśvamedha of Kumāragupta I.

The age of Kumāragupta I is the golden age of Indian literature and art. Sculpture flourished in all the principal cities. Kumāragupta I assumed the title of *Mahendrāditya*,

His Titles.

* See p. 308.

and several others, such as *Śrī-Mahendra*, *Śrī-Aśvamedha Mahendra*, *Ajita-Mahendra*, *Śrī-Mahendra-Siṁha*, *Siṁha Mahendra*, and *Mahendrakumāra*. During the Hūṇa wars he was obliged to debase the currency. Some of his heavier gold coins contain a very large amount of alloy, while some of his silver coins are really silver-plated copper. The coinage of Kumāragupta I falls into two groups. The first group is only an imitation of the coins of his grandfather and father. These are the "archer", the "horseman", the "*Aśvamedha*", the "lion-slayer" type, and the "tiger-slayer" types. The new types introduced by this emperor are the "swordsman" type, the "elephant-rider" type, the "peacock" type, and the peculiar coin on which the figures of both of his principal queens appear. His silver coins can be divided into three general classes. The first class is the earliest, in which corrupt Greek letters still survived, and they bear a striking resemblance to the silver coins of the later Western Satraps. These coins were struck for use in Kathiawad only. The coins of the second class are smaller than the first and thicker. The bust of the king and the figure of Garuḍa are very rudely executed. These coins appear to have been in use in the hilly districts which separate Mālava from Northern Gujarat. The corrupt Greek letters appear again. Kumāragupta I struck a new type of silver coins for use in Northern and Central India. These coins bear the true portrait of the king on one side, and on the other side we find a peacock. This coinage was imitated by the Maukharis of the United Provinces and the Varddhanas of Thaneswar in the sixth and seventh centuries. The silver-plated copper coins of Kumāragupta I have been found in large numbers in Kathiawad and were issued during a time of great financial pressure. His copper coins are very rare.

The Debased Currency.

His Silver Coins.

During the reign of Kumāragupta I, Indian sculpture attained the height of its excellence. The Jain image from Mathurā of 114 G.E., i.e. 433, the Buddha image discovered at Mankuwar dedicated in 449, the copper images of Buddha discovered at Nālandā and Sultanganj in the Bhagalpur District, together with images discovered at Sarnath near Benares, are the best known examples of this period.

Gupta Sculpture.

Kumāragupta I was succeeded, during the second Hūṇa war, by his eldest son Skandagupta, in the year 455.

VI. Skandagupta (455–468)*

Skandagupta, the eldest son of Kumāragupta I, by his first empress-consort, whose name we do not know, is one of the most important persons in Indian history. His very name was forgotten during the troublous times which followed his death and the subsequent dissolution of the vast fabric of the Gupta Empire. He alone seems to have realized the peril which hung over India in the shape of clouds of barbarian Hūṇas, and like a true patriot he devoted himself solely to the task of securing the safety of his country. During the old age of Kumāragupta I, this prince stemmed the tide of the first Hūṇa onslaught, and the victories obtained by the Gupta armies were due solely to his personal bravery. The Gupta panegyrist records with wonder that the prince-imperial had to sleep on the ground for a whole night during the first war. When internal dissensions had weakened the people of Magadha, when they had forgotten their sacred duty of defending the gates of India and become immersed in their petty jealousies, at a time when the last great Indian Empire was in its death agony, Skandagupta alone remained faithful to the old tradition of the ancient people of Magadha.

Character of Skandagupta.

The thirteen years of Skandagupta's reign were spent in incessant warfare. At first he drove out the Hūṇas from the empire and secured the safety of his subjects. He reformed the debased coinage of the last years of Kumāragupta I by issuing coins of pure gold, silver, and copper. But later on a rival emperor was set up in Magadha, in the person of his stepbrother Puragupta. The forces of the empire became divided, and the last great Gupta emperor fell fighting, with his enemies in front and in the rear, about 468. Skandagupta left no issue. After his death the Hūṇa barbarians swamped the Indian civilization of centuries and destroyed the empire of Samudragupta and Chandragupta II within a few years. They came in great waves and settled down in the Panjab and Rajputana. Gradually they became Indianized and merged

His Victories in the Second Hūṇa War.

The Rival Emperor, Puragupta.

Hūṇa Settlements in North-western India.

* See p. 308.

in the population, but their descendants continued to rule over the North-western Provinces of India for centuries.

Skandagupta issued coins of the "archer" type like his predecessors. After his accession he issued a special type of gold coins called the "King and Lakshmī" type. He claimed to have steadied the throne of the Goddess of Fortune of his family, who was ready to depart as her throne had become insecure, and therefore he claimed to have become wedded to that goddess. Skandagupta restored the gold coinage to the type and the weight of the ancient Indian *Suvarṇa* of 146 grains. Some of his coins were debased during the Hūṇa wars and contain a large amount of base metal. His silver coins fall into two distinct classes, the western and the northern. Three types of the western coinage are known, the "Garuḍa", the "bull", and the "altar" types. In his northern coinage he imitated the northern silver coinage of his father, Kumāragupta I.

Coinage of Skandagupta.

His Silver Coinage.

Besides the Hūṇa wars the only important event of the reign of Skandagupta was the restoration of the great dam of the Sudarśana Lake, which had been built during the reign of the Maurya emperor Chandragupta, turned into an irrigation tank by Aśoka, and repaired by the Scythian king Rudradāman I in 151. This dam was breached in the Gupta year 136 (456). At this time Parṇadatta was the Gupta viceroy of Kathiawad. He rebuilt this dam and made it 68 cubits in height. In the Gupta year 138 (458) a temple of Vishṇu was built on this dam by Parṇadatta's son Chakrapālita. The subsequent history of the Sudarśana Lake is not known. The fertile valleys which surround the base of the Girnar Mountain and the dense forest, still inhabited by lions and known to sportsmen as the Gir Forest, are now supposed to be the ancient bed of that lake.

Destruction and Restoration of the dam of the Sudarśana Lake.

VII. The Shadow Emperors (468–473)

A. PURAGUPTA (*c.* 468)

Puragupta.

Puragupta was the son of Kumāragupta I by his second wife, Anantadevī. He was the rival of Skandagupta and was the real cause of the destruction of the last Magadhan Empire. He issued coins of gold only, of which only one or two specimens are known. His reign must have been very short, but we know nothing about the events which immediately followed the death of Skandagupta. The withdrawal of the strong arm of the last great emperor of the Gupta dynasty brought about the inevitable result, for the prevention of which Skandagupta had sacrificed his life. Afghanistan, Panjab, and Rajputana were wiped out, as it were, from the map of India of the fifth century. We do not know anything of the history of these countries for six hundred years. The history of India henceforth is the history of the middle country and of Southern India.

Result of the Hūṇa Invasion

B. NARASIṀHAGUPTA (*c.* 469–472)

Puragupta was succeeded by his son Narasiṁhagupta, born of his wife Śrīvatsadevī. Narasiṁhagupta must have been a young man when he came to the throne. After the irruption of the barbarians, Bhaṭārka, governor of Kathiawad, virtually became independent, as that province was cut off from the rest of the Indian Empire. Narasiṁhagupta issued a few gold coins which are found in the United Provinces, Bihar, and Bengal. Henceforth the "archer" type is the only known type of later Gupta coinage. Narasiṁhagupta assumed the title of *Bālāditya* and reigned for a few years only, as we find that his son, Kumāragupta II, was on the throne in 473.

Loss of Kathiawad.

Short Reign.

C. KUMĀRAGUPTA II (473–476)

There are good reasons for believing that Kumāragupta II was an infant in arms when he succeeded to the tottering throne of Samudragupta. Three generations of kings had ascended the throne within five years: Puragupta, his son Narasiṁhagupta, and his grandson Kumāragupta II all reigned between 468 and 473. The Imperial seal of Kumāragupta II was discovered at Bhitari in the Ghazipur District, and some of his gold coins have been discovered in the United Provinces and Bihar. These coins are very rare, which indicates that the reign of Kumāragupta II was a very short one.

The Child King.

His Seal.

VIII. Budhagupta (476–495)

Origin of Budhagupta. After the death or deposition of the child emperor Kumāragupta II, the throne passed on to Budhagupta, who appears from his name to have been a descendant of Samudragupta. The Chinese traveller Yuan Chwang has recorded that Budhagupta was the son of Śakrāditya. In Sanskrit both the words *Śakra* and *Mahendra* mean Indra, the king of the Gods, and therefore Budhagupta may have been the son of *Mahendrāditya*, i.e. Kumāragupta I. **The Sarnath Inscriptions of Budhagupta.** Two inscriptions discovered at Sarnath, near Benares, prove that Budhagupta was in possession of Benares in 477. In 483 he was in possession of Northern Bengal, where Mahārāja Brahmadatta was his viceroy. Brahmadatta was succeeded by Jayadatta later on. In 484 Budhagupta was in possession of Mālava. At this time Mahārāja Suraśmichandra was the viceroy of the country between the Rivers Yamunā and Narmadā, and another Mahārāja named Mātṛivishṇu was the governor of Mālava under the former. We do not know what happened in Mālava during the reign of Budhagupta. But under his successor the Hūṇas, led by Toramāṇa, invaded that province and drove out the viceroys of the Guptas. **The Eran Coin of Budhagupta.** The last known date of Budhagupta is the year 494, which has been found on a coin discovered at Eran in Eastern Mālava. No gold coins of this emperor have been discovered, but most probably the coins bearing the name of *Prakāśāditya* were issued by him. Allan is inclined to assign the *Prakāśāditya* issues to Puragupta, but the reigns of **Prakāśāditya.** Puragupta, his son Narasiṁhagupta, and his grandson Kumāragupta II together came to an end within eight years, a period much too short for the comparatively numerous issues bearing the name of *Prakāśāditya*.

IX. The Later Emperors

A. BHĀNUGUPTA (*c.* 495–545)

Bhānugupta. We do not know when and how the reign of Budhagupta came to an end. One of his successors, named Bhānugupta, reigned over Northern India from Northern Bengal to Eastern

Image of the Boar Incarnation of Vishnu dedicated during the reign of the emperor Budhagupta at Eran in the Saugor district

Hūṇa Conquest of Mālava.

Mālava. During his reign the Hūṇas invaded Mālava through Rajputana. Goparāja, a noble of Magadha, accompanied the emperor in the last expedition dispatched from Magadha against the Hūṇas. The last battle with the barbarians was fought near the modern village of Eran in Eastern Mālava, where Goparāja was killed. A pillar marks the spot where the people of Magadha made their last stand against the Hūṇas; it was erected to commemorate the self-immolation of Goparāja's wife in the Gupta year 191, or 510–511. During the reign of Bhānugupta, in the year 543, Rājaputradeva was the governor of Puṇḍravardhana or N. Bengal. The emperor Bhānugupta is known from two inscriptions only, and the latest epigraphical date for this sovereign of the Gupta dynasty is the year 224, or 543 on the Damodarpur plate.

B. THE LATER IMPERIAL GUPTAS

We do not know much about the successors of Bhānugupta except their names. Three kings seem to have succeeded to the throne; but their dominions seem to have become restricted to Bengal and Bihar. They are known from their coins only, which have been discovered exclusively in Eastern India. A large number of coins of Chandragupta III, surnamed Dvādaśāditya, were discovered at Kalighat near Calcutta in 1774. Another sovereign, named Vishṇugupta, held the surname of Chandrāditya, and a few of his coins have been found in Western Bengal. A third king, Jayagupta, is known from two coins only.

Gradually the provincial governors and the officials of the Gupta Empire asserted their independence. The descendants of Govindagupta became independent in Magadha or Bihar and founded a separate dynasty known in history as the later Guptas of Magadha.

BIBLIOGRAPHY

FLEET, *Corpus Inscriptionum Indicarum*, Vol. III.

J. ALLAN, *Catalogue of Coins in the British Museum*, Gupta Dynasties.

R. D. BANERJI, *The Age of the Imperial Guptas*, chap. i.

V. A. SMITH, *Early History of India* (4th ed.), chaps. xi–xii.

H. C. RAYCHANDHURI, *Political History of Ancient India* (3rd ed.).

CHAPTER II

THE FIRST INDIAN RENAISSANCE AND THE CULTURE OF THE GUPTA AGE

The age of the early Imperial Guptas is generally regarded as the Augustan Age of Indian culture in the mediæval period. The reunion of the whole of Northern India under one rule gave a great impetus to trade both internal and external. Traders carried the products of India to far distant lands and brought back foreign gold in abundance. The material prosperity of the people increased by leaps and bounds, and their affluence found expression in marked improvement in all branches of culture. **Improvement in Trade.**

The emperors of the Gupta dynasty were Vaishṇavas and strong supporters of Hinduism. It is quite evident that Buddhism, which had become the predominant religion of India during the rule of the Scythians, declined for want of material support. **Decline of Buddhism.** There is no evidence of any persecution of Buddhists during the rule of the Imperial Guptas, but there cannot be any doubt that the state support went principally to the Brāhmaṇas. This royal patronage led to a revival of Sanskrit literature. The legendary stories about the mythical king Vikramāditya of Ujjain had their origin in the munificence and liberal patronage of Chandragupta II, who assumed the surname of Vikramāditya. **Vikramāditya.** The Brāhmaṇas gave their attention to the reform of the orthodox Brāhmaṇical religion. Modern Hinduism was evolved out of the older Aryo-Dravidian religion. The widespread worship of Vishṇu and Śiva and the delegation of sacrifices to the learned classes began in this age. **Religion.** The worship of images, with its gorgeous ritual, began during this period. With the reform of the Brāhmaṇical religion came the inevitable recasting of the sacred literature. The principal *Purāṇas* were rewritten in this period, and in their historical portions the name of the Gupta dynasty is given last of all, thus proving that the final redaction of this class of literature took place in the fifth and sixth centuries. **Final Redaction of the Purāṇas** Indian speculative philosophy apparently obtained a strong foothold in our theology during this period, and finally obtained supremacy for the Vedānta school all over India. There are strong reasons to believe that the dramas and poems of Kālidāsa were written in Ujjain in Mālava during the rule of the later Imperial Guptas, and a large number of works on grammar and rhetoric were composed at the same time.

Supremacy of the Vedānta School.

Literature.

Increased intercourse with the western world brought about a complete reformation of the Indian almanac and Indian astrology. Roman works on astronomy and astrology were very largely adopted by Indian writers on these subjects, and the agreement arrived at is still to be seen in the correspondence of the Indian and European names of weekdays and of the signs of the zodiac. While the works of earlier Greek and Roman astronomers were incorporated, the Julian reforms are not mentioned by Indian astronomers, proving thereby that this reconstitution of Indian astronomy took place before the decline and fall of the early Gupta Empire.

The Calendar.

Influence of Roman Astronomy.

One of the remarkable achievements of the Guptas was the reform of the Indian currency. The earliest Gupta coins, those of Samudragupta, are based on the standard of the later Kushan coins, i.e. the Roman standard. These coins weigh 118 to 122 grains. The Guptas also adopted the name *Denarius* from Latin numismatics and converted it into the Indian *Dīnāra*. The standard was slightly changed during the reign of Chandragupta II, when the Roman standard of 121 grains was given up in favour of a new standard of 126 and 132 grains. The Roman standard was finally abandoned during the reign of Skandagupta, who reverted to the ancient Indian standard of the *Suvarṇa* of 146 grains. This standard remained permanent till the overthrow of Śaśāṅka by Harshavarddhana after 619. The silver coins minted in Western India at first followed the weight of the Scythian standard of 32 grains, but during the reign of Skandagupta gradually rose to the Indian standard of the Kārshāpaṇa.

The Currency.

The Roman Standard.

Reversion to the Indian Standard.

Much better known than the renaissance of Indian literature and currency is the renaissance of Indian art. The increase in the material prosperity of the nations united under one rule has left an indelible mark on the history of the plastic art of the country. Indian sculpture shook off its subservience

The First Indian Renaissance.

to foreign traditions and motifs and asserted its personality. The stereotyped copying of the Indo-Greek school of Gāndhāra, which characterized the intervening school of Mathurā, was abandoned in favour of a fresh naturalism. The new schools of art characterized their production by the introduction of symmetry, perspective, and natural proportion. The traditions of the Gāndhāra school were partly preserved in the representation of stories from the life of Buddha, but the artists of the new school introduced fresh ideas while representing incidents of Puranic mythology. The great school of sculpture at Mathurā gradually declined and finally ceased to exist in the beginning of the sixth century. Its place in Northern India was taken by the schools of Benares and Pāṭaliputra. These two northern schools became the parents of three other mediæval schools in later years; namely, the Eastern school of mediævai sculpture in Bengal and Bihar, the Chedī-Chandella school of East-central India, and the school of Dhārā in Mālava.

Gupta Schools of Sculpture.

A Buddha—Late Mathura School of Sculpture—Gupta period (6–7th century A.D.)

The reorganization of the Indian Empire under the Guptas led to the formation of a bureaucracy as efficient and as well organized as the official system of Chāṇakya and Chandragupta Maurya. The gradations of these officials have not been recorded in Indian literature, and we have to rely entirely on epigraphical evidence. The names of the majority of the officials are to be found in the seals discovered by Bloch

Officials of the Gupta Empire.

and Spooner among the ruins of Vaiśālī and Nālandā. The highest class of officials were the *Mantrins* and the *Sachivas*, but the majority of them held the title of *Kumārāmātya*. The official system seems to have been inaugurated early in the reign of the Emperor Samudragupta. The Allahabad inscription of Samudragupta was composed by the Minister

Seal of a Kumārāmātya used in the 8th century by a descendant of a Gupta official in Eastern Bengal

of Peace and War (*Sāndhi-vigrahika*), and the Judge (*Mahā-daṇḍanāyaka*), the *Kumārāmātya* Harisheṇa. The name of Chandragupta II's minister was Śikharasvāmin, who was also a *Kumārāmātya*. His son Pṛithivīsheṇa, too, was a *Kumārāmātya*. It appears now that the rank of the *Kumā-rāmātya* was held by almost all officers at the beginning of their careers. Formerly scholars used to translate this term as "the Prince's councillor", but now it appears that the title or the rank was held by all members of the Imperial Council. Most probably all of them were ministers of the second class. Pṛithivīsheṇa was the minister (*Mantrin*) of

The Imperial Council.

the Emperor Kumāragupta I, but afterwards he became the Commander-in-chief (*Mahābalādhikṛita*). There were several gradations among the ministers who held the rank of *Kumārāmātya*. To the highest grade belonged those who were equal in rank to the Emperor himself (*Śrī-Paramabhaṭṭāraka-pādīya-kumārāmātya*). Evidently all princes of the imperial family were called *Yuvarājas*, and the heir-apparent was called *Yuvarāja-bhaṭṭāraka*, because there are two classes of *Kumārāmātyas* who were regarded as Princes of the Empire. To the second class of *Kumārāmātyas* belonged those who were held to be equal in rank to the heir-apparent (*Yuvarāja-bhaṭṭāraka-pādīya-kumārāmātya*). Those who were held to be equal in rank to the younger princes appear to have belonged to the third class (*Yuvarāja-pādīya-kumārāmātyas*). To the fourth class belonged ordinary *Kumārāmātyas*. We have here a gradation of officers corresponding to some extent to the nobility of the early Roman Empire. The *Kumārāmātyas* were thus a class of high officials some of whom were equal in rank to the Emperor himself, others to the heir-apparent, while the third class held the same rank as the Princes of the blood-royal. Other officers besides the *Kumārāmātya* were admitted to the rank of the Princes. The Commander-in-chief of the army was equal in rank to the heir-apparent (*Yuvarāja-bhaṭṭāraka-pādīya*). The next class of officials of importance were the *Uparikas*, who were employed as provincial Governors. An *Uparika* named Chirātadatta was the governor of Northern Bengal in the Gupta year 124 = 443, during the reign of Kumāragupta I. Two *Uparikas* named Brahmadatta and Jayadatta ruled the same province in 482 and at some later date during the reign of the Emperor Budhagupta. Both of them held the title of Mahārāja in addition to the rank of *Uparika*. An officer of the rank of *Kumārāmātya* was appointed to rule over the Suvvuṅga District in Eastern Bengal, and later on, when his descendants became independent, they continued for nearly five hundred years to use the seal of the *Kumārāmātya* received from the Imperial Secretariat at Pāṭaliputra in the fifth century. The minor officials are also known from their seals discovered at Basarh (Vaiśālī) and Nālandā. The most important among them is the Master

Gradations of Rank.

Rank of Imperial Generals

The Uparikas.

The Viceroys of Bengal.

The Governors of the Eastern Frontier.

General of Military Stores (*Raṇabhāṇḍāgārādhikaraṇa*), the officer in charge of the moral conduct of the people of Tīrabhukti (*Tīrabhuktau Vinayasthiti-sthāpaka*). The existence of such an official during the reign of the early Gupta emperors is remarkable in Northern India. Most probably this class of official had succeeded the *Dharmma-mahāmātras* of the Maurya period.

Other Important Officials.

With the rise of the Guptas, Brāhmanism once more reasserted its supremacy. Seals of temples which are noted even now for their sanctity have been discovered at Vaiśālī. The most important among them is the seal of the Great Temple of the Vishṇupāda at Gaya. This shrine appears to have come into existence early in the fourth century, and bears on it the emblems of Vishṇu, viz. the mace, the wheel and the symbols for the Sun (wheel) and the Moon (lotus). Another important religious establishment which grew up during the Gupta period was the temple of Śiva, called Āmrātakeśvara, at Benares. The most important Buddhist establishments of this period were great monasteries at Benares, Bodh-Gaya, and Nālandā. The recent archæological discoveries at Nālandā show that the abbots of the monastery carried on an extensive correspondence with kings all over India. Seals of a sister of the *Mahākshatrapa* Rudrasena I of Saurāshṭra, of King Bhāskaravarman of Assam and of the Emperor Harshavardhana of Thāneśvara have been found.

Religious Institutions.

The emperors of the Gupta dynasty may also be credited with the reorganization of Hindu society. Henceforth we no longer hear of Buddhist Greeks or Hinduized Scythians; all were incorporated in orthodox Hindu society. With the religious revival came a missionary zeal which converted the Indian and the foreigner without any distinction to Vaishnavism. The incorporation of the Hinduized barbarians into the different castes and sub-castes was regulated by the Gupta monarchs. This gave rise to the modern caste system of North-eastern India, which is essentially different from that of Central, Southern, Western, or North-western India. In Kashmir, Panjab, Sindh, Rajputana, and Malwa this earlier reorganization of the caste system was dissolved by the influx of the Hūṇas and Gurjaras, and therefore the caste systems of these countries are totally different from that of Bengal, Bihar, the United Provinces, and the eastern part of the Central Provinces. In North-eastern India the new sub-castes, which arose on account of the admission of the Hinduized barbarians into Hindu society, were generally grouped under the two lowest castes of the original Indo-Aryan society, viz. the Vaiśyas and the Śūdras.

BIBLIOGRAPHY

F. E. PARGITER, *The Dynasties of the Kali Age.*
R. D. BANERJI, *The Age of the Imperial Guptas.*

CHAPTER III

THE NORTHERN DYNASTIES OF THE EARLY MEDIÆVAL PERIOD

I. The Vākāṭakas

The most important dynasty of India contemporaneous with the early Guptas was that of the Vākāṭakas of Central India and the Northern Deccan. Their inscriptions are found over a wide area extending from Nachna Kuthara in the Ajaygaḍh State, near Sutna, to Poona. The Vākāṭakas were a powerful race of kings, and they ruled over Central India, the Central Provinces, and the Northern Deccan for at least eight generations. The dynasty was founded by a man named Vindhyaśakti. His son Pravarasena I was the first king of note and performed the horse-sacrifice. He was succeeded by his grandson Rudrasena I, who married the daughter of Bhavanāga, the king of the Bhāraśivas, a tribe of the Gangetic plains. According to an inscription discovered in the Ajanta caves, Pṛithivīsheṇa I, son of Rudrasena I, defeated the king of the Kuntala country, i.e. the modern districts of Dharwar and North Kanara. His son Rudrasena II married Prabhāvatī-guptā, the daughter of the emperor Chandragupta II, in the last quarter of the fourth century. This date proves that the

Extent of their Kingdom.

Pravarasena I.

Pṛithivīsheṇa I.

Rudrasena II, the Son-in-law of Chandragupta II.

Vākāṭaka kingdom must have been founded before the foundation of the empire of the early Guptas by Chandragupta I.

Rudrasena II must have died early, because we find the Gupta princess ruling over the Vākāṭaka kingdom as the regent for her minor son, the Yuvarāja Divākarasena. Prabhāvatīguptā visited Śrīśailam, the famous shrine of Mahādeva or Śiva in the Karnul District of the Madras Presidency. She reigned as regent for about thirteen years and was succeeded by her second son Pravarasena II. During the latter's reign the Vākāṭaka kingdom extended from Jubbulpur in the north to the banks of the Bhīmā in the south, and from Raipur in the east to the Western Ghats in the west.

The Sons of Prabhāvatīguptā.

Pravarasena II was succeeded by his son Narendrasena, who claims to have subdued the kings of Kośala, Mālava, and Mekala. He was succeeded by his son Pṛithivīsheṇa II, whose mother was the daughter of a king of the Kuntala country. The succession then seems to have passed on to a brother of Narendrasena, whose son Devasena handed over the kingdom to his son Harisena. The latter reigned in the beginning of the sixth century, when the Hūṇas were wresting Mālava from the Guptas. He is said to have defeated the kings of Kuntala (Northern Kanarese Districts), Avanti (Malwa), Kaliṅga (Southern Orissa), Kośala (Eastern Central Province), Trikūṭa (Bundelkhand), Lāṭa (Gujarat), and Andhra (the Northern Telugu Districts). In the middle of the sixth century the power of the Vākāṭakas was broken by the Kalatsuris or Kalachuris, a southern people who founded a powerful state in the Nasik and Aurangabad Districts.

Decline of the Vākāṭakas.

II. The Hūṇas

Very little is known about the history of the Indian branch of the Hūṇas. The earliest princes of this dynasty are no doubt mentioned as the chiefs of the Ye-tha or the Epthalites, who are called "white Huns" by Roman historians. The history of the Hūṇas is to some extent preserved in Chinese records, but that of the Indian branch is to be gleaned from their inscriptions and coins. The first known Hūṇa prince of India is Khiṅkhila. This king and his successors, Toramāṇa and Mihiragula, are mentioned in the histories of

Khiṅkhila.

Kashmir, and their coins have been found in that province as well as in the Panjab. The inscriptions of the last two chiefs have also been discovered at Gwalior and Eran.

The real date of the Hūṇa kings can be determined from the inscriptions of the brothers Mātṛivishṇu and Dhanyavishṇu discovered at Eran in Eastern Mālava. In the Gupta year 165 = 484–485, a *Garuḍa-dhvaja* or Staff of Vishṇu was dedicated by both of these brothers. But later on, in the first year of the reign of Toramāṇa, Mātṛivishṇu had passed away, and his younger brother dedicated an image of the Boar Incarnation of Vishṇu, thus proving that the conquest of Mālava by Toramāṇa occurred probably a few years after 484. It is therefore quite probable that the first year of Toramāṇa corresponds with the year 191 of the Gupta era, i.e. 510*–511. The first and second Hūṇa wars can therefore be relegated to the reign of Khiṅkhila, who can be taken to have been a contemporary of the emperor Skandagupta. Earlier writers on this subject used to think that Toramāṇa was a contemporary of Skandagupta, but recent discoveries have proved beyond doubt that Skandagupta died soon after the second Hūṇa war, and it is possible that Toramāṇa did not conquer Mālava before 511, or more than forty years after the death of Skandagupta. The first two Hūṇa wars were events contemporaneous with the Hūṇa invasion of Persia. The Persian king Firoz was killed in a battle with the Hūṇas in 484. The collapse of the Persian opposition enabled the Hūṇas to devote their entire energy to the subversion of the Gupta Empire. The Scythian feudatories of the Guptas in Afghanistan and the Panjab were very easily overthrown. The rich monasteries of the province of Gandhāra and the great university of Takshaśilā were destroyed, never to recover their ancient glory. Toramāṇa issued copper coins which bear the first two syllables of his name. The majority of these coins are found in the Western Panjab and Kashmir. He was succeeded by his son Mihirakula or Mihiragula, a name distinctly Persian in sound.

Date of Toramāṇa.

Hūṇa Wars of Skandagupta.

Hūṇas Conquer Persia.

Third Hūṇa War.

Destruction of Takshaśilā and the Buddhist Temples of Gāndhāra.

Indian tradition represents Mihirakula as a tyrant. At last, his cruelty having become unbearable, the Indian princes combined against him under Bālāditya, King of Magadha, and

* This is merely a theory.

Yaśodharman, King of Mālava. They obtained a complete victory over the Hūṇa king and compelled him to retire to Kashmir. It is said that Mihirakula was taken prisoner but was set at liberty by Bālāditya. This battle was fought some time before 533, and destroyed the influence of the Hūṇas in Central India. Mihirakula continued to rule over some parts of India in 547, as he is mentioned by the Christian monk Cosmas Indicopleustes as Gollas, a white Hun king, who was the lord of India and exacted tribute by oppression.[1] The provinces of North-western India and Afghanistan remained permanently in the occupation of the Hūṇas till these barbarian tribes intermarried extensively with the older inhabitants and finally produced the Rajput tribes of the later mediæval period.

Hūṇas overthrown in Central India.

Inscriptions of Mihirakula.

Mihirakula is known from two inscriptions. One of these was discovered inside the fort at Gwalior, and from it we learn that he was the son of Toramāṇa and ruled over Northern India for at least fifteen years. The second inscription was discovered at Kura in the Salt Range of the Panjab, and records the construction of a Buddhist monastery for the monks of the Mahīśāsaka school.

The later history of the Hūṇa chiefs and their Indianization is very obscure. The Panjab was in the occupation of the Hūṇas even at the time of the accession of Harshavardhana in 606.

Absorption of Hūṇas in India.

Karṇa, son of Gāṅgeya, the celebrated conqueror of Northern and Southern India, of the Kalachuri or Haihaya family of Ḍāhala, married a Hūṇa princess named Āvalladevī. After the eleventh century the Hūṇas disappeared from Indian history as a separate race or tribe.

III. The Maitrakas of Valabhi *

After the death of Skandagupta nothing is known of the history of Kathiawad or Gujarat for some time. Towards the end of the fifth century Bhaṭārka, a general of the Gupta Empire, obtained possession of the peninsula of Kathiawad and founded an independent kingdom which lasted till the end of the eighth century.

[1] This is merely a matter of conjecture, and historians do not agree as to the dates. The following books should be consulted for opposite views: V. A. Smith's *Early History of India* (4th edition), pp. 335–7.

* See p. 308.

Bhaṭārka and his eldest son Dharasena I were content with the modest title of *Senāpati*, or general, but three other sons of Bhaṭārka assumed the title *Mahārāja*. Dharapaṭṭa, the youngest son, was succeeded by his son Guhasena, who ascended the throne in the middle of the sixth century. Guhasena, his son Dharasena II, and his grandson Śilāditya I were content to call themselves *Sāmantas* or *Mahā-sāmantas*. Imperial titles were assumed for the first time by Dharasena IV some time before 645, i.e. during the reign of Harshavarddhana of Thāneśvar.

Earlier Chiefs of Valabhi.

After Śilāditya I the succession passed to Dharasena III, his younger brother's son, and then to Dhruvasena II, younger brother of the former. This prince was hard pressed by Harshavarddhana. At this time the Maitraka kings had conquered Mālava, and after the war with Harsha, Dhruvasena was married to the daughter of that emperor. During the wars with the kings of Thāneśvar, the Maitraka king Dhruvasena II received great help from the Gurjara king Dadda II (surnamed Praśāntarāga) of Broach. After the death of Harshavarddhana, the Maitrakas became powerless, and though they continued to assume the Imperial titles, they became dependent on their feudatories. Dharasena IV, son of Dhruvasena II, conquered Broach before 649. His kingdom included both Kathiawad and Central Gujarat. After his death the crown passed on to Dhruvasena III, a grandson of Śilāditya I. This prince held Kapadvanj in Central Gujarat, and was succeeded by his elder brother Kharagraha II. The next kings were Śilāditya III, a nephew of Dhruvasena III and Kharagraha II, in the middle of the seventh century. The four successors of Śilāditya III were all named Śilāditya, whose kingdom was confined to a portion of Kathiawad and Northern Gujarat. Śilāditya IV is known to have reigned from 691 to 701; his grandson Śilāditya V was reigning in 722, and his great-grandson Śilāditya VI in 760. The last known king of this dynasty is Śilāditya VII, who was alive and reigning in 766. Shortly afterwards the kingdom of Valabhi was overthrown and its capital destroyed by Arab raiders from Sindh.

Dhruvasena II, the Son-in-law of Harsha.

The Last Kings.

Destruction of Valabhi by the Arabs.

The Maitraka kings of Valabhi issued a silver coinage in

imitation of the silver coins of Chandragupta II, but the legends on these coins have not been read as yet. The type was adopted by the Rāshṭrakūṭas of Malkhed, and one Kṛishṇarāja of that dynasty issued silver coins of this type on which his name is perfectly legible.

Ruins of Siva Temple at Bhumra, Nagod State (6th century A.D.)

IV. The Kings of Uchchakalpa

Uchchakalpa is the old name of the northern part of the district of Jubbulpore including the states of Maihar and Nagod of the Baghelkhand Political Agency of Central India. The kings who ruled over this province were originally feudatories of the Vākāṭakas. Two kings of this dynasty issued grants of land inscribed on copper plates which are dated, but there is some difference of opinion among scholars about the era used in these dates. The dates of Jayanātha, the earlier king, are 174 and 177; if referred to the Gupta era these dates are

The Copper Plate Grants.

equivalent to 493 and 496, but the late Dr. Kielhorn was of opinion that they should be referred to the Kalachurī-Chedī era, which began in 248, or seventy-one years earlier. Kielhorn therefore regarded the Uchchakalpa dynasty as not belonging to the group of the feudatories of the Gupta Empire. Jayanātha was succeeded by his son Śarvanātha, whose dates range from the year 193 to 214, perhaps equivalent to 508 to 533. The majority of inscriptions of this dynasty are on copper plates discovered in the deserted city of Khoh, six miles to the west of Unchehra, the chief town of the small state of Nagod in Central India. The village of Bhumra, on the top of a plateau thirteen miles to the north-west of Unchehra, was the dividing line between the kingdom of Uchchakalpa and that of the Parivrājakas. From a boundary pillar set up during the reign of Mahārāja Hastin we learn that the Parivrājaka king of that name was the contemporary of Śarvanātha of Uchchakalpa. The kingdom of Uchchakalpa came very suddenly to an end about 550.

Their Dates.

Śarvanātha.

Boundary Pillar at Bhumra.

V. The Parivrājaka Mahārājas

The Parivrājaka chiefs were feudatories of the early Gupta Empire, and in their inscriptions they used the Gupta era and referred to it as such. Five generations of chiefs of this family are known, of whom the last two only issued grants of land. Hastin reigned for nearly half a century (475–511) and was a contemporary of the Uchchakalpa Mahārāja Śarvanātha, who reigned during the years 508–533. He practically asserted his independence though he did not assume Imperial titles. He issued small gold coins of the type of the South Indian "*Fanam*". No other feudatories of the Gupta Empire, except the later chiefs of Valabhi, dared to assume the Imperial right of issuing coins in their own name.

Mahārāja Hastin.

His Coins.

Saṅkshobha, the son of Hastin, issued a grant of land in 528. The fall of the Parivrājaka chiefs as well as of the kings of Uchchakalpa was probably due to the sudden rise of Yaśodharman of Mālava.

Saṅkshobha.

VI. Yaśodharman

This chief is known from three inscriptions discovered in the vicinity of the city of Mandasor, the ancient Daśapura, which was the capital of Western Mālava in the early mediæval period. Nothing is known about his antecedents. He claims to have crushed Mihirakula and overrun the entire country from the banks of the River Lauhitya (Brahmaputra) and the hill called Mahendra (Ganjam District) in the east to the Western Ocean, and from the Himalayas in the north to the Vindhya Mountains. Yaśodharman is known, from one inscription, to have been reigning in the Vikrama year 589 = 533.

Yaśodharman defeats Mihirakula.

His Date.

An earlier generation of writers supposed that Yaśodharman formed a coalition with the emperor Narasiṁhagupta Bālāditya and defeated Mihirakula at Kahror in Western Panjab about 528. This theory was based on Indian tradition as recorded by Yuan Chwang more than a century afterwards. But the recent discoveries of the inscriptions of Kumāragupta II and Budhagupta at Sarnath have proved beyond doubt that the emperor Narasiṁhagupta Bālāditya ceased to reign in 473. The theory is therefore no longer tenable, but it is quite possible that Yaśodharman allied himself with the chief named Bālāditya who is mentioned in the Sarnath inscription of Prakaṭāditya. The same chief is probably mentioned in the Deo-Banarak inscription of Jivitagupta II. We do not know anything about his successors. Probably some of them succeeded to the kingdom of Mālava, but his empire passed into the hands of other people. In the north the Guptas of Magadha, the Maukharīs of Kanauj, and the Varddhanas of Thāneśar occupied the country between the Satlej and the Brahmaputra, and the vast empire of Yaśodharman melted away as quickly as it had been formed.

Older Theory of the Defeat of the Hūṇas,

disproved by Sarnath Inscription.

VII. The Guptas of Magadha *

Govindagupta.

Govindagupta, the younger brother of Emperor Kumāragupta I, was the ruler of the western provinces of the Gupta Empire under the latter. An inscription referring to him has

* See p. 309.

been discovered in Mālava, from which we know that this prince was alive in the Mālava-Vikrama year 524 = 467. His descendants selected Magadha, the home province of the ancient Guptas, as the sphere of their activities. His son Harshagupta and his grandson Jīvitagupta I most probably served under Skandagupta and Budhagupta. His great-grandson Kumāragupta III is said to have fought with the Maukharī king Īśānavarman. At this time the Maukharīs were at the height of their power. Īśānavarman was reigning in the Vikrama year 611 = 554. This date is one of the fixed points in the chronology of the later Guptas of Magadha.

Kumāra-gupta III.

Damodaragupta, the son and successor of Kumāragupta III, also fell in a battle with the Maukharīs. He was succeeded by his son Mahāsenagupta, who turned the tide of victory in favour of his own dynasty and reconquered the whole of Northern Bengal. He defeated Susthitavarman of Kāmarūpa, or Assam, on the banks of the Brahmaputra, and re-established the former glory of the Gupta Empire. His sister Mahāsenaguptā was married to Ādityavarddhana of Thāneśvar, and her son Prabhākaravarddhana obtained supreme power in Northern India during the closing years of the sixth century.

Damodaragupta and the Maukharī War.

Mahāsenagupta and the Assam War.

Most probably Śaśaṅka was the eldest son of Mahāsenagupta. This prince started issuing gold coins of a new type in his own name and tried to restore the glory of the empire of the early Guptas. He combined with Devagupta of Mālava, and advanced upon the Maukharī stronghold of Kanauj. The ruling Maukharī chief, Grahavarman, who had married Rājyaśrī, the daughter of Prabhākaravarddhana, was defeated and killed by Devagupta, and Kanauj was occupied. At this time Prabhākaravarddhana died and was succeeded by his eldest son Rājyavarddhana. Before Śaśāṅka could join Devagupta, the latter had been defeated by Rājyavarddhana, who in turn was defeated and killed by Śaśāṅka. Rājyavarddhana was succeeded by his younger brother Harshavarddhana. This young prince succeeded in winning over Mādhavagupta, the younger brother of Śaśāṅka (?), and in forming a coalition with King Bhāskaravarman of Assam. Śaśāṅka was defeated and expelled from North-eastern India. The current accounts about his death heard by Yuan Chwang in

Śaśāṅka.

Attack on Kanauj.

Defeat and Death of Rājyavarddhana II.

Coalition against Śaśāṅka.

Magadha are incorrect. Śaśāṅka was reigning over Orissa in 619, i.e. thirteen years after the accession of Harsha, and the latter's attempts to destroy Śaśāṅka's power ended in failure. Śaśāṅka was helped by Pulikeśin II of the Chālukya dynasty of Badami, and Harsha was defeated in the southern part of Orissa.

Śaśāṅka allies himself with Pulikeśin II.

Mādhavagupta.

After the expulsion of Śaśāṅka from Eastern India, the kingdom of Magadha fell to the lot of Mādhavagupta, who reigned as a feudatory of the kings of Thāneśvar. His son Ādityasena assumed Imperial titles and became independent after the death of Harsha in 647. Ādityasena was alive in the year 66 of the Harsha era, i.e. 672. Like his ancestors he was a Vaishṇava. His mother, Queen Śrīmatī, erected a monastery at Aphsad in the Gaya District, close to a temple of Vishṇu built by Ādityasena. His wife, Queen Koṇadevī, excavated another tank on top of the Mandāra Hill in the Bhagalpur District of Bihar and Orissa. This tank is to be found at the foot of the steps leading to the top of the hill and is now called *Pāpahāriṇī.*

Ādityasena.

Vaishṇava Monastery at Aphsad.

Koṇadevī's Tank at Mandāra.

The subsequent history of the Guptas of Magadha is very obscure. Ādityasena was succeeded by his son Devagupta and his grandson Vishṇugupta. His great-grandson Jīvitagupta II was the last king of the Gupta dynasty, and after his death Eastern India became a prey to anarchy. Jīvitagupta II made a grant of land to the temple of the god Varuṇasvāmin at Deo-Banārak in the Shahabad District of Bihar. Eastern India was overrun by the neighbouring princes after the death of Jīvitagupta II.

The Last Kings.

VIII. The Maukharis of Kanauj

The Maukharis are a people of great antiquity and existed as a clan or tribe in the second century B.C. The founder of the dynasty was a chief named Harivarman. His son Ādityavarman was born of his queen named Jayasvāminī. Ādityavarman married Harshaguptā, who was evidently the daughter or sister of Harshagupta of Magadha. The latter was succeeded by his son Īśvaravarman, who defeated the king of the Andhras and advanced towards the south-west as far as

Conquest of Īśvaravarman.

Dhārā in Mālava and Raivataka Hill (Girnar). A reference to the Andhras is also to be found in the Harāhā inscription of Īśānavarman of 554. These Andhras appear to be the people of the Telugu country who lived on the borders of the Maukhari kingdom.

Īśānavarman, the son and successor of Īśvaravarman, defeated Kumāragupta III of Magadha and advanced in the east as far as the sea coast of Bengal. In the south he defeated the Śulikas of Northern Orissa and the Andhras of the Telugu country. On the west the Maukharīs carried on a long war with the Hūṇa chiefs of the Panjab. Śarvavarman, the son and successor of Īśānavarman, defeated and killed King Dāmodaragupta of Magadha in the east and also defeated the Hūṇas on the west.

Conquests of Īśānavarman.

War with the Guptas.

Śarvavarman.

There is a gap in the chronology of the Maukharī dynasty after Śarvavarman and Anantavarman. A king named Avantīvarman ruled over the country to the west of the Son, but his exact relationship to the last two kings cannot be determined. Avantīvarman's son Grahavarman married Rājyaśrī, the daughter of Prabhākaravarddhana of Thāneśvar. He was killed by King Devagupta of Mālava during the reign of his brother-in-law Rājyavarddhana. The Maukharīs disappeared as a local dynasty of Northern India with the rise of Harshavarddhana.

Avantīvarman.

Grahavarman.

IX. The Kings of Kāmarūpa

Very few records of the kings of Kāmarūpa have come down to us, and the earliest mention of them is found in the Nidhanpur plates of Bhāskaravarman. This Bhāskaravarman was the contemporary of Harshavardhana, and at the time of the latter's accession he was only a *Kumāra*. His grant enumerates a dynasty consisting of eleven kings, beginning with Pushyavarman Of these eleven kings Bhāskaravarman himself, and his father, grandfather, and great-grandfather are mentioned in the *Harsha-charita* of Bāṇabhaṭṭa. In the inscription of Ādityasena, Bhāskara's father Susthitavarman is mentioned as the contemporary of Mahāsenagupta of Magadha.

Bhāskaravarman.

His Ancestors.

Nothing is known about the remaining rulers of this dynasty. They claimed descent from the Asura king Naraka through his son Bhagadatta, who was a contemporary of Duryodhana of the *Mahābhārata*. The part which Bhāskaravarman played in Harsha's campaign in Eastern India will be narrated in the next chapter. The plates which inform us of these particulars were issued from Karṇasuvarṇa (in Western Bengal), and according to Yuan Chwang that town was the capital of Śaśāṅka. The grant referred to on the plates was made, apparently, in the reign of Harsha (606–649). Of King Bhāskara's successors we know nothing.

His Conquest of Western Bengal.

BIBLIOGRAPHY

Jouveau Dubreuil, *History of the Deccan.*

F. Kielhorn, "List of Inscriptions of Northern India", *Epigraphia Indica*, Vol. V, Appendix, and Vol. VII, Appendix i.

V. A. Smith, *Early History of India* (4th ed.), chap. xii.

D. R. Bhandarkar, "List of Inscriptions of Northern India" *Epigraphia Indica*, XXI, XXII.

CHAPTER IV

NORTHERN INDIA IN THE BEGINNING OF THE SEVENTH CENTURY

Harshavarddhana

In the closing decades of the sixth century the chiefs of Thāneśvar or Sthāṇvīśvara, near Kurukshetra, became very powerful. They succeeded in curbing the power of the Maukharis and interposing a powerful buffer state between the kingdom of Kanauj and the territories of the Hūṇas to the west. Ādityavarddhana of this family married the princess

The Kings of Thāneśvar.

Mahāsenaguptā of Magadha, whose father Dāmodaragupta had been killed in battle while contending with the Maukharī king Śarvavarman. His son Prabhākaravarddhana assumed Imperial titles and succeeded in imposing his suzerainty upon the whole of Northern India. He had two sons and a daughter. The last was married to Grahavarman, son of King Avantīvarman of Kanauj, of the Maukharī dynasty.

Early in the beginning of the seventh century we find Prabhākaravarddhana sending an army to the northern regions in order to chastise the Hūṇas. This army was placed under the command of his eldest son Rājyavarddhana. A second army, under the king's younger son Harsha, followed as a reserve. When the princes were absent, Prabhākaravarddhana fell ill, and Harsha, receiving this news, returned hastily to court. Prabhākaravarddhana died shortly afterwards and was succeeded by his eldest son Rājyavarddhana, on the latter's return from the Hūṇa campaign. The death of Prabhākaravarddhana acted as a signal to subordinate princes on all sides to assume independence. The princes of the Imperial Gupta dynasty were still ruling in different parts of the country. The king of Mālava, Devagupta, hastily formed an alliance with King Śaśāṅka of Bengal and fell upon the kingdom of Kanauj, then under the rule of Grahavarman, who was killed, while his wife Rājyaśrī was imprisoned. The capture of Kanauj was probably due to a surprise, as Devagupta attacked it while Śaśāṅka was still at a distance. As soon as news of the murder of Grahavarman and the imprisonment of Rājyaśrī was received at Thāneśvar, Rājyavarddhana advanced with a mobile column of ten thousand horse, leaving the infantry and the elephants in the charge of Harsha. The former easily succeeded in driving out Devagupta, but was in turn defeated by Śaśāṅka of Bengal, who had arrived in the interval. In a duel between Śaśāṅka and Rājyavarddhana, the latter was killed. Bānabhaṭṭa, the paid historiographer of the court of Thāneśvar, denounces this duel in very strong terms, and modern historians have followed him in calling the slaying of Rājyavarddhana a treacherous murder. But in the two grants of Harshavarddhana the event is correctly described as a duel. Rājyavarddhana is said in these two inscriptions to have given up his

Death of Prabhākaravarddhana.

Devagupta of Mālava.

Campaign in the Gangetic Doab.

Defeat and Death of Rājyavarddhana

life in the house or the camp of the enemy, according to dictates of law (*Dharm-ānurodhena*). Harsha did not assume the crown immediately after the death of Rājyavarddhana. According to the Chinese historical work named *Fang-chih*, Harsha administered the kingdom jointly with his widowed sister Rājyaśrī till 611. Subsequently when Harsha assumed Imperial titles an era was reckoned from the date of Rājyavarddhana's death, and denominated the era of Śrī-Harsha. This era is so called by the Musalman traveller Al-Bīrūni. Immediately after assuming kingship Harsha advanced towards Kanauj and succeeded in rescuing his sister, who had escaped to the Vindhya Hills where she was in hiding. The details of his campaign against Śaśāṇka have not been recorded. Evidently it was of long duration, and at first Harsha could make very little headway against his powerful opponent.

Campaign against Śaśāṅka.

The true history of the eastern war of Harsha can be gleaned only from contemporary records. Before beginning his campaign in Eastern India, Harsha took the precaution of allying himself with the kings of Kāmarūpa, the hereditary enemies of the Guptas of Magadha. Susthitavarman, who had been defeated by Mahāsenagupta, was succeeded by his eldest son Supratishṭhitavarman, but the real power fell to the prince Bhāskaravarman, a younger brother of the king. The kings of Kāmarūpa cherished a deep-rooted hatred of the Guptas of Magadha, and Bhāskaravarman sent an embassy to Thāneśvar under a reliable officer named Haṁsavega. Harsha allied himself with the king of Kāmarūpa and received valuable presents. Śaśāṅka was thus attacked from both flanks and compelled to retire from Magadha. At this time another traitor appeared in his camp. Mādhavagupta, who was most probably his younger brother, joined Harsha, and his defection compelled Śaśāṅka to leave Bengal and Bihar for Orissa. The kingdom of Śaśāṅka extended from the banks of the River Son to Southern Orissa. We find that thirteen years after the death of Rājyavarddhana, Śaśāṅka was still ruling on the eastern coast and was recognized as suzerain by Mādhavavarman II of the Śailodbhava family of the Koṅgoda District (Ganjam).

Harsha's Alliance with the King of Kāmarūpa.

Śaśāṅka driven out of Magadha and Bengal.

Throughout his reign Śaśāṅka continued to be a thorn in the

side of Harsha. He was never completely subjugated. After his defeat in Bengal, Śaśāṅka allied himself with the Chālukya king Pulikeśin II of Badami, who defeated Harsha on the eastern coast some time before 634. Harsha was repeatedly compelled to invade the Ganjam District, which in the seventh century was called the Koṅgoda *maṇḍala*. In 642 he had just returned home after a long campaign there. Yuan Chwang records this when telling us of his own invitation to Assam, as guest of Bhāskaravarman, on the eve of his departure for China.

Śaśāṅka's Alliance with Pulikeśin II.

Harsha's Campaign in Koṅgoda.

Harsha tried to penetrate into Southern India by another road. He advanced as far as the banks of the River Narmadā, but on the Khandesh side of that river the fords were strongly guarded by the Chālukyas under Pulikeśin II, and Harsha's attempts to conquer Southern India were once more foiled. On the western coast he invaded the kingdom of Valabhi in the peninsula of Kathiawad, and Dhruvasena II, the king, was compelled to fly to Broach. The Gurjara king Dadda II (Praśāntarāga) of Broach allied himself with Pulikeśin II and reinstated Dhruvasena II. Harsha gave one of his daughters in marriage to the latter and retired. Mālava and Kathiawad were thus not included in his kingdom. The whole of Bengal was temporarily occupied by King Bhāskaravarman of Assam, and Mādhavagupta of Magadha ruled over Bihar. The actual kingdom of Harsha therefore extended from the banks of the River Son to the Eastern Panjab.

Harsha's Campaign in South-western India.

Extent of his Kingdom.

In 641 Harsha sent to China an ambassador who returned in 643 with a Chinese mission. This mission remained in India till 645. Harsha died in 647, leaving no heir to inherit his kingdom. After his death the kingdom of Kanauj fell to his cousin Bhaṇḍī, the son of his mother's brother. Taking advantage of the anarchy which followed the great king's death, Arjuna, one of Harsha's ministers, attacked the Chinese embassy and plundered it. Wang-hiuen-tse, the head of the Chinese mission, fled to Nepal and brought back a Tibetan army with which he captured Arjuna and took him a prisoner to China.

Exchange of Missions with China.

Death of Harsha.

Fight with the Chinese Mission.

Harsha spent the whole of his youth in constant warfare. No special praise is devoted to him in any Indian work except his incomplete life by his court poet Bāṇabhaṭṭa. In his later days he turned religious and, like all Indian kings, spent huge sums of money on religious charities. For this munificence he is praised very lavishly by Yuan Chwang. A good deal of light is thrown on the state of India in the seventh century by the records of the Chinese traveller Yuan Chwang. Yuan Chwang wrote an account of India, called the *Si-yu-ki*, and his friend Hwui Li wrote his biography after his death. Both of these works contain detailed and interesting remarks about the state of India, its geography, history, condition of the people, trade routes, and the foreign relations of its kings. A certain amount of information regarding the early history of Harsha and his period is also available from the incomplete prose-poem of Bāṇabhaṭṭa, entitled the *Harsha-charita*. The genealogy of the dynasty can be obtained from the seals of Harsha discovered at Sonpat and Nālandā. Two grants of Harsha have been discovered, which supply the name of that king of Mālava who killed Grahavarman.

Materials for the History of the Period.

Harsha himself was a man of tireless energy. He moved quickly from place to place, and stayed at his capital during the rainy season only. Like Aśoka, Harsha became a Buddhist monk in his old age. He led the life of a devout Buddhist, and enforced the prohibitions of the Buddhist law with very great strictness. He tried to copy Aśoka to a very large extent. Rest-houses were built on the roads, and physicians were stationed in them. In spite of Harsha's patronage the Buddhist religion was then on the decline. He himself worshipped Śiva, Sūrya, and Buddha with equal devotion.

Harsha's Character.

Harsha held quinquennial assemblies at Prayāga or Allahabad, and Yuan Chwang was present at one of these held in 643. They were attended by all feudatory chiefs and nearly half a million people, and lasted for nearly three months. On the opening day an image of Buddha was worshipped. On the second and third days Śiva and Sūrya were worshipped. On the fourth day ten thousand Buddhists received costly gifts, and during the following twenty days gifts were distributed among the Brāhmaṇas. The next ten days were devoted to the distribution of similar gifts to the Jains. Yuan Chwang records that with the exception of Harsha's

The Quinquennial Assemblies

elephants and military accoutrements, which were necessary for maintaining order and protecting the royal estate, nothing was retained. The king gave away his ornaments and jewellery and even his clothes. Finally he begged second-hand garments from his sister Rājyaśrī and, having donned them, worshipped Buddha.

Yuan Chwang left India shortly after the assembly of 643, and the sources of the history of the period are thereafter very scanty. The empire founded by Harsha was not consolidated even at the time of his death. The great feudatory chiefs assumed independence immediately after his decease. Northern India became divided into a number of petty states and relapsed into that state into which it had fallen after the decline of the early Gupta Empire. Harsha was a great patron of literature and a poet of no mean order. He composed three dramas called the *Nāgānandam*, the *Priyadarśikā*, and the *Ratnāvalī*. The poet Rājaśekhara states that a poet called Bhāsa wrote the *Priyadarśikā* and sold it to Harsha. The commentary of Nāgojī Bhaṭṭa on the *Kāvya-prakāśa* contains a similar account. The poet Dhāvaka also is said to have sold the authorship of his work to Harsha. Both statements are unreliable. Harsha was a patron of Bāṇa, whose great works, the *Kādambarī* and the *Harsha-charita*, hold high places in Sanskrit literature. Harsha was also the patron of the poet Bhartṛihari, and Bāṇa's brother-in-law, the poet Mayūra, is also said to have lived at his court. Very few monuments built by Harsha or belonging to his reign have been discovered, and we do not know anything of the state of sculpture, painting, and art in general in the seventh century.

Harsha's Literary Attainments.

His Patronage of Literature.

BIBLIOGRAPHY

WATTERS, *On Yuan Chwang*, Vols. I and II.
Harshacharita, translated by Cowell and Thomas.
R. K. MOOKERJI, *Harsha* (Rulers of India Series).
V. A. SMITH, *Early History of India* (4th ed.), chap. xiii.

CHAPTER V

THE SOUTHERN DYNASTIES OF THE EARLY MEDIÆVAL PERIOD

In the beginning of the sixth century the history of Southern India assumed a definite form. Just as the mediæval history of Northern India begins with the rise of the early Guptas in the fourth century, so the mediæval history of Southern India begins with the decline of the Pallavas and the rise of the Chālukyas of Badami.

I. The Pallavas

According to some scholars, the Pallavas of Southern India were a people of northern origin and were most probably the same as the Pahlavas of the inscriptions of Rudradāman I. Very little is known about their migrations from the north to the south, where they established a powerful kingdom on the eastern coast. They are mentioned in the Pāṇḍu-Leṇā cave inscription of the nineteenth year of the Sātavāhana king Vāśishṭhīputra Puḷumāvi. It is now generally accepted that the power of the Sātavāhanas came to an end in the first half of the third century, and Professor Jouveau-Dubreuil is inclined to place that event in 236. The same scholar is also inclined to think that the Pallavas obtained their kingdom in Southern India by intermarriages with the Sātavāhana kings, and that they reigned at Amarāvatī, in the Kṛishṇā district on the eastern coast, in the first half of the third century. The earliest known Pallava kings are known to have reigned at Kāñchī, modern Conjeeveram, to the south of the Kṛishṇā. A king named Śivaskandavarman was reigning at Kāñchī, and his kingdom extended over nearly the whole of the Southern Deccan. It included the province of Sātāhaṇī, i.e. the home province of the Sātavāhanas. This proves that the Pallava kingdom extended from Amarāvatī, on the eastern coast, to Bellary, near Bijapur. Another inscription discovered in the Guntur district mentions a king named Vijayaskandavarman,

Origin of the Pallavas.

Date of the Extinction of the Sātavāhanas.

Śivaskandavarman.

his son Vijayabuddhavarman, and his wife Chārudevī, who made a gift to the temple of Nārāyaṇa at Dalura. Śivaskandavarman and Vijayaskandavarman appear to have been ruling in the third century. **Vijayaskandavarman.**

Early in the fourth century we find Vishṇugopa as the King of Kāñchī. He fought with Samudragupta. Very little is known about the Pallava kings of Kāñchī, but from Sanskrit inscriptions we know that a Pallava dynasty ruled in the Telugu country over the district of Karmma, which, later on, was included in the kingdom of the Eastern Chālukyas of Veṅgī. Six generations of kings of this dynasty are known to have ruled in the fifth century. **The Pallavas of Kāñchī.**

In the sixth century we find, reigning at Kāñchī, a new dynasty which begins with a king named Siṁhavishṇu, who conquered the Choḷa country and invaded South-eastern and South-western India. He was succeeded by his son Mahendravarman I, who was defeated by the early Chālukya king of Bādāmi. This king appears to have been a Jain at first and to have been converted to the Śaiva cult by the saint Appar. When the northern provinces of his kingdom were conquered by Pulikeśin II, Mahendravarman I retired to the Tamil districts. He was succeeded by Narasiṁha I, who defeated Pulikeśin II of Bādāmi in three pitched battles and destroyed the Chālukya capital at Bādāmi. This king is also said to have conquered the island of Ceylon and defeated the kings of the Pāṇḍya, Kerala, and the Choḷa countries. At this time Mahāvalipuram became the base of the Pallava navy, and a second expedition was sent to Ceylon in the second half of the seventh century. Narasiṁha I was succeeded by his son Mahendra II, about whom we know nothing. He was succeeded by his son Parameśvaravarman I, who assumed the title of Vikramāditya after defeating Vikramāditya I of the Chālukya dynasty, in the battle of Peruvalanallur in the Trichinopoly District. Vikramāditya I had invaded the Choḷa country and camped on the banks of the River Kāverī. The southern kingdoms combined against him and the king of Ceylon joined them. He retired discomfited. Parameśvaravarman was succeeded by his son Narasiṁha II, also named Rājasiṁha, who married a lady named Raṅgapatākā. Some of **Siṁhavishṇu of Kāñchī.** **Mahendravarman I.** **His Conversion by Appar.** **Narasiṁha I defeats Pulikeśin II.** **His Campaigns in South India and Ceylon.** **Parameśvaravarman I.** **Battle of Peruvalanallur.** **Narasiṁha II.**

the temples at Kāñchī were built during the reign of this king.

Narasiṁha II was succeeded by two of his sons, Parameśvara II and Mahendra III. Parameśvara II most probably

Parameśvara II.

built the temple of *Vaikuṇṭha-Perumal* at Kāñchī, and the building of the *Kailāsanātha* temple at the same place is

Nandivarman.

also attributed to him. He was succeeded by Nandivarman, who defeated the eastern Chālukyan king, Vishṇuvarddhana III of Veṅgī, and subdued the kings of the Śavaras and the Nishādas. This king reigned for at least fifty years. The Pallava kings who followed Nandivarman are known as the Gaṅga-Pallavas. Hultzsch and Venkayya take them to belong to a separate family altogether, but Professor Jouveau-Dubreuil holds that the first Gaṅga-Pallava king, Dantivarman, was a direct descendant of Siṁhavarman.

II. Early Chālukyas of Badami [1] *

Before the rise of the early Chālukyas, Western India was divided among the Kadambas, the Naḷas, and the Mauryas. Pulikeśin I became the king of a small tract of country to the south of the River Kṛishṇā. He belonged originally to a place called Indukānti and migrated to Badami, a place in the southern part of the modern district of Bijapur. This

Badami.

district most probably belonged to the Kadambas, from whom it was wrested in the middle of the sixth century. According to the inscription of his son, Pulikeśin I performed the

Later Genealogies of the Chālukyas.

horse-sacrifice. Like the early Guptas of Northern India, the early Chālukyas were orthodox Hindus, and had as their crest the image of the Boar (*Varāha*) incarnation of Vishṇu. In later times, when they had spread all over the Deccan, the Brāhmaṇas invented a special genealogy for them.

Pulikeśin I.

Pulikeśin I married Durlabhadevī of the Batpura family, and his power was confined to the surrounding country be-

Kīrtivarman I.

tween the Kṛishṇā and the Malaprabhā. He was succeeded by his eldest son Kīrtivarman I in 566. This prince laid the foundations of the subsequent greatness of the Chālukyas. He overran the whole of the eastern coast as far as Bengal in the north and the Pāṇḍya and Choḷa countries in the

[1] Also called the Western Chālukyas of Badami. * See p. 316

extreme south. In these regions he claims to have conquered the Magadha, Vaṅga, Aṅga, Kaliṅga, Gaṅga, Draviḍa, Choḷa, and Pāṇḍya countries. On the western coast he conquered Banavāse (northern part of the Mysore State), Mushika (southern part of the Travancore State), Kerala (the Malabar coast), and destroyed the kingdoms of the Naḷas (Bellary and Karnul), the Mauryas of Northern Konkan, and the Kadambas (Belgaum and Dharwar Districts). Kīrtivarman I married a princess of the Sendraka family. The date of his accession is fixed by the statements in the long inscription of his younger brother Maṅgaleśa in cave No. IV Badami. This inscription was incised in 578, which corresponded to the twelfth year of his reign.

Kīrtivarman I left two sons, but he was succeeded by his younger brother Maṅgaleśa in 596. The principal event of Maṅgaleśa's reign was the conquest of the northern part of the Deccan plateau, which was being ruled by the Kaḷatsurīs or Kaḷachurīs. During the lifetime of his elder brother, Maṅgaleśa excavated a large hall and temple for the family deity, Vishṇu, on the hillside below the citadel of Badami. Maṅgaleśa was killed during a war with his nephew Pulikeśin II, while trying to secure the succession for his own son. In his old age he set up a marble pillar at Mahākūṭa near Badami and inscribed the principal events of his reign on that pillar.

Maṅgaleśa.

Killed by his Nephew Pulikeśin II.

Maṅgaleśa died in 608 and was succeeded by his nephew Pulikeśin II, the greatest king of this dynasty. During the civil war between uncle and nephew, the conquered provinces had rebelled. The earlier part of the reign of Pulikeśin II was spent in suppressing that rebellion. He laid siege to Banavāse and to Elephanta, the capital of the Konkan. He subdued the Gaṅgas, the Lāṭas, the Gurjaras of Broach, and the whole of the Deccan plateau. In the north-east the kings of Kośala and Kaliṅga submitted to him, and the country thus conquered brought Pulikeśin II into contact with Harshavardhana, emperor of Northern India. On the eastern coast Pulikeśin II besieged and stormed Kāñchī. These events took place before 634. In 636 Harsha invaded Kathiawad, and Pulikeśin II allied himself with Śaśāṅka of Bengal and his feudatory, Sainyabhīta-Mādhavavarman II of Koṅgoda, and with the

Campaigns of Pulikeśin II.

Coalition against Harsha.

Façade of Cave No. II, excavated out of a hill at Badami, Bijapur district, Bombay Presidency, by Pulikeśin II of the Early Chālukya Dynasty

kings of Valabhi and Broach on the west. With this combination he was able to defeat Harsha with very great ease in 637 and 638. On the eastern coast Pulikeśin II installed his younger brother Vishṇuvardhana as the viceroy of the newly conquered territory, with his capital at Vēṅgī, and the latter founded the independent dynasty of the Eastern Chālukyas. Pulikeśin II obtained great influence in India and outside by thwarting the designs of Harshavardhana over Southern India. Khusru II of Persia exchanged presents and letters with him and sent an embassy which is supposed to have arrived in 635. **Exchange of Embassies with Persia.**

The end of Pulikeśin II was disastrous. The Pallavas of Kāñchī rallied under Narasiṁhavarman I and defeated Pulikeśin II at the battles of Pariyala, Manimaṅgala, Suramara, and other places, finally sacking Badami or Bātāpīpura, the Chālukyan capital. Pulikeśin II died during these wars. These events took place some time after the visit of Yuan Chwang to the Deccan in 640 and the accession of Vikramāditya I in 655. One of the most important events of the reign of Pulikeśin II was the foundation of a collateral branch of the Chālukyas in Gujarat. The splendid temples at Aihole and Pattadkal in the Bijapur District, especially the beautiful Meguti temple, were built during his reign. **Defeat of Pulikeśin II by the Pallavas.** **The Chālukyas of Gujarat.**

The supremacy of the early Chālukyas was re-established by Vikramāditya I, a son of Pulikeśin II, who inflicted a crushing defeat upon the Pallavas and captured their capital, Kāñchī. According to one of his inscriptions, this king defeated the Pallava kings Narasiṁhavarman I, Mahendravarman II, and Parameśvaravarman II. During these long struggles, extending from 642 to 670, the country between Badami and Conjeeveram (Kāñchī) was sacked and pillaged by the contending armies. After destroying the supremacy of the Pallavas, Vikramāditya I went to the extreme south and humbled the pride of the Choḷas, Pāṇḍyas, and Keralas. In his wars he was assisted by his son Vinayāditya and his grandson Vijayāditya. The Pallava war was actually over before 671, according to the Naosari grant of Śryāśraya-Śilāditya of the Gujarat branch. Vikramāditya I was succeeded by his son Vinayāditya in 680. **Vikramāditya I.**

Vinayāditya had fought under his father in the extreme south as well as in Gujarat. He was succeeded in 696 by his son Vijayāditya, who also had been engaged in the extensive campaigns of his grandfather. Vijayāditya assisted his father in his northern campaign and is said to have acquired for him the emblems of the Gaṅgā and Yamunā rivers. He built the great temple of Vijayeśvara at Pattadkal in the Bijapur District. That building is now called the temple of Saṅgameśvara. In 730 Vijayāditya granted a village called Kardama to a Jain teacher named Niravadya-Udayadeva, who belonged to the Devagaṇa of the Mūlasaṅgha and was a pupil of Pūjyapāda. The latter was probably the author of the *Jainendra-vyākaraṇa*. Vijayāditya was succeeded by his son Vikramāditya II in 734. This prince married two princesses of the Haihaya family. One of these princesses, Loka-mahādevī, built the great temple of Śiva at Pattadkal called the temple of Virupāksha. Her sister Trailokya-mahādevī built another temple called Trailokyeśvara in the same place. The outstanding exploit of Vikramāditya II was his conquest of Kāñchī. He defeated the Pallava king Narasiṁhavarman II and gave great wealth to the temple of Rājasiṁheśvara at Kāñchī. A defaced inscription of Vikramāditya II has actually been discovered in the temple of Rājasiṁheśvara at Kāñchī, thus proving that the statement in the Aihole inscription about his conquest of the Pallavas is no empty boast. During this period Gujarat was invaded constantly by the Arabs of Sindh. Sindh had been conquered by Muhammad bin Qāsim in 712, but the power of the kings of Valabhi was not destroyed till 770. Before 739 a Musalman army had invaded Gujarat. Vikramāditya II had already invaded Sindh, Cutch, Sorath, and Broach. The Arabs, who were known in India as Tājikas, advanced as far as Naosari, where they were defeated by Vikramāditya's kinsman and feudatory, Avanījanāśraya-Pulikeśin.

Buildings of the Early Chālukyas

Vijayāditya.

Vikramāditya II.

Defeats the Pallava Narasiṁhavarman II and occupies Kāñchī.

Arabs ravage Gujarat.

Vikramāditya II was succeeded in 747 by his favourite son Kīrtivarman II, who was the last king of this dynasty. Another son of Vikramāditya II was the ancestor of Taila II, who revived the Chālukya dynasty in 973. The inscriptions of Kīrtivarman II are to be found only south of the Bhīmā,

Vikramāditya II.

thus proving that he had already lost the Chālukya dominions in the Northern and Eastern Deccan to the Rāshṭrakūṭas. He was defeated by the Rāshṭrakūta king Dantidurga some time after 757.

The early Chālukyas of Bādāmī were orthodox Hindus, and under their fostering care the Brahmanical religion revived as it had done under the Guptas in the north. Sacrifices mentioned in the Vedas were performed by many of the earlier kings, and magnificent temples were erected at Badami Aihole, and Pattadkal in the Metropolitan District. This state patronage led to a gradual decline of Buddhism in the Deccan. The Digambara Jainism, however, became in the meantime the favourite faith of the masses. The early Chālukyas were great patrons of art, and the most magnificent fresco paintings of Ajanta, and the famous cave temples of Elephanta and Badami, were executed in their time. Their political relations extended as far as Persia in the west, and for nearly two centuries they were the absolute masters of the foreign trade of the western coast, because all ports of the Arabian Sea, from Cambay in the north to Mushika in the south, belonged to them.

Patronage of Brāhmaṇism.

Decline of Buddhism.

Early Chālukya Art.

Western Trade.

III. The Kadambas

The Kadamba dynasty of Banavāse was founded by Mayūraśarman, who took advantage of the internal disorder of the Pallava kingdom caused by the invasion of Samudragupta. The kingdom was therefore founded in the middle of the fourth century, and its capital, Banavāse, was an important centre of the Kanarese country. One of the kings defeated by the Vākāṭaka king Rudrasena II was that of the Kuntala country, which is another name of the Banavāse District. It is generally believed that Kaṅgavarman, the son of Mayūraśarman, was defeated by Rudrasena II.

Mayūraśarman.

Eight generations of kings of this dynasty ruled over the Kanarese country till they were overthrown by the early Chālukya king Pulikeśin I in the middle of the sixth century. Harivarman, the last of the line, is probably the Kadamba chief mentioned in the inscription of Pulikeśin I. The Kadambas survived as petty chiefs throughout the supremacy of the eastern Chālukyas of Badami, the Rāshṭrakūṭas of Malkhed, and the western Chālukyas of Kalyāṇī. In the eleventh and twelfth centuries they established independent kingdoms at Goa and Hangal.

IV. The Kaḷatsurīs or the Kaḷachurīs

Immediately before the rise of the early Chālukyas of Badami, a dynasty of kings who called themselves the Kaḷatsurīs or Kaḷachurīs ruled over Mālava and the Northern Deccan. We do not know anything about the origin of this line of kings except that they used the era of the Traikūṭakas. From inscriptions of the Kaḷatsurī king Śaṅkaragaṇa and his son Buddharāja, we learn that they ruled over a very large area. Śaṅkaragaṇa had his capital at Ujjain in Western Mālava, but his kingdom extended over the Northern Deccan as far as the Nasik District. His feudatory Nirihullaka ruled over the lower Narmadā valley in 580. Northern Deccan was conquered from Śaṅkaragaṇa's son Buddharāja by the early Chālukya king Maṅgaleśa some time before 601. Even in 609 Buddharāja was ruling over Mālava, and Vidiśā (Bhilsa) was included in his kingdom. In 610 Ānandapura (Anand in the Kaira District) was included in it, and he possessed complete control over the Bharukachchha *Vishaya*, i.e. the Broach District. The Kaḷatsurī power in Gujarat was destroyed by Pulikeśin II of Badami.

Saṅkaragaṇa.

V. The Rāshṭrakūṭas of Malkhed *

The Rāshṭrakūṭas existed as a subordinate dynasty during the height of the power of the early Chālukyas of Badami. Govindarāja I, the grandson of Dantivarman I, was probably a contemporary of Pulikeśin II, and attempted to secure independence at the time of the struggle between Pulikeśin and his uncle Maṅgaleśa. Dantivarman II or Dantidurga secured the country between the Godāvarī and Bhīmā during the reign of Vikramāditya II of the early Chālukya dynasty of Badami. Some time before 753 practically the whole of the Deccan

* See p. 317.

came into the possession of the Rāshṭrakūṭas. The earliest royal grant issued by Dantivarman II is dated A.D. 753. The latest date of Kīrtivarman II is 757. After 757 the Chālukya sovereignty was wiped out even in the Kanarese country. Simultaneously with the conquest of the Deccan, Southern Gujarat was conquered by Kakkarāja II, and we find Surat in his occupation as early as 757. In an inscription discovered in the caves of Ellora, Dantivarman or Dantidurga is credited with the conquest of the Kāñchī, Kaliṅga, Kośala, and the Śrīśaila country, i.e. the Karnul District. He was succeeded by his uncle Kṛishṇarāja I. He must have been an old man when he ascended the throne, because during his lifetime his son and heir-apparent, Govindarāja II, issued a grant of land in his own name in 770. He excavated the celebrated rock-cut temple of Śiva called Kailāsa at Ellora.

Dantivarman II. **His Conquest of the Eastern Coast.** **Kṛishṇarāja I.** **The Excavation at Ellora.**

Kṛishṇarāja I was succeeded by his son Govindarāja II, after a short reign. Govindarāja II was reigning in 779, and his feudatory Karkarāja was ruling over the Northern Deccan in that year. This king was deposed by his younger brother Dhruvarāja. Dhruva was a powerful prince, and during his reign the Rāshṭrakūṭas came into conflict with the Gurjaras of the Indian Desert. After the fall of the Chālukyas of Gujarat, the Arabs had been driven back to the delta of the Indus, and upon the foundation of a separate Rāshṭrakūṭa principality in Southern Gujarat the Gurjaras came into conflict with the former. Vatsarāja of the Gurjara dynasty of Bhinmal (in the Jodhpur State) overran the whole of Northern India. From a statement in the Jain *Harivaṁśa Purāṇa* we learn that in 783, a king named Indrāyudha was ruling in the north, Śrīvallabha, son of Kṛishṇarāja (I) in the south, and Vatsarāja in the west. Vatsarāja became so powerful that he defeated the king of Bengal and carried away the double white royal umbrellas of that king. He possessed a third umbrella, which had been taken from the king of Kośala. This powerful king was defeated by Dhruva, who captured the double white royal umbrellas of Bengal and compelled the Gurjara king to retire into the desert. Dhruvarāja's reign was short, and he was succeeded, some time before 794, by his son Govinda III.

Govinda II. **Dhruva.** **The Gurjara War.** **Vatsarāja and his Conquests.** **Dhruva defeats Vatsarāja**

Govinda III. By defeating his brother and rival Stambha or Khambayya, Govinda became the most powerful king in the Deccan. In the south he destroyed the western Gaṅga king Mārasalba and defeated Dantivarman of Kāñchī. At this time his aid was invoked by Dharmapāla of Bengal and his protégé Chakrāyudha. Nāgabhaṭa II, the son of Vatasarāja, had combined the petty Gujara tribes. Dharmapāla was defeated and Indrāyudha was replaced on the throne of Kanauj (see p. 232). At this juncture Chakrāyudha and Dharmapāla appealed to Govinda III, and the latter invaded Northern India. Nāgabhaṭa II suffered a crushing defeat at the hands of the allies and was forced to retire to his desert fastness. Govinda directed his nephew Karkarāja-Suvarṇavarsha, the viceroy of Gujarat, to prevent the recurrence of a similar feat by the Gurjara king. The northern campaign of Govinda III took place before 808. Govinda III raised the Rāshṭrakūṭas from the position of a mere local dynasty to that of the paramount power in India The Eastern Chālukyas of Veṅgī had submitted to him, and his dominions extended as far as the southern bank of the River Narmadā in the north and the Tuṅgabhadrā in the south. Govinda was succeeded by his son Amoghavarsha I in 814.

War with Gaṅgas and Pallavas. **The Gurjara Confederacy.** **Northern Campaign of Govinda III.** **Defeat of Nāgabhaṭa II and Dharmapāla.** **Extent of the Rāshṭrakūṭa Kingdom under Govinda III.**

Amoghavarsha I. Amoghavarsha I was undoubtedly the greatest king of the dynasty, and though he was not so fortunate in war as his father, he repeatedly humbled the Eastern Chālukya kings of Veṅgi. He was a great patron of learning, and spent the riches amassed by his ancestors in improving his kingdom. He founded the city of Mānyakheṭa, now a small village called Malkhed in the eastern part of the Nizam's dominions. The northern part of the Konkan was then under the rule of the Śilāra chief Pullaśakti. The celebrated port of Bharukachchha or Broach, on the Narmadā, came into the possession of the Rāshṭrakūṭas. In the north the Gurjara power revived under Bhoja I. Dhruvarāja II, the viceroy of Gujarat in 867, claimed to have defeated Bhoja I; but most probably he merely prevented an incursion of the Gurjara army to the south of the Narmadā. Amoghavarsha I could not prevent the conquest of Northern India by the Gurjaras under Bhoja I, who transferred his capital from Bhinmal to Kanauj.

Gurjara Invasion of Gujarat.

Amoghavarsha turned Jain and became one of the most liberal patrons of the Digambara sect. According to a Jain work called the *Uttara-Purāṇa*, he was the disciple of a Jain ascetic named Jinasena, the author of the *Pārśv-ābhyudaya*, which was composed during the reign of Amoghavarsha I. A Jain philosophical work entitled *Jayadhavala* was composed in 837. In a Jain mathematical work called the *Sārasaṁgraha*, by Vīrāchārya, Amoghavarsha I is called a follower of the *Syādvāda* doctrine of the Jains. He himself composed a small religious tract, called the *Ratnamālikā*, which exists in a Tibetan translation. He reigned for at least sixty-three years and was succeeded by his son Kṛishṇarāja II. **Amoghavarsha becomes a Jain.**

Kṛishṇa II married a daughter of Kokalla I, the founder of the Haihaya or Chedī kingdom of Central India. Evidently the death of Amoghavarsha I was followed by civil war between his sons, and during this period Kṛishṇarāja II was supported by his father-in-law. It appears, therefore, that for nearly a quarter of a century after the death of Amoghavarsha I the succession to the throne was disputed. During this period Kṛishṇa II was mentioned only once, in an inscription discovered in Gujarat. Kṛishṇa was on very good terms with the Chedīs or Haihayas, but during the earlier part of his reign his capital was burnt by the Eastern Chālukyas of Veṅgī, with whom he was constantly at war. In the northern part of his dominions, Kṛishṇa II suffered a reverse at the hands of the Gurjaras, who were most probably helped by his relations, the Rāshṭrakūṭas of Gujarat. He came to the throne in 878, and was still ruling in 911. He died at some time between 911 and 914, and was succeeded by his grandson Indra III. Indra III revived the power and glory of the Rāshṭrakūṭas, which had suffered a temporary eclipse during the reign of his grandfather. He invaded Mālava, the southernmost province of the Gurjara Empire of Kanauj, and sacked Ujjain. He then attacked the centre of the Gurjara Empire and destroyed its capital, *Mahodaya* or Kanauj. Mahīpāla I, the grandson of Bhoja I, fled towards the east and was pursued by Indra's general, the Chālukya chief Narasiṁha, as far as Prayāga or Allahabad. This was the first serious reverse suffered by the

The Civil War. **Wars with the Chālukyas of Veṅgī.** **The War in Gujarat** **Invasion of Mālava.** **Conquest of Kanauj.** **Flight of Mahīpāla I.**

Gurjaras of Kanauj, and the destruction of their capital cost them loss of prestige.

Indra returned to the Deccan and was shortly followed on the throne by his son Amoghavarsha II, who reigned for a year, and then by his younger brother Govinda IV, who reigned till 933. Govinda IV took to a vicious life, which ruined his constitution and weakened the government. After the death of Govinda IV, Amoghavarsha III was raised to the throne. He was a younger brother of Indra III, and therefore the uncle of Govinda IV. Amoghavarsha III had married Kuṇḍakadevi, a daughter of the Chedī king Yuvarāja I. While residing at Trīpurī he married his eldest daughter Revakanimmāḍi, the eldest sister of Kṛishṇa III, to the Western Gaṅga chief Buṭuga II. He died after a very short reign and was succeeded by his son Kṛishṇa III.

Govinda IV.

Amoghavarsha III.

Kṛishṇa III was the last of the Rāshṭrakūṭa emperors of Southern India. He ascended the throne some time between 933 and 940. One of his first acts was to depose the Western Gaṅga King Rāchamalla I and to place his younger brother Buṭuga II on the throne. Mārasiṁha II, one of the younger sons of Buṭuga II, conquered Northern India for Kṛishṇa III. In the north the latter extended his kingdom as far as the centre of the Chandella and Chedī kingdoms. He set up a pillar of victory at Maihar, between Allahabad and Jubbulpur. In the south Kṛishṇa III defeated the Pallava king Anniga and the Choḷa king Rājāditya-Muvāḍi-Choḷa at the battle of Takkola. In the south-east he advanced as far as Kāñchī and Tanjore. Kṛishṇa III reigned for more than a quarter of a century and was succeeded by his younger brother Khoṭṭiga. This prince was alive in 971, and was succeeded in the next year by his nephew Kakkarāja II or Amoghavarsha IV. Within a few years Indrarāja IV, the son of Kṛishṇa III, was placed on the throne by the Western Gaṅga chief Mārasiṁha II. Three kings had succeeded Kṛishṇa III within twenty years, and in the troublous times which followed, Taila II, the son of Vikramāditya IV, destroyed the power of the Rāshṭrakūṭas in the Deccan. The last Rāshṭrakūṭa king, Indra IV, died seven years after the victory of Taila II, in 982.

Northern Campaign of Kṛishṇa III.

Southern Conquest.

Khoṭṭiga.

Amoghavarsha IV

Indra IV.

Overthrow of the Rāshṭrakūṭas.

The defeat of the Rāshṭrakūṭas was followed by a division

of the Deccan plateau and the Konkan into a number of petty states. Taila II belonged to the western branch of the Chālukya dynasty, and his successors did not succeed in imposing their suzerainty upon all the powerful feudatory chiefs of the Rāshṭrakūṭa Empire. In Northern Gujarat another Chālukya family founded an independent kingdom at Anahilapāṭaka. The Konkan, or the flat country at the base of the Deccan plateau, was divided by the Śīlāhāras into two parts. The northern Śilāhāras had their capital at Thana or Sthānaka; the southern Śilāhāras ruled over Ratnagiri, and a third branch established itself at Karhad in the Satara District and in the Kolhapur State. The interior of the northern Kanarese District contained the powerful kingdom of the Raṭṭas of Saundatti. The Kādambas founded two kingdoms in the southern Kanarese country with their capitals at Hangal, in the Dharwar District, and at Goa. Some of these feudatories later on acknowledged the suzerainty of the Western Chālukyas of Kalyāṇī, but most of them remained semi-independent.

BIBLIOGRAPHY

SIR R. G. BHANDARKAR, *Early History of the Deccan.*
JOUVEAU DUBREUIL, *History of the Deccan.*
JOUVEAU DUBREUIL, *The Pallavas.*
R. GOPALAN, *Pallavas of Kanchi.*
R. D. BANERJI, "The Northern Conquests of Krishna III", *Journal, Bihar and Orissa Research Society*, Vol. XIV, 1928.

CHAPTER VI

THE EARLY MEDIÆVAL CULTURE OF SOUTHERN INDIA

The long rule of the Pallavas formed a link between the early and the mediæval art of Southern India. The Pallava art connects the Mathurā school of sculpture with that of Amaravatī, in which northern influence is undeniable. Very

Northern Influence on Pallava Art.

few remains of the early Pallava period have come to light; the majority of the specimens of Pallava architecture at Kāñchī and Māmallapuram belong to the later mediæval period. Fragments of sculpture discovered between the mouths of the Godāvarī and the Kṛishṇā on the eastern coast are the only known specimens of this period.

Pallava Architecture.

The Temples of Kāñchī.

The mediæval examples of Pallava architecture are the earliest known examples of southern architecture. They were the models on which Javanese temple architecture was based. The temples at Kāñchī are still used for public worship, and the way in which they have been modernized makes it very difficult for a student of art to imagine their pristine condition. The best examples of Pallava architecture of Kāñchī are the temples of Tripurāntakeśvara and Airāvateśvara. Of the other temples at the same place those of Kailāsanātha and Mukteśvara bear striking resemblance to the earlier group of the monolithic temples at Māmallapuram. The two temples by the sea-shore at Māmallapuram, though later in date than the monolithic temples excavated out of the rock, belong to the same type as the Rājasiṁheśvara and Mukteśvara temples of Kāñchī. We therefore possess a complete series of illustrations of early and late mediæval architecture of the Pallava period in the temples on the rock and sea-shore at Māmallapuram.

Māmallapuram.

Māmallapuram, or Mahābalipuram, is the name of a small island on the eastern coast nearly fifteen miles east of Chingleput and more than fifty miles to the south of Madras city. The island is divided from the mainland by a narrow creek navigable at all seasons of the year. On account of its natural harbour, this creek appears to have been one of the principal ports and dockyards for the Pallava navy. The ruins on the island consist of structures of two different classes, monolithic temples and cave temples.

The Monolithic Temples.

The earliest of the monolithic temples are small structures carved out of small boulders, such as *Draupadī's ratha*, which has a roof like that of a thatched hut. From this simple design grew up the more elaborate *Gopuram*-shaped roof, *Arjuna's ratha*, which is also a square structure like *Draupadī's ratha*. More ambitious structures like *Bhīma's ratha* and *Dharmarāja's ratha* grew out of this simple design. *Bhīma's ratha* is perhaps the largest monolithic temple on this island. It is oblong in shape, and its outline shows that it is the precursor of the ambitious *Gopurams* of the gigantic temples at Tanjore, Madura, and Śrīraṅgam. The cave temples at Māmallapuram resemble the group of early caves on the Trichinopoly rock. The *chef-d'œuvre* of Pallava art is the magnificent bas-relief near the Kṛishṇamaṇḍapam at Māmallapuram. The entire rock-surface available has been covered with representations of men and animals, among which the most striking figures are those of two elephants inside a large cave. The figures are realistic and show great vigour of execution.

Origin of the "Go-puram."

The Great Bas-relief of Māmal-lapuram.

At Māmallapuram and Kāñchī we see the beginnings of South Indian temple architecture, which developed later on into a special type on lines quite different from those of the northern architecture. What the early Guptas did for Northern India, was done for Western India by the early Kaḷatsurīs and the early Chālukyas of Badami. The early mediæval monuments of Western India fall into three isolated groups. The earliest group includes the mediæval caves of Ajaṇṭā; the second group the cave temples of Konkan, such as those at Elephanta, Mandapeśvara or Montpezir, and those of the second group at Kānherī. The third group consists of the caves of Badami and Aihole, and the celebrated temples of Pattadkal and Aihole in the Bijapur District of the Bombay Presidency. The temples and caves of the third group belong entirely to the period of the early Chālukyas of Badami, and form the second best group of examples of South Indian art.

Prototypes of Early Javanese Architec-ture.

The Cave Temples of Western India.

Elephanta.

Badami.

The best examples of early Chālukyan architecture are the caves and temples of Aihole, Pattadkal, and Badami. Cave No. IV at Badami is perhaps the best example of the Vaishṇava cave-temple in the whole of India. This magnificent work was carved out of the rock some time before 578 by Maṅgaleśa, the younger brother of Kīrtivarman I. Cave No. I of this group is a Śiva temple, and all caves of this group bear bas-reliefs of the western type which culminated in the bas-reliefs of the Kailāsa cave at Ellora. The beginnings of early mediæval South Indian painting are to be found in the Cave No. IV at Badami. All bas-reliefs of this cave were painted, and its ceiling was decorated with elaborate Tantric figures

Early South Indian Painting.

(*Yantras*) used in the worship of Vishṇu. These paintings betray an undeniable connexion with the decorative art found in the ceilings of the Ajaṇṭā caves.

Early Painting at Ajaṇṭā. The paintings in the Ajaṇṭā caves fall into three distinct groups. The paintings in the earliest groups have for the most part disappeared. They are to be found on the walls and the ceilings of caves with Brāhmī inscriptions. The fragments of votive inscriptions in painting of the second class indicate that they were executed during the reigns of the early Chālukya monarchs of Badami. These inscriptions are painted on the frescoes as labels. To the third class belongs the latest painting in the cave at the end of the horseshoe-shaped ravine in which the Ajaṇṭā caves were excavated. Painting exists on the ceilings of the front porch on the higher level or the second storey of the great Kailāsa cave at Ellora, and similar paintings are to be found in several of the Kāṇherī caves which were excavated along the great ravine to the south, or left, of Cave No. III. Such paintings on Deccan trap involved a special preparation of the ground. In the majority of the caves at Ajaṇṭā the rock-surface was smoothed. It was then plastered thinly with some adhesive substance which clung tenaciously to the rock.

Mediæval Painted Inscriptions.

Painting in the Kailāsa Cave, and at Kāṇherī.

Art of Ajaṇṭā. The art of Ajaṇṭā reveals a finished product after centuries of culture and cultivation. The lines of the drawing are very vigorous, the knowledge of the pigments and of the standard of the mixture betray very great skill. The subjects treated

Subjects. are various. Every available bit of space has been made use of. The art is mainly decorative; but mixed with dados, panels, arabesque works, and other details, there are long frescoes covering entire lengths of wall-space and devoted to the representation of Buddha's life. The subjects of the Ajaṇṭā paintings have not been scientifically analysed until recently, and reliable identifications were made by M. Foucher only in the present century. Eminent artists are of opinion that the line work of the majority of the Ajaṇṭā paintings is very vigorous and decisive, and this characteristic denotes a great

Character of the Ajaṇṭā Paintings South Indian. advance in India over the contemporary art of Italy and Southern Europe. The human figures and the scenery depicted in the frescoes at Ajāṇṭā are typically southern. The dress of the men and women, their forms and features, have no connexion with Northern India; the architecture, too, is southern, and possesses very little connexion with northern architecture of any period.

Belonging to the same period as the second group of the

Buddha the Teacher—Fresco from later caves, Ajaṇṭā—*circa* 6th century A.D.

Ajaṇṭā caves are the temples on the hill of Badami and those at Aihole and Pattadkal. The temples on the fort-rock at Bādāmī appear to be the earliest examples of early Chālukyan temple architecture. They are simply enlarged replicas of *Arjuna's ratha* at Māmallapuram. The temples at Aihole and Pattadkal are, however, adorned with magnificent sculptures, bas-reliefs, and decorative carvings. Of this group the temples

The Temples of Aihole and Pattadkal.

The Meguti Temple.

at Aihole are better known. The Meguti temple is perhaps the second dated temple of the early Chālukya period. It is slightly later in date than Cave No. IV at Badami, as it was erected in 634 during the reign of Pulikeśin II. The old temple, which is now called Lad Khan's temple, consists of pillars with thin slabs between them, and is built on the same plan as the early Gupta temples at Nachna-kuthara and Bhumra, i.e. it is partly two-storied, and the central part is surrounded by a closed veranda. The Jain temple near the temple of Virupāksha and the Meguti temple resemble *Dharmarāja's ratha* at Māmallapuram. Others show the beginning of a *śikhara* or spire, like the later temple at Nachna-kuthaṛa. The most remarkable temple of the entire group is the Durgā temple, which is built on the plan of the earlier Buddhist Chaitya-halls or Cathedrals. Sir John Marshall discovered similar ones at Sanchi and Taxila.

Lad Khan's Temple. **The Jain Temple.** **The Apsidal Temple of Durgā.**

The design of the excavations at Ellora divided them into three separate groups, each belonging to a separate religion. The right side of the entire façade was given to the Buddhists, and here we find Chaitya-halls like those at Kārlā or Kāṇherī; but in these Chaitya-halls we find that the great horseshoe-shaped opening in the centre has been reduced in size. The centre of the hill is occupied by the great Kailāsa temple, excavated by the Rāshṭrakūṭa king Kṛishṇarāja I. The Kailāsa is a unique Hindu temple. It is perhaps the largest excavation in the world and consists of a single-storied Maṇḍapa, a double-storied *Sabhā-maṇḍapa* with three side porches, in the centre of a huge courtyard surrounded by long halls or corridors on all three sides, full of bas-reliefs and images, while the fourth side is occupied by an artificially built porch. From its bold design and magnificent execution this stupendous monolithic temple is rightly an object of wonder. It is remarkable not only for its vast size, but also for the delicacy of its bas-reliefs, at the base of the double-storied *Sabhā-maṇḍapa*. The Hindu or Brāhmaṇical group contains many other magnificent temples which would have been regarded as stupendous in any other place, but at Ellora they are dwarfed by the massive proportions of the Kailāsa. Many of those magnificent cave-temples, such as the Daśāvatāra cave, the

Situation of Ellora. **The Kailāsa Cave.** **The Brāhmaṇical**

Rāmeśvara cave, and the Dhumarlena cave, contain large and important bas-reliefs. The extreme left of the Ellora Hill is occupied by Jain caves. These are full of decorative details which tire the eye and though some of them are very large, yet they are neither so attractive nor so elegant in outline as those just described.

and the Jain Caves at Ellora.

During this period the Hindu religion revived in Southern India also. The leader of Hindu reform in South-western India was Śaṅkarāchārya, a Brāhmaṇa of the Malabar country, the founder of the Advaita school of Vedānta philosophy. His disciples spread all over India and founded four great monasteries called Śaṅkara-maṭhas, at Puri in the east, at Joshimath, north of Haridwar in the Himalayas, at Sringeri in the south, and at Dwarka in the west. The abbots of these monasteries are called Śaṅkarácháryas. Another great scholar and reformer was Kumārila-bhaṭṭa.

In the extreme south of the Indian Peninsula the Hindu religion became divided, very early, into two warring factions, the Śaivas and Vaishṇavas, but both sects were hostile to the Jains and Buddhists. The Śaiva missionaries are called Aḍiyārs and the Vaishṇava ones Āḷvars. Buddhism was driven out of the Indian Peninsula by the activities of these missionaries, who preached to the masses, wrote, very often in the vernaculars, and ultimately became more powerful than the Brāhmaṇas, who followed the Vedic religion very strictly. These Āḷvārs and Aḍiyārs are now regarded as saints.

BIBLIOGRAPHY

J. FERGUSSON and J. BURGESS, *The Cave Temples of India*, London, 1880.

E. B. HAVELL, *Indian Sculpture and Painting*, London, 1908.

V. A. SMITH, *History of Fine Art in India and Ceylon* (2nd ed.) edited by K. de B. Codrington.

CHAPTER VII

INDIA OF THE SEVENTH CENTURY, AS DESCRIBED BY YUAN CHWANG (HIUEN-TSANG)

After the establishment of the Kushan Empire a continuous stream of pilgrims started from China in the hope of reaching the Buddhist Holy Land. They continued to come till the conquest of Western China by the Tibetans in the eighth century. Beginning from Sung-yun and ending with I-tsing, many of these Chinese travellers have left excellent accounts of the countries through which they passed, and of India.

Yuan-Chwang. Yuan Chwang is the best known among them on account of his long stay in India, his piety and learning, and the valuable collection of Buddhist Sanskrit manuscripts which he carried away from India to China. Yuan Chwang quitted China at the age of twenty-eight or twenty-nine, in September, 629,

His journey to India. crossed the Central Asian desert, and reached India through Tashkend and Samarkand. He then passed through Balkh and crossed the Hindu-Kush, arriving at Kapiśā near Kabul, where for the first time he saw Indians. In 631 and 632 Yuan Chwang resided in Kashmir. In 634 we find him residing at Chīnabhukti in the Eastern Panjab. The next two years he spent in the United Provinces, residing for the most part at Kanauj, the capital of King Harshavardhana. In 637 he reached Magadha, the Buddhist Holy Land, and visited all of the Buddhist *Tīrthas* then known. In 639 Yuan Chwang passed along the eastern coast to Kaliṅga and finally reached

His Travels in India. Kāñchī. In 641 he reached Badami and, after visiting some of the cave-temples, returned to Nālandā in 643. The remaining months of the year 643 were spent in the company of King Harshavardhana, whom he quitted in April, arriving at Khotan in September, 644. After a long and arduous journey across the Hindu-Kush, the River Oxus, and the Central Asian desert, Yuan Chwang reached China in 645, after a total absence of more than fifteen years.

The general description of India is to be found in the second

Chuan of the *Si-yu-ki*. From this description we learn that the southern part of Afghanistan, consisting of the valleys of Kabul, Ghazni, and Kandahar, which lay to the south of the Hindu-Kush range, was included in India. Indian cities were surrounded by a quadrangular wall, "broad and high, while the thoroughfares are narrow tortuous passages. The shops are on the highways and booths (or inns) line the roads. Butchers, fishermen, public performers, executioners, and scavengers have their habitations marked by distinguishing signs. They are forced to live outside the city and they sneak along on the left when going about in the hamlets. As to the construction of houses and enclosing walls, the country being low and moist most of the city walls are built of bricks, while walls of houses and enclosures are wattled bamboo or wood. Their halls and terraced belvederes have wooden flat-roofed rooms, and are coated with chunam, and covered with tiles burnt or unburnt. They are of extraordinary height, and in style like those of China. The (houses) thatched with coarse or common grass are of bricks or boards, their walls are ornamented with chunam; the floor is purified with cow-dung and strewn with flowers of the season; in these matters they differ from us. But the Buddhist monasteries are of most remarkable architecture. They have a tower at each of the four corners of the quadrangle and three high halls in a tier. The rafters and roof-beams are carved with strange figures, and the doors, windows and walls are painted in various colours. The houses of the laity are sumptuous inside and economical outside." [1]

Description of Indian Towns and Villages.

Buddhist Monasteries.

Yuan Chwang found Buddhism on the decline. Buddhists were divided into eighteen schools. "Wherever there is a community of Brethren it makes its own rule of gradation. The Brother who expounds orally one treatise (or class of scripture) in the Buddhist Canon, whether Vinaya, Abhidharma, or Sūtra, is exempted from serving under the Prior; he who expounds two is invested with the outfit of a superior; he who expounds three has Brethren deputed to assist him; he who expounds four has lay servants assigned to him; he who expounds five rides an elephant; he who expounds six

State of Buddhism in India.

[1] Watters, *On Yuan Chwang*.

rides an elephant and has surrounding retinue. Where the spiritual attainments are high, the distinctions conferred are extraordinary."[1]

Condition of Monasteries.

The eighteen schools always differed in opinion, and there were frequent controversies among them. "For offences against the Vinaya the Community of Brethren has a gradation of penalties. If the offence is slight a reprimand is ordered. For an offence next above this in gravity there is added a

The seven past Buddhas and Maitreya, dedicated by a Chinese pilgrim, with a Chinese inscription, at Bodh-Gaya, now in the Indian Museum, Calcutta (10th century A.D.)

cessation of oral intercourse with the Brethren. When the offence is serious the punishment is that the Community will not live with the offender, and this involves expulsion and excommunication. Expelled from a Community, the monk has no home; he then becomes a miserable vagrant, or he returns to his first estate."[2]

Caste and Kingship.

Yuan Chwang notices the four great castes, and says that intermarriage between the castes and between relations by the father's or the mother's side was prohibited. Widow-marriages were not known, but mixed castes were already in existence. Even at that time the kingship was already re-

[1] *Ibid.*, p. 162. [2] *Ibid.*, pp. 162-3.

stricted to the Kshatriyas, but men of other castes had rebelled and assumed the distinction of kingship. "The national Guard (lit. warriors) are heroes of choice valour, and, as the profession is hereditary, they become adepts in military tactics. In peace they guard the sovereign's residence, and in war they become the intrepid vanguard.

"The army is composed of Foot, Horse, Chariot, and Elephant soldiers. The war-elephant is covered with a coat-of-mail, and his tusks are provided with sharp barbs. On him rides the Commander-in-chief, who has a soldier on each side to manage the elephant. The chariot in which an officer sits is drawn by four horses, whilst infantry guard it on both sides. The infantry go lightly into action and are choice men of valour; they bear a large shield and carry a long spear; some are armed with a sword or sabre and dash to the front of the advancing line of battle. They are perfect experts with all the implements of war such as spear, shield, bow and arrow, sword, sabre, &c., having being drilled in them for generations."[1]

The Army.

Trials and Ordeals.

The criminal class was small. Offences against social morality, disloyal conduct, and unfilial offences were punished by the cutting off of noses, ears, or a foot. Fines were imposed for other offences. Ordeals were practised in place of trial in certain cases. The principal ordeals were by water, by fire, by weighing, and by poison. "As the Government is generous, official requirements are few. Families are not registered, and individuals are not subject to forced labour contributions. Of the royal land there is a four-fold division; one part is for the expenses of government and state worship, one for the endowment of great public servants, one to reward high intellectual eminence, and one for acquiring religious merit by gifts to the various sects. Taxation being light, and forced service being sparingly used, everyone keeps to his hereditary occupation and attends to his patrimony. The king's tenants pay one-sixth of the produce as rent. Tradesmen go to and fro bartering their merchandise after paying light duties at ferries and barrier stations. Those who are employed in government service are paid according to their work. They

Government.

[1] *Ibid*, p. 171.

go abroad on military service or they guard the palace; the summonses are issued according to circumstances and after proclamation of the reward the enrolment is awaited. Ministers of state and common officials all have their portion of land, and are maintained by the cities assigned to them."[1]

Description of Harsha.

Yuan Chwang visited the courts of two of the greatest monarchs of India of the seventh century. He was very favourably received by the Emperor Harshavardhana of Kanauj; he was loaded with favours and treated with marked honours, and in his description of the city of Kanauj the Chinese pilgrim repeats the story which is known from Bāṇabhaṭṭa's *Harsha-charita* about the king's ancestry and his wars with Śaśāṅka, the king of Eastern India. Yuan Chwang speaks very highly of Harsha and his government. "He forgot sleep and food in his devotion to good works. He caused the use of animal food to cease throughout the Five Indias, and he prohibited the taking of life under severe penalties. He erected thousands of topes on the banks of the Ganges, established Traveller's Rest-houses through all his dominions, and erected Buddhist monasteries at sacred places of the Buddhists. He regularly held the Quinquennial Convocation; and gave away in religious alms everything except the materials of war. Once a year he summoned all the Buddhist monks together, and for twenty-one days supplied them with regulation requisites. He furnished the chapels and liberally adorned the common halls of the monasteries. He brought the Brethren together for examinations according to merit and demerit. Those Brethren who kept the rules of their order strictly and were thoroughly sound in theory and practice he advanced to the Lion's Throne (that is, promoted to the highest place) and from these he received religious instruction; those who, though perfect in observance of the ceremonial code, were not learned in the past, he merely honoured with formal reverence; those who neglected the ceremonial observances of the Order, and whose immoral conduct was notorious, were banished from his presence and from the country. The neighbouring princes, and the statesmen, who were zealous in good works and

The Quinquennial Assemblies.

[1] *Ibid.*, pp. 176–7.

unwearied in the search for moral excellence, he led to his own seat, and called 'good friends', and he would not converse with those who were of a different character. The king also made visits of inspection throughout his dominion, not residing long at any place but having temporary buildings erected for his residence at each place of sojourn, and he did not go abroad during the three months of the Rain-season Retreat. At the royal lodges every day viands were provided for 1000 Buddhist monks and 500 Brahmins. The king's day was divided into three periods of which one was given up to affairs of government, and two were devoted to religious works. He was indefatigable, and the day was too short for him."[1]

In the extreme south Yuan Chwang visited the capital of Pulikeśin II, king of the Deccan, and the caves of Ajaṇṭā. **Pulikeśin II.** He mentions in this connexion that Harshavardhana had failed to conquer Mahārāshṭra. Yuan Chwang spent nearly two years at Nālandā, now called Bargaon, in the Patna District of Bihar and Orissa. **Nālandā.** He found that many foreign students came to study there in the university and were examined before they were admitted. He mentioned some celebrated Buddhist teachers of the university, such as Guṇamati, Dharmapāla, and Śilabhadra. On his arrival at Nālandā, Yuan Chwang was presented to Śilabhadra, who made him over to his nephew Buddhabhadra. Yuan Chwang **The System.** resided with Buddhabhadra and describes the system of the great monastery of Nālandā. Students came to the university **Students.** not only to learn Buddhism, but also to study the Vedas, grammar, logic, and medicine. Śilabhadra was the most learned teacher at Nālandā at the time of Yuan Chwang's visit. One hundred villages supported the university and the monastery.

BIBLIOGRAPHY

WATTERS, *On Yuan Chwang.*
BEAL, *Buddhist Records of the Western World.*
BEAL, *Life of Hinen Thsang.*

[1] *Ibid.*, p. 344.

CHAPTER VIII

THE ORIGIN OF THE RAJPUTS AND THE RISE OF THE GURJARA EMPIRE

Origin of the Rajputs.

The origin of the Rajput tribes is still shrouded in mystery, but there cannot be any doubt that the Rajputs are a mixed race. They include many tribes which cannot be of Indo-Aryan origin. The Pratīhāras or the Parihars are really descended from Gurjaras or Gujars, a low-caste tribe, many of whom are regarded with contempt in the Panjab even at the present day. The Gujars followed the Hūṇas and invaded India through the north-western passes. Some of their tribes settled in Afghanistan, and a portion of that country is still called Guzaristan. A district in the Panjab is still called Gujarat. The ancient country of *Lāṭa*, consisting of the Ahmedabad, Kaira, Broach, Surat, and the Baroda District of the Bombay Presidency, received its modern name of Gujarat after the settlement of the Gujars in it. Gujarat still contains a very large racial element who are still called Gujars. In the north the Gujar kings of Bhinmal, who later assumed the clan name proves that they cannot be of pure Kshatriya origin. Moreover, Tod mentions certain tribes who are decidedly of southern origin; these are the Chālukyas or Śolāṅkīs and the Śilāhāras. Inclusion of all these among the Rajputs proves that the modern caste was composed of converted Hūṇa and Gurjara tribes, with a small admixture of Dravidians. There might have been a substratum of true Aryan Kshatriyas among them, but it is rather doubtful. The better class Rajputs of the present day claim to have originated from the sacrificial fire of Brahman on the Aravalli Mountains or from the heroes of the *Mahābhārata*. The Yādavas, the Sammās, and the Rāshṭrakūṭas claim to be descended from Kṛishṇa. The claim of the Śiśodīyās or Guhilots of Mewad to be the direct descendants of Rāma, and that of the Rathors of Jodhpur to be descended from the Gāhaḍavālas of Kanauj has been proved to be doubtful. The ten tribes, such as the Chauhans

Their Mixture of Blood.

Imaginary Account of the Origin of Rajput Tribes.

and the Pratīhāras, who claim to be descended from the sacrificial fire of Brahman, are really Hinduized Gujar and Hūṇa tribes, for whom Brāhmaṇa priests discovered a mythical origin after having converted them. A similar divine origin has been provided by Brāhmaṇas in modern times for the Mughal emperor Akbar I, the Mongolian Koch rājās of Coochbihar, and the beef-eating Shans or Ahoms of Assam. **fabricated by Brāhmaṇas.**

The earliest Rajput princes known to us are the Gurjara kings of Broach who occupied that country shortly after the fall of the Gupta Empire. They were most probably feudatories of the Gurjaras of Rajputana. We know very little about them except that Dadda I was a subordinate chief. His grandson Dadda II protected Dhruvasena II of Valabhi against Harsha of Kanauj. He ruled from 628 to 640. His great-grandson Jayabhaṭa III is the last known chief of the dynasty and was ruling in 736. The Gurjara kingdom of Broach was probably overthrown in the second half of the eighth century by the early Arab invaders. **The Gurjara Kings of Broach.**

I. The Pratīhāras of Bhinmal and Kanauj *

The Pratīhāras or the Gurjara-Pratīhāras of Southern Rajputana most probably founded a kingdom at the beginning of the seventh century. Their relations with the early Gurjara kings of Broach are not yet definitely known. The history of the dynasty is now chiefly known from the records of the later kings who ruled at Kanauj. The earliest king of the Gurjara dynasty of the Indian Desert was Nāgabhaṭa I. He is said to have defeated the Arabs of Sindh. He was succeeded by his brother's son Kakustha, who was succeeded by his brother Devaśakti, who appears to be the first important king of this dynasty. **Nāgabhaṭa I.** Vatsarāja, the son and successor of Devaśakti, united the Gurjara tribes of the desert and made a vehement attack on the princelings of Northern India. **Vatsarāja.** From Bhinmal, in the southern part of the Jodhpur State, he conquered Kanauj and defeated the kings of Bengal and Kośala. **His Northern Campaigns.** His pretentions to the Imperial rank received a severe check at the hands of the Rāshṭrakūṭa king Dhruva, who defeated him and compelled him to retire to the confines of the Indian desert. **Defeat by Dhruva.**

* See p. 309.

Dhruva instructed his nephew Karkarāja, the feudatory chief of Gujarat, to keep an eye on the Gurjara king. This Vatsarāja was alive in 783, and is mentioned in the *Jaina-Harivaṁśa-Purāṇa* as the contemporary of King Vallabha, the son of King Krishṇa, and Indrāyudha of Kanauj (see p. 260). Vatsarāja's son and successor, Nāgabhaṭa II, also played an important rôle in the political history of Northern India. In the last quarter of the eighth century Dharmapāla of Bengal invaded Kanauj and deposed Indrāyudha, the reigning monarch, whom he replaced by his own nominee Chakrāyudha. Indrāyudha fled for shelter to Nāgabhaṭa II, who once more organized a confederacy of the Gurjara tribes of the Panjab and Rajputana and drove out Dharmapāla and Chakrāyudha from Kanauj. Govinda III, son of Dhruva, joined Dharmapāla and Chakrāyudha and, like his father, once more drove the Gurjaras out. Nāgabhaṭa was alive in 815 and was succeeded by his son Rāmabhadra, who was probably kept confined to the desert.

Mention in the Jaina-Harivaṁśa. **Nāgabhaṭa II.** **The War in Kanauj.** **Nāgabhaṭa II conquers Kanauj, but is defeated by Govinda III.** **Rāmabhadra.**

In the middle of the ninth century the Gurjara power revived once more under the leadership of Bhoja I, the grandson of Nāgabhaṭa II. Bhoja removed his capital from Bhinmal in the Indian Desert to Kanauj, the capital of Northern India in the Middle Ages. His kingdom extended from Karnal in the Eastern Panjab to Northern Bengal in the east, and from the Himalayas to the banks of the Narmadā. The whole of this territory was acquired by Bhoja himself, as his ancestral dominions consisted of a few hundred miles of barren land in the present State of Jodhpur. Bhoja I was the pioneer of Rajput influence in Northern India, and from this time onwards Rajputs ruled over the whole of Northern India with the exception of Bengal and Bihar. Rajput chiefs were given large tracts of lands in the newly conquered dominions and settled down in their new homes. By the rise of Bhoja the power of the Rāshṭrakūṭas of the Deccan was humbled, and the successors of Amoghavarsha I were compelled to seek the aid of the Arabs of Sindh, the hereditary enemies of the Gurjaras of the Indian Desert. During the reign of Bhoja I the Gurjaras invaded Gujarat, some time before 867, but were repulsed by Dhruva-Dhārāvarsha, the Rāshṭrakūṭa viceroy of Gujarat,

Bhoja I. **The Gurjara Empire.** **Rise of the Rajputs.** **The Gurjaras invade Northern Gujarat.**

On the frontiers of the Pāla kingdom in the east, a long struggle went on between the Gurjaras and the Pālas, the latter suffering a crushing defeat in the battle of Mudgagiri or Munger. Bhoja I ruled over Northern India for a long period, more than half a century, and was succeeded by his son Mahendrapāla I.

The War in Bengal.

The Battle of Munger.

During the reign of Mahendrapāla, the Pratīhāra Empire extended as far as the peninsula of Kathiawad, and Mahendrapāla thus succeeded in separating two hereditary enemies of his family, the Arabs of Sindh and the Rāshṭrakūṭas of Malkhed. In Eastern India, Southern Bihar and Northern Bengal acknowledged the rule of Mahendrapāla. The death of Mahendrapāla I, in the first quarter of the tenth century, was the signal for a scramble among his sons for the throne. Mahendrapāla I was succeeded in the first instance by his son Bhoja II, with the aid of the Chedī or Haihaya chief Kokalla I; but he was very soon dethroned by his half-brother Mahīpāla I, who, with the aid of the Chandella chief Harsha, succeeded in conquering the whole of the empire. During this struggle most of the feudatories assumed independence, the Chālukyas of Gujarat and the Paramāras of Mālava being among the first to do so. The Chandellas continued to recognize the Pratīhāras as their suzerains for some time longer. During the rule of Mahīpāla I, the Rāshṭrakūṭa power in the south revived under Indra III, a great-grandson of Amoghavarsha I. The internal dissensions and the rebellions of the feudatories enabled the Rāshṭrakūṭas to overrun Mālava with ease. Indra III rushed straight upon Kanauj, the capital of the empire, and Mahīpāla I was forced to fly for safety towards Allahabad, but nevertheless the Rajput Empire suffered a severe loss of prestige. Even after this campaign, Kathiawad continued to be ruled by Gurjara viceroys. A Chāpa chief named Dharanivarāha ruled over Wadhwan in 914. In 915-16 the Musalman traveller Al-Masa'udī, an inhabitant of Baghdad came to India. He describes the extent of the Pratīhāra empire, the vast standing army, maintained by the Emperors, and their hereditary feud with the Rāshṭrakūṭas of the Deccan. Mahīpāla I was ruling over the empire in 931, and was succeeded

Mahendrapāla I.

The Gurjaras in E. India.

The Civil War.

Bhoja II.

Mahīpāla I.

Rāshṭrakūṭa Revival.

Indra III invades Mālava and Kanauj.

shortly afterwards by his sons. According to some scholars, Vināyakapāla was a quite different person from Mahīpāla and was his successor. Mahīpāla I was succeeded, according to this view, by his brother Vināyakapāla or Herambapāla, who was in possession of the capital, Kanauj, in 931. He was succeeded by his son Mahendrapāla II. This prince is only known from a single inscription discovered at Partabgarh in Southern Rajputana, and was living in 948. Two years later Kanauj fell to the lot of Devapāla, a son of Mahīpāla I, who was recognized as the ruling king by Nishkalaṅka, the governor of the Jhansi District. This Devapāla is mentioned in an inscription of the Chandella king Yaśovarman dated 954. Two years later Devapāla was succeeded by another king named Mahīpāla II, who was recognized as suzerain by the Yādava chiefs of Northern Rajputana, and is known from a single inscription discovered at Bayana in the Bharatpur State. Four years later we find another son of Mahīpāla I, named Vijayapāla, on the throne, All of these four princes appear to have been sons of Mahīpāla I and to have succeeded him within a short period of twenty or twenty-five years. Vijayapāla is also known from one inscription only, which is a land grant issued by a subordinate chief named Mathana for the maintenance of a god installed by him in memory of his mother. This assumption of the royal functions indicates that the Gurjara feudatories had practically become independent. In this inscription Vijayapāla is only recognized as his suzerain by the Gurjara-Pratīhāra chief of Rājyapura (Rājor in Alwar) in 960.

Mahendrapāla II

Devapāla.

Mahīpāla II.

Vijayapāla.

The vast fabric of the Gurjara-Pratīhāra Empire was reduced to the small local kingdom of Kanauj during the reign of this king. In Gujarat the Chālukya Mūlarāja assumed Imperial titles in 974, and was followed shortly by the Paramāra Vākpatirāja in Mālava. The Chandellas of Jejākabhukti assumed royal titles from the time of Yaśovarman. The Chedīs or Haihayas of Ḍāhala had thrown off their allegiance long ago. Only the minor Gurjara chiefs continued to recognize Vijayapāla and his son Rājyapāla. Vijayapāla appears to have reigned for a long time, as we find his son Rājyapāla on the throne of Kanauj in 1018. In that year Sultan Maḥmūd of Ghazni

Feudatory Chiefs assume Independence.

Sultan Maḥmūd and Rājyapāla.

invaded India and came to Kanauj after destroying Mathurā. Rājyapāla, evidently, was not supported by the feudatory chiefs and was compelled to submit to the conqueror. The temples were destroyed and the inhabitants killed or reduced to slavery. Gaṇḍa, the Chandella king, now organized an attack on the helpless Rājyapāla on account of his tame submission to the Musalmans. By his order the Kachchhapaghāta chief Arjuna of Gwalior killed Rājyapāla in battle.

Destruction of Kanauj.

Rājyapāla defeated and killed by Rajputs

After the destruction of Kanauj, Rājyapāla had removed the capital to the south of the Ganges. At this time the country to the south of the Ganges had passed into the possession of the Chedīs of Ḍāhala. In 1019 Maḥmūd started from Ghazni to take revenge on the Hindu chiefs for the murder of Rājyapāla. But Trilochanapāla, the son of Rājyapāla, was compelled by Gaṇḍa to fight on the side of the Hindus, and the new capital, Bari, was destroyed in 1020. Pratishṭhāna, on the opposite side of Prayāga or Allahabad, was sacked, but remained in the possession of Trilochanapāla till 1027. After this the remnants of the once magnificent empire of the Pratīhāras were wrested from them by the Chedī king Gāṅgeyadeva of Ḍāhala.

Maḥmūd's Campaign of 1019.

Trilochanapāla.

Gāṅgeya destroys the Pratīhāra Kingdom.

The Pratīhāra Empire became divided among the following Rajput powers: (1) the Chālukyas of Gujarat, (2) the Paramāras of Mālava, (3) the Chāhamanas or Chauhans of Ajmer, (4) the Kachchhapaghātas of Gwalior, (5) the Yādavas of Mathurā, (6) the Chedīs or Haihayas of Ḍāhala, and (7) the Tomaras of Delhi.

Divisions of the Rajput Empire.

As the leaders of the New Hindus or Rajputs, the Pratīhāras saved Northern India from the ravages of a Musalman conquest, and thus prevented the conversion of the entire population to the Musalman faith. Even when they were unimportant chiefs in the Rajputana desert they fought repeatedly with the Arabs of Sindh; it is true, with varying fortunes, but they always succeeded in keeping them at bay, till decline set in among the Arabs. In this fashion the Pratīhāras saved Indian religion and civilization from total extinction. The Pratīhāra Empire extended very nearly over the same area as that of the Guptas, and its duration from the time of Bhoja I to that of Mahīpāla I was also very nearly

Importance of Rajput History.

the same, but from the cultural point of view the Pratīhāra period is far less interesting to students on account of the comparative rudeness of the age.

Nature of Pratihāra Government. The Pratīhāra Government was more or less feudal in nature, and its rapid dissolution was due to the "centrifugal tendency" which is still observable among the Rajputs. The succession of governors was most probably hereditary, and unless the emperor or the head of the great tribal organization was very strong, his authority was nominal in the distant provinces. The fall of the Gupta Empire was probably followed by a declaration of independence by provincial governors and subordinate chiefs; but during the decline of the Pratīhāra Empire, the great tribal chiefs, such as the Chandellas, continued to profess nominal obedience, even after attaining independence.

II. The Rajput Kingdoms of Afghanistan and the Western Panjab

The Shāhiyas of Kabul. The earliest Muhammadan chroniclers have recorded that a dynasty of Turkish kings who claimed to be descended from Kāṇishka was ruling in Kabul when the Arabs appeared in Afghanistan. One of the kings of this dynasty was overthrown by his Brāhmaṇa minister, and the kingdom passed on to the Brāhmaṇas. We do not know anything about the history of the Hindu kings of Kabul except from the bare statements in Musalman Chronicles and from a few coins. The coins provide us with the names of some of the kings of this dynasty. The best known king was Sāmantadeva, whose coins are found in very large numbers on the frontier. There appear to have been several kings of this name, as coins were issued with the name of Sāmantadeva on them more than a century afterwards. The names of other kings are Spalapatideva and Amṛitadeva. According to Al Bīrūnī, the first dynasty was overthrown by Kallar, who is identified with Lallīya of the *Rājataraṅginī* of Kalhaṇa. He was succeeded by Kamaluka. A king named Sāmanta also belongs to this dynasty. After their defeat by the Musalmans in the Kabul valley the Shāhīyas removed their capital to Und, the ancient form of which was Udabhāṇḍapura. Bhīma-shāhī married his granddaughter Diddā to the Kāśmīra king Kshemagupta in the middle of the tenth century. The last Shāhīya king, Trilochanapāla, was defeated and overthrown by Maḥmūd of Ghazni in 1021–2. The Shāhīyas, therefore, survived in the Western Panjab for nearly a century and a half after the fall of Kabul, which was conquered from them in 871 by Yaqūb bin Lāith of the Saffārī dynasty.

Removal of the Capital to Und.

Bhima.

Mahmūd destroys the Shāhiyas of Und.

III. The Rajputs of Sindh

In Sindh also the history of the fall of the Rajput power is preserved in Musalman chronicles only. The Rajput kings of Sindh carried on long wars with the Musalmans of Seistan and Kandahar in the beginning of the eighth century. The country was divided into three different parts, viz. Upper Sindh, Middle Sindh, and the Delta. In the beginning of the eighth century the Rajput kings exercised a loose sovereignty over the whole of Sindh. The country was divided into a number of provinces, under separate governors who held the strongest positions in the country. The people in Upper and Middle Sindh were Buddhists, and they did not resemble the Rajput rulers in any way. In Lower Sindh the different communities lived separately under the Rajputs and were mostly traders. Ḍāhir, who was the king of the whole of Sindh in 711, was a Rajput of the Sammā (*Śāmba*) tribe of the Yādava clan. He had refused to punish the people of the Port of Dewal, who had captured some vessel carrying presents from Ceylon to Ḥajjāj, the Arab governor of Persia. In retaliation, the Arabs under Muḥammad bin Qāsim, after attacking it on three different occasions, obtained possession of Dewal. Encouraged secretly by the Buddhists of Sindh, this small band of Arabs conquered the whole of Sindh, which became a Muhammadan province. The Arabs of Sindh destroyed the Maitraka dynasty of Valabhi after 766, and the early Gurjara kingdom of Broach. Their bitterest opponents were the Gurjaras of the Indian Desert and the early Chālukyas of Badami.

Position of the Rajputs in Sindh.

The Sāmba Yādavas.

Buddhist Treachery and the Musalman Conquest.

Fall of Valabhi.

IV. The Tomaras of Delhi

Sources of Tomara History. **The Kings.** **The Chāhamāna Succession.**

Like the Shāhīyas of Udabhāṇḍapura and the Rajputs of Sindh, the Tomaras are known to us solely from the Muhammadan chronicles and a few coins. An inscription of the Musalman period, discovered in Palam near Delhi, mentions that the Tomaras were ruling over the province of Hariyāṇaka before the Chāhamānas. From the coins of the dynasty we know that Sallakshaṇapāla, Anaṅgapāla, and Mahīpāla belonged to it. In the eleventh century the Chāhamānas of Ajmer conquered the Tomara kingdom, and at the time of the Muhammadan conquest of Northern India the kingdoms of Ajmer and Delhi were united.

V. The Chandellas of Bundelkhand *

Harsha. **Khājurāho.**

Among the dynasties which rose on the ruins of the Pratīhāra Empire, that of the Chandellas of Bundelkhand was the most powerful. Its kings are known in inscriptions as the Chandellas of Jejākabhukti, i.e. the district of Jejā or Jayaśakti (*Jijhoti* in modern Hindī). The first prince of this dynasty who obtained real independence was Harsha. He sided with Mahīpāla I or Kshitipāla, and succeeded in placing him on the throne after deposing his stepbrother Bhoja II. Harsha married a Chāhamāna princess named Kañchhukā, and was the real founder of the greatness of the Chandellas. The earliest capital of the Chandellas was Kharjuravāhaka, modern Khājurāho, near Nowgong, in the Chhatarpur State of Central India. The later Chandellas had two other capitals, e.g. Mahoba, and Kālañjar.

Yaśovarman. **Conquest of Kālañjar.**

Like the Gurjaras, the Chandellas also were either of partial Hūṇa descent or Hūṇas converted to Hinduism, who claimed semi-divine origin like the Pratīhāras and the Chāhamānas. Harsha's son Yaśovarman acknowledged the suzerainty of Vināyakapāla in 955. He was specially fortunate in his campaign against the Chedīs, from whom he obtained the celebrated hill fort of Kālañjar. Yaśovarman built one of the celebrated temples at Khājurāho, and in it he installed a

* See p. 312.

famous image of Vishṇu given to him by Devapāla, the son of the Emperor Vināyakapāla of Kanauj. This image was known as Vaikuṇṭha and was given to the King of Tibet. The King of Tibet presented it to the King of Kangra valley, and the latter gave it to Herambapāla or Vināyakapāla in return for some elephants or horses.

Yaśovarman's Temple at Khājurāho.

Temple of Śiva-Khījurāho, Chhatarpur State, Central India—built by Chandella kings in the 11th century A.D.

Dhaṅga.

Dhaṅga, the son of Yaśovarman, became the most powerful king in Northern India at the end of the tenth century. He built two temples of Śiva at Khājurāho called Marakateśvara and Pramathanātha in 1002. Dhaṅga joined the confederacy of the Hindu kings against Sabuktegīn, in favour of the Shāhīya king Jayapāla. He was succeeded by his son Gaṇḍa, who was the contemporary of Rājyapāla of Kanauj and Sultan

His Temples.

Ganḍa. Maḥmūd of Ghazni. In 1009 Gaṇḍa joined another confederacy of the Hindu princes in support of Ānandapāla, the Shāhīya king of Udabhāṇḍapura. In this campaign Rājyapāla, the Pratīhāra king of Kanauj, had joined the confederacy, and therefore Sultan Maḥmūd determined to punish him. The results of Maḥmūd's campaigns of 1018 and 1019 have already been narrated. Vidyādhara, the son of Gaṇḍa, led the army of the feudatories against Rājyapāla, and that unfortunate king, for his submission to Maḥmūd, was slain in battle by Vidyādhara's general, the Kachchhapaghāta chief Arjuna. In 1019 Maḥmūd returned to India in order to punish the Hindu princes for having slain Rājyapāla. The Muhammadan historians state that after the capture of Bari, the new capital of the Pratīhāras, Maḥmūd invaded the Chandella kingdom. But Gaṇḍa fled without hazarding an open encounter with the Musalmans, leaving his baggage and elephants behind. Nothing further is known about him.

Leads the Second Rajput Confederacy.

Vidyādhara leads the Rajputs against Rājyapāla

Maḥmūd invades Gaṇḍa's Kingdom.

The rise of the Chedī King Gāṅgeya caused a decline of the power of the Chandellas. Vijayapāla, the grandson of Gaṇḍa was forced to retire to the hills of Bundelkhand, and his son Devavarman was dethroned by Gāṅgeya's son Karṇa. The latter compelled Devavarman's younger brother Kīrtivarman to serve in his army. During the second half of the eleventh century, Kīrtivarman restored the independence of the Chandella kingdom with the help of the Brāhmaṇa general Gopāla. The well-known drama *Prabodha-chandrodaya,* by Kṛishṇamiśra, was first performed during the celebrations which followed the victories over Karṇa.

Devavarman.

Restoration of Independence.

Madanavarman, the grandson of Kīrtivarman, is one of the most important figures in the history of Northern India in the twelfth century. His long reign of nearly forty years was a period of prosperity. He was the contemporary of the great Govindachandra of Kanauj, Yaśovarman and Jayavarman of Mālava, and Gayakarṇa of Ḍāhala. During his reign the Chālukyas of Gujarat conquered Rajputana and came into conflict with the Chandellas. The kings Siddharāja Jayasiṁha and Kumārapāla of Gujarat were the contemporaries of Madanavarman. During his reign, too, the fort of Kālañjar was beautified with several temples, and the western

Madanavarman.

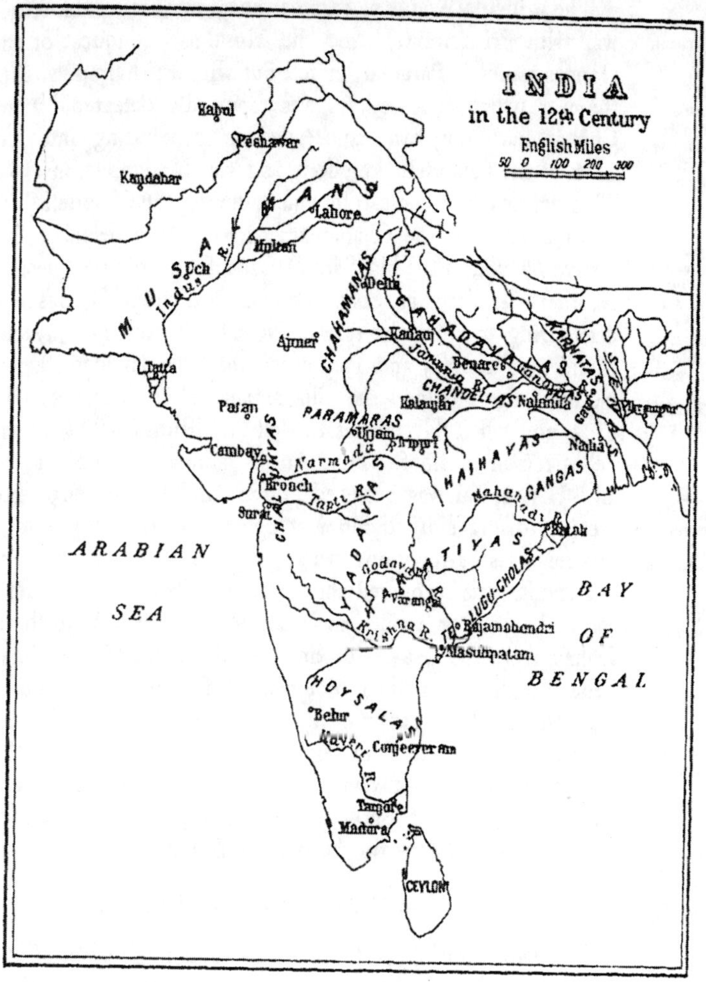

The Conquest of Eastern Mālava

frontier of the Chandella kingdom was extended as far south-west as Bhilsa near Bhopal. An image of Ṛishabhadeva, the first *Tīrthaṅkara* of the Jains, was dedicated, during the same reign, in the Jain temple at Khājurāho and is still worshipped at that place. Madanavarman was succeeded by his grandson Paramardin or Parmaldev.

The principal events of Paramardin's reign are his disastrous war with Pṛithvīrāja II and the Musalman conquest of the Ganges valley. Paramardin fell out with Pṛithvīrāja, and in the war which followed he was repeatedly defeated by the Chāhamāna king, who succeeded in penetrating into the heart of the Chandella kingdom, as far as Madanpur, in 1182. This defeat caused an estrangement among the Chandella, the Gāhaḍavāla, and the Chāhamāna kings. As a result of this quarrel, Muḥammad bin Sām of Ghor found the conquest of Northern India very easy. When Pṛithvīrāja II was endeavouring to stem the tide of Musalman invasion, Jayachchandra of Kanauj and Paramardin of Kālañjar stood aloof. None of them helped the Chāhamānas after their defeat in 1192, and when Jayachchandra fell at Chandawar the Chandellas remained aloof. The turn of Paramardin came last of all. His capital was besieged in 1201 and fell in 1203. He escaped disgrace by dying just before the fall of the fort. His reign lasted forty-one years.

Paramardin. **Pṛithvīrāja II conquers Bundelkhand.** **The Quarrels between the Kings of Northern India at the end of the Twelfth Century.** **The Musalmans capture Kālañjar.**

Kālañjar was recovered shortly afterwards by Paramardin's son and successor Trailokyavarman, who conquered Northern Ḍāhala from the last Chedī king Vijayasiṁha, and the Chandella kingdom remained independent for nearly a century after the death of Paramardin. Trailokya was succeeded by his son Vīravarman, who reigned in the second half of the thirteenth century and was followed by his son Bhojavarman. The descendants of Bhojavarman ruled as feudatory chiefs under the Musalmans till the reign of Akbar.

Trailokyavarman. **Later Chandellas.**

VI. The Paramāras of Mālava *

The Paramāra kings of Mālava fell under the sway of the Rāshṭrakūṭas in the first half of the tenth century, and then became independent in the second half under Vākpatirāja II, son of Sīyaka II, who was living in 974. He defeated the Kalachurī king Yuvarāja II in battle and invaded Gujarat and the Deccan repeatedly. During one of these invasions he was defeated and killed by the western Chālukya king Taila II. After his death he was succeeded by his younger brother Sindhurāja or Sindhula.

Early Kings. **Vākpati II.** **Defeated and killed by Taila II.**

* See p. 310.

Temple of Siddhanatha Śiva at Nemawar on the Narmada (Indore State), built in the new style of Bhoja I of Mālava (11th century A.D.)

Bhoja I. Bhoja I, the son of Sindhula, is celebrated in Indian history as one of the most learned princes of his age. He came to the throne in the beginning of the eleventh century and defeated the Chālukya king Bhīma I of Gujarat. In Eastern India he defeated a king named Indraratha or Indiradan. He was a contemporary of the Chedī kings Gāṅgeya and Karṇa and of Jayasiṁha II of the Western Chālukya dynasty of Kalyāṇī. **Confederacy against Bhoja.** Later on Bhoja defeated the Western Chālukya king Someśvara I. The Chālukyas of Kalyāṇī and Bhīma I of Gujarat combined with Karṇa of Ḍāhala, and Bhoja succumbed to this combined attack in the middle of the eleventh century. The immediate cause of the war with the Chālukyas of Gujarat was an unprovoked attack on that kingdom by Bhoja's general, a Jain named Kulachandra. **Cause of the War.** Bhīma I was at that time absent on a campaign against the Musalmans of Sindh. Kulachandra seized this opportunity to attack the Chālukya capital, Aṇahilapāṭaka, and sacked it. The loss to the people of Gujarat was so great that "the sacking of Kulachandra" has passed into a proverb. **Bhoja's Defeat and Death.** For this insult Bhīma I, later on, combined with Karṇa, King of Ḍāhala, and the Western Chālukya king Someśvara I, and overthrew Bhoja I in battle. Bhoja was killed and Mālava divided between Gujarat and Ḍāhala.

Bhoja was undoubtedly the greatest king of Mālava. He was a great patron of literature and established a university **Bhoja's Patronage of Literature.** at Dhārā, his capital, where special arrangements were made for the teaching of students. Celebrated works were incised on large slabs of stone and were built into the walls of the **Bhoja's College.** college halls. This building was turned into a Masjid by a Musalman saint named Kamāl Maulā, who reversed these inscribed slabs and turned them into pavement stones. **Recovery of Lost Works.** It is still called the College of Rājā Bhoja "Bhōja-śālā", and many of the lost works have been recovered from its pavement, such as the *Pārijātamañjarī-nāṭaka* of the *Upādhyāya* **Jain Teachers.** Madana. Bhoja was a Śaiva, but he encouraged discussions among the Jains, Buddhists, and Hindus. The Jain teachers **Vijñāneśvara.** Prabhāchandra Sūrī, Śāntisena, and Dhanapāla, as well as the celebrated legal commentator Vijñāneśvara, the author of the *Mitāksharā*, were among his contemporaries. Celebrated **Padmagupta.** poets like Padmagupta lived at his court, and scholars and poets, who enjoyed his patronage, wrote their works in the name of Bhoja, and at least twenty-three different works are ascribed to him. Works on various subjects, such as astronomy, astrology, rhetoric, *Yoga*-philosophy, law, engineering, grammar, lexicography, Sanskrit and Prakrit poetry, and veterinary science, have come down to us. Bhoja's successor was Jayasiṁha, whose exact relationship to his predecessor is not known. He was very shortly set aside by Udayāditya, a distant relative of Bhoja I.

His Literary Works.

Udayāditya.

After the fall of Bhoja I, the Paramāra kingdom became divided into many parts. Udayāditya and his sons reigned over South-western Mālava, while a separate line of kings ruled over Northern Mālava. Udayāditya, however, inflicted a crushing defeat upon King Karṇa of Ḍāhala in his old age and restored independence to the Paramāra dynasty. But from this date Mālava ceased to be a power of consequence in Central India. The third king of the other dynasty, Vijayapāla, was reigning in 1134. He was thus contemporary with the sons of Udayāditya. Two sons of Udayāditya ruled over Mālava after him, Lakshmadeva and his brother Naravarman. The successors of Naravarman were weaklings. Naravarman's son Yaśovarman was overthrown by the Chālukya king Siddharāja Jayasiṁha of Gujarat, after a long war, and for some time Mālava became a part of the kingdom of the Chālukyas. From 1142 to 1217 Mālava remained a dependency and was ruled by two different lines of feudatory chiefs, both descended from the sons of Yaśovarman. The independence of Mālava was restored by King Devapāla, a great-grandson of Yaśovarman. During the reign of this prince, Mālava and Gujarat were repeatedly invaded by the Musalmans. The last independent king of the Paramāra dynasty was Jayasiṁha V, who was overthrown by the Musalman generals of Sultan 'Alāuddīn Muḥammad Shāh Khalji in 1305.

Divisions of the Paramāras.

Vijayapāla.

The Chālukyas of Gujarat conquer Mālava.

Devapāla.

Jayasiṁha V.

VII. The Chāhamānas of Śākambharī and Ajmer

Like the Paramāras and the Chālukyas, the Chāhamānas of Śākambharī or Sambhar were a clan of Gurjara or Hūṇa

Viśāla-deva. descent. The dynasty became celebrated afterwards, on account of its long wars with the Musalmans of the Panjab. Its most celebrated king was Vigraharāja I or Viśāladeva, who advanced as far as the Siwalik range and placed his record on Aśoka's pillar in 1164. Vigraharāja extended his kingdom to the frontiers of Gujarat and is said to have defeated Jayasiṁha Siddharāja. In imitation of Bhoja I of Mālava he founded at Ajmer a college into the wall of which were built slabs of stone upon which many literary works were inscribed. One of these slabs contained portions of a drama called *Harakeli*, which is said to have been composed by Vigraharāja himself. The second work recovered from the ruins of this college, which was converted into a masjid by Sultān Muḥammad bin Sām of Ghor and is now called the *Ādhāi-din-kā-jhomprā*, is another drama called the *Lalita-Vigraharāja*, composed in honour of Vigraharāja by a poet called Somadeva, in 1153.

His College at Ajmer.

Recovery of Lost Works.

Someś-vara. Vigraharāja or Viśāladeva was succeeded by his nephew Pṛithvīrāja I. After a short reign this prince was succeeded on the throne by his uncle Someśvara, a brother of Vigraharāja, who married daughters of Chedī and Tomara kings. By the latter he had a son named Pṛithvīrāja II, and by the former another named Harirāja. This Pṛithvīrāja II became the king of Ajmer as well as of Delhi. The later Bardic Chronicles and the Hindi poem, the *Pṛithvīrāja-Rasā*, narrate many events about this king, but their statements are totally unreliable. This much can be gleaned from them, that the Chāhamāna king was not on good terms with either of his neighbours, Jayachchandra of Kanauj or Paramardin of Kālañjar. There is epigraphical evidence of Pṛithvīrāja II's war with the Chandella king. During this war Pṛithvīrāja II penetrated as far south-east as Madanpur, in the heart of Bundelkhand, and left his record in a temple at that place built in the time of Madanavarman.

Pṛithvī-rāja II.

Pṛithvī-rāja's Conquest of Bundel-khand.

Invasions of the Musal-mans. Sultān Muizzuddin Muḥammad bin Sām attacked the north-western frontier of the Chāhamāna kingdom twice. The Musalman army was defeated by Pṛithvīrāja II in 1191, but in the next year he was killed and his army in turn defeated. The death of the king was followed by the sack of Delhi in 1193. The conquest of Ajmer was the next step. According

Sack of Delhi.

to tradition, Pṛithvīrāja II is said to have carried away the daughter of Jayachchandra of Kanauj from the marriage meeting (*Svayambara-sabhā*), and for this reason the King of Kanauj did not help him or his successors. The Musalmans occupied Delhi and Ajmer and left a small tract around Sambhar to the son of Pṛithvīrāja II, but he rebelled with his uncle Harirāja and was defeated. The Chāhamānas then removed their capital to the hill fort of Ranthambhor, where they continued to reign till the end of the thirteenth century. The last king of this dynasty, Hammīra Siṁha, defeated one of the later kings of Mālava named Arjunavarman II, and built a temple inside the fort of Ranthambhor in 1269. Ranthambhor fell to 'Alāuddīn Muḥammad Shāh Khaljī in 1303.

Late Chāhamānas.

Fall of Ranthambhor

VIII. The Chālukyas of Gujarat *

The Chālukyas of Gujarat are better known to scholars as the Chālukyas of Aṇahilapāṭaka, which was the name of their capital. This place is called Aṇahilavāḍā in Gujaratī and Nahrwala in Muhammadan histories. It is now called Patan and is the head-quarters of the northern district of the dominions of His Highness the Gaikwad of Baroda. Mūlarāja, the founder of this dynasty, lived during the reign of the Pratīhāra emperor Vijayapāla (974). His father is simply called Rāji, and we do not know anything further about the ancestors of this line of kings. According to tradition, his accession took place in 961. He conquered the country from the Chāpa or Chāpotkaṭa princes. The history of this dynasty is very well known from a large number of historical works both in Sanskrit and in a language called the Ardha-Māgadhī, which is a literary dialect used by the Jains in their sacred books. After conquering Northern Gujarat with its capital, Aṇahilapāṭaka, Mūlarāja I added Surat and Broach in Southern Gujarat to his kingdom. Mūlarāja then conquered the Chūḍāsamā chief of Kathiawad, who oppressed pilgrims to Prabhāsa and was most probably a Musalman, as he is described as a beef-eater. Mūlarāja was a Śaiva and built several temples at Aṇahilapāṭaka. He invited Brāhmaṇas from Northern India to Gujarat, and the Audīchyas, Śrī-

Aṇahila-pāṭaka.

Mūlarāja I.

Conquest of Surat and Broach.

Conquest of Kathiawad.

* See p. 313

Brāhmaṇa Immigration from Northern India.

Rudramahālaya.

Gauḍas, and Kanaujīyā Brāhmaṇas of modern Gujarat state that they came from Northern India at the invitation of Mūlarāja. At Siddhapura, Mūlarāja I began the celebrated temple of Śiva called *Rudramahālaya*, but could not finish it. According to the Gujarat Chronicles, Mūlarāja I reigned for thirty-five or fifty-five years. He died in 996–997.

Bhīma I.

His Campaign in Sindh and Alliance with Karṇa.

Mūlarāja was succeeded by his son Chāmuṇḍarāja and his grandsons Vallabharāja and Durlabharāja. According to the Chronicles, all these three princes died within a couple of decades. Durlabha was succeeded by his nephew Bhīma I. Bhīma defeated the Musalman rulers of Sindh and helped the Rajput chiefs of Śivāsana, or Sehwan, in that country; but when he was absent, Kulachandra, the Jain general of Bhoja I of Mālava, invaded Gujarat and destroyed Aṇahilapāṭaka. Long after this event, Bhīma, smarting under the disgrace, entered into a treaty with Karṇa, King of Ḍāhala, and destroyed the independence of Mālava.

Muhammadan Description of Somanātha.

Sack of Aṇahilapāṭaka.

Attracted by stories of the enormous wealth of the shrine of Śiva at Somanātha or Prabhāsa, Maḥmūd invaded India in 1024. Muhammadan historians state that the temple was endowed with more than ten thousand villages. The water of the River Ganges was brought daily from Northern India for its worship. A thousand Brāhmaṇa priests were engaged for the performance of the daily ritual, and three hundred barbers were employed every day to shave the heads of the pilgrims who came to Somanātha. Three hundred and fifty men and women were employed as musicians and dancers at this temple. Maḥmūd left Ghazni in 1024. He passed through Multan and Sindh, crossed the *Thar* or the Indian Desert, and appeared before Aṇahilapāṭaka. Bhīma I fled, and his capital was sacked. Maḥmūd destroyed the fortifications and demolished the temples, after which he passed on to Verawal on the Arabian Sea and besieged the fort. After a long siege the fort was captured, and the temple of Somanātha was plundered. The accumulated riches of the shrine fell to the Musalmans, and the idol itself was partly burnt while a part of it was carried away to Mecca and Ghazni.

After the destruction of Somanātha, Bhīma took shelter in one of the islands of the Rann of Cutch. Maḥmūd pursued him and defeated his army. The Musalmans retired to Ghazni with their spoils, and Bhīma reoccupied his capital. Bhīma then successfully attacked the Paramāra chiefs of Abu, in which city his general Vimala built in 1032 the celebrated Jain temple, still the wonder of artists, and known as the temple of Vimala Śāha. The most important events of Bhīma's reign were the conquest of Mālava and the division of that kingdom between him and Karṇa of Ḍāhala (1041–51). These made Bhīma the most powerful monarch in Western India, and afterwards he defeated Karṇa in the latter's old age. Bhīma I reigned for more than forty years, and was succeeded by his son Karṇa in 1064.

Invasion of Abu.

Vimala Śāha's Temple at Abu.

Conquest of Mālava.

Karṇa enjoyed a long and peaceful reign of more than thirty years. He built a new capital near Ahmadabad called Karṇāvatī, and a temple of Śiva known as the Karṇameru. He subdued the Bhils of Asaval near modern Ahmedabad, built temples of Devī named Jayantī at Kocharva, and excavated a tank called Karṇasāgara. In his old age Karṇa married Miyaṇalladevī, a daughter of the Kādamba chief Jayakeśin I of the Kanarese country. He is said to have been killed by the Chāhamāna chief Duśśala in battle.

Karṇa.

His Public Works.

Karṇa was succeeded by his minor son Jayasiṁha some time after 1094. The earlier wars of Jayasiṁha were with the Paramāra chief Yaśovarman and one of his generals, Jagaddeva, who was related to the Kādamba chiefs of Goa. Jayasiṁha, surnamed Siddharāja, was one of the most powerful patrons of the Jain religion. He destroyed the bandit chiefs of the Ābhīra or Āhīr, Chāvḍā or Chāpotkaṭa, and Chūḍāsamā clans in the interior of Kathiawad and placed a viceroy at Sorath or Junagadh. A new era, called the *Siṁha-Saṁvatsara*, was founded by him in 1113. It was used in Kathiawad for nearly two hundred years. The temple of Neminātha at Girnar was built by Sajjana, Jayasiṁha's viceroy of Kathiawad. Jayasiṁha constructed *Sahasraliṅga* Lake, and after the defeat of Yaśovarman and his son Jayavarman of Mālava he added that country permanently to Gujarat. The conquest of Mālava brought him face to face with the rising power of the Chandellas under Madanavarman. In the Chandella war Siddharāja Jayaśiṁha was defeated, and Northern Mālava as far as Bhilsa

Jayasiṁha Siddharāja.

The Siṁha Era.

Annexation of Mālava.

Defeat by the Chandella Madana.

was added to the Chandella kingdom. Siddharāja completed the temple of *Rudramahālaya*, and his name is honoured throughout Gujarat as the greatest king of the country. The

Hemachandra Sūri.

great Jain scholar Hemachandra Sūrī, or Hemāchārya, was his constant companion and adviser. In 1143 Siddharāja Jayaśiṁha died and was succeeded by his distant relative, an illegitimate descendant of Bhīma I, named Kumārapāla, who was selected by the Council of Nobles.

Kumārapāla.

At the time of his accession Kumārapāla was more than fifty years of age. He fought and defeated the Chāhamāna

Chāhamāna War.

king Arṇorāja of Śākambharī. On the way he sacked Chandrāvatī, the capital of the Paramāras of Abu. In the south Kumārapāla defeated Mallikārjuna and the Śīlāhāra king of Northern Konkan or Thana. The kingdom of Gujarat became an extensive empire under him; on the east it was bounded by the Chandella kingdom and Gondwana; in the south it bordered

Extent of his Kingdom.

on the empire of the Yādavas of Devagiri, and on the west the Arabian Sea became its limit. Kumārapāla is said to have completed the new temple of Somanātha, which was begun

New Temple of Somanātha.

by Bhīma I. Kumārapāla was almost entirely under the influence of his Jain minister Hemachandra Sūrī, while two other influential advisers, Rāmachandra and Udayachandra, were also Jain teachers.

Jain Influence at the Court.

Hemachandra was born at Dhandhuka in the family of a merchant in 1088. At an early age he became a Jain monk. Under Siddharāja Jayasiṁha, he was one of the advisers, but

Hemachandra Sūri.

under Kumārapāla he became the chief minister. He wrote a large number of works on literature and religion. He died in 1172 at the age of eighty-four.

The Emperor Kumārapāla died at the ripe age of eighty-one in 1174 and was succeeded by his nephew Ajayapāla, who

Ajayapāla

was not inclined to favour the Jains. He distrusted the Jain ministers of Kumārapāla and appointed a Brāhmaṇa named Kapardin, who was an assistant of Hemachandra. Of a cruel and over-bearing disposition, he was murdered by a door-keeper, in 1177, after a reign of only three years and was

Mūlarāja II.

succeeded by his infant son Mūlarāja II. Mūlarāja II died after two years and was succeeded by Bhīma II.

The new king was a distant relation of Ajayapāla, but some

of the Jain chroniclers regard him as a son of that monarch. Bhīma II is credited with the long reign of sixty-three years. Some of his inscriptions were issued as late as 1240. During this period the great northern kingdoms were conquered by the Musalmans, and as early as 1178 the Sultans of Ghor invaded the kingdom of Gujarat. Rivals arose in the persons of Jayantasiṁha, who was living in 1223, and Tribhuvanapāla, who was living in 1242. Bhīma II was called "The Simpleton", and during his reign the Bāghelās of Southern Gujarat, descended from a sister of Kumārapāla, obtained ascendancy. Lavaṇaprasāda of this clan is mentioned as a minister of Bhīma II. His son Vīradhavala became a powerful feudatory chief. Vastupāla was the minister of Vīradhavala as well as his son Vīsaladeva. Vastupāla and his brother Tejaḥpāla were fabulously rich, and they built a magnificent temple of white marble at Delvāḍā (Dilwara), near Mount Abu, in 1230. In 1232 they built another temple of the *Tīrthaṅkara* Neminātha on Śatruñjaya Hill, and a third on the top of Girnar Mountain. Vīradhavala died in 1238 and was followed by Vīsaladeva who assumed Imperial titles in 1243. He died in 1261 and was succeeded by his nephew Arjuna in 1262. Arjuna's son Sāraṅgadeva reigned for twenty-two years and was succeeded by a distant relative named Karṇadeva in 1296. Karṇa II was insane, and during his reign the powerful nobles became absolutely independent. In 1297 Alp Khān, the elder brother and general of Sultān 'Alāuddīn Muḥammad Khaljī, invaded Aṇahilapāṭaka, and Karṇa II fled to Devagiri, leaving his family and capital unprotected. His principal queen became the concubine of Sultān 'Alāuddīn Muḥammad Khaljī. This woman, who was called Kaulādevī (Kamalā-devi), afterwards incited 'Alāuddīn to hasten the ruin of the land of her birth. She urged him to snatch away her daughter by her first husband, who was hidden in the jungles of Baglana. The Sultan sent Mālik Kāfūr to capture Karṇa and bring his daughter Devalādevī. For two months the insane king Karṇa II succeeded in keeping the Musalmans at bay, as he had received an offer of marriage for his daughter from Śaṅkaradeva, the Yādava king of Devagiri. But while on her way to Devagiri, Devalādevī was captured by Mālik Kāfūr near the caves of Ellora.

Bhīma II. **Musalman Invasions.** **Jayantasiṁha and Tribhuvanapāla.** **Rise of the Bāghelās.** **Vastupāla.** **His Temples at Abu, Śatruñjaya, and Girnar.** **Arjuna.** **Sāraṅgadeva.** **Karṇa II.** **Kamalā-Devī.** **Mālik Kāfūr sent to bring Karṇa's Daughter.** **Capture of Devalā.**

IX. The Haihayas or Chedīs of Ḍāhala *

The Haihayas, also known as Kalatsuris or Kalachuris, were most probably a southern people who had settled in Northern India in the later mediæval period. The earliest known kings of this clan are Śaṅkaragaṇa and Buddharāja, who ruled in Northern Deccan. After their overthrow, one branch of the clan seems to have migrated to Central India.

Their Origin.

The real founder of the greatness of the Chedīs was Kokalla I, who established a kingdom in the Jubbulpur District, formerly known as the Ḍābhāla or Ḍāhala. We do not know anything about Kokalla's ancestry. He was related by marriage to the Chandellas of Kālañjara and the Rāshṭrakūṭas of the Deccan. Kokalla helped Kṛishṇa to fight the eastern Chālukyas of Veṅgī, the Gurjaras, and the Rāshṭrakūṭas of Gujarat. In the north he helped Bhoja II, son of Mahendrapāla I of Kanauj, to gain the throne by defeating his half-brother Mahīpāla I.

Kokalla I. **His Alliance with Kṛishṇa II.** **Assists Bhoja II to get Kanauj.**

After the death of Kokalla I, the Chedī kingdom passed to his son Mugdhatuṅga-Prasiddhadhavala. Mugdhatuṅga fought under his brother-in-law Kṛishṇa II in the Kuntala or the Karṇāṭa province, and wrested the village of Pālī from the Somavaṁśī kings of Orissa. He was succeeded by his sons Balaharsha and Yuvarāja I. The succession appears to have been disputed, and Yuvarāja I was helped to the throne by the Chandella king Yaśovarman. Yuvarāja I is noted in history as having imported into Northern India a large number of Śaiva ascetics of the Mattamayūra sect from Gujarat and Mālava. In Mālava they had founded two important monasteries at Upendrapura (Uṇḍor) and Raṇapadrapura (Rāṇoḍ). Many monasteries were built and endowed for them by Yuvarāja I. He invaded Bengal through Magadha, and introduced a new style of architecture into Central India. He built a circular temple of Śiva at Gurgi, a place twelve miles to the east of Rewa city, and one of the Śaiva ascetics from Mālava built another temple of the same type at Chandrehe on the Son, thirty miles south of Rewa. He married a Chālukya princess named Nohalā, who built a monastery for

Mugdhatuṅga. **Yuvarāja I.** **The Mattamayūra Ascetics, brought to the Chedī Country.** **Campaign in Bengal.** **The Circular Temples.**

* See p. 311

Temple of Prabodhaśiva, built in the new Chedi style, Chandrehe on the Son, Rewa State (10th century A.D.)

Nohalā's Monastery at Bilhari. Other Buildings.

the Śaiva ascetics at Bilhari, in the Jubbulpur District. The monasteries at Bilhari, Gurgi, and Chandrehe were vast buildings of stone, each surrounded by a high stone wall and provided with artificial lakes. Yuvarāja I had at least one son and one daughter. The son, Lakshmaṇarāja, succeeded him on the throne, and the daughter, Kuṇḍakadevī, was married to the Rāshṭrakūṭa king Amoghavarsha III.

War with the Pratīhāras.

His Campaigns.

Relationship with the western Chālukyas.

Lakshmaṇarāja is said to have defeated the Pratīhāras of Kanauj and visited Somanātha near Verawal on the western coast, where he offered an image of the Nāga Kāliya to the god. He fought with the Pālas of Bengal in the east, the kings of Kāśmīra in the north-east, and the Pāṇḍya country in Southern India. Lakshmaṇarāja had two sons and a daughter. The daughter, Bonthādevī, was married to the Western Chālukya king Vikramāditya IV. Lakshmaṇarāja invited another Śaiva ascetic of the Mattamayūra sect and made him abbot of the great Śaiva monastery at Bheraghat on the Narmadā, now called the Marble Rocks. These Śaiva ascetics continued to exercise very great influence in Central India till the Muhammadan conquest.

Decline of the Chedis.

Yuvarāja II.

Kṛishṇa III conquers Ḍāhala.

Defeat by the western Chālukyas and the Paramāras.

With the death of Lakshmaṇarāja a period of decline set in. Lakshmaṇarāja was succeeded by his sons, Śankaraṅgaṇa and Yuvarāja II, one after the other. Yuvarāja II suffered a crushing defeat at the hands of his nephew Kṛishṇa III or Kaṇṇaradeva. The Rāshṭrakūṭas destroyed Tripurī, the Chedī capital, and advanced as far as Jura near Maihar, where Kṛishṇa III set up a pillar of victory. Yuvarāja II was also defeated by the western Chālukya king Jayasiṁha II of Kalyāṇī, and the Paramāra king Vākpatirāja II of Mālava. He was succeeded by his son Kokalla II, who was reduced to great straits by the Chandella king Vidyādhara.

Revival of the Chedis under Gāṅgeya.

Extent of his Conquests.

The power and prestige of the Chedis or Haihayas of Ḍāhala was revived by Gāṅgeya, the son and successor of Kokalla II. In the east Gāṅgeya conquered Benares and Tīrabhukti or Northern Bihar. He overran Northern India as far as Kāśmīra and Kaṅgra, and Southern India as far as Kuntala or Karṇāṭa. He was ruling over Champaran or Tīrabhukti (Northern Bihar) in 1019, i.e. immediately after the death of Rājyapāla of Kanauj. He was mentioned as the king of Middle India by the Musalman historians of the period of Sabuktegīn. According to the inscriptions of his descendants, Gāṅgeya was fond of residing at Allahabad, indicating thereby that the country to the south of the Ganges had passed out of the control of the Pratīhāras of Kanauj. Gāṅgeya assumed the title of Vikramāditya, and started issuing gold coins on the model of the coins of the Pratīhāra emperor Mahīpāla I. He died on the 22nd of January, 1041.

Gāṅgeya as Vikramāditya.

His Coins.

Gāṅgeya was succeeded by his son Karṇa, the most important figure in the history of Northern India in the eleventh century. Karṇa performed the annual funeral obsequies of his father in 1042 at Prayāga or Allahabad, and gave a village in the Benares District to a Brāhmaṇa, which proves that the Benares and Allahabad districts had been already conquered from the Pratīhāras. He defeated the Chandella Devarman and compelled his younger brother Kīrtivarman to serve in his army. Karṇa destroyed the remnants of the Pratīhāra Empire by conquering Yaśaḥpāla, the successor of Trilochanapāla. He then turned his attention to Mālava, and after some time he united his forces with the Western Chālukya king Someśvara I and with Bhīma I of Gujarat. The allies defeated the aged king Bhoja I of Mālava, and that country was divided between Gujarat and Ḍāhala. Later on Karṇa also defeated Bhīma I. Kīrtivarman and Vapullaka defeated the Musalmans of Sindh in the battle of the Yellow Mountain (Jungshahi). Early in his reign Karṇa invaded Bihar but was repulsed from the town of Gayā. In the south Karṇa defeated the Choḷa king Rājendradeva Parakeśarīvarman of Tanjore and the Pāṇḍya king of Madura.

Karṇa.

Annexation of Kanauj, and of Mālava.

Conquest of Gujarat.

Campaign in Bihar.

After conquering the whole of Northern India, Karṇa was crowned a second time in 1052, eleven years after his accession, and the regnal years in his inscriptions are counted from the date of his second coronation. Karṇa's empire extended from Bengal in the east to the Panjab, and from the Himalayas to the banks of the Narmadā and the Godāvarī in the south. In his old age Karṇa suffered serious reverses. The Chandella kingdom recovered its independence under Kīrtivarman. Udayāditya, a distant relation of Bhoja I, became independent in Mālava. According to Hemachandra, Bhīma I ultimately

His Second Coronation.

Karṇa's Reverses.

defeated Karṇa, while the Kāśmīrian poet Bilhaṇa has recorded that Karṇa was defeated and killed by Someśvara I of Kalyāṇī.

Karṇa built a new capital, close to Tripurī (modern Tewar), and called it Karṇāvatī. He built a splendid temple of Śiva, called the Karṇameru, at Benares. At Amarkanṭak he built a triple-shrined temple of Mahādeva of a new type which still exists, and the temple of Virāṭeśvara at Sohagpur in Southern Rewa is ascribed to him. Unlike his father, he did not issue gold coins. He married a Hūṇa princess named Āvalladevī. Karṇa was the last Rajput king who tried to found an empire in Northern India. Though he succeeded at first, he failed in the end. Union had become impossible for the Rajput tribes and their kings in the eleventh century, and this was the cause of their final overthrow at the end of the twelfth.

Karṇa-meru.

Temples at Amarkanṭak and Sohagpur.

In his old age Karṇa abdicated in favour of his son Yaśaḥkarṇa. Under this king the Haihayas lost most of the conquests of Gāṅgeya and Karṇa. The Paramāras of Mālava became powerful under Naravarman, the son of Udayāditya. A new kingdom was founded in Kanauj by Chandradeva of the Gāhaḍavāla family, and the Ganges valley was lost to the Chedīs. Yaśaḥkarṇa invaded the Andhra country, went as far as Drākshārāmam on the Godāvarī, and allied himself with Nānyadeva of the Karṇāṭaka dynasty of Mithilā. He invaded Champaran also, but was forced to retire. He was succeeded by his son Gayākarṇa after a long reign, during which the collateral branch of the Haihayas became independent in Southern Kośala.

Yaśaḥ-karṇa.

The Gāhaḍavālas.

Campaign in the Andhra Country and Champaran.

Gayākarṇa married a granddaughter of King Udayāditya of Mālava, a lady named Alhaṇādevī, the daughter of the Guhila chief Vijayasiṁha of Mewad, who had married Śyamaladevī, the daughter of Udayāditya. After the death of her husband Alhaṇādevī rebuilt the temple and monastery of Vaidyanātha at Bheraghat. Gayākarṇa died some time between 1151 and 1155 and was succeeded by his son Narasiṁha. Narasiṁha was succeeded shortly afterwards by his brother Jayasiṁha. During his reign the feudatory chiefs of Kakareḍī, a village still existing on the borders of the states of Panna and

Temple of Vaidyanātha rebuilt by Alhaṇādevī.

Narasiṁha

Rewa, assumed the royal prerogative of issuing grants of land. Jayasiṁha died some time between 1175 and 1180 and was succeeded by his son Vijayasiṁha, the last descendant of Kokalla I to rule over Ḍāhala. Vijayasiṁha was overthrown and killed between 1196 and 1200 by Jaitugi I of the Yādava dynasty of Devagiri. **Vijaya-siṁha.**

The Chedīs of Ratnapura continued to rule as independent princes in the jungle country between Orissa and the Central Provinces till the rise of the Tughlaqs. They had two capitals, Ratnapura and Jājallapura, and in Muhammadan histories they are called the Rais of Jajnagar. At the end of the twelfth century the Chedīs of Ratnapura were driven farther south, and they founded a new capital called Raipur, where Haribrahmadeva was ruling in the middle of the fifteenth century. The Haihayas remained virtually independent in this area till their conquest by the Bhonsles of Nagpur in the middle of the eighteenth century. **The Later Haihayas or Chedīs.**

X. The Gāhaḍavālas of Kanauj *

The Gāhaḍavāla kingdom was founded by Chandradeva in the last decades of the eleventh century. Chandradeva, the founder, was a man of humble origin, and the Gāhaḍavālas themselves were half-caste Gurjaras like the Chandellas or the Chāhamānas. He had to fight for a long time with the Chedīs under Yaśaḥkarṇa. His kingdom was surrounded on all sides by more powerful kingdoms, all of which were hostile. To the east lay the kingdom of the Pālas, and a new kingdom was founded in Mithilā by a Karṇāṭaka adventurer named Nānyadeva. To the south lay the Chedīs and the Chandellas; to the west the Musalman kingdom of the Panjab and the Chāhamāna kingdom of Delhi and Ajmer. Chandradeva was a contemporary of Rāmapāla of Bengal. He died after 1097 and was succeeded by his son Madanapāla, who reigned for seven years. **Chandra-deva.** **The Karṇāṭaka Kingdom of Mithilā.** **Chandra-deva's Contem-poraries.** **Madana-pala.**

Govindachandra, the son and successor of Madanapāla, was the most powerful king of the Gāhaḍavāla dynasty. He was associated with his father in the kingdom from 1104 and ascended the throne some time before 1114. He ruled over **Govinda-chandra.**

* See p. 313.

Turushka-daṇḍa. the area now known as the United Provinces, and he levied a special tax called the *Turushka-daṇḍa* either to buy off the Musalmans or to meet the expenses of the wars with them. During the decline of the Pālas of Bengal, Govindachandra did his best to help Rāmapāla's son and grandsons. He invaded Magadha on several occasions and annexed a portion of it. Govindachandra was the contemporary of the Chandella Madanavarman, Lakshmaṇasena of Bengal and the Chedī kings, Gayākarṇa, and his son Narasiṁha.

Wars with the Senas.

Annexation of South Bihar.

He was succeeded by his son Vijayachandra after 1155. Vijayachandra ruled till 1169 and was succeeded by his son Jayachchandra in 1170. Jayachchandra is said to have been related by marriage to Pṛithvīrāja II of Delhi and Ajmer. Tradition records that a daughter of Jayachchandra was carried away from the marriage assembly by Pṛithvīrāja II. For this reason Jayachchandra did not even try to help his son-in-law in his wars with the Musalmans. After the death of Pṛithvīrāja II in 1192, Sultān Muḥammad bin Sām invaded the kingdom of Kanauj and defeated Jayachchandra in the battle of Chandawar in 1194. Jayachchandra was killed, and the Ganges valley was occupied by the Musalmans.

Vijayachandra.

Jayachchandra.

Battle of Chandawar.

After the death of Jayachchandra, his son Hariśchandra was set up as the king in Kanauj and ruled till 1202. The kingdom of Kanauj was imperfectly conquered, and isolated chiefs continued to offer resistance to the Musalmans till the reign of Ghiyāth-ud-din Bilbun. The Gāhaḍavāla kings of Kanauj issued coins in gold, silver, and copper, in imitation of the coins of Gāṅgeyadeva.

Hariśchandra.

BIBLIOGRAPHY

Bhagwan Lal Indraji, "History of Gujarat", *Bombay Gazetteer*, Vol. I, Part I.

A. K. Sur—Gāhadvālas of Kanauj, *Indian Historical Quarterly*.

R. C. Mazumdar—Gurjara Pratihāras, *Journal of Department of Letters*, (Calcutta University), Vol. X.

V. A. Smith, "The History of Kanauj", *Journal of the Royal Asiatic Society*, 1909.

Luard and Lele, *The Paramāras of Mālava*.

V. A. Smith, "Chandella History and Coinage", *Ind. Ant.*, 1908.

R. D. Banerji, "The Haihayas of Tripuri and their Monuments", *Memoirs of the Arch. Survey*, No. 23.

H. C. Roy, *Dynastic History of Northern India*, Vol. I.

CHAPTER IX

THE EARLY MEDIÆVAL KINGDOMS OF NORTH-EASTERN INDIA

State of the Eastern Provinces of North India.

Anarchy in Bengal.

Election of a King.

After the death of Śaśāṅka the countries of North-eastern India were divided into a number of small kingdoms. Many of the petty chiefs who ruled over these kingdoms were descendants of the governors or officers of the early Gupta Empire. One of them was Lokanātha, who continued to use the seal of a Gupta official (*Kumārāmatya*) even in the eighth century. The Guptas of Magadha exercised a loose control over Bengal till their overthrow during the reign of Jīvitagupta II. The removal of the nominal sovereign led to a period of anarchy described by the Tibetan historian Tārānātha. Bengal became the prey of its neighbours. It was overrun by Yaśovarman of Kanauj and Harshadeva of Assam. According to the *Rājataraṅgiṇī*, the Kāśmīrian king Lalitāditya-Muktāpīḍa came to Bengal in the eighth century. The last invasion of Bengal during this period of anarchy was that of the Gurjara king Vatsarāja. During this period of anarchy the people of Bengal decided to elect a king in order to secure peace and settled government. The man selected to this end was Gopāla, the son of a successful soldier named Vapyaṭa.

I. The Pālas of Bengal *

Gopāla I.

Dharmapāla.

Gopāla ascended the throne in the first half of the eighth century, and his reign seems to have been passed in constant warfare. He was succeeded by his son Dharmapāla, the founder of the real greatness of the Pāla dynasty. Dharma-

* See p. 314.

pāla was an able monarch, and he extended the frontiers of the kingdom to the west of the Son. The original seat of the Pālas was in Magadha or South Bihar, but to that state Dharmapāla added Northern and Western Bengal. Eastern Bengal was not connected with the original Pāla kingdom. The first **The War in Kanauj.** act of Dharmapāla was to extend the sphere of his influence towards the west. At that time Kanauj was ruled by a prince named Indrāyudha. Dharmapāla succeeded in dethroning this prince and placing his own nominee, Chakrāyudha, on the throne. **Indrāyudha's Alliance with Nāgabhaṭa II.** Indrāyudha sought the help of the Gurjara king Nāgabhaṭa II. Nāgabhaṭa sided with the deposed king, and a long war ensued in which Dharmapāla and Chakrāyudha were defeated. They sought help from the Rāshṭrakūṭa monarch **Dharmapāla's Alliance with Govinda III.** Govinda III, with whose aid Dharmapāla succeeded in regaining his ascendancy over Northern India and forcing the kings of the Panjab and Northern Rajputana to acknowledge Chakrāyudha as king of Kanauj. Dharmapāla's reign is the most glorious period of the history of Bengal. With the co-operation of the Rāshṭrakūṭas, the Bengal army compelled the Gurjaras to retire once more into the confines of the **Expulsion of the Gurjaras.** Indian Desert. The defeat of the Gurjaras was so crushing that for a generation they did not venture out of their homes. Dharmapāla reigned for nearly forty years, and this long period was spent in incessant warfare, and he had no time to cultivate the arts of peace. He had inherited a small **Devapāla.** kingdom consisting of South Bihar, but he bequeathed to his son a large kingdom extending from the Brahmaputra to Benares.

The Rāshṭrakūṭa War. During Devapāla's reign, the Bengal army fought with the Rāshṭrakūṭas in Central India, and repelled an invasion of **The Kāmboja Invasion.** Tibeto-Burman tribes, known as the Kāmbojas, in the north. Devapāla's cousin Jayapāla conquered Orissa and Assam for him. The long reign of Devapāla was spent in the promotion of a distinctive culture in Bengal. The Pāla kings were Bud- **Patronage of Buddhism.** dhists, and during their rule Buddhism flourished in the North-eastern Provinces of India. The sacred shrines of Magadha were rebuilt by Devapāla, and the royal favour caused a revival of art and architecture. **Devapāla's Buildings.** Devapāla rebuilt some of the monasteries at Nālandā, and probably also the great temple at Bodh-Gaya or Mahābodhi, in the form in which it was seen by Cunningham and Rajendra Lala Mitra in 1872. He was a munificent patron of learning, and his court became the refuge of Buddhist scholars from all countries. Upon the destruction of Takshaśilā by the Hūṇas, Nālandā became the principal centre of Buddhist learning, and for four hundred years Bengal and Bihar were the only countries in which Buddhism flourished with the aid of the state. In all other countries in India a Brāhmaṇical revival or the Jain religion had practically driven out all forms of Buddhism, and Bengal became the centre of fresh missionary activities. The restoration of the Buddhist shrines led to the evolution of a new type of temple architecture, and with it a new school, which remodelled the plastic art of the country, arose in Bihar. The artists of the new school brought back naturalism and a proper sense of proportion to the sculpture of Magadha, and they have left a number of specimens which rank very high in the history of Indian plastic art.

New Style in Temple Architecture.

Eastern School of Sculpture.

Meanwhile the fame of the Buddhist scholars of Bengal travelled abroad, and Buddhist kings of other countries sought the alliance and the favour of Devapāla. In his old age Devapāla received an embassy from the Buddhist king of Suvarṇadvīpa or Java, named Balaputradeva, and at his request granted five villages in the Pāṭaliputra or Śrīnagara division (*bhukti*) in the districts (*vishayas*) of Gaya and Rājagṛiha. Balaputradeva was desirous of erecting a temple within the holy precincts of Nālandā, and requested Devapāla's favour by sending an ambassador to him.

Embassy from Java.

The Javanese Temple at Nālandā.

Devapāla died after a reign of nearly forty years. The succession then devolved upon Śūrapāla I, or Vigrahapāla I, son of Devapāla's cousin and grandson of Dharmapāla's younger brother Vākpāla. The closing years of the reign of Devapāla were troubled by the rise of the Gurjaras of Rajputana, and the suzerainty of the Pālas in Northern India was destroyed by the Pratīhāra Emperor Bhoja I. Shortly afterwards the Gurjaras invaded Magadha, and the Pālas were defeated in the battle of Mudgagiri or Munger. Śūrapāla I was succeeded after a very short reign by his son Nārāyaṇapāla, during whose reign Bihar and Northern Bengal became

Vigrahapāla or Śūrapāla I.

Bhoja I conquers.

Battle of Mudgagiri.

Mahendrapāla I in Magadha. a province of the Gurjara-Pratīhāra Empire. Mahendrapāla I, son of Bhoja I, was recognized as the ruling sovereign in these provinces. The long reign of Nārāyaṇapāla saw the dismemberment of the Pāla Empire in the east. In Eastern Bengal a Buddhist dynasty arose in Vikramapura, and the Pāla kingdom was reduced to Southern and Western Bengal.

Nārāyaṇapāla. Nārāyaṇapāla reigned for nearly fifty-five years. He was the son of a Chedī or Haihaya princess, and he brought a number of Śaiva ascetics from that country. In the earlier part of his reign Nārāyaṇapāla built one thousand temples of Śiva and placed them under the management of these Pāśupata Āchāryas, for whom he gave a village in Tirhut. Śaiva Influence.

The three successors of Nārāyaṇapāla, Rājyapāla, Gopāla II, and Vigrahapāla II, were princes of very little importance. During their reign Northern Bengal was conquered by a people of foreign (probably Tibetan) extraction who called themselves "Kāmbojas". One of the kings of this Kāmboja dynasty built a large and beautiful temple of Śiva. It was erected in 966 (?) at a place now called Bangarh, in the Dinajpur District of North Bengal.

Kāmboja Conquest of North Bengal.

Temple of Bangarh.

The fortunes of the Pāla dynasty were restored by Mahīpāla I in the second half of the tenth century. This king, a son of Vigrahapāla II, immediately after his accession conquered the whole of Magadha, Tīrabhukti, and Eastern Bengal. He was a great patron of Buddhism. Under him the kingdom of Bengal flourished. Art improved, and sculpture obtained a new tone. The great temple of Buddha at Nālandā was restored in the eleventh year of this king's reign, and the Buddhist temples at Benares were rebuilt and repaired by his kinsmen Sthirapāla and Vasantapāla. Mahīpāla I did not take any part in the great confederacies formed by the Rajput princes in aid of the Shāhīyas of Udabhāṇḍapura. In the latter half of his reign the Gurjara-Pratīhāra kingdom was destroyed by the Chandellas and the Chedīs, and Mahīpāla I came into conflict with the Chedī king Gāṅgeyadeva, who obtained Tīrabhukti after defeating him. About this time, shortly after 1020, a general of King Rājendra Choḷa I of Tanjore invaded Bengal through Orissa. He defeated a king of Daṇḍabhukti (Dātan in the Midnapur District) named Dharmapāla,

Mahīpāla I.

Restoration of Buddhist Shrines at Nālandā and Benares.

Gāṅgeyadeva in Tirhut.

then passed on to Southern Rāḍha (Howrah and Hooghly Districts), where the king Raṇaśūra was defeated. He then proceeded towards Eastern Bengal, where the last king of the Chandra dynasty, Govindachandra by name, was defeated. The Choḷa general then turned towards Northern Rāḍha and reached the banks of the Ganges. Here he was prevented from crossing the Ganges and capturing the capital. After a long reign of more than fifty years, Mahīpāla I was succeeded by his son Nayapāla at the end of the first quarter of the eleventh century.

The Choḷa Invasion.

Nayapāla.

Nayapāla reigned for a very short time only, and during his reign the Hindu holy place of Gaya rose to be a fine city under Viśvarūpa, the governor of the Gaya District, and in the fifteenth year of the reign of Nayapāla he built the series of temples around the shrine supposed to contain the footprint of Vishṇu at that city. During the closing years of the reign of Nayapāla, Magadha was attacked by the celebrated Chedī Emperor Karṇa. An account of the conflict is preserved in the Tibetan biography of Atīśa or Dīpaṅkara Srījñāna. When Karṇa invaded Gaya, Atīśa was residing at Mahābodhi or Bodh-Gaya and was about to depart to Tibet. The Chedī troops destroyed Gaya but were afterwards defeated by the Pāla army. When the troops of Karṇa were being slaughtered in large numbers, Atīśa intervened and settled the terms of a treaty between the two kings. Atīśa left for Tibet immediately afterwards, and Nayapāla was succeeded by his son Vigrahapāla III.

The Buildings of Vishṇupāda.

Chedī Invasion.

Intervention of Atīśa.

Vigrahapāla III.

The new king was a weak prince, and he permitted the formation of an independent kingdom in South-eastern Bengal, under the Yādava chief Jātavarman. Both Jātavarman and Vigrahapāla III had married daughters of the Chedī king Karṇa, and had fought against him in South Bihar. Vigrahapāla III was succeeded by his son Mahīpāla II after a reign of fourteen years. From this time the Pāla monarchy declined very rapidly. Mahīpāla II was a tyrant and had alienated the sympathies of the great feudal nobles. He offended also the great aboriginal chiefs of the caste called Kaivarttas, of Northern Bengal. One of their chiefs named Divvoka or Divya rose in rebellion, and Mahīpāla II had to

The Yādavas of Eastern Bengal.

Mahīpāla II.

Kaivartta Revolt.

Kaivartta Kingdom in Northern Bengal. face the rebels with an inadequate army, as the great nobles would not attend on him. In the fight which followed he was killed, and an independent Kaivartta kingdom was founded in Northern Bengal by Divvoka.

At the time of Mahīpāla II's death his brothers Śūrapāla II and Rāmapāla were imprisoned, and though Śūrapāla II is recognized as the successor of Mahīpāla II in the official records of the Pāla dynasty, his reign appears to have been nominal. We do not know how he died, but shortly afterwards

Rāmapāla. Rāmapāla assumed the offensive against the Kaivarttas. By promising large grants of land he won over the great feudatories to his side and traversed Western Bengal and Bihar. His principal ally was his maternal uncle, the Rāshṭrakūṭa chief Mathana or Mahaṇa, and the latter's nephew the *Mahāpratīhāra* Śivarāja.

The commander-in chief of the Pāla army, Śivarāja made

Śivarāja's Reconnaissance. a reconnaissance by crossing the River Ganges or Padmā and secured much useful information. At this time Divvoka

Defeat and Capture of Bhīma. had been succeeded by his nephew Bhīma. Rāmapāla threw a bridge of boats across the Ganges or the Padmā and crossed with his army, afterwards defeating the Kaivartta army and capturing Bhīma. After a reign of forty-five years Rāmapāla

Kumārapāla. was succeeded by his second son Kumārapāla.

The Southerners. Though the Pāla kingdom was restored by Rāmapāla, the dynasty was on the eve of extinction. A mercenary band of southerners settled in Eastern Bengal, and their chief, Vijaya-

Independence of Provincial Governors. sena, drove away the last Yādava king, Bhojavarman, who fled to the Pāla king. Though Orissa and Assam still acknowledged the suzerainty of the Pālas, the kings were losing all control over other provinces.

Shortly after the accession of Kumārapāla, the governor of

Campaign in Assam. Assam, Tingyadeva, rebelled, and Kumārapāla sent his minister and general Vaidyadeva to subdue that province.

Gopāla III. Kumārapāla died before the return of his general, and the nobles placed his infant son, Gopāla III, on the throne. The boy king was set aside by his uncle Madanapāla, the last king of this dynasty to rule over Bengal. After the murder of Gopāla III the great feudatory chiefs assumed independence, and Madanapāla was driven out of Northern Bengal by

Vijayasena in the eighth or ninth year of his reign. He continued to rule over Magadha or South Bihar for nine or ten years more, and finally invited Govindachandra of Kanauj to help him; but the good fortune of the Pālas had deserted them, and no king of that dynasty came back to Gauḍa. The history of the later Pālas is very well known from the *Rāmacharita* of Sandhyākaranandin. The author was Minister of Peace and War under Rāmapāla.

Vijayasena. **Madanapāla.** **Rāmacharita.**

The Pālas ruled over Bengal and Bihar with varying fortune for over four hundred years. They were not Rajputs, and therefore they did not take part in the constant intertribal feuds of Rajput tribes. Though they were staunch Buddhists they were tolerant of other faiths, and many of their grants were made in favour of Brāhmaṇas. Their steady patronage of Buddhism was the cause of the rise of many new forms of that religion, e.g. Tantric Buddhism, which spread to neighbouring countries like Burma and Tibet. Hindu caste-system became disorganized. Hundreds of valuable works were written under their patronage by Buddhist scholars and are being recovered every day from Nepal and Tibet.

The Position of the Pālas in N. India.

II. The Khaḍgas of Eastern Bengal

A dynasty of kings whose names ended with the word Khaḍga ruled over the lower part of the valley of the old Brahmaputra in the eighth and ninth centuries. Three generations of kings of this dynasty are known from two inscriptions discovered at Ashrafpur in the north-eastern part of the Dacca District. The last king, Jātakhaḍga, probably acknowledged the suzerainty of the second Pāla king, Dharmapāla. He had probably a son named Rājarāja-bhaṭa, who succeeded to the throne. Nothing is known of this dynasty after Rājarāja. Plastic art appears to have been in a very flourishing condition in Eastern Bengal in the eighth century, which was not the case in Bihar and in Western Bengal.

Jātakhaḍga. **Condition of Art in Eastern Bengal.**

III. The Chandras of Vikramapura

During the rise of the Pratihāras a line of Buddhist kings established an independent kingdom at the apex of the Ganges Delta, with their capital at Vikramapura. Their names end with the affix *Chandra*, and therefore they are known as the kings of the Chandra dynasty. In their inscription they say that they were the original rulers of Rohitagiri (Rohtasgaḍh in Bihar). Trailokyachandra of this family founded a kingdom in Chandradvīpa, in Southern Bengal, as a subordinate ruler under the king of Eastern Bengal or Harikela. His son Śrīchandra became the absolute master of Eastern Bengal and had his capital at Vikramapura. Several grants of lands made by this king have been discovered in different parts in Eastern Bengal. The dynasty came to an end with the rise of Mahīpāla I in the middle of the tenth century. A king named Govindachandra was ruling over the Delta in the second decade of the eleventh century, and was defeated by the Choḷa army sent to the Ganges by Rājendra Choḷa I.

Vikramapura. **Trailokya.** **Śrīchandra.** **Govindachandra.**

IV. The Senas

The Senas were a people of southern origin who came from the Karnarese districts of the Bombay Presidency. In their inscriptions they called themselves Karṇāṭa Kshatriyas. In the middle of the eleventh century the Karnāṭas founded two independent kingdoms in North-eastern India, one under Vijayasena and the second under Nānyadeva. The first two chiefs of the Sena dynasty were rulers of small principalities in Western Bengal. Taking advantage of the weakness of the Yādavas of Eastern Bengal, Vijayasena captured Vikramapura and made it his capital. Vijayasena gradually became supreme in Eastern Bengal, and during the rule of the successors of Rāmapāla he gradually enlarged his territories till he became a neighbour of the Pāla kings. When Madanapāla usurped the throne, the feudatory chiefs of the Pāla kingdom refused to obey him, and at this time Vijayasena attacked Northern Bengal and obtained possession of the southern part of the

Their Origin. **Vijayasena.** **Conquers Gauḍa.**

Rajshahi District. He was succeeded after a long reign by his son Vallālasena, born of his queen Vilāsadevī of the Śūra family of Western Bengal. Vijayasena had strengthened himself by marrying this princess, and according to tradition he was an ally of Anantavarman Choḍagaṅga of Orissa. He became the rallying point of the followers of the orthodox Brāhmaṇical religion throughout Bengal and Bihar and its champion against the Buddhists. The Pālas were now looked down upon in Bengal as kings of low origin, and the southerners, the Senas, became very popular. Vijayasena built a temple of Śiva, called Pradyumneśvara, and excavated a tank in front of it at Deopara in the Rajshahi District.

Vallālasena. **Senas as Champions of the Brāhmaṇical Religion.** **Vijayasena's Temple of Śiva.**

Vallālasena had managed the affairs of the state during the extreme old age of his father. He is credited with causing the modern divisions among the Brāhmaṇas and other higher castes of Bengal which form the basis of *Kulinism*. Subdivision in each caste was based on purity of descent and erudition and became the origin of later obnoxious differences among the sub-sects of each caste. Vallāla was a man of advanced age when he came to the throne, and he died after a reign of twelve years. He died in 1118–9 and was succeeded by his son Lakshmaṇasena, the most important and powerful king of the Sena dynasty.

Vallālasena. **His Short Reign.**

Lakshmaṇasena, who was born of the queen Rāmadevī of the Chālukya family, consolidated the Sena kingdom. He recovered the province of Mithilā and drove the Pālas out of Gaya. In their last extremity, Madanapāla and his sons sought protection from their relation, Govindachandra of Kanauj. Govindachandra had married Kumāradevī, the granddaughter of Mathana, Rāmapāla's maternal uncle. He took up the cause of his wife's relatives and a long war, lasting till 1147, ensued. During this period Lakshmaṇasena annexed South-western Bihar permanently, but the country to the west of the Son was annexed by the Gāhaḍavālas. Govindachandra advanced along the valley of the Ganges, and in 1126 he was in possession of the Patna District. This devastating war continued for twenty years more, and in 1146 Govindachandra advanced as far as Munger. During the war Lakshmaṇasena invaded the Gāhaḍavāla kingdom and advanced as

Lakshmaṇasena invades Magadha. **Govindachandra's Invasion of Magadha.** **Lakshmaṇasena invades Allahabad.**

Condition of Bihar at the end of the Twelfth Century. far as Benares and Prayāga or Allahabad. Hostilities ceased with the death of Lakshmaṇasena and Govindachandra in the middle of the twelfth century, but Bihar remained a debatable land. **Lakshmaṇasena's Era.** Lakshmaṇasena founded a new era, which is called the *Lakshmaṇa-Saṃvatsara* and is still used in Mithilā.[1] He re-named the old city of Gauḍa after himself, calling it **Lakshmaṇāvatī or Gauḍa.** Lakshmaṇāvatī. He was a great patron of literature and art, and was himself a poet. Many of his poems are still preserved in Sanskrit anthologies. The famous lyric poet Jayadeva probably flourished in his time. During his reign the Vaishṇava religion of the Bhāgavata sect prevailed in Bengal, and many good images in metal as well as in stone were made by the artists of the province. He died some time before 1170, and his death was followed by a long war of succession.

Lakshmaṇasena probably left three sons, Mādhavasena, Keśavasena, and Visvarūpasena, all of whom succeeded him on the throne. These kings resided at Vikramapura, and Gauḍa or Lakshmaṇāvatī, the old capital of Bengal, was forsaken. **The Civil War.** Most probably there was a war of succession after the death of Lakshmaṇasena. Bihar, the frontier province of the Sena kingdom, was left to look after itself, and a line of subordinate kings governed the Gaya District. **Jayachchandra conquers Gaya.** Jayachchandra of Kanauj invaded Bodh-Gaya in the eighth decade of the twelfth century and occupied the Gaya District for some time, but in 1202 the feudatories of the Sena kings were still ruling there. **The Musalman Conquest of Bihar.** After the death of Jayachchandra in 1194, the Musalman raiders found Bihar an easy conquest. The small province was divided between the Pālas, Gāhaḍavālas and the Senas, who were at war with each other. The Sena kings lived too far away (at

[1] There is another theory about the origin of the era of Lakshmaṇasena and the chronology of the Sena kings. Many scholars rely on the evidence of two works of doubtful origin, called the *Dānasāgara* and the *Adbhūtasāgara*, which are said to have been composed by Vallālasena in the Śaka years 1090 and 1091 = 1169–70. Scholars who believe in the authenticity of these two works think that Lakshmaṇasena ascended the throne in 1170, and fled to Eastern Bengal after the attack on Nadia by Muḥammad bin Bakhtyār Khaljī. These scholars disregard the contemporary evidence of the Gaya inscription of Aśokachalla, according to which Lakshmaṇasena must have died before the year 51 of the era of Lakshmaṇasena = 1170. They are unable to account for the association of the name of Lakshmaṇasena with the era which was founded fifty years before the date of his supposed accession. The astronomical calculation of the initial year of the era associated with his name, the Bodh-Gaya inscription of the year 51 of that era, and another record in the same place, of the year 74 of the same era, prove conclusively that this era was founded by Lakshmaṇasena in 1119, from the date of his accession, and that before 1170 the king had ceased to reign.

Vikramapura in the delta of the Ganges) and were too weak to exercise any real authority over the distant provinces, so that when the Musalmans came, the latter subdued each town and every petty chief at leisure, and no effort was made by the successors of Lakshmaṇasena to repel them. Even after the conquest of Bihar and Northern Bengal the Sena kings continued to rule over Southern and Eastern Bengal till the beginning of the fourteenth century. A king of this dynasty, named Danauja-Mādhava, was ruling over Eastern Bengal in 1282 and met the Emperor Bilbun. He was succeeded by another king named Madhusena, who was reigning over Eastern Bengal in 1289. We do not know anything about the successors of Madhusena, and, according to tradition, a second king of the name of Vallāla was ruling over Eastern Bengal when it was conquered by the Musalmans in the fourteenth century.

Danauja-Mādhava.

Vallāla II (?).

V. The Yādavas of Eastern Bengal

The empire founded by Mahīpāla I seems to have crumbled into decay within a single generation. Eastern Bengal became independent under Rajput kings of the Yādava clan. This kingdom was founded by a successful soldier named Jātavarman, who had migrated from the Panjab. He married Vīraśri, a daughter of the celebrated king Karṇa of Ḍāhala, and conquered Assam. He fought against the Kaivartta king Divya, but failed in an attempt to reconquer Northern Bengal for the sons of his brother-in-law Vigrahapāla III.

Jātavarman.

Jātavarman was succeeded by his son Sāmalavarman, who married one Mālavyadevi, most probably a daughter of King Udayāditya of Mālava. Sāmalavarman was the contemporary of the Pāla king Rāmapāla. His son Bhojavarman, the last king of the dynasty, was driven out from Vikramapura by Vijayasena.

Sāmalavarman.

Bhojavarman.

VI. The Bhañjas of Orissa

A line of kings with the affix Bhañja ruled over the whole of Orissa, from the banks of the Mahānadī to the south-western frontier of Bengal. The most powerful king of this dynasty

Raṇa-bhañja. was Raṇabhañja I, who reigned for more than fifty years and lived in the ninth century. His successors divided his kingdom among themselves, and two modern states are still ruled over by chiefs who add the same affix to their names. The Bhañjas ruled over a district called the Khiñjalī *maṇḍala*, which has not been definitely identified as yet. They were most probably feudatories of the Kesarī or Kara kings of Orissa and obtained independence after their fall.

VII. The Eastern Gaṅgas of Kaliṅga *

The Gaṅgas of Kaliṅga. In the middle of the eleventh century the eastern Gaṅgas were ruling over Kaliṅga to the north of the delta of the Godāvarī. Rājarāja I of this dynasty married Rājasundarī, a daughter of the Choḷa king Rājendra Choḷa II (i.e. Kulottuṅga I). Anantavarman Choḍagaṅga. This union strengthened the dynasty and enabled Anantavarman Choḍagaṅga, son of Rājarāja I, to extend his kingdom towards the north. Anantavarman Choḍagaṅga was crowned king in 1078 and was to some extent the contemporary of the Pāla kings Rāmapāla, Kumārapāla, and Madanapāla, as well as the Sena kings Vijayasena, Vallālasena, and Lakshmaṇasena. He ruled over Orissa and part of the northern Sarkars of Madras for seventy years, and during this long reign he saw the fall of the Pālas and the rise of the Senas. Subjugation of Orissa. He subjugated the petty chiefs of Orissa and the northern Sarkars. His Navy. He created a powerful navy which repeatedly attacked the southern frontier of Bengal. According to tradition, he was the ally of King Vijayasena and helped him to destroy the last vestiges of Pāla authority in Southern Bengal.

His Successors. Anantavarman Choḍagaṅga was succeeded by four of his sons, Kāmarṇava, Rāghava, Rājarāja II, and Anaṅgabhīma I, in that order. During this period—sixty years—the kings of Orissa failed to take any action against the aggressions of the Musalmans of Bengal. Musalman Raids. The frontiers of the kingdom of Orissa were ravaged continually by the Musalmans of Bengal, and these plundering raids are called "the conquest of Jajnagar" by Musalman historians. Revival of the Gaṅgas. The Eastern Gaṅga kings did not revive sufficiently to repel attacks or to retaliate, till the rise of Anaṅgabhīma II and Narasiṁha I in the thirteenth century.

* See p. 315.

The Gaṅga kings of Orissa were great patrons of art and literature. Orissa evolved a separate school of art for itself, and the greatest patrons of art were her kings of the Kara or Kesarī dynasty. The kings of this dynasty ruled over the tract around Bhuvaneśvara. The celebrated temples of Liṅgarāja, Brahmeśvara, and Vaital Deul were built by them. The Eastern Gaṅgas are credited with the later buildings in all parts of Orissa. According to tradition, Anantavarman Choḍagaṅga built the present temple of Jagannātha at Purī and the temple of Rājarājeśvara at Mukhaliṅgam. A Bengali scholar named Bhavadeva Bhaṭṭa built the temple of Ananta-Vāsudeva, near the temple of Liṅgarāja, during the rule of the Eastern Gaṅgas. The sculpture of Orissa shows no affinity with that of the Bengal school or any of the Central Indian schools. Though the temple type betrays a certain amount of resemblance to the mediæval temples of the Chedī-Chandella group, the architects of Orissa designed their temples on a different and a grander scale, which has remained unsurpassed anywhere in India.

The Temples of Bhuvaneśvara.

Bhavadeva Bhaṭṭa builds the Temple of Ananta-Vāsudeva.

Orissa Temple Types.

BIBLIOGRAPHY

R. D. Banerji, *History of Orissa*, Vol. I.

G. N. Sarkar, " Early History of Bengal," *Journal of the Department of Letters* (Vol. XVI), Calcutta University.

R. D. Banerji, " Pālas of Bengal ", *Memoirs of the Asiatic Society of Bengal*, Vol. V.

R. D. Banerji, " Pāla Chronology ", *Journal of the Bihar and Orissa Research Society*, Vol. XIV.

R. D. Banerji, " Lakshmanasena ", *Journal and Proceedings of the Asiatic Society of Bengal* (New Series), Vol. IX.

H. C. Roy, *Dynastic History of Northern India*, Vol. I.

CHAPTER X

THE LATE MEDIÆVAL DYNASTIES OF THE SOUTH

I. The Western Chālukyas of Kalyāṇī

Overthrow of the Rāshṭrakūṭas. Taila II, who overthrew the last Rāshṭrakūṭa king, came to the throne in 973. He destroyed the independence of Kakkaraja II in 973, and defeated Indrarāja IV, a grandson of Kṛishṇa III in 982. He was a descendant of Vikramāditya II of Badami. Immediately afterwards Taila II came into conflict with the Paramāras of Mālava, and carried on a long war **Capture and Death of Muñja.** against Muñja or Vākpatirāja II, who was finally defeated, captured, and killed. The Western Chālukya kingdom was confined to the South-western Deccan, and the great Rāshṭrakūṭa feudatories became independent in the north-west. After a reign of twenty-four years, Taila II was succeeded by **Satyāśraya.** his son Satyāśraya, and his grandsons Vikramāditya V and Jayasiṁha II, in succession.

During the reign of Jayasiṁha II, a popular religious leader founded a sect, now known as the Liṅgāyats, who practise **The Liṅgāyats** a new variety of the Śaiva religion. They do not recognize Brāhmaṇas or caste; but have their own priests, who are called *Jaṅgamas*. Jayasiṁha II is said to have been converted from Jainism to the Śaiva religion. The founder of this faith was Vāsava, an inhabitant of Bagewadi, still a place of importance in the Bijapur District. Vāsava held an important position under the Kaḷachuris of Kalyāṇī. Jayasiṁha II lived in troublous times. He was a contemporary of the Paramāra king Bhoja I and of the great conqueror Rājendra Choḷa I of Tanjore. He was defeated by Rājendra Choḷa I at Musangi **Battle of Musangi.** or Muyangi, and the latter advanced as far as Banavase through Mysore. Jayasiṁha II was succeeded by his son **Someśvara I.** Someśvara I in 1041. Someśvara founded Kalyāṇī and made it the capital of the Chālukyas. He also reigned in troublous times. Central India was in tumult on account of the wars of Karṇa of Ḍāhala. The Choḷas had risen in the south and invaded the Deccan plateau repeatedly. Rājādhirāja I (Rājakeśarīvarman), son of Rājendra Choḷa I, invaded the Chālukya kingdom, and his successor Rājendradeva Parakeśarīvarman defeated Someśvara I at the battle of Koppam. Again Vīrarājendra Rājakeśarīvarman defeated Someśvara I and his sons Vikramāditya VI and Jayasiṁha III in the decisive battle of Kudalsangamam. These successive Choḷa wars weakened the Chālukyas. Bilhaṇa, the court-poet of the Chālukyas, states that Someśvara I advanced as far as Kāñchī, which was then one of the capitals of the Choḷas, but this does not seem to be true. Someśvara I was succeeded by his eldest son Someśvara II, who was deposed by his younger brother Vikramāditya, after a reign of four years, in 1076.

The Choḷa Wars.

Battle of Koppam.

Battle of Kudalsangaman.

Someś-vara II.

Vikramāditya VI ascended the throne in 1076, and later on a special era was founded from that date and is known in history as the *Chālukya-Vikrama Era*. He was the greatest king of this dynasty, and he found it possible to restore the prestige of his family and recover some of the lost territories. During the temporary decline in the fortunes of the Choḷas in the third quarter of the eleventh century, Vikramaditya was able to recover a part of the Mysore plateau. Towards the end of Vikramāditya VI's long reign, war broke out with the Choḷas, and Rājendra Choḷa II invaded the Deccan plateau. This invasion was actually stopped by the Sinda chief Achugi II. After a reign of fifty years Vikramāditya VI was succeeded by his son Someśvara III in 1126. His reign appears to have been a tranquil one. He is reputed to be the author of works dealing with polity, administration of justice, medicine, astrology, arms, chemistry, and rhetoric. During this period the feudatories of the Chālukya kingdom became practically independent. Someśvara III died, after a reign of thirteen years, in 1138 and was succeeded by his sons Jagadekamalla II and Taila III. Taila III was defeated and captured by the Kākatīya king Prola in 1155, and immediately afterwards the Kaḷachurī chief Bijjala, who was his commander-in-chief, usurped the kingdom.

Vikramā-ditya VI.

Chālukya-Vikrama Era.

Someś-vara III.

Jagadeka-malla II.

Taila III.

Captured by Prola.

Usurpation of Bijjala.

Bijjala abdicated in 1167, and his sons came to the throne in succession. They reigned over the Chālukya kingdom till

1183. The feudatories refused to acknowledge them as their sovereigns. The sons of Bijjala became unpopular by persecuting the Lïṅgāyats, and Someśvara IV, the son of Taila III, obtained possession of the capital in 1183. By this time the eastern and northern provinces of the Western Chālukya kingdom had been conquered by the Yādavas of Devagiri and the southern part by the Hoyśaḷas.

The Conquest of the Kingdom by the Yādavas.

II. The Eastern Chālukyas of Veṅgī

Their Origin. The Eastern Chālukya dynasty was founded by Vishṇuvarddhana I, surnamed " the hunchback ", who was a younger brother of Pulikeśin II of Badami. He appears to have asserted independence in 651. His dominions lay in what is now the eastern part of the territories of the Nizam of Haidarabad. The kings became independent after the fall of the main Chālukya dynasty of Badami, and they were the bitterest enemies of the Rāshṭrakūṭas of Mānyakheṭa, with whom they were always at war.

Vijayasiddhi. Jayasiṁha I was ruling in the middle of the seventh century. Vijayasiddhi, grandson of Jayasiṁha I, reigned for twenty-five years and was living in 673. From the inscriptions of this dynasty its genealogy has been completely recovered, but the chronological record is a mere string of names. Very little is known about its kings, their exact dates, or the principal events of their reigns. Their history is being slowly recovered from references to them in inscriptions of other dynasties. Six generations after Vijayasiddhi, we reach the next certain date, in the reign of Vijayāditya III, who was a contemporary of the Rāshṭrakūṭa king Kṛishna II. Vijayāditya III attacked the Rāshṭrakūṭa kingdom and burnt a city named Kiraṇapura. His nephew Chālukya Bhīma I also defeated Kṛishṇa II. Chālukya Bhīma II, the great-grandson of Chālukya Bhīma I, claims to have defeated the Choḷas in the south and the Rāshṭrakūṭas under Govinda IV in the west. In the second half of the tenth century the Chālukya kingdom of Veṅgī was conquered by the Choḷas, and for more than a quarter of a century was ruled by them. The Chālukya inscriptions show a gap of twenty-seven years between Dāna,

Vijayāditya III. **Chālukya-Bhīma I.** **Chālukya-Bhīma II.** **Choḷa Supremacy.**

the eldest son of Chālukya-Bhīma II, and his son Śaktivarman Chālukya-chandra. The fortunes of the Chālukya dynasty were restored by Vimalāditya, a son of Dāna, who married a daughter of the Choḷa king Rājarāja I. This lady was the younger sister of the celebrated conqueror Rājendra-Choḷa I. Vimalāditya was living in 1011. His son Rājarāja Vishṇu-varddhana, by the Choḷa princess Kundavadevī, married a daughter of his maternal uncle Rājendra Choḷa I. Their son Rājendra Choḷa II married his cousin Madhurāntakī, a daughter of the Choḷa king Rājendradeva, son of Rājendra Choḷa I. He ascended the throne of Veṅgī as Rājendra Choḷa II, but on account of his descent from Rājendra Choḷa I he was crowned king of the Choḷa kingdom in 1070 as Kulottuṅga I. Henceforth the Chālukya and Choḷa kingdoms became united, and the son and grandson of Kulottuṅga I reigned at Tanjore. Subsequently, with the decline of the Choḷa power, the central part of the territories of the eastern Chālukyas of Veṅgī was occupied by the Kākatīyas of Varaṅgal, but the Chālukya-Choḷa chiefs continued to rule in the deltas of the Godāvarī and Kṛishṇā till the fourteenth century.

Choḷa Marriages.

Vishṇu-varddhana.

Kulottuṅga I.

The Chālukya-Choḷas.

III. The Malabar Country

The coast land at the apex of the Indian Peninsula is the most fertile district of Southern India. The coast is full of creeks which are natural ports, and from time immemorial this country has attracted the attention of foreign merchants and traders. The Greeks and the Romans traded on this coast for a long time. and Roman coins are found there in large numbers. The country is mentioned by Ptolemy, and a considerable Roman settlement is said to have existed in Roman Imperial times at Cranganore. During the period of the Western Roman Empire large settlements of early Christians and Jews were founded on the western coast. The Kadambas ruled over the northern part of the Malabar District, but after their decline and fall their territory was divided into a number of Nayar principalities, about which very little definite information is available. In tradition these Nayar chieftains are called Perumals. The division of the

The Western Coast.

Roman Settlement at Cranganore.

The Kadambas.

The Perumals.

country into a number of petty kingdoms led to its invasion by many foreign kings. The conditions of Malabar remained unsettled till the rise of the kings of Vijayanagara in the fourteenth century, but the extensive foreign trade of the ports kept the country very rich in spite of repeated foreign invasions.

IV. The Choḷas of Tāñjuvur (Tanjore)*

Like the people of the Kerala or the Malabar coast, the Choḷas were one of the great divisions of the ancient Dra- **The Early Choḷas.** vidian race which had maintained its independence from the very dawn of Indian history. The Choḷas ruled over the eastern coast of the Indian Peninsula, which they controlled jointly with the Pāṇḍyas of Madurā. The history of the early Choḷas still remains unknown except for scanty references in early Tamil literature. After the reform of the ancient Dravidian religion and the recognition of Brāhmaṇa supremacy **Their Brāhmaṇical Genealogy** in Southern India, a special genealogy of the mediæval Choḷa kings was created by the Brāhmaṇas of Southern India. This genealogy is to be found in Choḷa inscriptions.

Among the mediæval Choḷa kings the best known and the **Parāntaka I (907–946).** earliest is Parāntaka I, who commenced to reign in 907 and was alive in 946. He was the real founder of Choḷa supremacy in Southern India. He defeated the Pāṇḍya king Rājasiṁha of Madurā, confirmed the Gaṅga king Pṛithivīpati II in his kingdom, and invaded Ceylon. Parāntaka's son Rājāditya **Rājāditya.** Muvāḍi-Choḷa came in contact with the Rāshṭrakūṭa king Kṛishṇa III. The latter was defeated at the battle of Takkola, but Rājāditya was killed. Half a century later Rājarāja I, **Rājarāja I (985–1012).** the grandson of a younger brother of Rājāditya, laid the foundation of the great Choḷa Empire. Already the Choḷas had become a maritime power in Southern India. Rājarāja **Naval Battle at Kandalur Śalai.** had come to the throne in 985, and before the twelfth year of his reign he had defeated the Malabar navy in the battle of Kandalur Śaḷai. Within a few years he had reduced the entire country at the foot of the Ghats and destroyed the indepen- **His Conquests.** dence of the Eastern Chālukyas of Veṅgī, the Pāṇḍyas of Madurā, the Gaṅgas of Mysore, and the chiefs of the Malabar

* See p. 318.

coast. He extended his kingdom to Kaliṅga in the north and Ceylon in the south, and defeated Satyāśraya of the Western Chālukya dynasty. Before 1012 the Choḷa navy had commenced to conquer the islands of the Indian Archipelago, and the conquests of Rājarāja I were consolidated into a vast overseas empire by his son and successor Rājendra Choḷa I. Rājarāja I died in 1012. He built the great temple of Śiva at Tanjore, and called it Rājarājeswara after himself. On the walls of the temple is inscribed the record of his conquests. In 1006 Chuḍāmaṇivarman, king of Kaṭāha (Kedah in the Malay Peninsula), began a Buddhist temple at Negapatam. It was completed by his son Māravijayottuṅgavarman. At the request of the former Rājarāja I granted a village for this temple.

Overseas Empire.

Great Temple at Tanjore.

The Malayan Temple at Negapatam.

Rājendra Choḷa I, son and successor of Rājarāja I, was one of the greatest monarchs of India. He ascended the throne early in 1012, and broke the power of the Western Chālukyas by defeating Jayasiṁha II at the great battle of Musangi or Muyangi. Henceforth the war between the Choḷas and the Chālukyas became a long record of victories for the Choḷas. In the north Rājendra Choḷa I defeated a king named Indiradan or Indraratha of Gondwana and the combined kings of Central India at the battle of Chakrakoṭṭa in the Bastar State of the Central Provinces. One of his generals raided Orissa and Bengal, advancing as far as the southern coast of the Ganges, opposite the city of Gauḍa. In the south he captured Banavase and the fertile plains of the Malabar coast. His greatest achievement was the conquest of the Burmese coast lands, the Malay Peninsula, and some islands of the Indian Archipelago. His navy conquered for him the Laccadives (Lakshadvīpa) and Maldives (Māladvipa), off the Malabar coast, and the Nicobar Islands in the Bay of Bengal. A great victory was obtained by the Choḷas in Farther India over a king named Saṅgrāmavijayottuṅgavarman, the king of Kaṭāha. This king was most probably a member of the Śailendra dynasty of Java and a descendant of Chuḍāmaṇivarman, the contemporary of Rājarāja I. The territories wrested by the Choḷas from this king consisted of the extensive kingdom of Śrīvijaya, which at one time included

Rājendra Choḷa I.

Battle of Musangi.

Battle of Chakrakoṭṭa.

Northern Campaign.

Campaigns in Farther India and the Archipelago.

War in Kedah.

Śailendra Dynasty of Sumatra and Java.

Sumatra and Java with its capital at Palembang. The long list of the conquests of Rājendra Choḷa in Farther India has provided a subject for controversy, as it is extremely difficult to identify most of them on account of the change of name in Burma, the Malay peninsula, and the Eastern Archipelago. Among the localities in Farther India mentioned in the Rājarājesvara temple inscription of the nineteenth year of the king's reign, Śrīvijaya (Sumatra), Pāppalam or Māppappalam, a seaport in Rāmanna-deśa or Burma, Kaḍāra (Kedah in the Malay Peninsula), and Nakkavaram (the Nicobar Islands) can be properly identified. Places such as Laṅkāśoka and "Mayirudingan surrounded by the sea", with many others, cannot be identified as yet. Rājendra Choḷa I died in 1042 and was succeeded by his son Rājādhirāja.

Death of Rājendra Choḷa I.

The new king was immediately called upon to face a series of campaigns both in the north and in the south. Three kings of the south, Māṇābharaṇa, Vīra-Kerala, and Sundara-Pāṇḍya, combined with four kings of Ceylon named Vikramabāhu, Vikrama-Pāṇḍya, Vīra-Śālamegha, and Śrī-Vallabha-Madana-rāja. This formidable confederacy was broken up by the king before the fourth year of his reign. Vīra-Pāṇḍya and Vīra-Kerala were beheaded. In the north Someśvara I of the western Chālukya dynasty was defeated at Koppam, and the king's younger brother built a pillar of victory at Kollapuram. The Eastern Chālukya king Vijayāditya of Veṅgī and a king named Gaṇapati were defeated in the north. It appears now that a very widespread conspiracy among northern and southern kings came into existence, immediately after the death of Rājendra Choḷa I, to overthrow Choḷa supremacy, but their attempts were frustrated. The Ceylonese campaign appears to have been undertaken by the king's younger brother Rājendradeva either during this reign or afterwards. Vīra-Śālamegha was beheaded, and two sons of Mānābharaṇa were brought back as hostages. Rājādhirāja I was succeeded by his younger brother Rājendra some time between 1052 and 1053.

Rājādhi-rāja (1042-52). **Confederacy of Southern and Ceylonese Kings.** **Battle of Koppam.** **War in the Telugu Country.** **Campaign in Ceylon.** **Death of Rājādhi-rāja.**

Rājendradeva was present in most of the campaigns of his elder brother and shares with him the credit of defeating the Western Chālukyas at the battle of Koppam. His daughter Madhurāntakī was married to Rājendra, the son of the Eastern

Rājendra-deva (1052-63).

Chālukya king Rājarāja. Rājendradeva reigned for at least twelve years and was succeeded by his brother Vīrarājendra Rājakeśarīvarman, who ascended the throne in 1063.

Eastern Chālukya Connexion.

Immediately after his accession Vīrarājendra Rājakeśarīvarman was faced with the rising power of Vikramāditya VI of the western Chālukya dynasty. Vikramāditya tried to interfere in the Eastern Chālukya kingdom of Veṅgī, and therefore after the death of Rājarāja that kingdom was bestowed on Vijayāditya VII instead of passing to the former's son Rājendra Choḷa II, who was Vīrarājendra's nephew and the daughter's son of Rājendra Choḷa I. Vīrarajendra finally defeated Vikramāditya VI and his brother Jayasiṁha III at the great battle of Kudalsangamam at the apex of the Kṛishṇā-Tuṅgabhadrā *Doāb*. On another occasion also he sacked the city of Kampili and defeated Someśvara II. Finally he annexed the Kanarese countries to the Choḷa Empire and deprived Someśvara II of his throne with the aid of the latter's brother Vikramāditya VI. In the north Vīrarājendra advanced as far as Chakrakoṭṭa and expelled a king named Devanātha. Vīrarājendra was also compelled to undertake a campaign in Farther India and defeat the king of Kaṭāha or Kaḍara in the Malay Peninsula. He is known to have reigned at least seven years, and was succeeded by his son Adhirājendra.

Vīrarājendra (1063-70).

Eastern Chālukya Succession.

Battle of Kudalsangamam.

Western Chālukya Succession.

Campaign in Malay Peninsula.

According to Western Chālukya inscriptions, Adhirājendra, the son of Vīrarājendra, was placed on the throne by Vikramāditya VI. Adhirājendra lost his life, and the throne passed on to Rājendra Choḷa II of Veṅgī, who was the grandson of Rājendra Chola I and the great-grandson of Rājarāja I. After his accession at Tanjore, Rājendra assumed the title of Kulottuṅga Choḷa I. He ascended the throne of his maternal ancestors in 1070. Vikramāditya VI tried to interfere in the Choḷa succession but did not succeed. Early in his reign Kulottuṅga Choḷa I defeated the Paramāra king of Dhārā, i.e. Udayāditya of Mālava, at Chakrakoṭṭa and captured Wairagaḍh (Vayirākara). His next campaign was undertaken in the south, where he destroyed an unnamed king and crowned himself once more on the banks of Kāverī. He subdued the rebellious Pāṇḍya princes, the chiefs of the Malabar, and reduced the entire country as far as the Gulf of Mannar. After reducing the Choḷa

Kulottuṅga Choḷa I (or Rājendra Choḷa II) (1070-1118).

War with Udayāditya of Mālava.

Southern Campaigns.

Empire to obedience, Kulottuṅga I turned his attention to the north. Some time before the twenty-sixth year of his reign, i.e. 1095–6, he invaded Kaliṅga. His grandson Anantavarman-Choḍagaṅga had ascended the throne in 1078. Towards the close of Kulottuṅga's reign Gaṅgavāḍī, or the southern part of the Mysore plateau, was recovered for the Western Chālukyas by Hoyśaḷa chiefs. After a long reign of forty-nine years, Kulottuṅga I died in 1118 and was succeeded by his son Vikrama Choḷa *Tyāgasamudra.* Though Kulottuṅga I succeeded in ascending the throne of his maternal grandfather and in retaining it for nearly half a century, there was great disaffection throughout the Choḷa Empire, where many descendants of Rājarāja I were living. These dissensions brought about the decline of the Choḷa power in Southern India, a decline which began at the accession of Kulottuṅga I. During his reign there were two Buddhist temples at Negapatam, one of which had been built in the twentieth year of the reign of Rājarāja I. Kulottuṅga I made grants to both of these temples. Inscriptions testify to the fact that Buddhism was a flourishing religion in Southern India at this time. There existed a temple of Buddha and another of Tārā at Ḍambal near Gadag in the Dharwar District, to which a grant of land was made by the local merchants in 1095 during the reign of Vikramāditya VI, when his queen Lakshmadevī was the vicereine of Ḍambal. In 1063 one of his ministers established or built temples of Buddha, Lokeśvara, and Tārā at Balligave in Mysore. The age of Kulottuṅga I was a period of religious revival, as the great Vaishṇava reformer Rāmānuja was his contemporary and had to fly to Mysore to avoid the displeasure of the king.

Invasion of Kaliṅga. **Loss of Mysore.** **His Death.** **Dissensions among Choḷa Princes.** **Grants to Buddhist Temples at Negapatam.** **Condition of Buddhism.** **Buddhist Temples at Gadag and Balligave.** **Rāmānuja.**

Vikrama Choḷa *Tyāgasamudra* and his descendants gradually grew weaker. The Pāṇḍyas of Madurā, the chiefs of Kerala or Malabar, and the kings of Ceylon gradually threw off their allegiance. Later on the Chālukya-Choḷa chiefs became independent in the Telugu country. Kulottuṅga III commenced to reign in 1178. During his long reign of thirty-seven years the Hoyśaḷas of Dorasamudra and the Pāṇḍyas of Madurā practically conquered the whole of the Choḷa kingdom. The Choḷas had become so weak in his time that during his reign Parā-

Vikrama Choḷa. **Loss of the Empire.** **Kulottuṅga III (1178–1216).**

kramabāhu of Ceylon sent two armies to interfere in a disputed succession in the Pāṇḍya kingdom of Madurā. The Ceylonese armies advanced to the neighbourhood of the Choḷa capital and were driven out with great difficulty. His son and successor Rājarāja III commenced to reign in 1216. **Rājarāja III.** A Pallava chief named Kopperuñjiṅga became very powerful. **Kopperuñjiṅga.** From his head-quarters at Sendamangalam in the South Arkat District he conquered the Telugu country and captured Rājarāja III. The Choḷa king was saved by the generals of the Hoyśaḷa king Narasiṁha II and managed to retain his throne till 1245. The last king of the Choḷa dynasty was Rājendra Choḷa III, **Rājendra Choḷa III.** who managed to exist as an independent prince till 1267. Nothing is known about his successors.

A highly decentralized system of administration existed in Southern India from ancient times. **Choḷa Administration.** The inscriptions of the Choḷa kings of Tanjore give evidence of the continuation of this system in detail. The unit of government was the union of villages called *Kurram*. **Union of Villages, &c.** A number of Kurrams formed a *nadu* (district), a number of districts formed a division, and a province (*maṇḍalaṁ*) consisted of several such divisions. The viceroys **Viceroys.** were mostly princes of the royal family or members of some overthrown dynasty. Registers of royal orders were regularly kept and all arable or waste lands carefully surveyed. **Survey of Land.** The survey records were kept at head-quarters. The unit of linear measurement was the length of the footprint of Kulottuṅga I. The royal dues were taken either in kind or in gold, and the amount was fixed by an estimate before the cutting of the crop, and a revision after it. **Revenue.** The revenue was collected by the village assemblies. Royal orders were written by the private secretary and confirmed by the chief secretary. **Secretariat.** The list of taxes and imposts is very long and cannot be understood at the present date. The chief source of the income of the State was the land-revenue, together with petty imposts either external or internal. **Imposts.** There were local treasuries even in the Kurrams, where unspent balance of the revenue was kept. Taxes were remitted when necessary. The unit of the currency was the golden *Kāsu*, **Currency.** weighing one-sixth of an ounce. An extensive system of irrigation existed in the Tamil country. **Irrigation** Dams were thrown across the rivers and all tanks and wells utilized for the fields when necessary. Main channels distributed the waters of the Kāverī over a large area. There was a large artificial reservoir in Gaṅgai-Koṇḍa-Choḷa-puram, the new capital built by Rājendra Choḷa I. The village assembly was both deliberative and executive and passed the highest sentences, including that of death on criminals. Checks were imposed upon it by district officials and viceroys. The king was the highest appelate authority in the country.

Justice.

The Choḷas were great builders. Rājarāja I built the great temple of Rājarājeśvara at Tanjore, which still excites the admiration of visitors. This temple is the earliest example of post-Pallava architecture of Southern India and became the prototype of all later South Indian temples. Plastic art took a new shape in the extreme south under the Choḷas, and metal images of this period show a wonderful equipoise and elasticity in their execution. Rājendra Choḷa I built a great temple in his new capital at Gaṅgai-Koṇḍa-Choḷa-puram in the Trichinopoly District, which was destroyed in modern times. There were great trunk roads from the River Mahānadī in Orissa to Koṭṭaru near Cape Comorin. Kulottuṅga I planted military colonies along this road, which was 64 cubits in breadth and along which public ferries were maintained across all rivers.

Temple of Rājarājeśvara at Tanjore.

Choḷa Art

Temple of Rājendra Choḷa I.

Roads.

Ferries.

V. The Pāṇḍyas of Madura

From time immemorial Madhura or Madurā, the Mathurā of the south, had been the centre of the Pāṇḍyas, a race of pure Dravidians who claimed to be descended from Aryan gods after the reform of the ancient Dravidian religion. Except for scanty references in early Tamil literature, we do not know anything about the early or the mediæval kings of Madurā. The early Pāṇḍya kings issued copper coins with the symbol of the fish, and contemporary inscriptions from the fourth to the ninth centuries mention the existence of the Pāṇḍya kingdom. With the rise of the Choḷas, the Pāṇḍyas lost their independence, which they did not succeed in regaining till the end of the twelfth century. The first independent Pāṇḍya king was Jaṭāvarman Kulaśekhara, who began to reign in

Madurā.

The "Fish" Coins.

1190. His successor Sundara Pāṇḍya I came to the throne in 1216 and conquered the Choḷa capitals of Tanjore and Udaipur. His inscriptions are found in the Choḷa country proper, i.e. the districts of Tanjore and Trichinopoly. Sundara Pāṇḍya I reigned till 1238 and was succeeded by Sundara Pāṇḍya II. The fall of the Choḷas brought the Pāṇḍyas face to face with the rising power of the Hoyśaḷas of Dorasamudra. The Hoyśaḷas advanced into the heart of the Choḷa country and captured the hill fort of Trichinopoly and the Island of Śrī-Raṅgam in the River Coleroon. Though the last Choḷa king, Rājendra Choḷa III, drove away the Hoyśaḷas for some time, they returned and reoccupied Śrī-Raṅgam. The highlands along the base of the Eastern Ghats were permanently annexed by them, and the coast land only remained in the possession of the Pāṇḍyas. Jaṭāvarman Sundara Pāṇḍya I, who came to the throne in 1251, invaded Ceylon and advanced as far as Nellore in the north, where he defeated the Kākatīya king of Varangal. He also defeated the Hoyśaḷa king Someśvara at Śrī-Raṅgam.

Jaṭāvarman Kulaśekhara. **Sundara Pāṇḍya I.** **Sundara Pāṇḍya II.** **The Hoyśaḷa Conquest.** **Jaṭāvarman Sundara Pāṇḍya I.**

The later Pāṇḍyas seem to have become feudatories of the Hoyśaḷas of Dorasamudra, and when the first Musalman invasion of Southern India took place, in the beginning of the fourteenth century, the collapse of the power of the Hoyśaḷas prostrated Madurā and the Pāṇḍya country at the foot of the Musalman general. Pāṇḍya chiefs continued to rule over Madurā till the end of the sixteenth century, and their history belongs to the history of the Musalman period. The last known king was Jaṭilavarman, who was reigning in 1567, or two years after the destruction of the empire of Vijayanagara at the battle of Talikota.

The Musalman Conquest. **Jaṭilavarman.**

VI. The Yādavas of Devagiri*

The downfall of the Rāshṭrakūṭas of Mānyakheṭa in 982 did not bring the whole of the western part of Southern India under the Western Chālukyas of Kalyāṇī. The feudatories of the Rāshṭrakūṭas remained almost unaffected, and in many cases became practically independent. Such were the Yādavas of the Belgaum District. Upon the fall of the Western

The Early Yādava Chiefs.

* See p. 319.

Chālukyas, the Yādavas became the paramount power in Western India and ruled over an empire which was as extensive as that of the Rāshṭrakūṭas.

The Yādavas were Marathas proper and lived in the heart of the Maratha country, extending from Nasik to Devagiri (modern Daulatabad). The celebrated Brāhmaṇa scholar Hemādri has left an account of the Yādava dynasty. According to the genealogy given by Hemādri, Bhillama V restored or brought about the independence of this dynasty at the end of the twelfth century. The inscriptions of the family leave no doubt about the fact that Bhillama V was the first of its chiefs to assume the Imperial title. During the troublous times which followed the decline of the Chālukya monarchy, Bhillama gained the upper hand in the northern part of the Deccan and gradually made himself master of the country to the north of the Kṛishṇā. He is said to have founded the city of Devagiri, where he crowned himself in 1187. The Yādavas came into conflict with the Hoyśaḷa chiefs of Dorasamudra, and though they succeeded in defeating them at first, they were finally defeated by the Hoyśaḷa king Vīra Vallāla I at the battle of Lakkundi in 1191. Bhillama died in the same year and was succeeded by his son Jaitugi or Jaitrapāla I.

Bhillama V.

Battle of Lakkundi.

Foiled in their attempts to conquer the Northern Kanarese districts, the Yādavas of Devagiri turned their attention to the north-east, where internal dissensions among the Chedīs or Haihayas of Tripurī or Ratnapura had weakened the once powerful kingdom of Ḍāhala. Some time after 1196 Jaitugi I defeated a Chedī king, and the Kākatīya chief Rudra of Anamakonda. The Kākatīya kingdom was given to Gaṇapati, a nephew of Rudra, and the Yādavas became the paramount power in the southern part of Central India also.

Defeat of the Chedīs.

Siṁhaṇa.

Jaitugi I was succeeded by his son Siṁhaṇa or Simghaṇa, the most powerful king of the dynasty. Siṁhaṇa destroyed the independence of Jājalladeva III of Ratnapura. In the south he defeated the Hoyśaḷa king Vīra-Vallāla II and extended his kingdom to the south of the Kṛishṇā. He destroyed the independence of the southern Śīlāhāras of Kolhapur by defeating Bhoja II and storming the almost impregnable fort of

Defeats the Chedīs of Ratnapura and the Hoyśalas.

Praṇālaka (modern Paṇhālā). In the north Siṁhaṇa defeated the Andhra king Kokkala of the Telugu country and Arjunavarman of Mālava. He also invaded Gujarat several times. His son Rāmachandra advanced as far as the banks of the River Narmadā. According to Somadeva, the author of the *Kīrttikaumudī*, Lavaṇaprasāda of Gujarat was forced to submit to Siṁhaṇa on account of the revolt of certain chiefs in the northern part of his kingdom. The second Yādava invasion of Gujarat took place some time before 1138, during the reign of Viśāladeva. Thus, during the reign of Siṁhaṇa, the Yādava Empire in the Deccan became as extensive as that of the Rāshṭrakūṭas. With the exception of the extreme south, the whole of the Central and Western Deccan, including Khandesh, was included in his kingdom. Siṁhaṇa died in 1246 after a reign of thirty-nine years, and was succeeded by his grandson Kṛishṇa or Kaṇṇara.

Conquest of Kolhapur. **Defeat of Arjunavarman of Mālava.** **Second Invasion.** **The Yādava Empire.** **Kṛishṇa.**

Siṁhaṇa was a great patron of literature and art. Under him the post of *Śrīkaraṇa*, or private secretary to the king, was held by a man named Soḍhala, whose son Śārṅgadhara wrote an exhaustive work on music called *Saṅgīta-ratnākara* and the king Siṁhaṇa himself is said to have written a commentary on this work. Chāṅgadeva, the grandson of the celebrated astronomer Bhāskarāchārya, was the chief astronomer in the court of Siṁhaṇa. Chāṅgadeva built a temple of Bhavānī at Pāṭnā near Chālisgāon, and a college for the study of *Siddhānta-Śiromaṇi* and other works composed by his grandfather at a place called Changdev after him, near Bhusawal. In 1207 the college was endowed with lands by two Maratha feudatory chiefs of Siṁhaṇa. In 1222 an astrologer named Anantadeva built a temple at Bāhal in Khandesh, and in its inscription he styles himself the Chief Astrologer of Siṁhaṇa.

Soḍhala. **Work on Music.** **Astronomical College at Changdev.** **Anantadeva.**

Jaitrapāla or Jaitugi II, Siṁhaṇa's son, had died in his father's lifetime, so the succession devolved upon his son Kṛishṇa or Kaṇṇara, who ascended the throne at Devagiri in 1247. Kṛishṇa was a great patron of the Brāhmaṇas and performed many Vedic sacrifices. Jāhlana, the son of Kṛishṇa's minister Lakshmīdeva, compiled an anthology called *Śuktimuktāvalī* or Sanskrit verses. Amalānanda wrote a commentary called *Vedānta-kalpataru* on Vāchaspatimiśra's *Bhāmatī* during

Kṛishṇa revives Vedic Ceremonies. **Encouragement of Literature.**

the reign of Kṛishṇa. After a reign of thirteen years, Kṛishṇa was succeeded by his younger brother Mahādeva. Mahādeva defeated the Chālukya-Vāghela king Viśāladeva and the Hoyśaḷa King Narasiṁha III. He defeated Queen Rudrāmmā of the Kākatīya dynasty, destroyed the independence of the Śīlāhāras of Northern Konkan and placed the country under a Yādava viceroy. The oldest temple of Viṭhobā at Pandharpur, in the Sholopur District, was built during the reign of Mahādeva in 1272. Mahādeva was succeeded by his son Amaṇa, but the latter was set aside by Kṛishṇa's son Rāmachandra in 1272.

Mahādeva. His Conquests. Annexation of Northern Konkan. Temples. Amaṇa.

Rāmachandra was the last independent king of the Yādava dynasty of Devagiri. He defeated the Kākatiya king Pratāparudra of Varangal and Bhoja II of Mālava. During his reign the Yādavas succeeded in driving out the Hoyśaḷas from the northern part of Mysore. The celebrated scholar Hemādri was the chief minister and private secretary of Mahādeva and Rāmachandra. He was a Brāhmaṇa and one of the greatest scholars of the mediæval period. His great work on Hindu religion, law, and custom, called the *Chaturvarga-Chintāmaṇi*, is divided into four parts, to which a fifth or an appendix was added later. Hemādri is said to have composed a large number of works on many different subjects. Bopadeva, the author of the well-known grammar, *Mugdhabodha*, was a protégé of Hemādri. Most of the Hindu temples in the Deccan are attributed to Hemādri, and he is reputed to have been the creator of a new style in temple architecture, a style called "Hemāḍpanti". Vāgbhaṭa, the writer on medicine, was a contemporary of Hemādri, and the Maratha saint Jñāneśvara composed his celebrated commentary on the Bhagavadgītā in Marathi during the reign of Rāmachandra in 1290.

Rāmachandra. Hemādri. Boapdeva. Hemāḍpanti Temples. Vāgbhaṭa. Jñāneśvara.

In 1294 Rāmachandra was surprised by 'Alāuddīn Muḥammad Khaljī, who had advanced secretly from Kara, near Allahabad, and appeared before Devagiri. Rāmachandra was unprepared and threw himself into the fort of Devagiri with a small force. The city was then besieged by the Musalman army. Rāmachandra's son Śaṅkara was advancing towards Devagiri to relieve his father, but he was defeated on the way and Rāmachandra surrendered. As soon as 'Alāuddīn had

Invasion of 'Alāuddīn Khaljī. Surrender of Rāmachandra.

departed, Rāmachandra refused to pay the promised tribute, and after the accession of 'Alāuddīn to the throne of Delhi, the Musalman general Mālik Kāfūr was sent against Devagiri (1307). Rāmachandra was again defeated and this time was sent as a prisoner to Delhi. On his release he returned to his country, and in 1309 entertained Mālik Kāfūr, then on his way to Southern India. Rāmachandra died in the same year and was succeeded by his son Śaṅkara, who at once declared his independence. As a consequence, Mālik Kāfūr came to Devagiri in 1312, defeated Śaṅkara, and destroyed the Yādava kingdom. Harapāladeva, son-in-law of Rāmachandra, tried to resist the Musalman occupation of the country; but he, too, was defeated and killed in 1318.

Invasion of Mālik Kāfūr.

Śaṅkara.

Harapāla.

VII. The Hoyśaḷas of Dorasamudra *

The Hoyśaḷas, who are also called Poyśaḷas, Poyśaṇas, and Hoyśaṇas, claimed to be descended from the Moon. The early chiefs were feudatories either of the Western Chālukyas or the Choḷas. Vishṇuvarddhana was the first really independent prince of this dynasty. He did not assume Imperial titles, but he defeated the Choḷa feudatories Narasiṁhavarman and Adiyama. In the west he defeated the Kādamba chief Jayakeśin II of Goa, and his minister Gaṅgarāja defeated the army of the Western Chālukya king Vikramāditya VI. Finally he defeated the Gaṅgas in the decisive battle of Talakad. The Hoyśaḷas now occupied the important positions between the Choḷas in the south-east and the Western Chālukyas in the north-west. Vishṇuvarddhana descended from the Deccan plateau and occupied Coimbatore. Some time before 1131 he destroyed some of the Perumals of the Malabar country and conquered the Tuluvas of the South Karara District. In the north he advanced as far as Chakrakoṭṭa in the Bastar State of the Central Provinces and invaded Kāñchī. Gradually he annexed the whole of the Kanarese Districts as far as Lakkundi in the Dharwar District. Later, he advanced the northern frontier of his kingdom as far as the River Kṛishṇā and sacked Madurā in the south. By his marauding expeditions Vishṇuvarddhana acquired great wealth. His queen Śāntala-

Their Origin.

Vishṇuvarddhana.

Battle of Talakad.

Invasion of Southern India.

* See p. 319.

Temples. devī erected a Jain temple at Śravaṇa-Begoḷā. His minister Gaṅgarāja erected a tomb in memory of his wife in 1121. Vishṇuvarddhana was succeeded by his son Narasiṁha I.

The reign of this king coincides with the fall of the Western Chālukya monarchy, and Narasiṁha reigned peacefully over the dominions acquired by his father. The original Hoyśaḷa

Bas-relief from Belur, Hasan district, Mysore—Hoyśala sculpture; Kṛishṇa tending cattle in Gokula (12th century A.D.)

Change of Capital. capital was Belāpura, modern Belur, in the Hassan District of Mysore. Vishṇuvarddhana removed it to Dorasamudra, also called Dvārasamudra, modern Halebid, about ten miles north-east of Belur. Hulla, a minister of Narasiṁha I, was a great patron of Jainism, and the Hoyśaḷas have left splendid buildings at Belur and Śravaṇa-Belgoḷā. In the concluding

Wars with western Chālukyas and Yādavas. decades of the twelfth century Vīra-Vallāla II, son of Narasiṁha I, conquered the northern part of the Dharwar District and defeated Brahma, the general of the Western Chāḷukya king Someśvara IV. He also defeated Jaitrasiṁha, minister of the Yādava king Bhillama V. The country to the south of the Kṛishṇā was added to the Hoysaḷa kingdom, and Vīra-Vallāla defeated the Yādava army at the battle of Lakkundi. A reference to this battle is to be found in a Harihar inscription of Narasiṁha II, dated 1224. The Yādavas were pursued as far as Yelburga in the Nizam's dominion. Vīra-Vallāla died after 1211 and was succeeded by his son Narasiṁha II.

Battle of Lakkundi.

During the reign of his son Narasiṁha II, the Yādavas of Devagiri under Siṁhaṇa recovered their lost territories. Narasiṁha II lost his father's conquests to the north of the Tuṅgabhadrā. In the south he claims to have re-established the Choḷa king, and he most probably placed Rājarāja III on the throne after liberating him from Kopperuñjiṅga. The certain dates of Narasiṁha II range from 1223 to 1231. He was succeeded by his son Someśvara or Sovīdeva. The decline of the Choḷa monarchy enabled the Hoysaḷas to conquer a portion of the plain or coast land below the Eastern Ghats, and Someśvara captured the Island of Śrī-Raṅgam in the River Coleroon. The Hoysaḷas now came into closer contact with the Pāṇḍyas of Madurā, and a long war ensued for the possession of Śrī-Raṅgam. Someśvara died in 1254 and was succeeded by his son Narasiṁha III. His certain dates range from 1254 to 1286. During his reign the people of the Hoysaḷa kingdom contributed to the Jizya tax levied on all Hindus of the Kanarese country living at Benares. The uneventful and long reign of Narasiṁha III was spent in protracted wars against the Pāṇḍyas of Madurā. He was succeeded by his son Vīra-Vallāla III, the last king of the Hoysaḷa dynasty.

Narasiṁha II.

Yādava War.

Wars in Tanjore.

Capture of Śrī-Raṅgam.

Narasiṁha III.

Payment of the Jizya.

Vīra-Vallāla III.

The certain dates of Vīra-Vallāla III range from 1310 to 1339, but he could not exercise much authority after 1310. He appears to have ascended the throne in the last decade of the thirteenth century. But shortly afterwards 'Alāuddīn Khaljī invaded Devagiri, and after its fall the turn of the Hoysaḷa kingdom arrived very soon. In 1310 Sultān 'Alāuddīn Muḥammad Shāh Khaljī deputed Mālik Kāfūr and Khwājā Hājī to conquer Dorasamudra. The Musalman army marched from Devagiri and besieged Dorasamudra. Vīra-Vallāla III sur-

Musalman Invasion.

Submission of Vira-Vallāla III. rendered, and Dorasamudra was occupied and sacked by the Musalmans. From Dorasamudra the Musalman army proceeded against Madurā. After the return of the Musalman army, Vīra-Vallāla III continued to pay tribute. He removed his capital from Dorasamudra to Belur and finally to Tondanur. He was a man of considerable ability whose submission to the Musalmans was all along nominal. After the fall of the Khaljīs and before the rise of the Tughlaqs, he organized a formidable confederacy of Dravidian Hindu chiefs and regained the whole of the Kanarese and Tamil country with the exception of a small tract of land around Madurā. Saṅgama and his five sons, of the Yādava clan, who afterwards founded the empire of Vijayanagara, were his principal colleagues. But the aged monarch did not live to see the final expulsion of the Musalmans from the extreme south. **His Murder.** In 1339 he was captured and flayed alive by Sultān Damaghan of Madurā.

Like the Western Chālukyas, the Hoyśaḷas were great builders. In spite of centuries under Musalman rule, their **Hoyśaḷa Temples.** temples at Śravaṇa-Belgoḷā, Belur, and Halebid still excite our admiration. The Hoyśaḷas encouraged sculpture, while **Art.** the decorative art as practised by them is of a class of its own. The earliest sculptures of Vijayanagara were directly **Origin of Mediæval South Indian Art.** inspired by the Hoyśaḷa school, splendid examples of which have been discovered all over the Mysore State.

BIBLIOGRAPHY

Sir R. G. Bhandarkar, *Early History of the Deccan.*

Fleet, "Dynasties of the Canarese Country", *Bombay Gazetteer*, Vol. I, Part II.

F. Kielhorn, "Synchronistic Art", *Epigraphia Indica*, Vol. VIII, Appendix ii.

S. K. Aiyangar, *Ancient India.*

CHAPTER XI

THE MEDIÆVAL HISTORY OF KĀŚMĪRA

The early history of Kāśmīra still remains shrouded in mystery. In spite of the existence of Kalhaṇa's history of that country, the date of no event prior to the accession of Durlabha of the Karkoṭa dynasty can be ascertained. Durlabha was the son-in-law of Bālāditya, the last king of the dynasty founded by Gonanda. He was a man of humble origin, and succeeded to the kingdom of Kāśmīra on the extinction of the ruling dynasty. **Early History of Kāśmīra uncertain**

I. The Karkoṭa Dynasty

Durlabha, the first king of this dynasty, is known from Chinese history and was a contemporary of Yuan Chwang. He is said to have controlled the roads from China to the Kabul valley. Yuan Chwang visited Kāśmīra between 631 and 633. At that time the plains below the hills, such as Taxila, Hazara, and the Salt range, were included in the kingdom of Kāśmīra. Durlabha is also known from his copper coins. He was succeeded by his son Pratāpa II, who issued coins resembling those of his father, and was in turn succeeded by three of his sons, who are better known in Indian literature. The third son, Lalitāditya-Muktāpīḍa, known in Chinese history as King Mu-to-pi, sent an embassy to the Chinese emperor Hiuen-Tsung (713–755). He defeated a king of Kanauj named Yaśovarman and extended his power towards the Kabul valley. His minister, a native of Tokharistan, held, according to Stein, the Chinese title "Tsiang-kiun" or general. In India this title was supposed to be his proper name, and in consequence the Kāśmīrians called him Chaṅkuṇa. Muktāpīḍa defeated the Turkish tribes of North-western Kāśmīra and North-eastern Afghanistan, as well as the Tibetans and the Dards. The Chinese pilgrim Ou-k'ong visited Kāśmīra shortly after Muktāpīḍa's death, in 759–763. Muktāpīḍa built a Buddhist *Vihāra* at Parihāsapura and another at Hushkapura, **Durlabha.** **Pratāpa II.** **Lalitāditya.** **Chaṅkuṇa.** **Ou-k'ong.**

the city founded by Huvishka. He died during an expedition into the snow-bound Himalayan regions and was succeeded by his eldest son Kubalayāpīḍa. The death of Muktāpīḍa was followed by a number of short and weak reigns. Finally his grandson Jayāpīḍa ascended the throne. His coins bearing the name Vinayāditya are well known. Jayāpīḍa was succeeded by two of his sons and finally by an illegitimate grandson called Chippaṭa-Jayāpīḍa, who was raised to the throne when a child. The uncles of the king, whose mother was of low origin, became very powerful, and after his death placed a number of his cousins on the throne. Finally the throne passed on to Avantivarman, the son of one of Chippaṭa-Jayāpīḍa's maternal uncles.

Kubalayāpīḍa.

Jayāpīḍa-Vinayāditya.

Chippaṭa-Jayāpīḍa.

II. The Utpala Dynasty

Avantivarman, the founder of the Utpala dynasty, was a powerful and energetic king. He consolidated the kingdom, which had suffered economically as well as politically during the reign of the successors of Lalitāditya. Even the forest chiefs of Kāśmīra had thrown off allegiance to the king. Avantivarman founded the town of Avantipura and built a number of splendid temples, the ruins of which have been brought to light recently. His minister Śūra founded a town named, after himself, Śūrapura. He was representative of the turbulent class of nobles called Ḍāmaras, who brought about the downfall of the Hindu kingdom of Kāśmīra. Avantivarman regulated the course of the River Vitastā, and his engineer Sūya dug fresh channels to the river in order to drain waterlogged lands and prevent floods.

Avantivarman.

Foundation of Avantipura.

Irrigation Works.

Avantivarman was succeeded by his son Śaṅkaravarman, who had to fight with his cousin Sukhavarman in order to gain the throne. Śaṅkaravarman conquered the sub-montane forest districts from rebel chiefs and advanced towards Kangra. He attacked and defeated a chief of the Gurjara tribe of the Central Panjab named Alakhāna (Al-Khān). He thus came into conflict with Alakhāna's suzerain, the Pratīhāra emperor Bhoja I of Kanauj, whom he claims to have defeated. Śaṅkaravarman was attacked by Lallīya Shāhī, the ruler of Kabul,

Śaṅkaravarman.

who had allied himself with the Gurjaras, but the result of the war is not known. On his northern frontier Śaṅkaravarman defeated the Dards and the Turks. He levied new imposts and did not spare even the temple-endowments and Brāhmaṇa-corporations, while he made excessive demands for forced labour and oppressed the cultivators. He died during an expedition into the Hazara country.

Gurjara War.

Wars in the North west.

After the death of Śaṅkaravarman, his licentious queen Sugandhā placed two of his sons on the throne, one after the other, and finally ascended it herself; but the council placed on the throne Pārtha, a great-grandson of Avantivarman's half-brother Śūravarman, and a mere child. The new king's father was a cripple, and he tried to rule the land on behalf of his son with the help of the army. Queen Sugandhā tried to recover the kingdom in 914 but was defeated and killed. In 921 the child king Pārtha was deposed, and his crippled father Nirjitavarman ruled for two years. He was succeeded by another child king, a half-brother of Pārtha, but as the new-comer could not pay enough money to the army he was deposed and Pārtha restored. As a result of heavy bribes to the army, his half brother Chakravarman was also placed on the throne for a short period, but finally the crown was sold by the officers and the soldiers to the minister Śambhuvardhana.

Sugandhā (904-906).

Pārtha (906-921).

Nirjitavarman (921-923).

Śambhuvardhana (935-936).

A powerful Ḍāmara, named Saṅgrāma, now took up the cause of Chakravarman and marched with a large army upon Śrīnagara in 936. The officials were defeated with great slaughter at the battle of Padmapura, and Chakravarman was again placed on the throne. He introduced a number of low-caste Ḍomba women into the seraglio, and for this reason he was murdered in 937. He was succeeded by a son of Pārtha, called Avantivarman, who is better known as the Mad Avanti. He murdered his father Pārtha in the Jayendra *Vihāra* and starved his half-brother to death. Avanti died of consumption two years later, in 939, and was succeeded by his illegitimate son Śūravarman II. The commander-in-chief, Kamalavardhana, rebelled and forced Śūravarman II to fly. The Brāhmaṇas chose Yaśaskara, whose father was the treasurer to Gopālavarman. This Brāhmaṇa king ruled over Kāśmīra for nine years, and during this period the country enjoyed

Chakravarman (936-937).

Unmatt-Avanti (937-939).

Śūravarman II (939).

Yaśaskara (948-949).

peace. He was succeeded by his infant son Saṅgrāma, who was murdered by the powerful minister Parvagupta.

III. The Gupta Dynasty

Parva-gupta (949-950). Parvagupta had aspired to the throne since the days of the Mad Avanti. He was a clerk of low origin, but after the murder of Saṅgrāma, in 949, he ascended the throne. His rule lasted for two years only, and he died in 950 to be succeeded by his son Kshemagupta, a grossly sensual youth who was addicted to many vices. He married Diddā, the daughter of a chief of the Lohara country, which lies in the small hill-state of Punch. Diddā's father Siṁharāja had married a daughter of King Bhīma Shāhī of Kabul. Diddā was a very intelligent and capable woman. She inherited political capacity and energy from her mother's ancestors, and she ruled over Kāśmīra for more than half a century. Her husband was a mere puppet in her hands, and he obtained the nickname of Diddā-Kshema. He associated his queen with him on the coinage, and the coins of his reign, all issued under their joint names, are the only examples of pure Indian (non-Muhammadan) coins bearing the name of a queen-consort. During the lifetime of her husband, Diddā built a temple of Śiva, named Bhīmakeśvara after her mother's father.

Kshema-gupta (950-958).

Diddā.

Abhi-manyu (958-972). Kshemagupta died in 958 after a reign of nine years, and was succeeded by his infant son Abhimanyugupta, to whom Diddā became guardian. She drove away the minister Phalguṇa and then quarrelled with her husband's relations. When pressed hard she was saved by a faithful minister named Naravāhana, whom she afterwards compelled to commit suicide. Finally a revolt of the Ḍāmaras compelled Diddā to recall Phalguṇa. In the meantime her son Abhimanyu died, and she placed her grandson Nandigupta on the throne in 972. At this time Diddā built a temple called Diddā-maṭha. Three years afterwards Nandigupta was murdered, and two other grandsons of the old queen were placed on the throne, one after the other. The queen now openly lived with her paramour Tuṅga, a Khasa, or Mongolian, of Prunts, who had begun life as a cowherd. After the death of Bhīmagupta, her last surviving

Nandi-gupta (972-973).

grandson, in 980, Diddā herself ascended the throne and began to issue coins in her own name. Diddā and Tuṅga ruled over Kāśmīra in peace till 1003, the former maintaining herself on the throne, in spite of the enmity of the Ḍāmaras and the Brāhmaṇas, by means of her masterly diplomacy. She was able to bequeath the throne to her father's family, nominating her nephew Saṅgrāmarāja as her successor. The crown of Kāśmīra passed on to the new king without bloodshed. **Diddā (980–1003).**

IV. The First Lohara Dynasty

Saṅgrāma, son of Diddā's brother, was a weak king, and during the earlier part of his reign Tuṅga remained predominant. During his reign the map of Northern India underwent a change. Already Sabuktegīn had established a Musalman kingdom at Ghazni, while the Brāhmaṇa Shāhīyas had been obliged to retire from Kabul to the secluded Indus Kohistan. Here also, during the opening years of the eleventh century, they were repeatedly attacked by the Musalmans, who finally conquered the whole of the Panjab. The last Hindu king of Udabhāṇḍapura was Trilochanapāla Shāhī. Tuṅga himself led a Kāśmīrian contingent to the help of Trilochanapāla. This campaign took place in 1013. The combined Hindu army was defeated, and the Musalmans spread over the fertile plains of the Panjab. On his return to Kāśmīra, Tuṅga was murdered with his son. Saṅgrāma died in 1028 and was succeeded by his son Harirāja. During his reign Sultan Maḥmūd of Ghazni invaded Kāśmīra up to the foot of the hills. The Musalman army failed to take the fort of Lohkoṭ and retired as soon as winter came. **Saṅgrāma (1003–28).** **Musalman Conquest of Afghanistan.** **Kāśmīrian Contingent in the Musalman War.** **Harirāja (1028).** **Maḥmūd invades Kāśmīra.**

Harirāja died after a reign of twenty-two days, and his licentious mother Srīlekhā attempted to obtain the throne. Both the widowed queen and a relative of Harirāja, named Vigraharāja, were defeated by the royal bodyguard, who placed another son of Saṅgrāma, named Ananta, on the throne. During the reign of Ananta the princes of the Shāhīya royal family of Udabhāṇḍapura found shelter in Kāśmīra and exercised a good deal of power in that country. A Shāhīya chief named Rudrapāla invaded the Dard country and repelled an in- **Ananta (1028–76).**

Sūryamatī. vasion of barbarian chiefs. Ananta married Sūryamatī, a daughter of the king of Kangra. This queen built a temple of Sadāśiva on the River Jhelum, and during the old age of Ananta the administration was taken over by her, and the kingdom saved from bankruptcy. Haladhara, an able minister, was placed in charge of the administration. Acting upon the advice of Sūryamatī, Ananta abdicated in favour of his son Kalaśa, but immediately afterwards both the king and the queen regretted this step. Ananta regained a certain amount of power and retained it till 1076, when he retired to the sacred town of Vijayeśvara. Kalaśa burnt the town and insisted on sending his aged father to exile. After a violent quarrel with the queen, the aged Ananta committed suicide in 1081.

Kalaśa (1076–89)

Kalaśa now asserted himself and made himself suzerain of the surrounding valleys. During his reign his eldest son Harsha, who had been nominated by his grandfather as his successor, conspired against his father. Harsha was arrested in 1088. His life was spared but he was not allowed to succeed. Kalaśa died in 1089 and was succeeded by his younger son Utkarsha. Harsha now conspired with his step-brother Vijayamalla and managed to escape from prison. Utkarsha was imprisoned after a reign of twenty-two days, and Harsha made himself the master of the kingdom. Vijayamalla fled to the Dard country and was killed. Harsha was a man of extravagant habits, and very soon the treasury was exhausted. He then started to plunder the treasures of the temples and finally to melt images made of gold and silver. He imposed many new taxes. He invaded Rājapurī and many other places, but all of his expeditions ended in failure. A successful general named Uchchala invaded Kāśmīra in 1101. He was joined by disaffected nobles, but was defeated by Harsha. At this time Uchchala's brother Suśśala invaded Kāśmīra and drove away the royal forces. This unexpected aid enabled Uchchala to rally his forces, and he marched upon the capital. Harsha was attacked in Śrīnagara on two sides. The city gates were opened by treachery and the palace burnt. Harsha fled from his capital and took refuge in the villages. He was killed before the end of the year 1101.

Utkarsha (1089).

Harsha (1089–1101).

Insurrections under Uchchala and Suśśala.

Harsha's licentious character and passionate nature often

brought unexpected troubles on him. He was a strong man and fond of display. "Cruelty and kind-heartedness, liberality and greed, violent selfwilledness and reckless supineness, cunning and want of thought—these and other apparently irreconcilable features in turn display themselves in Harsha's chequered life." [1] Harsha employed Musalman generals, who are called Turushkas by Kalhaṇa. **His Character.**

V. The Second Lohara Dynasty

After the death of Harsha, the kingdom of Kāśmīra devolved on Uchchala. The new king subdued the Ḍāmaras and secured the attachment of the lower classes. Harsha's grandson Bhikshāchāra was set up as a rival king and was countenanced by the chief of Rājapurī. Suśśala, however, now invaded Kāśmīra, and in 1111 Uchchala was defeated and murdered. A king named Śaṅkharāja then occupied the throne for a single day, and he was followed by Uchchala's half-brother Salhaṇa. Suśśala now pushed forward and occupied the capital, becoming king in 1112. He then led an expedition against Rājapurī for harbouring Bhikshāchāra. In 1119 the principal Ḍāmaras rose against Suśśala and besieged him in his capital, compelling him to retire to Lohara, upon which Bhikshāchāra became king. But the descendant of Harsha was too fond of the pleasures of life to attend to his kingly duties. In the capital, rivalry was rife among the ministers, and the Ḍāmaras oppressed the cultivators. Trade ceased and money became very rare. In spite of these troubles an expedition was sent against Suśśala into the country of Lohara. Musalmans were employed in this army, which was defeated by Suśśala in 1121. Suśśala immediately marched upon the capital and occupied it without resistance. Bhikshāchāra now retired to Rājapurī, whence his Ḍāmaras continued to harass the plains of Kāśmīra. During these wars Bhikshāchāra displayed great bravery. In 1123 Śrīnagara was besieged and a terrible famine devastated the capital, as all food grains were burnt during the siege. Suśśala was murdered in 1128 by an adherent of Bhikshāchāra, but the late king's supporters were

Uchchala (1101-11). **Suśśala (1112-20).** **Bhikshāchāra (1120-1).** **Suśśala (restored) (1121-8).** **Jayasimha (1128-49**

[1] Stein's Introduction, *Chronicles of the Kings of Kasmir*, Vol. I, p. 112.

strong enough to place Jayasiṁha, his son, on the throne. Bhikshāchāra was soon afterwards defeated by the foreign troops of the king, whose ministers gained over the disaffected Ḍāmaras with bribes. Bhikshāchāra had then finally to retire from Kāśmīra, but he continued to trouble Jayasiṁha till 1130, when he was killed. After the fall of Bhikshāchāra, Jayasiṁha's relatives rebelled in Lohara, the family stronghold. One by one the forts were retaken and the Ḍāmaras subdued. Jayasiṁha restored the monasteries and temples. He ruled till 1149, and led an expedition against the Musalmans of the Panjab.

Fall of Bhikshāchāra.

End of Kalhaṇa's Chronicle.

Kalhaṇa's *Chronicles of the Kings of Kāśmīra* narrates events till the twenty-second year of Jayasiṁha. The later Chronicles of Kāśmīra are very brief. Its kings continued to rule over the valley till the middle of the fourteenth century, when the queen Kota was deposed by a Muhammadan usurper named Shāh Mīr. The Brāhmaṇas continued to occupy the principal posts under the early Musalman Sultans of Kāśmīra, and Sanskrit was used as a court language till the end of the fifteenth century. Kāśmīra thus remained isolated from the rest of India, even under her Musalman kings. Her history shows that, isolated from the neighbouring provinces, Kāśmīra developed a culture of her own. Her people were very conservative and the type of coins of Kadphises and Kāṇishka I were issued by kings up to the time of Jayāpīda (Vinayāditya). The influence upon Kāśmīra of Indo-Greek art and architecture lasted till the end of the eighth century A.D., and can be seen in the ruined temple of the Sun (Mārtaṇḍa), built by Muktāpīda (Lalitāditya). The script of the country also remained almost unchanged and the modern Śāradā alphabet is very much like the North Indian alphabet of the Gupta period (fifth century A.D.).

Later Hindu Kings.

BIBLIOGRAPHY

KALHANA's *Rajatarangini*, translated by M. A. Stein.

Cambridge History of India, Vol. III, chap. xii.

H. C. ROY, *Dynastic History of Northern India*, Vol. I, chap. iv.

CHAPTER XII

THE MUHAMMADAN CONQUEST OF NORTHERN INDIA

The Musalmans did not succeed in conquering the whole of India at any time. The subjugation of Northern India took more than five centuries to accomplish—from the fall of Alor in Sindh in 712, to the capture of Ujjain by 'Alāuddīn Muḥammad Khaljī in 1305. The conquest of Northern India itself may be divided into five different stages: (1) the Arab conquest of Sindh; (2) the expulsion of the Shāhīyas from Kabul; (3) the destruction of the Shāhīya kingdom of Und by Sultān Maḥmūd of Ghaznī and the conquest of the Panjab (4) the conquests of the kingdoms of Delhi and Kanauj by Sultān Muizzuddīn Muḥammad bin Sām; and (5) the conquest of Ranthambhor, Mālwa, and Gujarat by Sultān 'Alāuddīn Muḥammad Shāh Khaljī in the beginning of the fourteenth century.

Five Stages of the Musalman Conquest.

The Arab conquest of the province of Sindh is fully described in the Persian history called *Chāchnāmah*. In spite of its mutilation it bears the stamp of truth. Therefore in the case of the Musalman conquest of Sindh we possess a fairly accurate narrative, though its material comes from one side only. In the earlier part of the eighth century Sindh was ruled by Brahmana princes. The leading nobles belonged to the Sammā clan, a branch of the great Yādava tribe. The Rajputs were immigrants into Sindh and were Hindus, but the majority of the people, as well as many of the great nobles, were Buddhists. There was no love lost between the rival sects, and the principal cause of the success of the Arabs was the treachery of the Buddhist inhabitants of the country, who openly refused to co-operate with their government in its fight against the Musalmans.

The Chāchnāmah.

The Hindus and the Buddhists.

At last the great port of Dewal was stormed by a small Musalman army under the command of Muḥammad bin Qāsim. Dewal was captured, and the Musalman army conquered Lower, Middle, and Upper Sindh with great ease

Sieges of Dewal.

Death of Dāhir. in 711. Dāhir, the king of the country, was defeated and killed, while the neighbouring princes seem to have looked on the Musalman conquest of Sindh with great indifference. **Siege of Bhakkar.** The remnants of the Rajput army threw themselves into the important fort of Bhakkar near Alor. Alor was the capital of Upper Sindh, just as its neighbour, Sukkur, is at the present day. Bhakkar is an island near Sukkur in the bed of the Indus, and was regarded as one of the strongest forts in Northern India. When the Rajputs saw that all was lost, they sent their women to a neighbouring island. **The "Jauhar".** They were finally defeated outside Alor in 712. Their survivors committed their wives and daughters to the funeral pyre on an island and then sallied forth and were killed to a man. This ceremony is known as the *Jauhar* ceremony and was performed many times in the Rajput cities of India. After the fall of Alor, Sindh remained a Musalman kingdom right up to the British conquest of the Panjab and Northern India.

Musalman Conquest of Baluchistan. The second step was taken in the middle of the ninth century. Though Persia was conquered in the middle of the seventh century and the southern coast of Baluchistan occupied in 643, Afghanistan remained independent under Hindu kings till the middle of the ninth century. Herat in the west and Balkh in the north had been conquered long before, but Kābul had remained unconquered under the Shahīyas till the fourth decade of the ninth century. **Conquest of Kābul.** It was finally conquered by Yāqūb bin Laith in the middle of that century. The Shāhīya kings retired towards India, but for a long time they held the fertile valleys of the Kābul River.

The third step towards the conquest of India was taken about the close of the tenth century. After the decline of the Arab emperors of the Ābbāsi dynasty of Baghdad, the outlying provinces of the Arab empire became independent. Khorāsān and the country to the north of the Oxus had fallen to the share of the Sāmānī dynasty. **The Sāmānī Dynasty.** King 'Abdul Mālik, the fifth king of this dynasty, had a favourite Turkish slave named **Ālaptegīn.** Ālaptegīn. By degrees this slave became governor of Khorāsān. After the death of 'Abdul Mālik, he opposed the succession of Mansūr and was obliged to fly from the country. He left Khorāsān with a body of trusted adherents and found refuge in the city of Ghaznī to the south-west of Kābul. Here he founded a new kingdom without much opposition from the Hindus. His slave named Sabuktegīn became king of Ghaznī in 977. With the help of his Turkish adherents he started to plunder the villages and towns in the kingdom of the Shāhīyas of Und. We do not possess any Indian account of the long wars of the Shāhīyas with Sabuktegīn and his son Sultān Maḥmūd, and have to rely solely on Musalman accounts. In early Musalman histories Jayapāla is called the Rāja of Bathinda, which is perhaps the same as Bhatinda in Central Panjab. But the references to the Shāhīyas and their wars with the Turushkas in the *Rājataraṅginī* leave no doubt that Jayapāla was one of the Shāhīya kings of Und. The first raid of Sabuktegīn took place in 986. Jayapāla invaded the territories of Ghaznī in retaliation. He was defeated in the valley of Laghman and compelled to surrender a number of elephants and to pay a large sum of money. On his return to the capital, Jayapāla refused to submit to the conditions of the treaty, and called on the principal Rajput chiefs of India for aid against the Musalmans. Dhaṅga, the Chandella king of Kālañjar, and his son Gaṇḍa headed the Rajput confederacy. The Rajputs were defeated by Sabuktegīn in the battle of the Kurram, and Jayapāla was compelled to cede the country to the west of the River Indus. Sabuktegīn now assumed the title of king and started issuing coins in his own name. During the remainder of his life he was busy with the affairs of the Sāmānī kingdom, and died in 997.

Conquest of Ghaznī.

Sabuktegīn.

Jayapāla.

Battle of Laghman.

The First Rajput Confederacy.

Battle of the Kurram Valley.

Sabuktegīn's eldest son, Maḥmūd, assumed the title of Sultān. Maḥmūd had accompanied his father in his wars and received his education in many campaigns. He was a bigoted Musalman but an able general. The weakness of the Hindu kingdoms of Northern India became apparent to him at once, and he declared a *Jihād*, or holy war, against the infidels of India. The fabulous wealth of the cities attracted him powerfully, and he invaded India more than twelve times. Most of these expeditions were plundering raids; but Maḥmūd planned them deliberately, and almost all of them were undertaken with the object of destroying some celebrated Hindu holy place. He fought

Maḥmūd.

His Holy Wars.

with his Hindu neighbour, the Shāhīya king of Und, and destroyed that kingdom. The only provinces which he annexed to his kingdom were the Panjab and Sindh. He invaded the territories of Jayapāla of Und in November, 1001, and defeated the troops of the Shāhīya king in the battle of Peshawar. Jayapāla was captured with his family, but was released on promising to pay tribute. The old king was too proud to submit to these indignities—he ascended the funeral pyre and left the throne to his son Ānandapāla, who for a long time resisted the encroachments of the Musalmans of Ghaznī. Confederacy after confederacy of Rajput chiefs assembled at Peshawar. The supreme command of the Hindu army was placed in the hands of Viśāladeva, the Chāhamāna king of Ajmer. The combined armies of the Pratīhāras of Kanauj, the Chandellas of Kālañjar, the Paramāras of Mālava, the Tomaras of Delhi, the Kachchhapaghātas of Gwalior, and the Chāhamānas of Ajmer were once more defeated by the Musalmans near Peshawar (1008). Maḥmūd pursued the Hindu army into the heart of the Panjab and destroyed the celebrated temple of Jvālāmukhī at Kangra (1009). The twelfth expedition of Maḥmūd was directed against Mathurā and Kanauj. The splendour of the buildings of Mathurā touched the heart of the Musalman king; but they were ruthlessly destroyed, and the noblest monuments of the Kushan period perished in fire. From Mathurā, Maḥmūd passed on to Kanauj; the narrative of this expedition will be found in the section on the Gurjara-Pratīhāras of Kanauj (see pp. 234-5). The thirteenth expedition was undertaken against the Chandella king Gaṇḍa for the murder of the Pratīhāra king Rājyapāla. Gaṇḍa fled, leaving his elephants and camp equipment. An expedition was undertaken to plunder and destroy the celebrated temple of Somanātha at Prabhāsa-pattana or Verawal; this has been described in the section on the Chālukyas of Gujarat (see. p. 248).

Annexations. **Battle of Peshawar.** **Ānandapāla.** **Second Battle of Peshawar** **Invasion of Mathurā and Kanauj.** **Destruction of Mathurā.** **Campaign against the Chandellas.** **Destruction of Somanātha.**

The untold wealth obtained by Maḥmūd by the plunder of the rich cities and temples of India was spent by him in beautifying his capital. Some of the monuments built by Sultān Mahmūd at Ghaznī still exist. Mahmūd was a great patron of literature. Firdausī, the author of the *Shāhnāmāh*,

Buildings of Ghaznī. **Firdausī.**

was a member of his court. But the most distinguished literary man of the period was Ābū Raihān Muḥammad bin Aḥmad, commonly called Al-Bīrūnī. Al-Bīrūnī was born in Central Asia and was brought against his will to Ghazni. After the fall of the Shāhīyas of Und in 1021, he settled down in the Panjab and studied Sanskrit. He made a special study of astronomy, mathematics, physics, chemistry, and mineralogy. He was one of the ablest scholars in the world, and the accuracy of his scientific method has elicited the admiration even of modern scholars. After the death of Maḥmūd, Al-Bīrūnī completed his celebrated work, the *Taḥqīq-i-Hind*, and he lived in the court of Maḥmūd's son Masa'ūd till 1048.

Al-Bīrūnī.

His Account of India.

The successors of Maḥmūd continued to rule over Eastern Afghanistan, the Panjab, and Sindh for more than one hundred and fifty years after his death. Their closest neighbours were the Tomaras and the Chāhamānas. Bahrām, one of the descendants of Maḥmūd, murdered two chiefs of the valley of Ghor, and in revenge 'Alāuddīn Husain, the next chief of Ghor, attacked Bahrām in 1150 and compelled him to take refuge in the Panjab. The city of Ghaznī was destroyed, and in 1173 the successors of Maḥmūd ceased to have any control over Afghanistan. The chiefs of Ghor gradually rose in importance. Muizzuddīn Muḥammad bin Sām, also known as Shihābuddīn Muḥammad Ghorī, conquered Multān in 1175. In 1178 he invaded Gujarat through Sindh, but was defeated by the generals of Mūlarāja II. In 1186 Sultān Mūhammad defeated Khusrū Mālik, the last king of the dynasty of Maḥmūd, and annexed the Panjab. Sultān Muḥammad bin Sām now attacked the dominions of Pṛthvīrāja II of Delhi. The armies met at Tarain or Talawari, a village near Karnal, where the Musalman army was defeated. Musalman historians state that the Hindu army was composed of contingents sent by all the Hindu kings of Northern India, but this statement is not correct. The Gāhaḍavālas of Kanauj and the Chandellas of Kālañjar must have stood aloof. After his defeat Sultān Muḥammad bin Sām retired in safety and was not pursued by the Rajputs. The first battle of Tarain took place in 1191. Muḥammad bin Sām attacked the Rajput kingdom of Delhi again in 1192. This time he succeeded in defeating the

Murder of the Chiefs of Ghor.

Destruction of Ghaznī.

Muḥammad bin Sām.

Annexation of the Panjab.

War with the Chāhamānas.

First Battle of Tarain.

Second Battle of Tarain.

Chāhamāna army on the same field. Pṛithvīrāja II was killed. Musalman historians say that the Rajput king fled from the field of battle, but was captured and killed. After the fall of the king, Delhi and Ajmer were occupied in 1193 by the Musalmans, without much opposition from the Chāhamānas. The conduct of the Indian campaign was now entrusted to Sultān Muḥammad's ablest general, Qutbuddīn Aibak. With the exception of the Chāhamāna capitals of Delhi and Ajmer, the kingdom, with its principal forts, such as Ranastambhapura or Ranthambhor, and Bayana or Vijayagaḍh, remained in the hands of the Chāhamānas, who transferred their capital to Ranthambhor.

Capture of Delhi and Ajmer.

Nature of the Conquest.

Jayachchandra, the Gāhaḍavāla king of Kanauj, was attacked in 1194. He had remained aloof during the wars of the Chāhamānas with the Musalmans, and when his turn came no other king of India came forward to help him. He was defeated at the battle of Chandawar, near Etawah, and killed. Jayachchandra was succeeded by his son Hariśchandra at Kanauj, which defied the Musalmans till the reign of Iltutmish. Hariśchandra was reigning in 1202, when he issued a grant of land. The country between the Ganges and the Yamunā was easily occupied by the Musalmans, and Musalman chiefs were given fiefs and occupied the principal forts there, from which they plundered the territories of Hindu chiefs. Kanauj fell finally in the beginning of the thirteenth century.

Battle of Chandawar.

Conquest of the Antarvedi.

Musalman Feudal Chiefs.

The Musalmans found the conquest of Bengal and Bihar much easier than that of Kanauj. During the long wars between the Pālas, the Senas, and the Gāhaḍavālas, Magadha, or South Bihar, had become some sort of no-man's-land. The Gāhaḍavālas had conquered the western part of the province, the Senas had occupied its south-western part or the modern district of Gaya, and the Pāla kings were still holding out in the hilly country in the south-eastern part. After the fall of the Gāhaḍavālas, the *Mahānāyakas* of Jāpila had occupied the fort of Rohitāśva or Rohtasgadh. Muḥammad bin Bakhtyār, whose personal title appears to have been Īkhtiyāruddīn, had occupied Chunar, gathered round himself a body of Musalman freebooters, and started plundering the whole of Magadha. Īkhtiyāruddīn Muḥammad bin Bakhtyār had no connexion

State of Magadha at the end of the Twelfth Century.

The Robber Baron Muḥammad bin Bakhtyār.

either with Sultān Muḥammad bin Sām or with his general Qutbuddīn Aibak. After the Musalman conquest of Delhi, he had presented himself before the muster-master at Delhi, but being rejected, he entered the service of Hazābruddīn Ḥasan-i-Adīb, the feoffee of Budaun. Afterwards he migrated to Oudh and entered the service of Ḥasāmuddīn Aghulbak, from whom he received Bhagawat and Bhuili, near Chunar. From here he plundered the most important places in Magadha and advanced as far eastwards as Maner, the ancient Maniari, near Patna. During one of these plundering expeditions he attacked the fort of Bihar and the neighbouring University of Nālandā. Govindapāla, the last descendant of Dharmapāla, defended the fort, but he was defeated and killed. The monasteries of Uddaṇḍapura or Bihar and Nālandā were plundered and destroyed by fire. The contemporary Musalman historian Minhāj-us-Sirāj has recorded naïvely that the greater number of inhabitants of that place were Brāhmaṇas with shaved heads, i.e. Buddhist monks, and that the whole of the place was a college, full of books. From Bihar Muḥammad started plundering in Bengal, but Lakshmaṇāvatī or Gauḍa did not fall till 1203. The Senas remained independent in Eastern Bengal till the beginning of the fourteenth century, and the Paramāras of Mālava and the Chālukyas of Gujarat continued to rule unmolested till the rise of Sultan 'Alāuddīn Muḥammad Shāh Khaljī.

His Early Life.

Plundering Raids in Magadha.

Destruction of Uddaṇḍapura and Nālandā.

Occupation of Western Bengal.

After the destruction of Nālandā in 1199, Ikhtiyāruddīn Muḥammad bin Bakhtyār received recognition from Qutbuddīn Aibak of Delhi. The sons of Lakshmaṇasena did not make any serious attempt to resist the advance of the Musalmans. Thus ended the Musalman conquest of Northern India. It consisted simply of the occupation of the principal forts, the rest of the country remaining practically independent under the Hindu chiefs. Want of unity and coherence among the Hindus of Northern India was one of the principal causes of their downfall. They lacked the qualities which distinguished the Dravidian Hindus of the south, such as Harihara I or Krishṇadevarāya of Vijayanagara.

Muḥammad recognized by Sultan Qutbuddīn Aibak.

BIBLIOGRAPHY

ELLIOT and DOWSON. *History of India as told by its own Historians*, Vols. I and II.
S. LANE-POOLE, *Medieval India.*
I. PRASAD, *History of Medieval India*, Allahabad, 1925.
Cambridge History of India, Vol. III, chaps. i–iii.
R. C. MAZUMDAR, *The Arab Invasion of India.* Journal of Indian History, Vol. X.
M. NAZIM, *Mahmud of Ghazna*, Cambridge, 1931.

GENEALOGICAL TABLES

THE WESTERN KSHATRAPAS

- Ysāmotika.
  - Chashṭana.
    - Jayadāman.
      - Rudradāman.
        - Damaysada (Damajadaśrī) I.
          - Satyadāman.
        - Jīvadāman I.
        - Rudrasiṁha I.
          - Rudrasena I.
            - Pṛithivīsena.
            - Damajadaśrī II.
          - Saṅghadāman
          - Dāmasena.
            - Vīradāman.
              - Rudrasena II.
                - Viśvasiṁha.
                - Bhartṛidāman.
                  - Viśvasena.
            - Yaśodāman I.
            - Vijayasena.
            - Damajadaśrī III.
        - Daughter *m.* Andhra king Puḷumāvi.

- Svāmi-Jīvadāman.
  - Rudrasiṁha II.
  - Svāmi-Rudradāman II.
    - Svāmi-Rudrasena III.
    - Daughter.
      - Svāmi-Siṁhasena.
        - Svāmi-(Rudra)sena IV.
      - Svāmi-Satyasiṁha.
        - Svāmi-Rudrasiṁha III.

GUPTAS

Śrī-Gupta.

Ghaṭotkacha.

1. Chandragupta I = Kumāradevī.

2. Samudragupta = Dattadevī.

3. Rāmagupta.

Kuveranāgā = 4. Chandragupta II = Dhruvadevī or Dhruvasvāminī
(Vikramāṅka or Vikramāditya).

Rudrasena II = Prabhāvatī
(Vākāṭaka king)

Divākarasena.

(?) = 5. Kumāragupta I = Anantadevī

Govindagupta.

(?) Ghaṭotkachagupta.

6. Skandagupta.

10. Budhagupta.

11. Bhānugupta.

7. Puragupta = Śrīvatsadevī.
Prakāśāditya (?).

8. Narasiṁhagupta = Mahālakshmīdevī.
Bālāditya.

9. Kumāragupta II.

MAITRAKAS OF VALABHI

Senāpati Bhaṭārka.

Senāpati Dharasena I.

1. Droṇasiṁha.

2. Dhruvasena I.

3. Dharapaṭṭa.

4. Guhasena.

5. Dharasena II

6. Śilāditya I.
Dharmāditya.

Ḍerabhaṭa.

7. Kharagraha I.

8. Dharasena III.

9. Dhruvasena II.

10. Dharasena IV
(first *Mahārājādhirāja*)

Śilāditya II.

12. Kharagraha II.
Dharmāditya.

11. Dhruvasena III.

13 Śilāditya III.

14. Śilāditya IV.

15. Śilāditya V.

16. Śilāditya VI.

17. Śilāditya VII.

LATER GUPTAS OF MAGADHA

- Kṛishṇagupta.
  - Harshagupta.
    - Jīvitagupta I.
      - Kumāragupta III.
        - Dāmodaragupta.
          - Mahāsenagupta.
            - (?) Śaśāṅka
            - Mādhavagupta = Śrīmatīdevī.
              - Ādityasena = Koṇadevī.
                - Devagupta = Kamaladevī.
                  - Vishṇugupta = Ijjādevī.
                    - Jīvitagupta II.
          - Daughter *m.* Ādityavarddhana of Thāneśvar.
            - Prabhākaravarddhana.
              - Rājyavarddhana.
              - Rājyaśrī *m.* Grahavarman.
              - Harshavarddhana.

GURJARA-PRATIHARAS OF BHINMAL AND KANAUJ

- Devaśakti.
  - Vatsarāja.
    - Nāgabhaṭa II.
      - Rāmabhadra.
        - 1. Bhoja I (Mihira, Prabhāsa, or Ādivarāha).
          - 2. Mahendrapāla I.
            - 3. Bhoja II.
            - 4. Mahīpāla or Vināyakapāla.
              - 5. Mahendrapāla II.
              - 7. Mahīpāla II.
              - 6. Devapāla.
              - 8. Vijayapāla
                - 9. Rājyapāla.
                  - 10. Trilochanapāla
                    - ⋮ Yaśaḥpāla.

PARAMĀRAS OF MĀLAVA

- Upendrarāja.
  - Vairisiṁha.
    - Sīyaka I.
      - Vākpati I.
        - Vairisiṁha II.
          - Sīyaka II.
            - 1. Vākpati II.
            - Sindhurāja.
              - 2. Bhoja I.
                - 3. Jayasiṁha I (?).

- 4. Udayāditya (a relation of Bhoja I)
  - Lakshmadeva.
  - 5. Naravarman.
    - 6. Yaśovarman.
      - Ajayavarman.
        - Vindhyavarman.
          - Subhaṭavarman.
            - 8. Arjunavarman.
              - 9. Devapāla.
                - 10. Jayasiṁha II (A.D. 1269).
                  - ⋮ Jayasiṁha.
      - 7. Jayavarman.
      - Lakshmīvarman (feudatory of the Chālukyas of Gujarat).
        - Hariśchandra.
          - Udayavarman.

THE HAIHAYAS OF ḌĀHALA

- 1. Kokalla I.
  - 2. Mugdhatuṅga.
    - 3. Bālaharsha.
    - 4. Yuvarāja I.
      - 5. Lakshmaṇarāja.
        - 6. Śaṁkaragaṇa.
        - 7. Yuvarāja II.
          - 8. Kokalla II.
            - 9. Gāṅgeya, *Vikramāditya.*
              - 10. Karṇa = Āvalladevī (a Hūṇa princess).
                - 11. Yaśaḥkarṇa.
                  - 12. Gayākarṇa-Alhaṇādevī (a granddaughter of Udayāditya of Mālava).
                    - 13. Narasiṁha.
                    - 14. Jayasiṁha.
                      - 15. Vijayasiṁha = Gosāladevī.
                        - Ajayasiṁha.

CHANDELLAS OF BUNDELKHAND

- Nannuka.
  - Vākpati.
    - Jayaśakti (Jejā).
    - Vijayaśakti (Bijā).
      - Rāhila.
        - 1. Harsha = Kañchhukī.
          - 2. Yaśovarman = Puppā
            - 3. Dhaṅga.
              - 4. Gaṇḍa.
                - 5. Vidyādhara.
                  - 6. Vijayapāla.
                    - 7. Devavarman.
                    - 8. Kīrttivarman.
                      - 9. Sallakshaṇavarman.
                        - Jayavarman.
                      - 10. Pṛithvīvarman
                        - 11 Madanavarman
                          - Yaśovarman.
                            - 12. Paramardin.
                              - 13. Trailokyavarman.
                                - 14. Vīravarman.
                                  - 15. Bhojavarman.

CHĀLUKYAS OF GUJARAT

- Rāji.
  - Mūlarāja I.
    - Chāmuṇḍarāja.
      - Vallabharāja.
      - Durlabharāja.
      - Nāgarāja.
        - Bhīma I.
          - Kshemarāja
            - Haripāla.
              - Tribhuvanapāla.
                - Daughter.
                  - Ānāka.
                    - Lavaṇaprasāda (founder of the Bāghelas).
                - Mahīpāla.
                  - Ajayapāla.
                    - Mūlarāja II.
                    - Bhīma II.
                - Kīrttipāla.
                - Kumārapāla.
          - Karṇa.
            - Jayasiṁha Siddharāja

GĀHADAVĀLAS OF KANAUJ

- Yaśovigraha.
  - Mahīchandra.
    - 1. Chandradeva.
      - 2. Madanapāla.
        - 3. Govindachandra.
          - 4. Vijayachchandra.
            - 5. Jayachchandra.
              - 6. Hariśchandra.

PĀLAS OF BENGAL

- Dayitavishṇu.
  - Vapyaṭa.
    - 1. Gopāla I = Deddadevī.
      - 2. Dharmapāla = Raṇṇādevī.
        - Tribhuvanapāla.
        - 3. Devapāla.
          - Rājyapala.
      - Vākpāla.
        - Jayapāla.
          - 4. Vigrahapāla I (Śūrapāla I) = Lajjādevī.
            - 5. Nārāyaṇapāla.
              - 6. Rājyapāla = Bhāgyadevī.
                - 7. Gopāla II.
                  - 8. Vigrahapāla II.
                    - 9. Mahīpāla I.
                      - 10. Nayapāla.
                        - 11. Vigrahapāla III = Yauvanaśrī.
                          - 12. Mahīpāla II.
                          - 13. Sūrapāla II.
                          - 14. Rāmapāla.
                            - Rājyapāla.
                            - 15. Kumārapāla.
                              - 16. Gopāla III.
                            - 17. Madanapāla = Chitramatikā.
                              - 18. Palapāla.
                                - 19. Govindapāla (accession, A.D. 1161).
                      - Sthirapāla (?).
                      - Vasantapāla (?).

EASTERN GAṄGAS OF KALINGANAGARA

- Vajrahasta.
  - Rājarāja I = Rājasundarī (a daughter of Rājendra Choḷa II).
    - Anantavarman Choḍagaṅga (1078–1142).
      - Kāmārṇava.
      - Rāghava.
      - Rājarāja II.
      - Anaṅgabhīma I.
        - Rājarāja III.
          - Anaṅgabhīma II.
            - Narasiṁha I.
              - Bhānudeva I.
                - Narasiṁha II (1296).
                  - Bhānudeva II (contemporary of Ghiyāthuddīn Tughlaq Shāh).
                    - Narasiṁha III.
                      - Bhānudeva III.
                        - Narasiṁha IV (1384–1402).

EARLY CHĀLUKYAS OF BADAMI

- Jayasiṁha.
  - Raṇarāga.
    - Pulikeśin I.
      - Kīrtivarman I.
        - Pulikeśin II.
          - Chandrāditya.
          - Vikramāditya I.
            - Vinayāditya.
              - Vijayāditya.
                - Vikramāditya II.
                  - Kirtivarman II.
                - Bhīma.
                  - Kīrtivarman III.
                    - Taila I.
                      - Vikramāditya III.
                        - Bhīma II
                          - Ayyaṇa.
                            - Vikramāditya IV.
                              - Taila II (founder of the Western Chālukyas of Kalyāṇī).
          - Ādityavarman.
        - Vishṇuvarddhana (founder of the Eastern Chālukya dynasty of Veṅgī).
      - Maṅgaleśa.

THE RASHTRAKUTAS

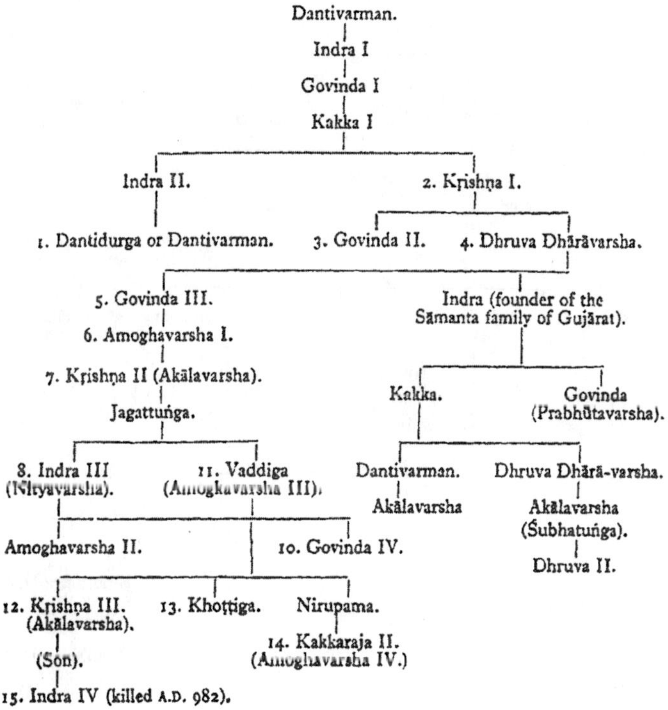

CHOḶAS OF TANJORE

- Āditya I.
  - Parāntaka I.
    - Rājāditya.
    - Gaṇḍarāditya.
      - Madhurāntaka.
    - Ariñjaya.
      - Parāntaka II.
        - Āditya II.
        - Rājarāja I.
          - Rājendra Choḷa I.
            - Rājādhirāja I.
            - Rājendra II.
              - Rājmahendra.
              - Madhurāntakī — Kulottuṅga I
            - Vīrarājendra.
              - Adhirājendra.
              - Daughter, married Vikramāditya VI of Kalyāṇī.
            - Ammaṅga *m.* Rājarāja I (of Veṅgī).
          - Kuṇḍavā *m.* Vimalāditya, Eastern Chālukya king of Veṅgī.
            - Rājarāja I (of Veṅgī).
              - Kulottuṅga I (ruled as Rājendra Choḷa II at Veṅgī).
                - Vikrama Choḷa.
                  - Kulottuṅga II.
                    - Rājarāja II.
                      - Rājādhirāja II.
                        - Kulottuṅga III.
                          - Rājarāja III.
                            - Rājendra Choḷa III.

YĀDAVAS OF DEVAGIRI

- Sevaṇa.
  - Mallugi.
    - Amaragaṅga.
      - 1. Bhillama.
        - 2. Jaitugi or Jaitrapāla I.
          - 3. Siṁhaṇa.
            - Jaitugi II.
              - 4. Kṛishṇa.
                - 7. Rāmachandra.
                  - 8. Śaṅkara.
              - 5. Mahādeva.
                - 6. Amaṇa.
    - Karṇa.

THE HOYŚAḶAS OF DORASAMUDRA

- Vinayāditya.
  - Ereyaṅga.
    - Vīra Vallāla I.
    - Vishṇuvardhana.
      - Narasiṁha I.
        - 1. Vīra-Vallāla II.
          - 2. Narasiṁha II.
            - 3. Someśvara.
              - 4. Narasiṁha III.
                - 5. Vīra-Vallāla III.

INDEX